Looking for Balance

The *Studies in Asian Security* book series promotes analysis, understanding, and explanation of the dynamics of domestic, transnational, and international security challenges in Asia. The peer-reviewed publications in the Series analyze contemporary security issues and problems to clarify debates in the scholarly community, provide new insights and perspectives, and identify new research and policy directions. Security is defined broadly to include the traditional political and military dimensions as well as nontraditional dimensions that affect the survival and well-being of political communities. Asia, too, is defined broadly to include Northeast, Southeast, South, and Central Asia.

Designed to encourage original and rigorous scholarship, the books in the Studies in Asian Security series seek to engage scholars, educators, and practitioners. Wide-ranging in scope and method, the Series is receptive to all paradigms, programs, and traditions, and to an extensive array of methodologies now employed in the social sciences.

# Looking for Balance

CHINA, THE UNITED STATES, AND
POWER BALANCING IN EAST ASIA

Steve Chan

STANFORD UNIVERSITY PRESS
*Stanford, California*

Stanford University Press
Stanford, California

Printed in the United States of America on acid-free, archival-quality paper

Library of Congress Cataloging-in-Publication Data
Chan, Steve, author.
    Looking for balance: China, the United States, and power balancing in East Asia / Steve Chan.
        pages cm. — (Studies in Asian security)
    Includes bibliographical references and index.
    ISBN 978-0-8047-7820-6 (cloth: alk. paper)
    ISBN 978-0-8047-8860-1 (pbk.: alk. paper)
        1. East Asia—Foreign relations—China.    2. China—Foreign relations—East Asia.
3. East Asia—Foreign relations—United States.    4. United States—Foreign relations—East
Asia.    5. China—Foreign relations—United States.    6. United States—Foreign relations—
China.    7. Balance of power.    I. Title.    II. Series: Studies in Asian security.
JZ1720.A57C47 2012
327.1′1205—dc22

                                                                                    2011008955

Typeset by Newgen in 10.5/13.5 Bembo

The way to great learning is through manifesting virtue, endearing [invigorating] the people, and reaching for the greatest benevolence . . . Their states having been properly administered, the world would be at peace.

Excerpt from *Daxue*,
customarily attributed to Confucius,
introduced originally as a chapter in the *Classic of Rites*
and after the Song Dynasty adopted as the first of *Four Books*,
widely accepted as the leading text of traditional Chinese education

# Contents

# Acknowledgments

I acknowledge with gratitude the College Scholar award and Dean's Fund for Excellence from the University of Colorado, as well as an award from the Sasakawa Peace Foundation administered by the East–West Center. Preliminary reports on various parts of the book were presented at conferences held at Texas A&M University, Missouri State University, and University of South Carolina in the United States, as well as at the National Cheng Chi University and Chung Cheng University in Taiwan, and Macquarie University in Australia. I also gave presentations on parts of my project at Hong Kong University, the University of Sydney, and the Korean Political Science Association in Seoul. I am grateful for the comments and criticisms from colleagues in the audience on these occasions. Finally, I am indebted to the editors of the Stanford series on Asian security, especially David Leheny's thoughtful and extensive suggestions, Geoffrey Burn's helpful guidance on publication, and constructive feedback from anonymous reviewers.

**Looking for Balance**

# 1

# Introduction

As I write these words, the People's Republic of China is celebrating its sixtieth anniversary. Since 1949, the government in Beijing has undoubtedly made huge progress in improving the living conditions of the Chinese people; over one-fifth of humanity is no longer facing the constant danger of hunger and starvation. Life in China has changed enormously for the better. There have of course also been trying times, especially during the "lost decade" of the Cultural Revolution, when the country faced the abyss of political and economic breakdown. Since its economic reforms launched in 1978, however, China has sustained the most rapid and protracted economic growth in modern history. Its economy has grown at about 10% annually in real terms in the years that followed—meaning that it has increased more than thirteen times in just over three decades (Bergsten et al. 2008, 106).

This economic expansion has increased China's technological and military capabilities. China's comparatively high growth rates, combined with its large size, have caused concerns abroad about a power shift in regional and even global political economy. There has been a surge in scholarship discussing China's rise and the concomitant prospects of power transition presaging its possible challenge to America's preeminence (e.g., Brown et al. 2000; Goldstein 2005; Ross and Zhu 2008; Shambaugh 2005). One salient theme of this debate among Americans has been whether to contain or engage China. Another strand of this discourse has been whether China's rise has inclined its neighbors to balance against it.

The participants in this discourse are of course fully aware that an *imbalance* of power has characterized East Asia and the international system. The United States has been the preeminent power, even during the Cold War. Since the Soviet Union's demise, its preeminence has been further strengthened. Even though China's recent growth has improved its relative position, the United States still has a vast lead in different measures of national power and will likely continue to enjoy a large advantage in the next few decades, especially in military capabilities. The failure of other states to balance against the United States presents an enigma to balance-of-power theorists. A similar puzzle presents itself in the reactions of China's neighbors to its reemergence as a major power. They have not ramped up their defense spending or scrambled to form a countervailing coalition in response to increasing Chinese capabilities. This book tries to explain this phenomenon—the non-occurrence of the expected outcome according to balance-of-power reasoning.

Several scholarly and policy-relevant concerns motivate my approach to this book. First, I try to ground my analysis on theories of international relations and political economy. In addition to extensive surveys of the literature on balance-of-power theories (and theories on power balances and balancing), I attend to recent rationalist theories about the origins of war and the conditions for peace, focusing especially on the idea of credible commitment.

Second, I try to introduce historical parallels in order to compare China's rise with other major power shifts. Not all such cases occasioned war or defeated hegemonic bids. Our thoughts tend to be warped by hindsight bias and the ease of recalling a few dramatic cases, such as Napoleon's France and Hitler's Germany. We tend to overlook cases in which "the dog did not bark," or occasions when the expected did not happen—such as when Mikhail Gorbachev decided not to continue his predecessors' policy of contending with or balancing against the United States. Few American scholars count his decision, the Soviet Union's demise, or the absence of war afterward, as a disconfirmation of balance-of-power theories.

Third, my analysis gives as much attention to the United States as it does to China. In this sense, my treatment is also different from the usual approach, which tends to focus on Chinese conduct and motivations without considering how these are influenced by others whose actions impinge on Chinese interests and perceptions. China's foreign policy clearly cannot be studied in isolation—how the United States acts influences how China acts. When it comes to balance-of-power dynamics in East Asia, the United States is the proverbial "elephant in the room." In bringing the United States explicitly into my discussion, I also call attention to the tendency by some analysts to apply different logics of analysis and rules of evidence when studying different countries. In such cases, the proper names of the countries being studied rather than the theoretical variables in question come to drive an analyst's conclusions.

Moreover, I take the position that theories based primarily on Europe's or America's experiences cannot be automatically assumed to be generalizable to Asia or China but at the same time, Asia's or China's experiences are also not necessarily unique (Hui 2005). Neither Chinese uniqueness nor American exceptionalism provides a fruitful basis for engaging scholarship or policy. Finally, to paraphrase Karl Marx, people make choices even if they make them under circumstances not of their choosing. Therefore, structural conditions constrain officials' policies but do not necessarily determine them. How China's neighbors react to its reemergence as a major regional power depends in large part on what Beijing does with its power, and the outcome is hardly preordained, as is sometimes implied in some deterministic formulations of balance-of-power theories. Commenting on the victory of the Kingdom of Qin during China's Warring States era—the culmination of "universal" domination over the dynamics of balance of power—Victoria Hui (2004, 202) offered this important caveat: history is open-ended, and one should not mistakenly think that contingent outcomes reflect universal laws.

The larger conclusions from this book can be summarized as follows. Although theorizing about balance of power has had a very distinguished tradition and continues to influence international relations scholarship, it also has some debilitating limitations. This perspective overlooks important cases in history when balancing against an aspiring hegemon did not happen or when hierarchy prevailed over anarchy. Even more important, it places too much emphasis on military capabilities and diplomatic alignments as a response to ongoing or prospective power shifts, treating these changes as zero-sum challenges and giving insufficient attention to the fundamental causes driving these changes. To put it starkly but simply, my argument is that China's neighbors are not balancing against its rising power. There are sound reasons for the non-occurrence of this outcome expected from the balance-of-power perspective. The fundamental one is that officials are not myopic. They realize that balancing policies—by increasing their country's armament or seeking foreign allies—are at best short-term solutions and at worst self-defeating actions. They are short-term solutions at best because, in the long run, the fundamental drivers of a country's economic growth—and thus its national power—are located within it, and external attempts to bend its developmental trajectory are likely to have only a limited and transient effect. Balancing policies can be self-defeating because they entail important opportunity costs and induce reactions that trigger cycles of escalating recrimination. The default strategy is not to balance because balancing policies require a strong domestic consensus to pay the current and prospective costs of these policies (Schweller 2004, 172). My argument goes even further, suggesting that balancing policies would entail forfeiting possible gains that could accrue from cooperation, gains that states are wary of foregoing in the absence of demonstrable hostility from a stronger neighbor. In this latter sense, my argument agrees with Stephen Walt's (1987) balance-of-threat theory.

Significantly, if states react to threat perception and not simply to power shifts, then there is something they can do about how others see them. This proposition suggests that officials do not have to make worst-case assumptions about others' intentions. If so, the balancing phenomenon does not have to be a constant feature of international relations, even though power shifts are always occurring. Rather, this phenomenon indicates choice, not destiny. I claim that this choice is fundamentally tied to an elite's strategy for garnering and sustaining domestic popularity and control. East Asian elites have collectively pivoted to a strategy of elite legitimacy and regime survival based on economic performance rather than nationalism, military expansion, or ideological propagation. In this respect, my interpretation differs sharply from other analysts whose studies emphasize Chinese nationalism, defense modernization, and an ambition to assert Beijing's cultural and political preeminence in East Asia. I see that such factors often have no less an influence on the formulation and conduct of U.S. foreign policy; this was particularly true during the administration of George W. Bush.

Whereas American officials and scholars continue to be concerned about military capabilities and security, or what Richard Rosecrance (1986) has called a "strategic vision" of national interest, East Asian countries—China included—have turned to an internationalist outlook that assigns priority to economic growth. To the extent that this model of governance has become pervasive in East Asia with few exceptions (e.g., North Korea, Burma), it has had a region-wide effect of dampening those forces that would have otherwise abetted the balance-of-power dynamics exemplified by competitive armament and exclusive alignment. To borrow from a summary observation made nearly two decades ago, I count myself among those who "are persuaded that the events of recent years are not moving in the direction of typical realist predictions, but rather away from them." Richard Rosecrance and Arthur Stein (1993, 11–12) went on to note, "Looking at the past, [the contributors to our volume] are impressed by the number of occasions in which other than strictly 'realist' determinants appear to have influenced or even decided national policy. Collectively, they believe that domestic factors have been neglected as determinants of grand strategy and that ideas, institutions, or interdependence play important roles in shaping national policy." A singular focus on balance of power—defined primarily in terms of military capabilities—in scholarship, policy statements, and popular discourse reflects American ambitions and obsessions more than it does Asian reality.

How can a rising power, or for that matter an extant hegemon, try to reassure other states about its benign intentions so that they will not balance against it? Its ability to communicate a credible commitment to honor agreements and to eschew opportunistic behavior naturally becomes a focus for understanding how international cooperation can be initiated and sustained—even when all the parties involved are fully aware of the power asymmetries that characterize their relations and realize that the more powerful among them will not entirely foreswear their advantages. I interpret the burgeoning commercial and financial ties among the East Asian countries as a form of credible commitment to cooperate and as a harbinger of such cooperation in the future. This does not mean that states with close economic relations would not go to war, but only that the probability of militarized conflict is reduced among such states.

Instead of policies traditionally understood as balancing efforts, I see more evidence of East Asian countries engaging in behavior that has been variously described as engagement, enmeshment, or entanglement—or to employ liberal terms, collaboration, cooperation, and integration. The key distinction is between organizing countervailing power to *balance* against a country on the one hand, and instituting networks of shared interests and interlocking relations to *defuse* its power on the other hand. The other important point to bear in mind is the synergy between self-restraint and restraint by others. The idea of balance of power has historically included both an associational aspect (self-restraint based on common expectations and norms, as in the case of the Concert of Europe after the Napoleonic Wars) and an adversarial aspect (the Concert members' power competition to avoid relative loss), even though the latter aspect has dominated contemporary American scholarship on balance-of-power theories, in contrast with the English School.

Whether by self-restraint or reciprocal restraint, the exercise of power can be tamed in different ways. Washington's construction of multilateralism offers one example of credible commitment to cooperate (Ikenberry 2001). This multilateralism integrated the United States with its West European allies after World War II and at the same time checked preemptively the latter countries' potential challenge to U.S. leadership in the future, thereby underscoring both associational and adversarial motivations. In contemporary East Asia, bilateral and multilateral hostage-giving and hostage-taking provides another example of jump-starting and then sustaining cooperation that would have otherwise been impaired by mutual distrust. This perspective emphasizes economic interdependence rather than military collaboration as a basis for building confidence and maintaining stability.

Whereas in standard formulations of balance-of-power theories balancing policies entail armament and alignment, such policies are not necessarily motivated exclusively or even primarily by balancing considerations. Defense spending can stem from domestic pork barrel politics, the influence of the military–industrial complex, and military Keynesianism to stimulate and manage the macro economy. Defense treaties can also have purposes other than the declared rationale. These treaties can be a *pactum de contrahendo*, intended as much to restrain an ally as to deter an adversary (Schroeder 1976). The North Atlantic Treaty Organization (NATO) was, for example, developed as much to deter the Soviet Union as it was designed to manage West Germany's rearmament and to sustain Washington's military preponderance by a policy of integrating the other NATO members' armed forces and subordinating them to U.S. leadership and control. If by bipolarity one means that the two bloc leaders need not depend on their allies for their own security, then why should the United States and the Soviet Union have bothered to protect their respective allies by entering into defense treaties with them during the Cold War? By this definition, these allies should not have mattered in the power balance between these bloc leaders—and the current U.S. global position, with its unassailable primacy, would have made these allies even more dispensable. Regime affinity, cultural identity, and other such variables are not typically admissible evidence in standard realist balance-of-power reasoning, and cannot therefore be invoked to explain such seemingly bizarre phenomena. If the preponderant power in a unipolar world can take on all military challengers, why again should Washington bother with entangling alliances?

In a recent special issue of the journal *World Politics*, John Ikenberry, Michael Mastanduno, and William C. Wohlforth (2009, 10) quoted Paul Kennedy's 2002 observation about the extent of U.S. global preponderance: "Nothing has ever existed like this disparity of power, nothing . . . I have returned to all of the comparative defense spending and military personnel statistics over the past 500 years that I compiled for *The Rise and Fall of the Great Powers*, and no other nation comes close." The United States, spending nearly half of the globe's military expenditures, is so much more powerful than the other major states that it seems odd to speak about its balancing against other states as opposed to the reverse. When balance of power is invoked to justify U.S. foreign policy, this concept is often intended to endorse the maintenance and even expansion of U.S. dominance rather than redressing the power asymmetries characterizing its relations with other states.

It is moreover often taken for granted that the United States is a status-quo power whereas others, such as a rising power like China, are dissatisfied challengers of the international order, or at least potentially so. Hence, there is much reference in both U.S. official and scholarly discourse about somehow transforming China into a "responsible stakeholder." Less attention has gone to considering the proposition that "The structural and contingent features of contemporary unipolarity point plausibly in the direction of a revisionist unipole, one simultaneously powerful, fearful, and opportunistic" (Ikenberry, Mastanduno, and Wohlforth 2009, 13). Robert Jervis (2009, 204) put matters more directly, remarking "What is most striking about American behavior since 9/11 is the extent to which it has sought not to maintain the international system but to change it. One might think that the unipole would be conservative, seeking to bolster the status quo that serves it so well. But this has not been the case." The more preponderant a country's power over others becomes, the freer it feels to pursue its ideological proclivities and the greater the role its domestic politics is likely to play in this pursuit. Significantly, remarks such as those just quoted are in the minority. Most American scholars tend to accept almost reflexively the assertion that the United States is a status-quo power and that all rising powers—with the exception of the United States overtaking Britain—are at least potentially revisionist, and they treat these assumptions for analysis as conclusions from it.

Of course, one does not have to be a realist or a balance-of-power proponent to acknowledge that weaker states are concerned about being dominated (or abandoned) by stronger ones—just as the latter countries are concerned about their strength relative to their peers. If "balancing" is taken to mean statecraft generally, it is surely possible for the secondary and even minor powers to engage in various forms of strategic behavior to manage, even manipulate, their relations with those that are more powerful (Bobrow 2008a). It is therefore not always self-evident who is being balanced by whom (such as in Pakistan's complicated relations with the United States, China, India, and Afghanistan). Moreover, although armament and alignment policies represent the quintessential forms of balancing behavior, they can very much have a domestic source, such as powerful lobby groups influencing military spending and foreign patrons being sought in order to protect a regime from its domestic opponents (e.g., Saudi and Yemeni rulers facing challenges from Islamic fundamentalists). It is not difficult to imagine that national security and the imperative of balance of power can be invoked for domestic parochial or partisan reasons. This being the case, domestic factors can influence both the nonoccurrence and the ostensible occurrence of balancing behavior. These factors can affect officials' incentives and hamper their efforts to address an emergent foreign threat. At the same time, just because officials sometimes appear to engage in this behavior and even say so in their public statements, it does not necessarily follow that their behavior is in fact being motivated primarily by foreign rather than domestic considerations. Officials have been known to misrepresent—that is, to lie—about their motivations and intentions.

The preceding discussion raises naturally the question, "What [is the] price [of] vigilance?" (Russett 1970). How much security is enough, and can excesses in military expenditures undermine not just civilian consumption but also the long-term prospects of a country's economy? As already mentioned, East Asian countries have adopted a conception of security that extends beyond a narrow definition of military strength, giving priority instead to economic performance, one that provides the foundation for this strength. This view is associated traditionally with liberalism. At the same time, prominent realists have also warned that excesses in extending national power can have a boomerang effect. Tempering the definition of "national interest" and moderating the pursuit of power have been recurrent themes in the writings of Hans Morgenthau, Kenneth Waltz, Stephen Walt, and Christopher Layne. Despite my criticisms of realism and balance-of-power theories, I am in the company of these realists. Saying so, in turn, acknowledges that this book is not just about China and other states' reactions to its rise.

China offers a mirror to reflect on U.S. policies. Waltz (1986, 1988), for example, has warned that a concentration of power is dangerous and that it can provoke balancing behavior from other states. He and other realists have thus counseled that the United States should adopt the role of an offshore balancer rather than getting directly involved in East Asian countries' security. Still other "postclassical realists" would argue that military security does not and even should not always trump economic capacity as a policy priority, and that leaders can favor the latter over the former in making an intertemporal tradeoff so that a country may be better off in the long run both in its security and economic capacity (Brooks 1997). Whether such advice is sound can be debated. It is not helpful, however, to describe policies that have the intent and effect of sustaining and even increasing U.S. military preponderance—a situation of imbalance—as balancing. It is also unhelpful to overlook the question whether an excessive emphasis on armament and alignment can actually produce a less favorable power balance in the long run.

To state briefly my other major arguments in the following paragraphs, I claim that states' interactions can produce multiple equilibriums, rather than just one single or dominant one (a situation of balanced power), as balance-of-power theorists are inclined to assert. That is, a situation of balanced power is a contingent outcome rather than a universal law. As attested by ancient China's dominance in East Asia and, more recently, America's attainment of global primacy, outcomes other than balanced power are possible.

Moreover, as Kenneth Waltz (1997, 915) explained, "State actions are not determined by structure. Rather, as I have said before, structures shape and shove; they encourage states to do some things and to refrain from doing others. Because states coexist in a self-help system, they are free to do any fool thing they care to, but they are likely to be rewarded for behavior that is responsive to structural pressures and punished for behavior that is not." If so, one needs to inquire about when—and why—states living in a self-help system are likely to decide that cooperation pays greater dividends than competition. To invoke the well-known prisoner's dilemma game (Jervis 1978), what conditions can get states to move away from the saddle point of mutual defection and to get them to settle on some other more rewarding, self-sustaining process based on a long-term view of the benefits to be gained by cooperation?

This question suggests that structure is not everything or even the most important thing. This view contrasts with those balance-of-power theorists who are inclined to give primary and even exclusive attention to power shifts stemming from the natural and even inevitable differences in the growth rates of states. It proposes that one needs to instead consider the interactions of structural influences and agential strategies (Hui 2005). What a state, like a rising China, does or does not do matters in influencing other states' views—and, as already mentioned, the policies that others, especially the United States, adopt toward China also matter when it comes to Chinese conduct.

Agential strategies can involve attempts to reassure others so that they are not alarmed by one's power gains to mount balancing policies. As already mentioned, balance of power involves not just the competitive logic of reciprocal restraint by states to check one another's power. It also entails the associational logic of self-restraint supported by those norms and institutions that foster mutual trust and coordination. Moreover, I argue that agential strategies are fundamentally about a regime's or elite's ideas about how best to secure domestic political support, legitimacy, and therefore control. In other words, these strategies pertain fundamentally to what a regime or elite calculates to be the most promising approach to hold on to power. The strategies selected can make a huge difference in a state's external relations. When many states in a region adopt similar strategies, their aggregate decisions have region-wide ramifications. That in contrast to the Middle Eastern elites, East Asian leaders have pivoted their regime survival and popularity on economic performance has been consequential in steering their external relations away from balance-of-power dynamics. I therefore problematize the occurrence of such dynamics, treating this phenomenon as a matter of contingency, reflecting elite choices rather than universal reaction to the international system's supposed structural imperative. In so doing, I connect states' foreign conduct to their domestic sources.

Finally, as already mentioned, I shall try to introduce historical contrasts and parallels in order to situate China's recent rise in a broader context, even though space limitation does not allow an extended treatment of precedents such as those offered by China's own preeminence in East Asia roughly between the fourteenth and nineteenth centuries and the predicaments faced by the Second Reich after Germany's unification in the wake of the Franco-Prussian War of 1870. Two reasons motivate my inclination to attend to such a historical and comparative orientation.

First, I reject the often implicit and sometimes explicit claim of Chinese uniqueness or American exceptionalism—and indeed, the ethnocentric and even self-serving treatment that one sometimes encounters in the literature. Thus, for instance, some analysts suggest that China's recent relative power gains have altered its incentives and constrained U.S. influence (observations that verge on being truisms), without even a simple acknowledgment of the implications introduced by these views for the contrasting case of the Soviet Union's collapse and Russia's relative decline to U.S. power and incentives. Selective attention causes analysts to address the policy and theoretical implications of China's relative power gains without, however, considering similar cases such as Germany's and Japan's recent overtaking of the Soviet Union/ Russia in their economic capabilities, even while adopting the position that material capabilities should always trump regime intentions or ideology in explaining the foreign policies of states.

Second, by introducing other historical cases of ascending and declining powers and the alternative experiences and outcomes associated with their capability changes, one can conjecture about "what could have happened but did not" and try to discern the possible relevance of these conjectures for informing the case of contemporary China. For instance, why did the other states not block the United States from achieving regional hegemony in the Western Hemisphere? As another example, the recent decline of the Soviet Union/ Russia and China's recent ascendance should present a quasi-experiment for comparing U.S. responses. Has Washington reduced its armament and alliance commitments in Europe and acted conversely in Asia? If balancing power has motivated U.S. policies, one should see these policies moving in opposite directions in these two regions. Balance-of-power theories cannot have things both ways.

When I remarked above that I reject the view of Chinese uniqueness or American exceptionalism, I have in mind more than just an interest in engaging in historical comparisons and empirical generalizations. I hope to avoid the tendency to emphasize the other's exoticness and one's own special status—a tendency that often borders on cultural stereotyping. Readers of this book will not encounter discussions of the Middle Kingdom Syndrome, China's concept of *tianxia* ("all under heaven"), imperial China's tributary system, or strategizing as reflected by the board game *wei ch'i*. These ideas are not entirely irrelevant to China's contemporary international relations, but these references serve more the purpose of conjuring up some cultural disposition without explicating the interpretive logic necessary to show the usefulness or validity of the suggested extrapolation. It is about as useful as invoking Manifest Destiny, the Monroe Doctrine, the idea of Fortress America, the analogy of American football, Alfred Thayer Mahan's treatise on sea power, and even Thucydides's history of the Peloponnesian War to illuminate current U.S. foreign policy.

Any country with a long history and a rich culture, including China, offers contested ideas and competing, even divergent, doctrines and schools of thought. Indeed, strategic thoughts often embody bimodal injunctions, such as to be cautious *and* audacious, confident *and* vigilant, uncompromising *and* flexible, optimistic about eventual victory *and* realistic about short-term setback (Bobrow 1965, 1969; Bobrow, Chan, and Kringen 1979). Chinese diplomatic discourse and military treatises feature both lofty Confucian rhetoric on the efficacy of moral suasion and hard-nosed, *realpolitik* recognition of military coercion (Feng 2007; Johnston 1995)—just as contemporary analyses of and pronouncements about U.S. policies often incorporate both liberal and realist themes and arguments. Such elements can coexist.

Moreover, there is often a gap between one's self-image (one that may even be shared by foreigners) and a more complicated record of history. China's interstate history is replete with wars and military campaigns that belie the Confucian dogma stressing "soft power" based on ethical teachings and cultural appeal. Actual practice has often departed from ritualistic rhetoric and official orthodoxy. Notwithstanding arguments to the contrary, the Chinese have not always eschewed maritime initiatives, shunned commercial contact with foreigners, or insisted that the latter be treated unequally under the tributary system (e.g., Dreyer 2007; Fairbank 1968; Levathes 1994; Reid and Zheng 2009; Rossabi 1983). Nor has China always managed to maintain a hierarchical system within its borders or in East Asia. Its regional hegemony has not always been accompanied by peace; there have been numerous wars, especially when dynastic authority has declined and imperial rule weakened (e.g., Hui 2008; Wang 2009). Even China's Great Wall, both as a physical and ideational construct, shows the considerable distance that can separate myth-making from historical reality (e.g., Waldron 1990). As these and earlier remarks suggest, I am generally skeptical about sweeping cultural, historical, and even psychological attributions, such as those suggesting ostensible Chinese nationalism, ethnocentrism, yearning for order, or proclivity for authoritarian rule (e.g., Pye 1968) as a basis for understanding contemporary Chinese foreign policy.

There was at one time much American interest in whether Lin Piao's 1965 article commemorating the 20th anniversary of China's victory against Japan's invasion, entitled "Long Live the People's War," publicized a blueprint for Chinese conquest of the world. More recently, there has been a debate about whether the idea *tianxia* offers a Chinese vision of a just world order or camouflages a justification for Beijing's hegemonic ambitions (e.g., Callahan 2008; Zhao 2005). This debate was triggered by Zhao Tingyang's *Tianxia Tizi* (*The Tianxia System*) in which he suggests that the traditional Chinese concept of "all under heaven" presents a more harmonious alternative to Western conceptions of world order. In this book, I will not engage in such textual interpretation and doctrinal analysis as widely practiced by researchers on China's foreign relations. Because others have already written extensively on various official theories or pronouncements (e.g., Shih 2005), I will not address topics such as Mao Tsetung's views on the "three worlds," Deng Xiaoping's advice of "*taoguang yanghui*" ("conceal brightness, cultivate obscurity"), Jiang Zemin's "*duoji shiji*" ("multipolar world"), or the ideas of "peaceful development" and "harmonious society" propounded by Hu Jintao and Wen Jiabao. These declarations present a particular worldview, profess a policy agenda, and even offer some insights about self-image and grand strategy. My predilection, however, is to give more emphasis to actual conduct than the leading figures' public statements—to eschew the practice, if you will, of "slow journalism." As it will also become evident in the following discussion, rather than echoing conventional views prevalent in American and even Chinese scholarship, I am inclined to question and even challenge them. My interpretations and arguments often depart from the mainstream.

Instead of dwelling on the more idiosyncratic or discrete aspects of Chinese foreign policy, such as reporting on or dissecting the nuances of public pronouncements or private interviews, my approach favors generalizations about policy conduct that set China and, indeed, East Asia, in a comparative and historical context. Thus, for instance, I try to show that leaders in East Asia have pursued a model of elite legitimacy and political economy different from that chosen by their counterparts in the Middle East and, to a lesser extent, Latin America. Moreover, my approach attends specifically to the intersection of politics, economics, and security considerations, showing how defense spending can hamper economic competitiveness, and how economic interdependence can build trust and discourage militarization. I have not cited extensively from Chinese language sources—not because of any language handicap, but rather because English language sources have become widely available on the internet. Moreover, Chinese scholars have acknowledged forthrightly that there has been a dearth of distinctively Chinese international relations theories—with much research and teaching heretofore having relied heavily on translations of books written by U.S. scholars (Qin 2007). Academic publications in China have usually applied conceptual categories and interpretative logic prevalent in American discourse—an important indication of U.S. "soft power."

The rest of this book unfolds as follows. In Chapter 2, I take up a review of the pertinent literature on balance of power, power balance, and balancing policies. This review points to areas of tension in this literature. The concept of balance of power has been used not only for international relations theories, but also as a symbol—even as an imperative—in framing discourse and justifying policies.

In Chapter 3, I survey the evidence on whether China's neighbors have been balancing against it. I focus specifically on data pertaining to their defense spending, trade with China, and alignment with the United States, as indicated by the deployment of U.S military personnel on their soil. Both over time and across space, these data contradict the claim that China's neighbors have been balancing against it.

In Chapter 4, I develop an econo-political explanation of why East Asian states have eschewed balancing policies. The opportunity costs of these policies are significant, both economically and militarily, and these costs have become even larger today than in the past because of the severity of guns-versus-butter tradeoff and the prospective reaction of globalized financial markets. I argue that governing elites in East Asia have increasingly staked their legitimacy and regime survival on their economic performance and that this decision is consequential in moving their regional relations in a cooperative direction.

In Chapter 5, I push my argument further and suggest that economic interdependence serves as a substitute for traditional military means of demonstrating resolve, commitment, and reassurance. I pursue my claims by way of four extended "mini case studies" that highlight the contradiction between East Asian reality and the usual balance-of-power expectations. These cases pertain to Taiwan's burgeoning commerce with China, North Korea's declining alignment with China and Russia contrasted with the persistence of the U.S.–South Korean alliance even though Pyongyang has fallen far behind Seoul in capabilities, Japan's decision to eschew nuclear armament and to maintain its defense budget at about 1% of its gross domestic product, and finally, the massive amount of U.S. public debt that China has purchased. To considerable degrees, albeit in different ways, these phenomena suggest nonverbal communication to reassure, or in North Korea's case, to demonstrate resolve.

Chapter 6 presents a series of discussions on the sources of changing power balances, the policy ensemble available to a declining power, and the communication that states can undertake to reassure each other that they are interested in protecting their security rather than expanding their power. It discusses briefly the U.S. ascent to hegemonic status in the Western Hemisphere, Britain's multifaceted attempts to manage its decline prior to World War I, and the Soviet Union's retrenchment policies that brought an end to the Cold War. It also takes up the topic of how a state can establish its trustworthiness in others' eyes. Prussia was able to avoid balancing reactions from other European powers in the Danish-Prussian War of 1864 by signaling self-restraint, invoking common norms, and appealing to their self-identity (Goddard 2008/09).

Chapter 7 continues the theme of credible commitment to build trust and to reassure other states. It specifically introduces institutions of multilateralism as a form of self-binding that makes a hegemon's power more predictable and legitimate in the eyes of others. These institutions were fostered by Washington after 1945, an approach that encouraged long-term cooperation from its Western allies without necessarily foreswearing America's power advantages. East Asia today is still far from reaching the level of multilateralism that characterizes the North Atlantic security community or the European Union. Nevertheless, there is an emergent and increasingly strong network of interlocking bilateral and multilateral financial and economic interests that buttress trust and reinforce cooperation. I present this network in the context of self-enforcing arrangements that make cooperation possible and sustain it in the long run. These developments that entrench cooperative interests and ideas do not necessarily banish power politics but contribute importantly to taming its practice.

Chapter 8 offers concluding comments, advancing three claims. First, by the logic of balance-of-power theories, China is unlikely to initiate a bid for regional hegemony, and if it does, it is unlikely to succeed. Second, rather than adopting the posture of an offshore balancer, the United States has pursued extra-regional hegemony—a policy that has contradicted the expectations and advice of many prominent realists. Third, this U.S. policy has been based historically on a grand bargain, exchanging the "follower" states' political deference to Washington for its military support and economic patronage. This bargain, however, is becoming increasingly strained due to a reduced need by Washington's traditional allies for its military protection and their diminished dependence on the U.S. market and desire for the U.S. dollar. At the same time, the pursuit of extra-regional hegemony will exacerbate further America's guns-versus-butter tradeoff in more challenging economic circumstances. These remarks suggest that China's rise is not the only or even the most important development that may destabilize international relations.

To summarize my thesis, too much emphasis has been given to competitive (or adversarial) logic in interstate relations and not enough to cooperative (or associational) logic. Balance-of-power theorists tend to accept structural anarchy as an axiomatic truth, thus overlooking the prevalence of political order and hierarchy (Lake 2009). They, and some who study domestic politics, contend that it is difficult to reach deals because people (and states) have difficulty making credible commitment. I suggest instead that Asia Pacific countries have had considerable success in overcoming this commitment problem, thereby fostering the macro trends and foundations for regional cooperation.

My claim rests on interlocking international and domestic bargains that have been struck, implicitly or explicitly. These bargains indicate a series of exchanges and were intended to promote confidence in self-restraint and mutual restraint. As just remarked, post-1945 relations between the United States and its allies signaled a grand bargain, exchanging the former's provision of security protection and market access in return for the latter's political subordination. The Yoshida doctrine exemplified one such bilateral agreement. External bargains often have "domestic clauses" (Wagner 2007), with Japan's peace constitution (imposed by the U.S.) providing another obvious example. Alliances such as those of Japan and South Korea with the United States serve not only the purpose of deterring foreign threats but also enable a dominant power to restrain its allies from seeking military independence. Thus these alliances signal Japan's and South Korea's self-restraint by self-binding to the United States, reassuring other states about their intention to eschew military power (most obviously, again, in Japan's capping of its defense budget at 1% of its gross domestic product and its abstention from nuclear weapons).

These external bargains have facilitated internal bargains between several East Asian states and their respective societies in their formative years after 1945. Unlike their counterparts in the Middle East and Latin America, East Asian elites have turned earlier and more decisively to a strategy for regime legitimacy and survival emphasizing economic performance. After the success of this strategy by Japan and the first wave of newly industrializing countries (NICs) became evident, they were joined by others in the region (with China and Vietnam as the latest NICs). Armament and alliance fell out of favor because they contradict an export-led model of economic growth. This model's contagion in turn forged a wider regional network of economic exchanges based on self-enforcing arrangements. Some bilateral parts of this network—most obviously burgeoning commerce across the Taiwan Strait—again communicate a credible commitment to eschew violence and disruption. China's purchase of massive U.S. debt similarly signals "superfusion" and credible commitment by both sides to refrain from defection.

Credible commitment is a distinct, unifying idea for my arguments. It is especially germane to international contexts characterized by rapid and sharp power shifts (which are likely to tempt opportunistic behavior). It requires the powerful states and those that are becoming more powerful to abstain from behaving aggressively or arbitrarily. This commitment does not necessarily entail formal agreements (defense treaties and neutrality pacts have sometimes turned out to be not credible) but can be made credible by self-binding behavior in contexts where all the interested parties are fully aware of the heavy opportunity costs of defection, even if such understanding is not spelled out in writing. Whether written or not, credible commitments stand behind and sustain domestic and international bargains. Significantly, self-binding extends to a regime's pact with its important domestic constituents—such as those that have a vested stake in promoting economic growth and foreign commerce. A state's commitment to eschew aggrandizement becomes more credible to foreigners when its external policies are thus checked by its own domestic interests and coalitions. Foreigners are better able to count on this state's domestic interests and coalitions to self-mobilize against its possible external aggression.

Unlike most studies on balance of power stressing the security imperative imposed by a country's external environment, I argue that a country's security policies are not structurally determined but rather reflect choices influenced by domestic interests and institutions. Naturally, external conditions can also influence a regime's domestic agenda and coalition. This view echoes Robert Putnam's (1988) formulation of two-level games, whereby officials have to attend to both domestic and foreign considerations. When I referred above to the interlocking nature of international and domestic bargains, Putnam's synergistic strategies naturally come to mind. Many of East Asia's initial internal bargains featured a regime agenda offering economic performance first, political rights later. These domestic deals would have been difficult to reach were it not for the political support, military protection, and economic assistance provided by the United States during the earlier years of the Cold War. East Asian states are developing new arrangements whereby they integrate and even reorient themselves with China. Mass values and attitudes in most East Asian countries favor economic growth as a national priority, suggesting that policies that jeopardize this goal, such as those that entail economic boycott or military containment of China, would face a political headwind. Therefore, international and domestic bargains interact: a regime's domestic incentives and interests affect its international relations, and vice versa.

A regime's own motivation to maintain its political legitimacy and viability returns us to the ideas of self-restraint and mutual restraint. Leaders are not myopic; they understand that behaving aggressively or arbitrarily will affect others' perceptions and incentives, inclining them to retaliate. Therefore, cooperative and competitive logics interact. Self-restraint stems from anticipation of mutual restraint—the implicit threat that states can adopt balancing policies to check another state's abuse of power. This prospective (unobserved) retaliation—such as another state's response to one's armament by counter-armament—renders bargains self-enforcing. Mutual defection, as shown by the metaphor of the prisoner's dilemma, produces a suboptimal outcome for both states. An awareness of the severe opportunity costs of armament and alliance has restrained East Asian countries from behaving according to balance-of-power reasoning. The shadow of the future disposes them to eschew balancing policies and inclines them to cooperate.

Interlocking international and domestic bargains, involving self-restraint and mutual restraint, buttress East Asia's regional stability and cooperation. The longer these bargains are sustained, the greater the prospect of continued cooperation. Ideas (especially successful ideas about the most effective strategy to secure regime legitimacy), interests (especially vested stakes in furthering returns from continued cooperation), and institutions (especially those favoring international cooperation and opposing the military–industrial complex) tend to entrench themselves over time. Therefore, in the absence of major shocks or catastrophic policy setbacks, it will become more difficult to overturn these ideas, interests, and institutions undergirding East Asia's stability and prosperity. Even though the spirit of Camelot has not yet taken hold, the ghost of Hobbes has surely receded.

# 2

## Balance of Power, Power Balance, and Balancing

Not so long ago, East Asia was expected to enter a period of interstate rivalry reminiscent of European *realpolitik* of a bygone era (e.g., Betts 1993/94; Friedberg 1993/94). Intense nationalism, weak regional institutions, disparate levels of economic development, diverse regime types, and recent conflicts contributed to this pessimistic prognosis. Like Mark Twain's death, however, this announcement has turned out to be, at the very least, premature.

Scholarship on East Asian relations often reflects a realist premise, even if only implicitly. Attention usually turns to China's recent rise, the implications of this development for the region's power balances, and other states' reactions to China's reemergence as a major power. I argue that despite China's recent gains in relative power, its neighbors have not balanced against it. This non-occurrence is intriguing because it contradicts realists' expectations—especially since, as I discuss in Chapter 3, balancing behavior should have been an easy prediction for them.

This chapter reviews the pertinent literature. It follows the useful distinction offered by Daniel Nexon (2009) along the lines of balance-of-power theories, theories of power balances, and balancing theories. It should become clear from this review that although almost all balance-of-power theories share a realist perspective, not all realists embrace these theories (Levy 2002). Moreover, theories of power balances and balancing theories do not necessarily subscribe to the inevitability of balance-of-power dynamics in interstate interactions. To the extent that these theories assign primacy to nonmaterial factors in their explanations, they fall outside the realist tradition. Before turning to these theories, I discuss the ways in which balance of power has been used in conventional discourse.

## Different Meanings of Balance of Power

Balance of power has been used in various ways, sometimes in an inconsistent and even contradictory fashion (Claude 1962; Haas 1953). Quoting A. F. Pollard, Colin Elman (2003, 8) wrote "[T]he term balance of power may mean almost anything; and it is used not only in different senses by different people, or in different senses by the same people at different times, but in different senses by the same person at the same time." This confusion has hampered meaningful discourse based on shared meaning, and has contributed to a vigorous debate about whether the entire research program on this topic has been degenerative in the Lakatosian sense (Vasquez 1997; Vasquez and Elman 2003). One usage of this concept refers to a given situation, describing the actual or likely distribution of capabilities among the relevant states. This usage, however, can point to an equilibrium or parity in these capabilities—and to a lack thereof. Thus, commentators sometimes talk about the contemporary balance of power in East Asia when they are fully aware that there is an asymmetry of power favoring the United States. That balance of power has been used to describe *any* distribution of national capabilities—and not necessarily one characterized by an equal distribution of such capabilities—is often a source of confusion.

Balance of power has also been used to refer to an ordering principle for international relations. It can be presented in this sense as either an empirical generalization or a normative desideratum, and sometimes in both senses, as shown in the writings of scholars such as Hans Morgenthau (1948) and Hedley Bull (1977). Significantly, that some use this concept in this way is an admission that international relations can be simultaneously adversarial and associational. In contrast to the English School, U.S. scholarship has privileged competitive logic over cooperative logic. The former is emphasized in Kenneth Waltz's structural realism, which argues that systemic forces of anarchy compel states to undertake armament and/or alliance in order to ensure their own survival. In his words (1979, 121), "balance-of-power politics prevail whenever two, and only two, requirements are met: that the order be anarchic and that it be populated by units wishing to survive." These conditions in turn are supposed to produce recurrent situations in which power distribution becomes balanced. The basic motivation for states' behavior in Waltz's theory is their pursuit of security. His theory is therefore sometimes described as defensive realism. In contrast, John Mearsheimer's (2001) offensive realism contends that states pursue power rather than just security, which suggests that great powers seek aggrandizement unless they are checked by countervailing forces.

Balance of power has been given another meaning in the literature. It is often used to refer to policies intended to offset a security deficit. Accordingly, balancing theories refer customarily to attempts by the weak to protect themselves from possible predation by the strong. Yet this term has also been used to describe or advocate policies that have the intent or effect of sustaining and even increasing the power advantage that the strong already enjoy. Thus, Hans Morgenthau (1951, 5, 11) advocated U.S. policies to equilibrate power in Europe and to maintain U.S. supremacy in the Western Hemisphere, both in the name of balance of power. Similarly, when American commentators speak about the balancing policies being pursued in East Asia, many of them clearly do not have in mind policies intended to bring about a situation of more balanced power between the United States and China.

In using balance of power to refer to policies, traditional discourse has stressed "internal balancing," a state's attempt to strengthen itself by increasing its own military capabilities, and/or "external balancing," a state's attempt to form or enter into a defensive coalition against a stronger adversary. Recently, this concept has been used to describe statecraft generally, so that the term "soft balancing" has sometimes been used to characterize the behavior of states that have actually refrained from taking up increasing armament or joining a countervailing alliance in response to preponderant American power. This broadened conception accommodates a variety of policies, practically all of which can be construed as balancing against another country—even if this country is not the strongest one in a regional or global context, and even though the policies in question may involve offensive actions aimed at altering the status quo. The North Atlantic Treaty Organization's attack against Serbia and the U.S.-led coalition's invasion of Iraq have occasionally been justified as efforts to preserve a balance of power inside the former Yugoslavia and in the Middle East, respectively. Balancing then becomes a generic term referring to weaker states' attempts to manage more powerful ones, and in some cases, even to efforts by an existing hegemon to contain the power of a rising competitor, as some scholars have discussed U.S. policies toward China. Balancing can even be directed against a country—such as Serbia or Iraq—that cannot plausibly be construed as a current or prospective competitor to the hegemon.

Analytic confusion is compounded when different labels are used to describe similar behavior depending on the proper names of the countries involved. Therefore, when a secondary or minor state aligns itself more closely with a stronger or rising power such as China, it is described as accommodating the latter—or, as in the case of Germany's or the Soviet Union's allies and associates, appeasing and even bandwagoning with it. These terms are not usually applied when such states align more closely with the United States, clearly the most powerful country even before World War I. They are instead typically said to be joining the United States in balancing against Germany, the Soviet Union, or China, even though the balance of power has not favored the latter countries. This usage could perhaps be understood had the motivation for balancing come from a target country's perceived threat rather than the power it is seen to possess (or to be developing). Such practice becomes more questionable when applied in what is purported to be intention-free analysis focusing on material conditions—that is, on states' objective power rather than their perceptions and intentions. Moreover, implicit in this labeling exercise is the assumption—one that goes against intention-free analysis—that some designated countries are greedy, revisionist, or expansionist but others are not.

These remarks point to another use of balance of power by scholars and officials as a symbol to frame discourse and advocate policies. It can be used to justify a course of action, confer meaning to an evolving situation, and shape a policy or research agenda. As a symbol, this concept is often used to conjure up both the idea of historical inevitability and the impression of tough-minded prudence in conducting interstate affairs. There is a tension between these two dispositions; if states always behaved according to balance-of-power logic, there would be no need for pundits to advise officials to adopt balancing policies. In the context of contemporary East Asia, balance of power as a symbol projects another irony.

As Benjamin Schwarz (2005, 27) remarked about the prevailing American discourse:

> Hardliners and moderates, Republicans and Democrats, agree that America is strategically dominant in East Asia and the eastern Pacific—China's backyard. They further agree that America should retain its dominance there. Thus U.S. military planners define as a threat Beijing's efforts to remedy its own weak position in the face of overwhelming superiority that they acknowledge the United States holds right up to the edge of the Asian mainland. This probably reveals more about our ambitions than it does about China's. Imagine if the situation is reversed, and China's air and naval power were a dominant and potentially menacing presence on the coastal shelf of North America. Wouldn't we want to offset that preponderance?

One would suppose that if balancing policy means anything, it means attempts to offset such preponderance.

Although not matching exactly the hypothetical scenario Schwarz invoked, the United States did of course threaten to go to war against the Soviet Union during the Cuban Missile Crisis, even though there was no doubt that in 1962 it had enjoyed a vast nuclear superiority and a conventional home-court advantage. Setting aside considerations of contested sovereignty and nationalist emotions, it is rather odd that balance-of-power rhetoric has been applied differently when framing the discourse on U.S. policies toward and Chinese designs on Taiwan in contrast to Soviet policies toward and American designs on Cuba. Nikita Khrushchev's introduction of nuclear-armed missiles to Cuba has typically been interpreted by Americans as an offensive rather than defensive move, as an effort to extend Moscow's influence into the American backyard rather than as an attempt at extended deterrence, seeking to protect an ally in the aftermath of the U.S.-organized Bay of Pigs Invasion. In contrast, Washington's policies toward Taiwan and the U.S. military presence in South Korea, Japan, and previously Taiwan are supposed to have served only defensive purposes, and Beijing should therefore not have felt threatened or even become concerned. My point here is not about the validity of the respective intentions being attributed but rather about the matter-of-fact treatment of this pivotal issue in analyses that are supposed to focus only on the balance of power—that is, the objective distribution of states' capabilities—as distinct from the balance of threat.

Although American officials and scholars often invoke balance of power as a symbol or rhetorical device, the actual logic applied in their arguments often belies this concept's traditional meaning and the straightforward policy implications offered by balance-of-power theories. As Christopher Layne (2009a, 121) remarked forthrightly, despite its overwhelming military capabilities, "Washington rejects the notion that China has any justifiable basis for regarding the American military presence in East Asia as threatening to its interests." Former U.S. Secretary of Defense Donald Rumsfeld claimed that any Chinese effort to increase military capabilities necessarily represents aggressive Chinese intention because in his view, "no nation threatens China" (quoted in Layne 2009a, 121). In a similar vein, former U.S. Secretary of State Condoleezza Rice (2000, 56) averred, "China resents the role of the United States in the Asia-Pacific region. This means that China is not a 'status-quo' power, but one that would like to alter Asia's strategic balance in its own favor." Efforts to create a situation of more balanced military capabilities are seen to suggest aggressive intention, and a country's status-quo orientation is judged by its alignment with American interests rather than its adherence to international norms.

Despite their rhetoric, statements made by U.S. officials and policy documents indicate Washington's intention to maintain an imbalance of power in favor of its global preponderance and to forestall a more equal balance of power in East Asia or anywhere else. The Pentagon's 1992 *Defense Planning Guideline* stated clearly, "[W]e must maintain the mechanisms for deterring potential competitors from even aspiring to a larger regional or global role" (quoted in Layne 2009a, 121). The 2002 *National Security Strategy of the United States* also professed an intention to prevent any country from "surpassing, or even equaling, the power of the United States." These statements articulate a policy seeking to consolidate global dominance (Bacevich 2002; Craig 2004), not to equilibrate interstate capabilities as suggested by balance-of-power logic (S. Chan 2010a).

Balance-of-power theories are distinguished from theories of power balances and balancing theories to mitigate confusions such as those just noted. Balance-of-power theories comment on the ordering principles of international relations. The proponents of the current dominant perspective of these theories claim that states (or at least the major ones) act to prevent any one of them from gaining hegemony, and that their aggregate actions in the long run tend to produce a recurrent phenomenon of power being balanced among them. These theories stress the enduring mechanisms induced by the international system's structural properties, such as the processes of competition, socialization, and emulation among states (Waltz 1979). These processes are responsible for producing regular patterns of balanced power and balancing behavior. As Nexon (2009, 335) noted, balance-of-power theories contain theories of power balances and at least partial theories of balancing. Whether the consequent power balances and balancing behavior produce international peace or stability, or even the long-term survival of states, is an empirical question on which balance-of-power theorists often have different opinions. There is disagreement about what should be the proper dependent variable(s) for balance-of-power theories, which in turn engenders criticisms that these theories evade empirical refutation.

Historical evidence from the nineteenth and twentieth centuries is mixed on whether a situation of power parity facilitates peace (Singer, Bremer, and Stuckey 1968). The proposition that balanced power confers a "peace dividend" is contested by the power-transition theory (Organski and Kugler 1980). In some realist writings, war is a possible—even legitimate—means to maintain or restore a balance of power (e.g., Gulick 1955, 35–37). It has been argued that balance-of-power theory "suggests why one expects to observe balancing behavior—not whether balancing will be conducive to peace" (Goldstein 2003b, 197); and that "[b]alancing hypotheses predict either state strategies of balancing or an outcome of balance (or nonhegemony), not peace" (Levy 2003, 132).

However, as Harrison Wagner (1993, 90–91) noted, at least Kenneth Waltz's (1979) writing has concerned peace and stability, such as when Waltz postulated that war and instability are less likely to occur in a bipolar system than in a multipolar system. The prospects for peace and stability are supposed to be enhanced in a bipolar system because the two coalition leaders are much more powerful than their respective allies. This fact in turn renders external balancing (alliances) unnecessary and makes internal balancing (armament) by the two bloc leaders the decisive factor in their power balance. Compared to bipolar systems, multipolar ones are considered more unstable and war-prone because they rely more on external balancing, and the uncertainties associated with alliance politics are in turn supposed to incline states to accept more risks in their foreign policy (Bueno de Mesquita 2003; Little 2007a, 206–207).

However, balancing policies are not guaranteed to achieve their intended objective, whether it is peace, stability, or balanced power. Still, it seems fair to ask what objectives states hope to achieve according to balance-of-power theories (I will return to Waltz's idea that balanced power is a systemic outcome that can occur without deliberate attempts by officials). If not international peace or stability, then would the prevention of hegemony and the perpetuation of survival be the desired outcomes? If so, balance-of-power theorists have to explain the absence of overt balancing by major states against current U.S. preponderance and the recurrence of hegemony in the ancient world of Mesopotamia, Greece, Rome, China, and pre-Columbian America (S. Kaufman, Little, and Wohlforth 2007; Wohlforth et al. 2007).

Barry Buzan and Richard Little (2000, 232) asserted forcefully: "The undeniable fact is that hierarchy was the dominant structural form during the ancient and classical era, and anarchy the exception. Most of the full international systems during this era spent most of their time under some form of imperial sway . . . Numerous cases in this era offer reasons to question the neorealist argument that anarchy is self-sustaining: in South Asia, East Asia, the Middle East, and the Mediterranean, anarchic systems regularly and repeatedly collapsed into empires or suzerain systems." Neorealist expectation is also challenged by the "death rate" of states—which has declined sharply in the past century—and by the continued existence of weak states that are unable to undertake balancing (Johnston 2003b, 111). It is one thing to claim that in individual cases, states may fail to act as expected by theories pitched at the systemic level or that their actions do not produce the results expected. It is a different matter when aggregate patterns over extended historical epochs and in different regions do not support these expectations.

Theories of power balances attend to the persistence of or changes in states' relative power, and address their causes and consequences. The distribution of power among states can result from a variety of factors, with deliberate attempts at balancing being just one plausible cause. Thus, theories of power balances do not necessarily entail balancing policies. Indeed, as already mentioned, there is no guarantee that balancing policies will produce a situation of balanced power. Domestic effort mobilization, entrepreneurial dynamism, and a capacity to innovate technology are among those more important factors that influence the long-term power shifts among states. Some theories of power balances—such as the hegemonic stability theory, the power-cycle theory, and the power-transition theory (e.g., Doran 1991; Kindleberger 1973; Organski and Kugler 1980)—obviously do not expect balanced power to be a regular or "normal" phenomenon in interstate relations. When an existing or would-be hegemon refrains from aggrandizement, this behavior may be due to reasons (e.g., rising nationalism on the part of its potential victims, escalating financial or reputational costs of conquest, peaceful or isolationist public opinion) other than power balance (Nexon 2009, 350). Nor do the proponents of those other theories just mentioned necessarily expect balanced power to produce international peace or stability.

Finally, balancing theories address states' policy choices in response to ongoing or prospective power shifts. Officials' menu is not limited to internal or external balancing. A variety of domestic and foreign factors influence their choices and the effectiveness of their responses. Failing to balance or balancing inadequately, and alternative ways of managing a current or would-be hegemon are empirically possible. Some proponents of balancing theories argue that armament and alliance are not necessarily the most probable response by states when reacting to power shifts. These theories do not necessarily suggest power balancing as states' primary motivation or stipulate balanced power as the most likely outcome of their conduct. Stephen Walt's (1987) balance-of-threat theory offers one example, stressing that states react to their perception of others' intentions rather than others' capabilities. Randall Schweller's (1994) theory of greedy states that bandwagon with a stronger power provides another example pointing to a motivation other than survival or self-protection. These greedy states hope to benefit from a stronger power's wars of conquest; a situation of more balanced power is not their intention, nor is it the successful outcome of their policies. Some balancing theorists even seek to explain why balancing policies sometimes fail to occur or are tardy or lethargic due to a regime's domestic politics or ideological disposition (e.g., David 1991; Schweller 2006; Zakaria 1998).

## Balance-of-Power Theories

In contrast to liberalism and constructivism, realism insists on the primacy of material conditions in interstate relations. As Jeffrey Legro and Andrew Moravcsik (1999, 18) remarked: "For all . . . realists, material resources constitute a fundamental 'reality' that exercises an exogenous influence on state behavior no matter what states seek, believe or construct. This is the wellspring of the label 'realism.' Realism, we maintain, is only as parsimonious and distinctive as its willingness to adhere firmly to this assumption. This assertion, above all else, distinguishes realism from liberal, epistemic, and institutional explanations, which predict that domestic extraction of resources and interstate interactions will vary not with control over material resources, but with state preferences, beliefs, and information."

Thus, even though realists may differ on other matters, they agree (or should agree) that ultimately material conditions determine the capabilities of states, and that these capabilities determine states' policies and the outcomes of these policies. Realists also emphasize the competitive logic of interstate relations, even though they may disagree about whether this competition is motivated by self-preservation or aggrandizement. Balance-of-power dynamics provides a dominant leitmotif in defensive realism. States are expected to prevent any one of them from gaining too much power, thereby achieving an advantage that can be used to conquer them later. Jack Levy (2002, 147) stated this expectation in a form that he thought would be acceptable to most balance-of-power theorists: "[T]he emergence of any single state with the potential to dominate the international system will generate a blocking coalition of other great powers, and . . . consequently hegemonies over the system will not form."

As he pointed out, this expectation reflects an Anglo-American bias, as it usually overlooks the failure of balance-of-power dynamics to prevent the Dutch, the British, and the Americans from attaining global primacy. British discourse on balance of power has typically focused on the European continent instead of dwelling at a global level dominated by nineteenth-century Britain. Similarly, many American realists are drawn to study power balances in regions other than the Western Hemisphere and often do not bother to consider the logic of their analysis for preponderant U.S. global power. This logic often privileges material capability with the claim that states' intentions are always subject to change and therefore cannot be relied upon. Yet some self-acknowledged realists are not averse to introducing considerations such as peaceful public opinion, democratic government, and status-quo orientation when discussing U.S. policy intentions.

Appeal is also sometimes made to the maritime status of the Netherlands, Britain, and the United States, with the claim that as maritime powers they are not nearly as threatening to other states as continental powers. These states could supposedly act as offshore balancers, but they have not been the target of others' balancing policies. This exceptional logic runs into a problem with Venice and more recently, Japan, which is also a maritime power, whose expansion before World War II encountered fierce resistance from others, including the other maritime states just mentioned. Moreover, prior to the nineteenth century, China had often maintained uncontested hegemony in East Asia even though it was a continental power. Indeed, as Victoria Hui (2005) showed, the history of China's Warring States era indicates that a balance-of-power system was hardly inevitable. The Kingdom of Qin was able to defeat its rivals and unify China (G. Chan 1999; Lewis 1999). The emergence of Qin as a victorious hegemon showed that strategies matter as much as structure (i.e., the interstate environment) in influencing interstate outcomes and dynamics. States can pursue self-strengthening policies, seeking to mobilize human and material resources, or conversely, accept short-term expediencies by adopting self-weakening policies such as resorting to hiring expensive mercenaries, contracting unsustainable loans, or relying on tax farming and the sale of public offices, which produce long-term deleterious effects (Hui 2004, 181). I will return to this issue in discussing the guns-versus-butter tradeoff in Chapter 4.

For now, I address briefly the proposition that maritime countries are more likely to pursue and indeed should pursue a policy of offshore balancing. This view supposes that not only should their insular status make them less threatening to continental powers, but this geographic feature should also make them less vulnerable to being invaded and conquered by continental powers (e.g., Jervis 1978, 195–196; Layne 2009a, 127; Mearsheimer 2001, 135–136). As already mentioned, one implication of this reasoning is that powerful, even preponderant, maritime powers are less likely to encounter balancing efforts from other great powers because they do not pose as much of an existential threat to them as continental powers do. Historical evidence based on at least formal alliances directed against the leading maritime power—compared to major continental powers—strongly supports this implication (Levy and Thompson 2010).

Another implication, one that is less often invoked, is that maritime powers should be under less pressure to develop their military capabilities for security reasons. In turn, it suggests that as a maritime power, the United States should be under less pressure to undertake armament than China, which is a continental power located close to other large continental powers. In fact, the opposite is true: the United States has spent more on its military in proportion to its economy. This phenomenon questions the adequacy of using a country's supposed maritime status to explain its behavior. One might plausibly characterize Britain's traditional diplomacy toward continental Europe as offshore balancing, but this characterization does not fit nearly as well with current U.S. policies toward Europe, East Asia, or the Middle East. Both Britain and the United States have in fact pursued extra-regional or global hegemony. Although Britain has been a leading maritime power, the British Empire has simultaneously been a land power—especially when the British Raj in India competed with Russia for influence in South Asia. Moreover, although the United States has vastly more naval and airborne assets than other states, it also has more conventional military capabilities to wage land warfare and occupy countries such as Afghanistan and Iraq. It is not just a maritime power because it is also simultaneously a land power, having fought protracted and distant campaigns in Korea and Vietnam—a feat no other country can match.

The suggestion that a maritime state is less threatening to other states encounters a double challenge from the situation involving Japan before World War II. Japan's neighbors—including China—were surely threatened by Tokyo's aggression, and Japanese leaders themselves felt that their national security was being seriously threatened by the other maritime powers (especially the United States) that were undertaking an economic blockade against it. Therefore, continental powers are not the only source of existential threat to other states; this threat can also come from maritime quarters—as evidenced also by the Anglo-Dutch and Anglo-American rivalries during earlier epochs. The struggles waged respectively by Athens, Carthage, Venice, and the Netherlands against Sparta, Rome, and the Ottoman and Spanish empires further complicate analyses based on a dichotomy of sea and land powers, albeit in different ways.

The discussion thus far hints at a distinction that was taken up explicitly by Emerson Niou, Peter Ordeshook, and Gregory Rose (1989), who suggested that balance-of-power theories address two kinds of stability: system stability and resource stability. They defined the former to mean that no essential state will be eliminated, and the latter to refer to power shifts that can include the transfer of resources from one country to another. In this conception of balance of power, system stability does not rule out war—so long as no essential states are eliminated. From this perspective, the resource changes that result from war and conquest may in fact be necessary to maintain system stability. Indeed, states in Niou and colleagues' theory can voluntarily transfer resources to others in order to ensure their indispensability as essential actors and therefore guarantee their survival. The weakest among the interacting states can do so, for example, by building up the strength of the dominant power to nearly fifty percent of the system's total resources, so that this development would incentivize other states to protect it—lest its elimination would tip the power balance to cross the critical fifty percent threshold to the collective detriment of everyone except the emergent hegemon. In this theory, resource instability may augur either war or peace, and can in fact contribute to system stability under some circumstances (Niou, Ordeshook, and Rose 1989, 317). This distinction between system stability and resource stability is quite useful, and offers an impressive example of a balance-of-power theory that also incorporates a theory of power balance and a balancing theory. It also introduces several knotty questions that invite further critical examination.

Briefly, what does it take for a state to qualify as an essential state? Even a minor power that is capable of tipping the balance between two contesting major powers or blocs can be an essential state. Yet in conventional discussions of bipolarity during the Cold War, it was widely accepted that the United States and the Soviet Union were so powerful that they did not need to depend on their allies for their security. Their assured second-strike nuclear capability would guarantee their security (if not survival in the case of a total nuclear war), even if all their allies were to defect to the other side. If so, why should they pledge to defend their allies—and indeed, why would they want to enlarge their respective coalition and go against the logic of minimum-winning coalition to obtain maximum gain (Wagner 1993)? Moreover, if wars that eliminate essential powers are the ones that transform the interstate system, and if World War II had had this effect in eliminating Germany as an essential power, would Germany's reunification cause the system to transform back to multipolarity? Waltz (1988, 618) remarked, "[C]hanges of structure and hence of system occur with variations in the number of great powers." Can these changes occur without a systemic war, such as when the system became unipolar after the Soviet Union's peaceful demise? And can system transformation occur in the wake of a relatively brief war and without an essential state being eliminated as in the case of the Seven Weeks' War between Prussia and Austria in 1866 (Bueno de Mesquita 1990)? This war presaged Germany's emergence as a potential hegemon in Europe. In what ways and to what extent does resource instability as reflected by ongoing power shifts among the major states—such as the rise of China and the disintegration of the Soviet Union—demote or promote their status as a great power or essential state? Finally, when a dominant state approaches having fifty percent of the world's military capabilities, as the United States has done in recent years, Niou and colleagues' (1989) logic expects both system stability and resource stability because the other states should be energized to ensure that it does not cross the tipping point so as to endanger their individual and collective survival. Yet, thus far we have not seen much evidence of major states balancing against the United States.

Balance-of-power theories have usually emphasized the competitive or adversarial logic of interstate relations. There is another conception that is less familiar to American scholars, one that gives greater emphasis to the associational relations among states even though their concomitant adversarial relations are not overlooked. The English School views states not just as participants in an international *system* but also as members of an international *society*. This associational conception recognizes that the great powers do not only seek to check one another's capabilities and strategies; they also cooperate to maintain stability in international relations—such as when the United States and the Soviet Union collaborated to limit nuclear proliferation. Peace treaties, spheres of influence, and concerts of great powers exemplify attempts to institutionalize "a mutual interest in common security" (Little 2007a, 67). Accordingly, a balance of power can involve not just reciprocal attempts to restrain others, but also the practice and institutions of self-restraint. Little's literature review showed that Hans Morgenthau's (1948) and especially Hedley Bull's (1977) writings addressed both the associational and adversarial aspects of international relations.

Nevertheless, arguments that suggest that the pursuit of excessive power can be self-defeating do not necessarily have to reflect a concern for associational considerations; they can reflect anticipation of other states' adverse reactions. Kenneth Waltz (1988, 625) warned, "In international politics, success leads to failure. The excessive accumulation of power by one state or coalition of states elicits the opposition of others." Thus, according to structural realism or defensive realism, the motivation for self-restraint derives not so much from a normative or associational concern as from a prudent consideration of the competitive or adversarial logic.

In addition to Morgenthau and Bull, others such as Alastair Iain Johnston (2003b, 145) have commented on a tension in classical realism between impulses stemming from structural pressure and motivations reflecting historical contingency. The latter motivations can suggest an associational orientation such that, for example, Morgenthau (1948) "lament[ed] the disappearance of a time in European interstate relations when individual kings and absolute rulers with virtual automaticity heeded norms of behavior for fear of the social punishments from violation—e.g., shame, shunning, loss of prestige and status . . . He even

[left] open the possibility that definitions of power and interest are culturally contingent, implying at least that there is a variation in how actors are socialized to conceptualize legitimate ways of pursuing legitimate interests . . . " Reflecting on East Asia's historical experience rather than Europe's, David Kang (2007b) pointed similarly to the strong societal or associational ties that had bound the secondary states to China—although, clearly, their relations were characterized by an imbalance rather than a balance of power in the China-centered tributary system (Fairbank 1968). The associational perspective on balance-of-power politics has very much been overshadowed by the adversarial perspective, which dominates current U.S. discourse on this topic. It has, however, animated the diplomacy of important historical figures, such as Metternich and Bismarck (e.g., Hamerow 1972; Kissinger 1973).

In Chapter 7, I will discuss Washington's construction of multilateralism after 1945, efforts that have had the intent and the effect of limiting the indiscriminate use of its overwhelming power in return for greater legitimacy for and voluntary compliance with its preponderance by its West European allies (Ikenberry 2001). I will also introduce the idea of self-enforcing arrangements in East Asia based primarily on deep and wide financial and economic interests (Yarbrough and Yarbrough 1992). These arrangements have taken on an associational orientation, reflecting both an increasingly common outlook and shared stakes. Chinese officials' participation in international institutions has produced some tentative evidence of their having been socialized in "the ASEAN way" (Johnston 2003b). The associational logic does not imply the arrival of a security community (e.g., Adler and Barnett 1998; Deutsch et al. 1957) but does suggest that the sharp edges of power competition and balancing can be tempered by self-restraint and mutual partisan adjustment (Lindblom 1965) in East Asia and elsewhere. Associational and adversarial aspects can coexist, and their relative influence on interstate relations can rise and fall over time and vary across specific ties.

## Theories of Power Balances

How can one explain why an imbalance rather than a balance of power has been more often the norm than the exception? Theories of power balances and, more indirectly, balancing theories address this question. The former attend to conditions that affect changes in national capabilities. The latter are about conditions that can ease or hamper efforts to offset a potential adversary's capabilities. They also address the broader question of how states may manage an aspiring or existing hegemon—balancing being just one among many (not mutually exclusive) policies with which they can end up. For both types of theories, the pertinent conditions can be located abroad or at home. As two scholars remarked almost twenty years ago, "[T]he 'balance' between countries may be as much determined by their domestic orientations as by their international power" (Rosecrance and Stein 1993, 21). Neither type expects a situation of balanced power to be a regular or inevitable outcome.

Power-transition theory, power-cycle theory, the theory of long cycles, the theory of imperial overstretch, and the theory of rent-seeking distribution coalitions exemplify the first type of theories that seek to explain changes in the relative capabilities of major powers (e.g., Doran 1991; Doran and Parsons 1980; Gilpin 1981; Kennedy 1982; Modelski 1987; Modelski and Thompson 1996; Olson 1982; Organski and Kugler 1980). These changes can be due to a state's greater capacity to extract and mobilize domestic resources, to its policy reforms enabling faster growth, or to the advantages of backwardness that latecomers enjoy because they can adopt the innovations and learn from the experiences of others. They can also stem in part from a reversion to normal circumstances, such as the Phoenix factor pointing to a country's economic recovery from its wartime devastation. This regression toward the mean is similarly applicable to periods after national stagnation or disarray due to foreign encroachment or a country's own poor governance (such as China's "lost decade" due to its Cultural Revolution). Conversely, institutional sclerosis, partisan politics, and national overextension can reduce and even reverse leading states' growth. Because they start with larger power shares, these states tend to suffer a relative decline because, starting with a smaller base, it is easier for the latecomers to achieve higher percentage gains, thereby improving their relative status. As suggested by this partial catalog of influences on states' growth rates, not all theories of power balances are realist. Indeed, to the extent that these important influences originate from domestic sources, traditional realist attempts at balancing through countervailing armament or alignment are largely ineffective in affecting long-term power shifts.

Some realists expect power balances to be restored, although they do not expect this restoration to be necessarily the result of officials' policies. Thus, for example, Christopher Layne (1993, 11) argued, "Unipolarity is likely to be short-lived because new great powers will emerge as the uneven growth process narrows the gap between the hegemon and the eligible states that are positioned to emerge as its competitors." This statement does not imply that the eligible great powers have deliberately sought to balance against the hegemon, although it does not rule out this possibility either; it simply predicts that a situation of greater equilibrium will eventually return regardless of states' policies. It echoes Kenneth Waltz's view (1997, 914) that "Morgenthau's understanding of balances of power differs fundamentally from mine. For Morgenthau, balances are intended and must be sought by the statesmen who produce them. For me, balances are produced whether or not intended." Whether resulting from deliberate policies or unintentional systemic processes, it is clear that by "balances" Waltz had in mind a situation of more equalized distribution of power, and not just any distribution of power. Although seemingly obvious, this point is germane because some American scholars present developments or policies with the effect or intent of sustaining and even extending U.S. preponderance under the rubric of balance-of-power theories.

Does one country's faster growth than another necessarily mean that the former is balancing against the latter? Few would disagree about East Asia's current or recent power balance. Since at least 1945, the United States has been the predominant power in this region. Clearly, there has not been a balance of power between the United States and China, especially in terms of military capabilities. Although China has made relative gains, the distribution of power continues to be highly asymmetric in favor of the United States. But does China's recent growth, which reduces the huge gap in America's favor, necessarily mean that it is balancing against the United States? According to Robert Ross (2006, 361), "If China is growing stronger in East Asia, then there is necessarily a relative decline of U.S. power. This is balancing." As stated, this view may or may not equate changes in power balances with the intent or outcome of balancing policies. Robert Art (2005/06, 180), however, stressed effect without necessarily implying any intent in stating his belief that one country's power gain would necessarily produce balancing against another country: "If China is engaged merely in a general increase in its military capabilities, with no specific adversary in mind, and if these changes result in enhanced Chinese military power in East Asia at the expense of the United States, then China is offsetting and thereby balancing U.S. power, even if it did not explicitly design its efforts to do so. Increases in a state's power relative to other states have consequences for the balance of power among them, irrespective of the state's intentions."

This view should be uncontroversial, so far as it suggests that the differences in states' growth rates can affect the power balance between them. However, it also removes intentionality, suggesting that balancing can occur even without a deliberate policy attempting to balance. It would subsume balancing theories under theories of power balances. By this reasoning, Japan's and Germany's post-1945 economic recovery and India's and Brazil's more recent economic expansions could also be described as balancing against the United States. Because power shifts are happening all the time, balancing would be a ubiquitous phenomenon—making falsification of the balancing idea virtually impossible since it is almost certain that at least some stronger countries are growing more slowly than weaker ones.

Following Art's logic, a state could even be seen as balancing against others simply because it has become stronger by virtue of its rivals' relative decline. Should the United States be said to have balanced against other states by default, due to the collapse of the Soviet Union? This reasoning suggests strongly that *any* power shift could be construed as balancing, not just that which has the effect of reducing the power asymmetry enjoyed by a hegemon. Objecting to this implication, Stephen Brooks and William Wohlforth (2005/06, 190) remarked that "if the United States were to build up its capabilities to conquer and subdue the EU and China, it would [also] be [seen as] balancing." Any increase or decrease of states' relative power—regardless of whether these changes have the effect of advancing, consolidating, or undermining hegemony, and regardless of whether these objectives are actually being sought by the relevant officials—can be taken as evidence that balancing is happening. In Robert Gilpin's (1981, 13) view, power shifts are inevitable because "the differential growth in the power of various states in the system causes a fundamental redistribution of power in the system." It is, however, a different matter to argue that such a redistribution of power means that balancing policies are occurring. Treating them as though they are the same would confirm balance-of-power politics by definition because some countries are always growing faster than others. It is therefore important to separate theories of power balances from theories of balancing as a policy or conduct.

Even if one acknowledges that states are sensitive to power shifts, it does not necessarily follow that their security would be reduced by a power shift to their relative disadvantage. This remark may sound astonishing but, after all, to many people power is a means to an end, which is security. Relative power gains by a counterpart may actually enhance one's security if they lessen the counterpart's sense of anxiety and vulnerability. Charles Glaser (1994/95, 75) thus explained, "following security-dilemma logic, all else being equal, increases in the adversary's security often increase one's own security because a more secure adversary has smaller incentives for pursuing an expansionist foreign policy, and therefore will pose a smaller threat. This argument does not depend on whether the increase in the adversary's security exceeds or trails the increase in the defender's security, because the change in the adversary's motives reflects its absolute security, not a relative measure of its security compared to the defender's." Consequently, a stronger China—especially one whose military forces have only limited offensive reach—can enhance its security without necessarily compromising U.S. security. As Thomas Christensen (2001, 28) observed, under some circumstances, "China's overall inferiority could actually encourage, rather than discourage, escalation." This logic suggests, for example, that rather than enhancing U.S. security, a prospective missile-defense system is likely to abet China's insecurity and encourage it to undertake countermeasures with possible net adverse consequences for the United States.

A strictly bilateral perspective that assumes zero-sum consequences can also be problematic. Would Chinese interests in maintaining peace on the Korean peninsula, restraining Japanese rearmament, and discouraging Taiwan's independence be helped or hindered by a diminished U.S. influence? This question suggests that when placed in a multilateral context, another state's relative loss does not necessarily translate into one's relative gain, and vice versa. When assessing the effects of differential growth rates on the power trajectories of various great powers, the power-cycle theory shows multilateral and often unexpected ramifications (Doran 1991; Doran and Parsons 1980; Tessman and Chan 2004). In a multipolar world, one's relative decline may be due to an ally's faster growth, so that the combined strength of one's coalition is increased. The policy implications of power shifts are difficult to discern *a priori* when interstate relations are characterized by complex interdependence (Keohane and Nye 1977), with partnerships and coalitions varying across issues and over time. This understanding accords with David Shambaugh's (2004/05, 91) observation, "China's rise need not inexorably result in the eclipse of the United States as a regional power." Surely, a stronger United States turned out to benefit Britain in World War I.

## Balancing Theories

Balancing theories concern states' actual policy conduct in their attempt to check a potential adversary—or their failure to do so. Realism does not expect states to always undertake balancing policies. To paraphrase Kenneth Waltz (1997, 915), states are free to do any foolish thing, but the systemic pressure of living in an anarchic world will shove and push them to balance against others' power for the sake of their own survival. Those that fail to obey this security imperative are eliminated from the interstate system. Competition, emulation, and socialization turn balancing behavior into the dominant tendency of interstate relations, with balanced power hypothesized as a long-term and regular outcome of their behavior.

The very idea of balancing suggests intentionality and, moreover, a target whose prospective capabilities are the object of one's concern. Balancing entails a focus on a specific country with the aim of deterring it, and if deterrence fails, defeating its aggression. In this traditional formulation, "Balancing means the creation or aggregation of military power through internal mobilization or the forging of alliances to prevent or deter the territorial occupation or the political and military domination of the state by a foreign power or coalition" (Schweller 2006, 9). This balancing takes two standard forms: a state's own efforts to build up its defense (or internal balancing) and its pursuit of allies to form a countervailing coalition (or external balancing).

One may conjecture that external balancing is more popular when states are less able to mobilize their internal resources and when the interstate system is characterized by multipolarity. Conversely, a more developed industrial and administrative structure should permit modern states to mobilize domestic resources more effectively than their predecessors, making internal balancing a more feasible option, at least for the more developed ones. Moreover, when bipolarity or unipolarity prevails, external balancing should matter less. The respective leaders of the two blocs in a bipolar world—and especially the global hegemon in a unipolar world—are more than a match for all their allies combined. The addition or subtraction of an ally, even a major one, should not change the basic power balance (Little 2007a; Wagner 1993). When a hegemon's overwhelming military strength means that it does not have to worry about its survival as a state, how can balance-of-power reasoning explain its continued pursuit of armament and alignment?

Balancing theories' conclusions sometimes contradict the claim that balancing is a ubiquitous and even automatic response when states face a rising or dominant power. John Mearsheimer (2001) argued that major states have two basic options: to balance or to pass the buck. Buck-passing is an attempt to get another state to take on the burden of deterring, and if deterrence fails, of defeating one's enemy. Mearsheimer dismissed bandwagoning as a viable policy because a state would be strengthening an associate that could one day turn against it.

Randall Schweller (1994), however, contended that bandwagoning behavior has been quite prevalent. States often join a stronger state thought to be waging a successful campaign of aggression in the hope that they can share the spoils of its victory. Schweller (1996) criticized traditional realist formulations for their hidden status-quo bias, suggesting that states are only interested in seeking survival in an anarchic system. It is more persuasive to view states as being motivated by both fear and greed. Greedy states seek to change the status quo for their own benefit, inclining them to jump on the bandwagon of a winning coalition.

Contrary to Mearsheimer's expectation, bandwagoning behavior is not unusual—and not just for the smaller states—because it appears that in their alliance relations, great powers have more often joined the stronger side (such as the United States during the Cold War) than opposed it (Sweeney and Fritz 2004). Indeed, one may ask what motivates the state that is the bandwagon. What should it seek after survival is assured? Still other scholars, most prominently Paul Schroeder (1994a), have pointed out that when faced with an emergent or even existential danger, most states—such as the victims of Napoleon's attack—have sought appeasement, hiding, binding, and even transcending. These ideas suggest that the menu for choices available to states is more extensive than just internal and external balancing.

More recently, soft balancing has joined the ranks of balancing theories (e.g., Art 2005/06; Brooks and Wohlforth 2005, 2005/06; Khong 2004; Lieber and Alexander 2005, 2005/06; Pape 2005; Paul 2005). It was introduced in response to a failure thus far by the other major states to increase their armament or to enter into a coalition to oppose predominant U.S. power. This non-occurrence has contradicted expectations from prominent realist scholars such as Kenneth Waltz (2000) and Christopher Layne (1993, 2006b). Michael Mastanduno and Ethan Kapstein (1999, 5) remarked, "What is most striking, in the context of neorealist balance-of-power theory, is the reluctance of other major powers to engage in an individual or collective strategy of balancing against the preponderant power of the United States in an effort to create an alternative international order." The major states acted contrary to balance-of-power reasoning (e.g., Brooks and Wohlforth 2008; Ikenberry 2001; Ikenberry, Mastanduno, and Wohlforth 2009; Johnston 1999; Mastanduno 1997). As Zhu Feng (2008) remarked, China has not balanced against the United States, and given the latter's preponderance, such action is unattractive and unlikely.

Soft balancing refers to an assortment of behaviors, ranging from active hindrance to passive acquiescence. Various forms of obstruction, boycott, or mere noncooperation (such as by withholding public approval of or lending legitimacy to U.S. policies) can be construed as soft balancing. It includes nonconfrontational tactics such as "territorial denial, entangling diplomacy, economic strengthening, and signaling of resolve to participate in a balancing coalition" (Pape 2005, 36). This formulation, as some have pointed out (e.g., Brooks and Wohlforth 2005), encompasses such a wide range of behaviors that it can become synonymous with traditional diplomacy. It stretches the concept of balancing beyond its traditional meaning, thereby stripping away what is most distinctive about balance-of-power theories as traditionally formulated. Moreover, if balancing is so broadly construed, it becomes difficult, even impossible, to refute empirically. The gains in connotation are greatly offset by the losses in denotation (Sartori 1970). As David Kang (2009, 21) observed, "The addition of terms such as *soft balancing, underbalancing,* and *prebalancing* does little to provide empirically testable claims but instead appears aimed more at saving a theory from falsification" (emphasis in the original). For these reasons, I adopt the traditional meaning of balancing when I argue that China's neighbors are not balancing against it.

Ted Hopf (1991) compared the incidence and severity of war during Europe's multipolar period in 1495–1521 (consisting of six powers: Austria, the Habsburg Empire, the Ottoman Empire, France, England, and Venice) with those during its bipolar period in 1521–1559 (pitting the Habsburg Empire against the Ottoman Empire) and concluded, "The international situation in sixteenth-century Europe became only marginally more stable after the shift from multipolarity to bipolarity. This record completely contradicts the predictions of polarity [advanced by Waltz]" (Hopf 1991, 486). These predictions assume implicitly that states are more inclined to take risks under conditions of greater uncertainty in a multipolar than in a bipolar world (Bueno de Mesquita 2003). Hopf found instead that "Contrary to Waltz's concerns about the baleful effects of alliance strategies under multipolar conditions, the great powers in sixteenth-century Europe did not pass the buck when confronted by challenges for hegemony in the system. Instead, they continually balanced against the state that appeared the most threatening at any given moment. The offense–defense balance may help explain this balancing behavior."

This conclusion suggests that the dominance of strategic defense is more powerful than polarity in influencing interstate peace and stability. If so, the rise of China—or for that matter, the attainment of global primacy by the United States—is not likely to be as consequential as the continuing viability of nuclear weapons as an effective deterrent. This remark in turn implies that U.S. efforts to build a missile-defense system would be destabilizing. Such efforts would threaten the other nuclear powers because an effective missile-defense system would nullify these countries' retaliatory threat, especially when they have relatively small nuclear arsenals such as in the case of China. Robert Pape (2005, 32) reported a Russian general's remark that Washington's claim that its national missile defense (NMD) will only target rogue states such as North Korea and Iran is "an argument for the naïve or the stupid . . . This system will be directed against Russia and against China." He concluded, "major powers have a basis to fear that U.S. NMD could evolve into a serious effort to acquire meaningful nuclear superiority, an effort that would make sense only if the United States had expansionist rather than status quo aims" (Pape 2005, 34). Whether or not the United States actually acquires this capability, others' perceptions of its intentions and motivations are important because this move can be seen to signify defection from the status quo ante of mutual assured destruction.

Hopf's analysis and other studies (e.g., Christensen and Snyder 1990; Kegley and Raymond 1994; Schroeder 1994a, 1994b; Schweller 1998, 2006) show that despite the tendency for balance-of-power theories to reflect European states' experiences, these theories' predictions have not often panned out, even for European relations (I will discuss this point in more detail later). The expected balancing behavior does not happen automatically—nor do the supposed hindrances to such behavior always work in the ways expected.

One source of the problem, albeit just one, is that just as an aspiring hegemon's neighbors react to its power accumulation and perceived ambitions, this state can also react to—even anticipate—its neighbors' behavior. During the period between 1798 and 1812, "it appears that other states sought to co-opt, reward, avoid, or bandwagon with France instead of balancing against Napoleon" (Rosecrance and Lo 1996, 482). By offering side payments and applying selective coercion, France was able to maintain at least one friendly link in Europe, thereby preventing a countervailing coalition from developing against it—until its invasion army suffered a devastating defeat in Russia. Thus, until quite late in the history of its serial conquests, France was able to follow a divide-and-conquer strategy and exploit the contradictions besetting its potential adversaries. "While each [of these potential balancers] would like a 'balance' to be constructed against France, each country would also wish to be friends with France, or at least to avoid military conflict with Napoleon's armies, diverting his expansion elsewhere" (ibid., 490). Except for the campaign at Austerlitz and the final confrontation at Waterloo, Napoleon was able to take on one opponent at a time. His rapacity and audacity finally forced the victims of his aggression to close ranks. However, even this development did not materialize until his military setback in Russia demonstrated that he was not invincible. Rosecrance and Lo (1996, 492) remarked perceptively that "In 1813–1814, the allies did indeed *balance against Napoleon's threat, but they also bandwagoned in favor of Russia's power*" (emphasis in the original).

Some balancing theories address the scope conditions under which balancing behavior is expected. For instance, Jack Levy and William Thompson (2005, 2010) argued that balancing behavior is most likely to happen in Europe, whose diplomatic history has inspired most of the current American scholarship on balance-of-power theories (this observation, however, does not deny that Chinese strategic culture has historically also endorsed the efficacy of force and the practice of balancing; e.g., Johnston 1995; Lewis 1999). In particular, these authors suggested that balancing behavior is most likely to pertain to continental systems that are both autonomous (i.e., not dominated or penetrated by a strong extra-regional power) and multipolar (i.e., consisting of several major powers). Interstate relations under these conditions present the "most likely" case for confirming balance-of-power theories. If empirical confirmation is not forthcoming in this case, it would be more damaging to these theories, even though confirmation under this narrow set of European circumstances does not necessarily permit generalization to other geographic, cultural, or historical settings.

Levy and Thompson argued that balancing has historically not occurred against leading maritime powers or economic hegemons, such as Britain and the United States, because these states pose less of a threat than land-based military powers that are more capable of conquering their continental neighbors (presumably the other great powers). Having investigated the period in Europe between 1495 and 1999, these scholars demonstrated that countervailing coalitions were more probable against a leading state possessing at least one-third of the combined land forces of the European powers. Thus, external balancing did not always occur against the strongest power or even the strongest land power, but only a continental one that had passed the one-third threshold in its land-based military. Suggesting that the balancing logic only applied to an autonomous European continental system but not a global system led by a maritime power, Levy and Thompson (2010) did not expect other major states to balance against current U.S. preponderance. In their view, compared to their continental counterparts, marine states have fewer capabilities and incentives to invade and occupy other major states.

Stephen Brooks and William Wohlforth (2008) suggested another scope condition. They argued that the United States has now gained such a preponderant advantage over the other major states that it can pursue policies without being hindered by external constraints. Moreover, one should not expect to see balancing against it. Others states, even major ones such as China and Russia, are deterred from this behavior because it would be extraordinarily costly for them and have practically no chance of succeeding. Thus, balancing only occurs within a certain range of a major state's capabilities—that is, when it has enough capabilities to motivate others to balance against it, but is not so capable that it can effectively thwart their efforts. This reasoning in turn raises a question. If the United States is now too strong to be balanced, why did the other major states not act earlier to contain its power? This question can be repeated for other historical cases such as the United States attaining regional hegemony in the Western Hemisphere, the Spanish *conquistadores'* rapid conquest of the Aztec and Inca empires, and the Kingdom of Qin's defeat of its rivals in ancient China to bring about that country's unification in 221 BCE. This question is also pertinent to contemporary China: why have its neighbors not balanced against its current rise?

Some studies have tried to account for states' failures to balance against an extant or rising power. For example, Randall Schweller (2006) showed that due to social cleavages and elite discord, France and Britain reacted slowly and inadequately to Germany before 1914. Norrin Ripsman and Jack Levy (2008) documented that these states sought temporary appeasement in order to buy time to prepare themselves militarily for a more successful showdown with Adolf Hitler in the late 1930s. Britain's decision to make the defense of Poland—an ally which it clearly did not have the capability to defend—as a *casus belli* is puzzling to balance-of-power theorists but can be instructive for developing balancing theories.

As Richard Rosecrance and Zara Steiner (1993, 128–129) noted, balance-of-power logic would have predicted a firm British response to Germany in 1938, but that response did not happen then. Britain made clear its intention to resist Germany only after a domestic political consensus had emerged belatedly in 1939, but by then it was too late to salvage the Eastern front due to the loss of Czechoslovakia (the Skoda factories had already been captured by Germany and the Czech army had been defeated) and the Soviet Union (which had signed a non-aggression pact with Germany). But 1939 was also too soon to confront Germany because Britain and France needed more time to ramp up their defense and secure American support. Balancing considerations should have inclined London to seek an alliance with the Soviet Union, or at least to get the Soviet Union into a fight with Germany. London instead issued its guarantee to Poland, giving "the Soviet Union the two-year respite that it desperately needed itself" (Rosecrance and Steiner 1993, 152). French and British weakness should have inclined them to appease: "From this standpoint, Neville Chamberlain appears as the ultimate neorealist" (ibid.).

Arthur Stein (1993) and Fareed Zakaria (1998) wrote similarly about the influence of domestic politics in the United States, especially popular and congressional isolationist sentiments that restrained the executive branch from undertaking a more expansive foreign policy agenda and a more overt and active role in opposing its eventual adversaries before both world wars. In Stein's analysis, domestic politics inclined Washington to understate its deterrence threat prior to World War II even though it had sufficient resources to undertake more vigorous actions against Germany and Japan and, conversely, to undermobilize its resources even though it had declared its doctrine of containment against the Soviet Union before the Korean War.

As a final example, Jack Snyder (1991) pointed to hypernationalism and logrolling politics in imperial Germany and Japan as important factors that contributed to these states' disastrous overextension—even though their leaders might have considered themselves to be only engaging in balancing against their imperialist rivals. This and other examples previously mentioned point to the influence of domestic politics and political culture on states' ability or willingness to undertake balancing policies. I will say more about the influence of a regime's domestic agenda on its foreign policy in Chapter 4.

External conditions can also help or hinder balancing policies. Countervailing alliances are hampered by the difficulty of organizing collective action (Olson 1965). States are tempted to pass the buck, get a free ride, and make side deals with an aspiring or extant hegemon. Conversely, this hegemon can offer side payments to break up an opposing alliance, and threaten to pick off any state that joins it. As shown by the histories of Napoleon's and Qin Shi Huang Di's conquests, this ability to bribe and punish can impede and disrupt countervailing coalitions. However, when a powerful extra-regional state is ready and able to serve as the anchor of a countervailing coalition, the obstacles to collective action can be more easily surmounted. The United States played this role in post-1945 Europe and Asia (Rosecrance and Lo 1996).

Other balancing theories analyze the question of target selection. Stephen Walt's (1987) theory of balance of threat argues that states do not necessarily try to contain the most powerful one among them; they rather balance against the most threatening state. Their threat assessment is based on various factors, including relative national capabilities, physical proximity, the efficacy of their defensive and offensive capabilities, and past relations. Walt's reformulation of balance-of-power theory into balance-of-threat theory addresses the otherwise inexplicable behavior of Britain, France, Japan, and even China, which had aligned with the United States to oppose the much weaker coalition led by the Soviet Union. Their alignment contradicts balance-of-power expectations. In Waltz's (1993, 74) words, "Balance-of-power theory leads one to expect that states, if they are free to do so, will flock to the weaker side. The stronger, not the weaker side, threatens them if only by pressing its preferred policies on other states."

Walt's turn to leaders' perceptions, however, departs from realism's traditional and distinctive emphasis on material conditions. Moreover, as Gideon Rose (1998, 168) warned, "[T]he link between objective material power capabilities and policymakers' subjective assessment of them remains murky. Critics might see the [neoclassical realist] school's emphasis on perceptions as a giant fudge factor, useful for explaining away instances where foreign policy and material power realities diverge." Indeed, how else could a balance-of-power theorist have accounted for the historical alignment of many East Asian states with the stronger United States against a weaker China? Neither maritime status (discussed previously, with the important caveat that this status is supposed to predict a leading maritime state's incentives and capabilities to attack and occupy the other major states, instead of the minor states that it has quite routinely invaded and colonized in the past) nor geographic proximity (to be discussed later) can easily explain this phenomenon.

Other scholars, focusing on successful hegemonic campaigns in the ancient world—such as those among the Greeks, the Assyrians, and the Chinese Warring States—have concluded that divisions and rivalries among prospective allies and inattention to an emergent power on an interstate system's periphery have accounted for failures to recognize and balance against an incipient threat in a timely and effective manner (S. Kaufman, Little, and Wohlforth 2007; Wohlforth et al. 2007). These factors might have also contributed to Britain's and France's failure to prevent the United States from gaining regional hegemony in the 1800s (Elman 2004; Little 2007b; Rock 2000; P. Thompson 2007). France's consent to the Louisiana Purchase (which increased the territorial size of the United States enormously) and Britain's nonintervention in the American Civil War would both be enigmatic from a balance-of-power perspective. Some have argued that cultural affinity and regime similarity had lessened the perceived threat posed by a rising United States to the declining British Empire. Such explanations, however, stress ideational rather than material factors.

In addition to Walt's balance-of-threat theory, Steve David's (1991) formulation of "omni-balancing" offers another example pertinent to target selection. It argues that unpopular leaders in the Third World are concerned with not only foreign threats but also more pressing domestic threats. They often subordinate the security of their state to the security of their regime or personal power. This motivation inclines them to align with a foreign power that could help them eliminate or contain domestic challengers, even though this patron may pose a serious threat to their state. Some Central and East European states did not respond to Germany's and Russia's power by balancing against Berlin and Moscow, because their incumbent elites were more concerned about domestic partisan politics and internal threats to their regime (e.g., Larson 1991; Miller and Toritsyn 2005). This tendency should also apply to American relations with countries in the Western Hemisphere, where it has undertaken repeated military interventions (e.g., Grenada, Panama, the Dominican Republic, Haiti), and more recently, in South Asia and the Middle East, where American support has buttressed unpopular regimes. During the 1950s, many East Asian countries aligned with the United States more because of their regimes' anticommunist ideology and interest in domestic survival than due to power-balancing considerations.

In one way or another, instead of giving primacy to material conditions, studies such as those just mentioned point to leaders' threat perceptions, regime priorities, historical antipathy, and cultural affinities to explain policies and conduct. Therefore, they depart from Waltz's structural realism, which has sought to distance international relations theories from motivational attributions. These nonmaterial factors also pertain to a current or prospective hegemon's strategy to achieve or maintain its dominance by fostering norms of deference and legitimacy. China's traditional tributary system and, more recently, America's post-1945 international order were both intended to promote other states' voluntary subordination to and the legitimization of the hegemon's leadership (Fairbank 1968; Ikenberry 2001, 2006).

Washington's policy of seeking extra-regional hegemony and undertaking forward military deployment around the world is puzzling from the perspective of some versions of realism. For example, neorealist formulations expect a concentration of power in any given state to cause balancing responses from other states. I have already quoted Waltz's (1988, 625) view that "excessive accumulation of power by one state or coalition of states elicits the opposition of others." Walt's (1987) balance-of-threat logic would also predict that aggressive moves to expand a country's power can increase other states' threat perception and thus cause them to balance against this perceived threat.

Anticipating other states' reactions, these theorists expect that a country with America's geographic position and military superiority would and should want to be an offshore balancer. Despite their different perspectives, both Waltz (1979) and Walt (1987) have warned that ambitious attempts to expand power can be self-defeating (Elman 2009, 66–68). Even John Mearsheimer (2001) implied that the drive to maximize power has limits (due in part to the stopping power of water) and predicted that Washington would (and indeed, should) adopt the role of an offshore balancer. He expected U.S. military disengagement from Western Europe and East Asia after the Cold War. However, Elman (2009, 72–73) and Layne (2009a, 127–129) differ on whether according to offensive realism, power-maximizing moves would be self-defeating.

Prominent realists—many (though not all) of whom are associated with balance-of-power theories—have advocated publicly against Washington's use of wars or military involvements to extend or shore up its extra-regional hegemony. Thus, Morgenthau (1965) criticized the Vietnam War, Mearsheimer and Walt (2003) opposed the Iraqi invasion, and Layne (2009a) objected to confronting China militarily over Taiwan. They were obviously concerned that Washington's policies could be self-defeating, either in balance-of-power or balance-of-threat terms. Even those who are not nearly as concerned about other states' adverse reactions to U.S. actions (e.g., Brooks and Wohlforth 2008) do not see these as self-strengthening moves.

Notwithstanding arguments from these and other realists, Washington has not pursued a policy of offshore balancing, as it did before World War II (see Christensen and Snyder 1990; Stein 1993), and has opted instead to extend and consolidate its extra-regional hegemony after 1945. It has not withdrawn from Western Europe and East Asia after the Cold War's end, and has instead increased its profile in the Middle East (especially Iraq), South Asia (especially Afghanistan and Pakistan), and Eastern Europe (in Russia's near abroad). Some of these developments have surely been spurred by events relating to 9/11, but policies designed to pursue and maintain extra-regional hegemony were already abundantly evident before this tragedy. My focus here is not about approving or disapproving U.S. policies; it is rather about how these policies correspond to expectations derived from balance-of-power theories and balancing theories.

Washington has clearly not favored the emergence of a multipolar world whereby it can assume the role of offshore balancer by passing the buck to others, such as Japan, India, and Russia, in order for them to do the "heavy lifting" of containing rising Chinese (or German or Russian) power. Rhetoric aside, it prefers to be the "lone sheriff" doing the heavy lifting itself, because buck-passing would require a multipolar world. An offshore balancer would seek deliberate aloofness, whereas, in contrast, a policy of extra-regional hegemony would advance close military coordination with and forward military deployment in allied countries. In so doing, states that enact this policy try to discourage other major states—whether they are current allies or potential competitors—from acquiring sufficient independent military capabilities to emerge as separate poles in a possible multipolar world.

Unlike continental powers with roughly comparable military capabilities that live in close physical quarters, the United States has been uniquely advantaged to play the role of an offshore balancer—even more so than Britain during its heydays. In this case, the non-occurrence of the expected contradicts balance-of-power theories and indeed, various strands of realism (Layne 2009a, 131). Balancing theories—such as Christopher Layne's (2006a) explanation,

which incorporates the liberal impulse of U.S. domestic politics and emphasizes U.S. desire for global ideological dominance and economic access to
other regions—try to account for Washington's distaste for offshore balancing.
Such explanations, however, address departures from balance-of-power expectations and should not be confused with balance-of-power theories—even
though, as remarked earlier, U.S. officials and some U.S. scholars frequently
use the argot of balance of power when discussing or promoting Washington's
extra-regional hegemony.

The preceding discussion leads to one final set of remarks about balancing
theories. These theories should pertain to not just the conduct of the weaker
states seeking to counteract the power of a dominant or rising state. They
should also have something to say about the conduct or strategy of the dominant or rising state. Thus, for instance, in their analysis of the anti-Napoleonic
coalition, Richard Rosecrance and Chih-Cheng Lo (1996) observed that the
formation of such a coalition was hindered not just by the usual impediments
to collective action, but also by the ability of the target of this balancing effort to "peel off" potential opponents from this coalition (or to persuade
them not to join in the first place) by offering them counterbids. Similarly,
Victoria Hui's (2005) analysis of Qin's conquest of its rivals showed that just
as the targets of potential domination try to contain an aspiring hegemon,
the latter can counteract to frustrate such attempts. Qin's officials sought to
break up *hezong*—a system of north–south alliances arrayed against it—by
various means of inducement and coercion, and to replace it with *liangheng*,
or an east–west set of alliances that enabled their country to attack nearby
states while befriending distant ones. Therefore, whether or not balance-of-
power dynamics will emerge should be subjected to "A dynamic theory [that]
consider[s] politics as a process of strategic interaction between competing
strategies and mechanisms rather than a parametric constant" (Hui 2005, 11).

## Asian Scholars' Divergent Views

Balance-of-power theories, as presented customarily in the writings of American scholars of international relations, are inspired primarily by European history (Levy 2003; Little 2007a). Barry Buzan and Richard Little (2000, 2, 3)
observed that "because mainstream IR theories are derived almost exclusively
from the model of the Westphalian international system established in the
seventeenth century, they inadvertently, but effectively, isolate the whole discourse of IR from the wider debates about world history." They went on
to remark that "Westphalia-based IR theory is not only incapable of understanding premodern international systems, but also that its lack of historical

perspective makes it unable to answer, or in many cases even address, the most important questions about the modern international system." Not all scholars of East Asian relations, however, share this opinion. We encounter different views about balance-of-power theories' pertinence to understanding East Asian states' reactions to China's rise (e.g., Acharya 2003/04; Friedberg 1993/94, 2005; Kang 2003/04, 2007b; Ross 1999). This divergence is hardly surprising, however, because no common agreement exists about what constitutes balancing policy.

According to Robert Ross (2006, 358), China's neighbors "reinforce the traditional realist and neorealist arguments that secondary states respond to great power capabilities rather than to threat assessment that incorporates an assessment of a great power's intentions . . . [Domestic] politics and intention-based threat perceptions are unnecessary variables to explain secondary state alignments. In this respect, balance-of-power realism explains alignment behavior of East Asian states as much as it does that of European states." He concluded that "there is nothing *sui generis* or culturally determined in East Asian international politics and that realism can explain alignment behavior among East Asian states as well as it does among European states" (Ross 2006, 355); and "balance-of-power politics is taking place in post-cold war East Asia" (ibid., 358). He concluded that China's immediate neighbors (such as Taiwan and South Korea) have become more accommodative to its rising power, but that East Asia's maritime states have sought closer alignment with the United States in order to check Beijing's rising power.

Ross's focus on secondary states corresponds with this book's interest in determining whether China's neighbors have responded to its recent rise by balancing against it. This shared focus takes exception to the claim by some balance-of-power theorists who argue that only great powers are capable of balancing each other and balance-of-power expectations should therefore be limited to the policies of just these countries. A concern with balancing motivation and behavior on the part of secondary and even minor states accords with the research reported earlier about how the neighbors of Prussia/ Germany and the Soviet Union/Russia have responded to them (e.g., Labs 1992; Larson 1991; Miller and Toritsyn 2005; Walt 1988). Ross's treatment of geography, however, departs from standard balance-of-power reasoning, which argues that *ceteris paribus*, the closer a country is to a strong or rising power, the more motivated it will be to balance against it. Geography is a *constant* and thus cannot in itself account for policy *changes* by China's neighbors. Being farther away from the reach of China's land-based military power, the maritime states in East Asia should have less of a security reason to balance against it (compared to those states located on or closer to China's borders) and should therefore be less motivated to seek closer alignment with the United States. Indeed, according to balance-of-power logic, because they are more exposed to preponderant American power, these maritime states should seek closer alignment with China in order to balance against the United States.

In contrast to Ross, David Kang (2003b) warned that theories based on European experiences do not fit East Asian reality. He observed that "First, East Asian states are not balancing China . . . Second, this accommodation of China is due to a specific constellation of interests and beliefs—a particular mix of identities and the absence of fear" (Kang 2007b, 4). Disagreeing with Ross, Kang (2007b, 201) argued that other states' perception of China's intentions and values rather than just its power would determine their reaction to its rise. "Furthermore, the East Asian states prefer China to be strong rather than weak because a strong China stabilizes the region while a weak China tempts other states to try to control the region" (Kang 2007b, 4). Historical evidence from East Asia's past also challenges balance-of-power expectations. In Kang's (2007b, 40) words, "evidence of balancing processes over six centuries is hard to find . . . [B]oth the outcome (stable hegemonic dominance) and the process evidence (no balancing and remarkable stability) decisively contradict balance of power theory." He concluded that "there is little evidence that South Korea will attempt to balance China, and even less evidence that South Korea fears China." Moreover, "the factors that explain South Korean foreign policy orientation toward China are as much about interests as they are about material power" (Kang 2009, 2, 3).

However, the extent to which past history can inform current relations—particularly the extent to which China's historical hegemony in Northeast Asia can be extended to the analysis of its relations with contemporary Southeast Asia—is questioned by other scholars such as Amitav Acharya (2003/04). Some have noted that China's hegemonic dominance in East Asia has not always prevailed (it has often broken down during periods of internal turmoil or fragmentation), and that war has been a rather constant feature in Chinese history (Hui 2008; Wang 2009). The practice and propagation of *para bellum* statecraft has also been prominent in traditional Chinese strategic thinking and is therefore not unique to Europe's Westphalian tradition (Johnston 1995).

David Shambaugh was also skeptical about realism's applicability to Asia. He singled out Mearsheimer's offensive realism, stating "It is a classic example of an international relations theorist, who is not well grounded in regional area studies, deductively applying a theory to a situation rather than inductively generating theory from evidence. As a China specialist, I do not recognize the

China that Mearsheimer describes, and I see no evidence of his 'Chinese hegemony' thesis and thus reject his policy prescription of preemptive containment" (Shambaugh 2004/05, 94). He concluded "Asia is currently witnessing the emergence of a regional community with a multilateral institutional architecture that is based on a series of increasingly shared norms about interstate relations and security" (ibid., 96). Moreover, "the evolving Asian system is oriented not around security affairs or major power relations, but around the increasingly dense web of economic, technological, and other ties being forged among Asian nations in the era of accelerating globalization" (ibid., 97). These remarks suggest that China's neighbors have been, as Kang observed, pursuing a policy of cooperation (see Khoo and Smith 2005 for a dissent), and disagree with the view that China's neighbors are adopting balancing policies out of a concern for their security. This book's arguments and evidence, especially in Chapters 3 and 7, support Shambaugh's position.

Advancing yet another view, Evelyn Goh (2007/08) introduced the ideas of "omni-enmeshment" and "complex balancing," arguing that Southeast Asian countries have undertaken a multidirectional and subtler form of diplomacy in order to engage and influence China. Although these countries have not followed traditional forms of balancing against China, Goh sees them nevertheless seeking to contain and deter Chinese aggression—albeit by means such as harnessing the U.S. military presence and integrating and socializing China in regional institutions and norms. The very idea of omnidirectional diplomacy, however, suggests that the institutional and normative restraints being fostered are not necessarily aimed at a specific country such as China. Moreover, this sort of multilateral diplomacy can be undertaken by any number of states, including China itself (e.g., Johnston and Evans 1999), to influence others. Additionally, an emphasis on institutions and norms typically highlights liberal and even constructivist approaches to international relations (e.g., Ba 2009), and does not correspond with the traditional wellspring of realism, with its core concern about balancing power and its insistence on material assets for providing national security. Furthermore, Goh's analysis suggests that the intent behind Southeast Asian states' diplomacy has been to sustain and support U.S. preponderance, thus suggesting evidence against the balance-of-power expectation of efforts that would seek to offset preponderance.

Naturally, states may seek to secure their relations by binding themselves to major powers so that they become more indispensable to others and so that their counterparts have reduced incentives to oppose them. Such a policy of alignment seeks to mitigate and diffuse others' power rather than attempting to aggregate power with them. The policy is available to an actual or potential hegemon and to others that are less powerful. Otto von Bismarck's complicated diplomacy pursued this strategy, intending to dampen other states' fears of a rising—though less than dominant—Germany (Goldstein 2003a; Hamerow 1972; Joffe 1995; Medlicott 1968).

As a final example, John Ciorciari (2009) argued that Southeast Asian countries have eschewed the traditional form of balancing policies based on military capabilities and collaboration. They have instead followed a "balance of influence" that emphasizes the inclusiveness or openness of their relations with other countries and the economic, institutional, and even ideational aspects of their relations. These emphases agree with Shambaugh's perspective described earlier. They also agree with Goh's ideas of omni-enmeshment and complex balancing, except that Ciorciari introduced explicitly the idea of balancing external influences, suggesting that China is not necessarily the only or even the dominant source of such external influences. Some states, such as Burma (Myanmar) and Cambodia, have maintained closer relations with China, whereas others, such as Singapore and the Philippines, have maintained closer relations with the United States. Yet while keeping, to a greater or lesser extent, such limited alignment, the Southeast Asian countries have avoided exclusive ties and have instead sought multidirectional engagement. Although their conduct may suggest a form of hedging, "'balancing' is too strong a concept to sum up maritime Southeast Asian behavior in recent years" (Ciorciari 2009, 165–166). My subsequent analysis, especially in Chapter 7, agrees with the view that "the most critical changes in the balance of influence have taken place not in military affairs—the traditional focus of balance of power theories—but instead in economic, institutional, and ideational spheres" (ibid., 158).

It is evident that states have at their disposal various policy options for managing an aspiring or existing hegemon (Bobrow 2008a). Evasion, entrapment, and even engagement are on their menu for choices. Moreover, they can buck-pass, bandwagon, transcend, and hide in the hope that a prospective predator will be distracted. Conciliation, accommodation, appeasement, and retrenchment are also part of their policy repertoire. Some may even withdraw to a sullen isolation and accept a protracted descent, as experienced at various times by the Spanish, Austro-Hungarian, Ottoman, and Chinese empires. But should buck-passing, bandwagoning with, and accommodation and appeasement of the dominant power be subsumed by the concept of balancing? This concept loses its distinctiveness when it is stretched to encompass these alternatives. A more extensive conceptual coverage is only purchased at the cost of imprecision and obfuscation. When the concept of balancing is applied to policies that align states more closely with the dominant power—such as when Japan, Singapore, and the other maritime Asian states are said to be balancing *with* the United States in order to check rising Chinese power (Ross 2006)—it contravenes the concept's traditional meaning, referring to the weaker states' armament or alignment directed *against* a dominant state or coalition for the purpose of offsetting their security deficit. Such conceptual elasticity makes it virtually impossible to falsify the claim that states are pursuing balancing policies.

John Vasquez (1997) criticized this protean quality, remarking that realism often presents analysts with a sucker's bet: "heads I win, tails you lose." He also warned about the tendency to assign a new label to behavior contradicting a theory so that it would appear to confirm it. The terms "soft balancing," "balancing with the dominant power," "omni-balancing," and "complex balancing" adopt the terminology of balancing without, however, adhering to its essential meaning. Naturally, this remark does not deny that the behavior being described by these terms may actually be occurring—only that this terminology has the effect of shielding the recognition that such behavior should have been seen as anomalous from balance-of-power theorists' dominant perspective. This linguistic device helps to salvage these theories from empirical challenges without adding any new theoretical content. It is anyone's prerogative to call a particular policy or behavior by whatever name he or she chooses. Felix Oppenheim (quoted in Schweller 1994, 81), however, had enjoined the "avoidance of unnecessary departures from common usage." Stable and distinctive categories, shared meaning, and an adherence to conventional usage help empirical cumulativeness and the advancement of a research program.

When debating about whether balance-of-power politics is occurring in East Asia, the issue engaging analysts is often not really about whether the East Asian states have been balancing against China or, for that matter, the United States—they have not, for the most part (North Korea's nuclear program offers what is arguably the most obvious example of balancing, although it is surprisingly rarely mentioned in this light). The more pertinent issue is whether and how balance-of-power theories should be revised to accommodate these states' anomalous behavior (Brooks and Wohlforth 2005/06, 191). As with the related debate about whether "realism is as realism does," one may legitimately ask whether proponents of balance-of-power theories should be able to conveniently move goalposts in claiming retrospective confirmation for their theories (Harrison 2009), or even to advance convenient scholarly legitimization for policies that actually contradict these theories' central tenet.

## Further Implications

Most of the studies on balancing just surveyed suggest that armament and alignment directed against a rising power are not a prevalent or even common phenomenon. Looking back to the histories of major interstate wars in the last two centuries, the aggressor states' own bellicosity and rashness contributed more to bringing about an overwhelming coalition against them than their eventual victims' own initiatives. By repeatedly attacking his neighbors, Napoleon Bonaparte frustrated attempts by Austria, Spain, Russia, and Prussia to appease and accommodate France's ambitions, to hide from its predation, and to even bandwagon with it. France's own blunders in alienating these countries and in forcing them to fight back did more than anything else, including British diplomacy, to cause the eventual formation of a countervailing coalition. This coalition did not become consolidated until after Napoleon's army had already suffered a serious defeat (Rosecrance and Lo 1996; Schroeder 1994a).

Following the precedent of Napoleonic France, imperial Germany confronted its neighbors in repeated crises before 1914, and its submarine warfare against neutral ships caused the United States, which had been sitting on the sidelines, to finally join World War I in 1917. This pattern was repeated by Hitler's Germany. By launching Operation Barbarossa in 1941 and thus starting a two-front war yet again, Germany brought about an alliance between the Soviet Union on the one hand and Britain and France on the other (e.g., Schroeder 1994a; Schweller 1998). These two sides would have liked to pass the buck in the hope that Berlin would be distracted to focus its predatory attention on the other side (Christensen and Snyder 1990). Thus, Hitler's own actions brought about a coalition that his enemies were not able to engineer themselves.

Tojo's Japan committed a similar fatal mistake; its attack on Pearl Harbor caused the United States to enter World War II. Even though there was little doubt that Franklin Roosevelt had wanted to intervene more decisively on the Allies' side, he had been restrained by a reluctant Congress and an isolationist public (Cole 1983; Stein 1993). Tokyo's action broke the policy impasse in Washington. In this case and others mentioned above, what the aggressor states did with their power—rather than the fact that they were powerful—was the decisive variable. Put differently, a powerful state has a hand in shaping its relations with others. It can act aggressively or reassuringly, thereby abetting or mitigating balance-of-power dynamics. States' own current behavior shapes others' future responses.

There is a reverse side to the above discussion that has tended to receive less attention. Policies seeking to check the Axis powers surely had an effect on officials in Berlin and Tokyo. Washington's assistance to London, including its Lend Lease program and its trade embargo against Japan arguably exacerbated Berlin's animosity and Tokyo's insecurity. Winston Churchill (quoted in Cole 1983, 106) reportedly remarked, "The President [Roosevelt] . . . said he would wage war, but not declare it, and that he would become more and more provocative. If the Germans did not like it, they could attack American forces . . . Everything was to be done to force an 'incident' . . . The President . . . made it clear that he would look for an 'incident' which would justify him to opening hostilities." At about the same time, Roosevelt's decision to deny strategic resources to Japan and to freeze its assets in the United States threatened to undermine Japan's economy and the ability of its armed forces to wage war. With the passage of time, Japan would become increasingly weaker while "the United States was building an incomparably larger fleet" (Barnhart 1987, 267).

Prior to World War I, the Anglo-German naval race undoubtedly contributed to the tension and mutual suspicion between these countries. Moreover, Germany and Austria-Hungary were anxious about the specter of a rising Russia (Copeland 2000; Schroeder 2004). These countries were fearful of the onset of a seemingly inexorable process of relative decline. The problem for Germany as a centrally located power was that it needed to be stronger than the two countries flanking it (Russia and France) but not so strong as to threaten Britain's role as a balancer (Niou, Ordeshook, and Rose 1989). It does not require too much imagination to recognize that China—located near Japan and Russia—finds itself in a comparable situation, having to defend itself without making them or the United States feel more insecure. How can a rising power effectively manage its neighbors' threat perceptions—and vice versa—goes to the very crux of balance-of-threat theories (Edelstein 2002).

The preceding remarks underscore three important points. First, ostensible balancing policies can exacerbate tension and suspicion, increasing the probability of a conflict that they were supposed to deter. They exacerbate the security dilemma, reminding us of Alexander Wendt's (1992, 410) warning that "Realism is a self-fulfilling prophecy." Actually, both self-fulfilling and self-negating effects are germane (Houghton 2009). Successful balancing policies are necessarily self-nullifying such that predicted disasters, such as war and aggression, are averted. Yet the non-occurrence of such a disaster is not sufficient proof that balancing policies have worked. Because other factors might have been responsible for or at least contributed to this outcome, one would have to reason counterfactually, imagining what would have happened had balancing policies not been undertaken. As an example, would the United States have tried to topple Fidel Castro again after the Bay of Pigs episode had it not been for Nikita Khrushchev's introduction of missiles to Cuba and the subsequent deal worked out for Moscow's withdrawal of these weapons in exchange for Washington's promise not to invade again (e.g., Thorson and Sylvan 1982)?

Second, it is not self-evident which countries are to be cast in the role of balancers and which as the targets being balanced. Although Germany and Japan were the aggressor states, an exclusive focus on their power accumulation would miss a big part of the picture preceding both world wars. From these countries' perspectives, the United States was clearly the predominant power—and Russia/the Soviet Union was getting stronger. It is therefore odd for some balance-of-power proponents to argue that the latter countries were necessarily balancing against the former countries' growing power. For those who insist on the primacy of material factors and intention-free analysis, it is difficult to understand why one would want to dismiss what must have appeared to be the two elephants in the room to officials in Berlin, Tokyo, and in 1914, Vienna—the United States was already the world's premier power and commanded a huge capability advantage over the other major states before both world wars, and Russia/the Soviet Union was on a steep upward trajectory that had already enabled it to overtake Austria-Hungary and that would eventually enable it to challenge Germany. Seen from Berlin, it was the combined power of the Triple Entente that urgently required an offsetting policy as Europe entered the second decade of the twentieth century (e.g., Albertini 1952–57; Fischer 1967). As I will discuss further in Chapter 6, the inability to make a credible commitment in the context of ongoing and expected power shifts looms large as a reason for conflict to occur.

Third, there is an "endogeneity" problem that confounds attempts at causal attribution connecting balancing policies to the occurrence or non-occurrence of war. A rising state may be discouraged from aggression because it expects such behavior to cause other states to balance against it. If so, the prospect of others' balancing against it has a moderating influence on this state's policies. Should one then say that balancing is still occurring—and even succeeding—even though it is only anticipated and thus unobserved? How can one be sure that the would-be target of balancing has expected balancing or that it has harbored aggressive intentions in the first place? Selection works also in the reverse direction such that, for example, an aggressor state's decision to launch a war is likely to reflect its calculation (anticipation) that other states will fail to take effective balancing against it. When they focus on those historical cases when war occurs, are scholars not "selecting on the dependent variable" (Levy and Thompson 2005)? Would they be studying a biased sample that overrepresents balancing failures and overlooks those instances when the "dog did not bark" (that is, occasions when anticipated balancing prevented war from breaking out in the first place)?

Scholars might have even overemphasized those occasions when ostensible balancing has contributed to the eventual outbreak of hostilities as a result of the dynamics of states' mutual recrimination spiraling out of control. In these cases that involve more evenly matched contestants—that is, more balanced power—it is more difficult for deterrence to succeed when compared to situations of lopsided asymmetry in the contestants' capabilities. This greater difficulty for deterrence to succeed, in turn, implies more occurrences of war, occurrences that could be interpreted as balancing failures.

To further complicate the picture, if a countervailing coalition forms after war breaks out (e.g., those organized by the victims of Napoleon's and Hitler's aggression), and if such a wartime alliance is successful in defeating the would-be hegemon, should one then conclude that balancing has worked? There is room for debate about whether the effectiveness of balancing policies should be judged by their ability to maintain the stability and even the peace of interstate relations (i.e., to deter the outbreak of war in the first place), or whether these policies' effectiveness should be judged by their ability to thwart a would-be hegemon's bid for dominance—even if it takes a war to do so. Some scholars, such as Richard Rosecrance (2003, 161) and John Vasquez (2003, 92) would argue that the eventual enemies of Napoleon and Hitler tried to appease rather than balance against them, that they were forced to fight back only after being attacked, and that the aggressors were defeated eventually not so much because of the other states' balancing efforts but rather because of the aggressors' own overexpansion and overreaching ambitions—that is to say, because these aggressors did not know when to stop.

To continue the above discussion, when an anti–Napoleonic coalition eventually formed, were its members balancing against France or bandwagoning with Russia? When minor powers such as Brazil joined World War II, were they balancing against Germany or bandwagoning with the United States? Should the delayed entry to both world wars by the United States be considered as evidence supporting balancing or buck-passing, since it occurred after the other belligerents had already been greatly weakened by their fighting? Moreover, if states are truly interested in balancing, should they not join the losing side in a war in order to cause a military stalemate or protracted deadlock? If so, should Italy's switching of sides in World War II be counted against balancing? Should the Soviet Union been expected to assist Japan in the final days of this conflict instead of declaring war against it? If there is not even agreement on whether such actions constitute balancing after the fact, falsifiable prediction of this phenomenon is even more questionable.

As suggested by my subsequent discussion, when victims of aggression join efforts to fight back after they have been attacked, this occurrence represents a rather low analytic bar for supporting balance-of-power claims. Whether states undertake balancing policies prior to the outbreak of armed hostilities presents, in my view, more compelling evidence for adjudicating these claims.

When one considers America's hegemonic ascendance in the Western Hemisphere and its subsequent primacy in a unipolar world, as well as the ambitious agendas of imperial Britain, Napoleonic France, and expansionist Germany and Japan, the opposition mounted by the other great powers have often been tardy and ineffective. One can add to these examples. Although seldom considered in this light, the end of the Cold War signified Soviet submission to American dominance. Mikhail Gorbachev's decision is puzzling from realists' and balance-of-power theorists' predominant expectation. Although the Soviet economy was under severe strain, he could have held out longer and persisted in his predecessors' policy of contesting with the West (Evangelista 1993; Wohlforth 2003). Richard Ned Lebow (1994, 268) argued, "The most fundamental tenet of realism is that states act to preserve their territorial integrity. Gorbachev's decision to abandon Eastern Europe's communist regimes wittingly called the integrity of the Soviet Union into question. It triggered demands for independence from the Baltics to Central Asia that led to the demise of the Soviet bloc. Soviet foreign policy under Gorbachev is outside the realist paradigm."

This episode of Soviet retrenchment and disintegration presents the occurrence of the unexpected from the realist perspective. One also encounters the non-occurrence of the expected from this perspective. Germany and Japan have thus far eschewed nuclear weapons and have continued to accept American soldiers and military bases on their soil (Mastanduno 1997). Their behavior refutes another cardinal tenet of realism, which suggests that great powers do not subcontract their security protection to another country. As another example, although some American analysts have been alarmed by China's recent accumulation of military capabilities, less attention has gone to considering whether, given its rapid economic expansion, Beijing could have ramped up its defense spending even more than it has. The United States has outspent China by a ratio of almost eleven to one in military expenditures (Brooks and

Wohlforth 2008, 29)—a disparity that can hardly be described as anything approaching a situation of power balance. Granted that estimates of military expenditures can be imprecise and subject to debate, this extent of asymmetry is not even remotely close to the power-transition theory's stipulation that to be considered a challenger to an existing hegemon, the next most powerful country should have at least 80% of its capabilities.

It also seems odd that China has accumulated about $1.154 trillion of U.S. government debt as of February 2011 and as much as "$1.5 trillion in dollar-denominated debt in March 2009" (Drezner 2009, 8), thereby helping to fund Washington's budget deficit and fiscal stimulus. Such behavior, in effect contributing to America's military programs, contradicts the logic of balancing. Structural realists or neorealists sharing Kenneth Waltz's perspective may argue that their prediction of the recurrence of balance-of-power dynamics is not about the foreign policies of particular states, that is, that their prediction pertains to systemic rather than unit-level phenomena and, as such, the foreign policy behavior of individual states does not prove or disprove their prediction. Yet as Alastair Iain Johnston (1999, 262) noted, "while *one* single-country test of realist propositions is not sufficient to confirm or undermine realist claims, realists ought to be concerned about the cumulative implications of *many* single-country major-power tests" (emphasis in the original). In Chapter 4, I will develop an econo-political explanation that addresses phenomena such as the seeming puzzles to balance-of-power theories noted above. But before then, I will show in Chapter 3 that contrary to conventional expectations, China's neighbors have not taken up balancing against it—just as China has not taken up balancing against the United States after the latter's ascendance to unipolar status (Johnston 1999).

# 3

## Looking for Balancing
### *The Non-Occurrence of the Expected*

Balancing in its original meaning refers to a state pursuing armament and/or alliances with the intention of offsetting a security deficit. It refers to policies seeking to increase one's own defense efforts and/or combine these efforts with those of others (e.g., Schweller 2006, 9). If balance-of-power theories' dominant perspective, emphasizing the adversarial and competitive logic of interstate relations, stands for anything, it stands behind the claim that such policies are the predominant way states respond to an unfavorable power balance.

This remark does not deny that states can pursue a variety of policies to manage an existing or would-be hegemon. These policies include binding, shirking, bandwagoning, buck-passing, accommodating, and even hiding and transcending. As Kenneth Waltz (2000, 38–39) told us, "that states try different strategies of survival is hardly surprising." At the same time, he (Waltz 1979, 117) emphasized, "If there is any distinctively political theory of international politics, balance-of-power theory is it."

The recent introduction of soft balancing into the vocabulary of balancing policies is a belated albeit accurate recognition of reality. Despite the ascendance of the United States to unprecedented global primacy, there is little evidence that other states have balanced against it. Yet soft balancing stretches the traditional meaning of balancing so that it can include nearly every behavior in the practice of statecraft. Short of enthusiastic and active support of U.S. policies, practically anything (such as foot-dragging, free-riding, and even just a failure to endorse the legitimacy of Washington's actions) can be construed as soft balancing.

As Stephen Brooks and William Wohlforth (2005/06, 188) observed, "the current debate [about soft balancing] is not really about the evidence pertaining to the states' behavior but rather about changing the definition of 'balancing' to fit this evidence." Richard Rosecrance (2001) also called attention to this revisionist tendency, noting that "specific realists" are being replaced by "generalist realists," for whom incentives to balance against potential or actual aggression can be trumped by incentives to wait and even bandwagon (Powell 1999). International relations can then be non-zero-sum and even increasing-sum. Rosecrance (2001) asked critically whether "realism has become cost-benefit analysis."

Although realists tend to agree on common axioms such as the primacy of states in the international system, this system's basic anarchic character, and the ultimate importance of material factors in shaping states' behavior and influencing the outcomes of their interactions, there are multiple "realisms" rather than a single "realism." Some realists, such as Stephen Brooks's (1997) postclassical realists, are open to an intertemporal tradeoff favoring the pursuit of current economic gains for the sake of achieving greater potential security in the future. Others, such as the neorealists, would argue that security concerns—whether those that pertain currently or in the long run—should always trump the pursuit of economic gains.

These neorealists, following the logic of Kenneth Waltz's (1979) pioneering work, give priority to the systemic influence of interstate structure, and they do not typically consider domestic factors in their analyses. Variables such as public opinion in countries bordering China and their commercial relations with China are germane to explaining why they are not balancing against it—but more so in balancing theories than balance-of-power theories, as discussed in Chapter 2.

To suggest that the prospective costs for China's neighbors to balance against it would exceed the prospective benefits hardly offers a ringing endorsement of realism. After all, realism in all its variants stands for more than such cost-benefit analysis, which can also characterize research in other analytic traditions such as liberalism. It is not enough to invoke arguments such as Taiwan and South Korea being too small to balance against China or their benefiting too much from their current commercial relations with China to balance against it. Economic costs did not stop Cuba and Rhodesia, to mention just two examples, from defying the United States and Britain respectively. Clearly, smaller countries—such as Turkey, Iran, and Pakistan in their relations with the Soviet Union (Walt 1988, 1987)—have balanced against their more powerful neighbor. One needs to explain why a country would wittingly enter into commercial relations with another that can possibly hold it up for political ransom (Hirschman 1945).

Neorealism, best exemplified by Kenneth Waltz's (1979) writing, offers a structural theory with spare details and is concerned with systemic outcomes over the *longue durée*. By their very nature, balancing theories are more about unit-level phenomena—specifically, the formation and execution of foreign policy by individual states. In this chapter, I will address this unit level and seek to accomplish the following goals. First, I argue that for several important reasons advanced by balancing theorists, it should be more likely that China's neighbors will balance against it. In other words, these factors tend to create a "most likely" situation for balancing and, accordingly, the credibility of balance-of-power predictions will be more severely strained if China's neighbors do not behave in the manner expected.

Second, I discuss the nature of the evidence on armament and alignment for discerning the presence and extent of balancing behavior. This discussion draws attention to the distinction between necessity and sufficiency. When the pertinent data meet the necessary conditions, one may say that it is plausible—although far from conclusive—that balancing policies are occurring. When, however, they do not even meet the necessary conditions, one can be reasonably confident that balancing policies are not occurring. Such plausibility probes address *prima facie* credibility and, as will be seen shortly, I resort to systematic data as opposed to anecdotal or selective evidence. These data are not infallible, but they help us to see general patterns over time and across space. Pattern analyses are less vulnerable to the errors, distortions, or vagaries that may characterize specific years or cases.

Third, I introduce data on defense spending, deployment of U.S. military personnel, and trade with China in order to discern whether other states are balancing against it. These multiple indicators offer convergent validation, and they all point in a direction that is anomalous from the dominant balance-of-power perspective. The patterns shown by these indicators will provide grist for explanation in the subsequent chapters: why are China's neighbors not balancing against it? Rather than closing this chapter with such an explanation, I will conclude with some general remarks about why it is so difficult—and even seriously misleading—to make definitive claims about who is balancing against whom.

## Variations in the Occurrence of Balancing

Recent work shows that balancing policies are hardly an automatic or inevitable response by the neighbors of a rising or threatening power. If anything, as Randall Schweller (2004, 172) argued, "underreacting to threats, unlike an effective balancing strategy, does not require overwhelming, united, and coherent support from elites and masses; it is a default strategy." Accordingly, balancing policies are not structurally determined but rather depend on contingent factors.

Schweller's remark points to an important distinction. It is one thing to fight back and/or to join a defensive coalition after a country has been attacked. It is another thing to undertake balancing behavior before an aggressor has started its war of conquest. That an anti-French coalition eventually emerged is not terribly surprising because Napoleon had launched repeated military campaigns against his neighbors (Schroeder 1994a). Similarly, that the United States joined the war effort against Japan and Germany can be readily explained after it had been attacked at Pearl Harbor and had met Hitler's declaration of war. Additionally, to say that the Soviet Union became a member of the anti-Axis alliance would be true but incomplete because, after all, it was Germany's invasion that forced Stalin's hand. These easy cases should not count as support for balance-of-power theories. Thoughtful analysts have instead directed their research attention to the prospective balancers' calculations and efforts before armed hostilities broke out. What did they do to deter or prepare for a potential war—as opposed to what they did after they found themselves already in war (Levy 2003, 135; Rosecrance 2003, 157; Vasquez 2003, 95–96)? In addition to Schweller (2006), Stein (1993) and Rosecrance and Steiner (1993) shared this concern in their studies. They concluded that domestic circumstances hampered British and American mobilization against the German threat.

Schweller's (2006) analysis of British and French reactions to Germany's resurgence during the interwar years (as well as France between 1877 and 1913) and of the War of the Triple Alliance (1864–1870, pitting Argentina, Brazil, and Uruguay against Paraguay) showed that these states had also failed to respond adequately to existential pressure. Weak elite consensus, elite cohesion, social cohesion, and strong regime/government vulnerability contributed to a failure to recognize an emergent foreign threat, and to an insufficient and tardy response to address it. Leaders of incoherent states are less able to assume the political risks and costs of mobilizing national resources. Elite agreement (about the existence, extent, and nature of foreign threat) and social cohesion (that people see themselves as a distinct "in group" worthy of the sacrifice of keeping it as a "going concern" against an "out group") figured prominently in Schweller's explanation of "unanswered threats." Their absence caused inaction or inadequate action to counter a foreign threat. Before both world wars, many conservative politicians in Britain and France feared the growing power of the working class, and they were wary of making political compromises with or concessions to labor for the sake of gaining its support for increased taxation to finance armament. Some even perceived socialists at home to pose a greater threat to them than Germany.

Political partisanship, loyalties to countries of origin, and the economic interests of different sectors and regions provided familiar storylines in explaining America's initial isolationism in both world wars and its eventual decision to join these conflicts (e.g., Beard 1936; Cooper 1969; Fordham 2007). In the debate preceding Washington's decision in 1917 to fight Germany, Democratic politicians were naturally more supportive of Woodrow Wilson than their Republican counterparts. Isolationist and anti-interventionist views were stronger among those legislators representing states with a large number of citizens of Irish and German descent. Conversely, support for U.S. intervention was more common among legislators representing the Northeast—which had benefited most from exporting its manufactured goods to Britain—followed by Midwesterners and then Southerners, whose respective exports of grain and cotton had produced less income.

As already mentioned, vulnerable elites and unstable regimes in weaker states may be motivated to seek support from a powerful foreign patron that is most likely to pose a security threat to their state (David 1991). Regime survival rather than national security is the dominant determinant of these states' foreign policy. Instead of balancing against a strong neighbor, states beset by civil strife, ethnic tension, or economic turmoil are often solicitous of assistance from this neighbor, and they can become dependent on its assistance. Accordingly, several East European and Central Asian states did not follow balance-of-power theorists' expectation in their relations with a resurgent Germany during the interwar years and with a more recently reinvigorated Russia (Larson 1991; Miller and Toritsyn 2005). Elites in Central American and Caribbean countries have also been wary of antagonizing Washington (with the well-known exceptions of Cuba, Grenada, and Nicaragua under the Sandinistas), even though they had suffered repeated military intervention and even occupation by U.S. forces (Lake 2009).

The presence and willingness of an extra-regional power to serve as a pivotal anchor for a possible countervailing coalition appears to be of greater importance in shaping the smaller states' policies than these states' size per se. The victims of Napoleon's aggression took so long to coalesce against him because there was no country that could serve as a credible counterpoise to rally and organize the opposition. Physically separated from the European continent,

Britain's role was more important financially than militarily. As Richard Rose-crance and Chih-Cheng Lo (1996) argued, it was Russia that eventually served as the catalyst and focal point for the opposing coalition after it had defeated Napoleon's expeditionary force. Because of their understandable fear of being picked off individually by France, members of this eventual coalition did not join a common cause until it became clear that Napoleon's army was not invincible.

Turning to World War II, Thomas Christensen and Jack Snyder (1990) described the dynamics among the eventual allies as buck-passing. Whereas London and Paris had wanted Hitler to direct his aggrandizement at the Soviet Union, Joseph Stalin was determined not to be sucked into a confrontation with Hitler, which accounted, in part, for the infamous Molotov-Ribbentrop Pact of 1939. During this time, the United States remained on the sidelines. In fact, Washington did not join both world wars until considerably after they had already begun, thus contributing again to the impression of buck-passing. Indeed, even after the United States became involved militarily, the Russians complained bitterly that the Western allies had delayed their Normandy invasion in the hope that the Russians would have borne the brunt of weakening the *Wehrmacht*. Buck-passing tends to embolden a potential aggressor by encouraging its belief that it can "run the table" on its opponents—that is, picking off each target individually by waging a campaign of serial conquest.

Therefore, whether or not there is a powerful great power standing ready and willing to intervene is a crucial factor in deciding the prospect of collective action. This pivotal state has to convince the other states that it has both the capability and the will to organize a countervailing coalition to oppose a rising or aggressive power. Only belatedly did Britain introduce troops to the continent to fight Napoleon, the Kaiser, and Hitler. Its capabilities and, more importantly, its intentions were in doubt. When London and Paris threatened to go to war in 1939 over Poland, Hitler was skeptical, remarking, "Why should Britain fight? You don't let yourself get killed for any ally" (quoted in Huth 1988, 5). He doubted London's sincerity to defend Poland because it was clearly incapable of rendering the necessary assistance. Neither Britain nor France had troops deployed where they could have made a difference in the Nazi invasion of Poland. Thus, British and French pledges sounded like empty talk that lacked inherent credibility.

Compared to the situation just described and the one that characterized U.S. policies before both world wars, Washington adopted a very different role after 1945. In both Europe and Asia, it took the lead in organizing alliances to contain Soviet and Chinese communism. That it had stationed its own troops and established forward bases on the soil of its allies made all the difference. Commenting on how this situation differed from the one that had faced Napoleon's victims, Rosecrance and Lo (1996, 487) observed, "the initial military dispositions of forces in the two periods were different. American forces were *already* on the Continent of Europe in 1945, on a front line dividing the Soviet sphere from the rest of Europe" (emphasis in the original). The United States was already committed rather than just promising to offer uncertain assistance at a later time. By making sunk investments and tying its hands (Fearon 1997), Washington demonstrated the credibility of its commitment.

States may fail to balance, or their response may be delayed to the extent that they are surprised by the sudden emergence of a new powerful state located at the periphery of the central system of international relations. This condition might have contributed to the Qin's ability to overcome a blocking coalition in its campaign to defeat its rivals successively at the end of the Warring States period (Hui 2005). It may also be pertinent to the absence of a blocking coalition aimed at preventing the United States from gaining regional hegemony in the Western Hemisphere. Other cases come to mind from city-states and empires during the pre-modern era (S. Kaufman, Little, and Wohlforth 2007; Wohlforth et al. 2007), such as among the ancient Assyrians and Greeks. Competition among the Greek city-states caused them to de-emphasize the threat from Persia and later, Rome. The indigenous peoples of Mesoamerica and South America were also torn by internal rivalries and insurrections against their overlords, so that some sided with the invading Spaniards and contributed to the latter's rapid and successful conquest despite their small numbers. And, as already mentioned, instead of blocking the ascent of the United States in the Western Hemisphere, British and French officials hoped that they might someday be able to recruit the Americans as an ally in their bilateral rivalry. The suddenness or rapidity with which a hegemonic threat emerges from an unfamiliar source may in part account for a failure to undertake timely and effective balancing policies. As well, intense competition among the prospective partners in a balancing coalition can contribute to this failure.

These reasons, however, are not generally applicable to the contemporary situation pertaining to China's rise. After all, the so-called China Factor has always loomed large in the minds of the region's officials. The United States has provided a pivotal focus for a countervailing coalition, which had already been organized before the onset of China's recent growth. Moreover, China's impressive growth has been an ongoing phenomenon for over three decades. It is difficult to argue that this development has escaped its neighbors' attention or that they have not had enough time to react to it. Finally, two other factors mentioned previously should abet rather than mitigate these neighbors' incentives to balance. China is a continental rather than maritime power—a consideration that is more likely to trigger balancing behavior according to Levy and Thompson (2005, 2010). As well, although China has developed enough power to cause concern among its neighbors, it is still far from attaining the level of preponderance that has, according to Brooks and Wohlforth (2008), made balancing against the United States a prohibitively costly and risky endeavor for other states. Balancing should be more likely when the target is not so overwhelmingly powerful that such efforts would be futile or even dangerous (because of the risk of being picked off by the hegemon), and when the target's power is sufficiently alarming to motivate a desire to contain it (there is no need to balance against a state with only a limited capability to harm others militarily). These structural variables should collectively increase the probability that China's neighbors will balance against it. When they do not, it is more difficult for balance-of-power theories to explain away this anomaly.

## Enabling Conditions for Balancing

Victoria Hui (2005) quoted Jon Elster approvingly, stating effectively that while people may be most motivated to undertake corrective action when they find themselves in the direst circumstances, their capacity to act is correspondingly most circumscribed by these circumstances. Balancing behavior entails favorable conditions whereby both the motivation and the capacity to act are the strongest.

Various strands of realism and balance-of-power theories place much stress on the anarchic nature of a system of competing states. Anarchy and the related competition for security are closely tied to the precept of sovereignty that denies a higher authority beyond the state and that insists on the juridical independence and equality of all states. Nationalism also fuels interstate rivalry and by its sharp delineation of in- and out-groups, abets status rivalry, accentuates stereotyping, and deepens and perpetuates perceived grievances. It is not difficult to imagine that whenever and wherever sovereignty and nationalism have receded (as in contemporary Western Europe) or have never taken root (as in international systems in the pre-modern era), the motivation for undertaking balancing behavior would be more muted if not entirely removed. Conversely, wherever nationalism and sovereignty still hold strong sway (such as in contemporary East Asia), balancing behavior should be more likely.

Naturally, the very idea of balancing presupposes a target to be balanced against and a reason for undertaking this action. These two parts are usually tied in practice, so that the target of balancing is typically a neighbor that is gaining strength, and the motivation for undertaking balancing is to seek counterstrength in order to maintain some semblance of power parity. Underlying balance-of-power theories is the view that any state with too much power is a potential threat to one's security and survival, because one can never be certain about that state's future intentions—that is, whether it would someday use its superior capabilities for aggrandizement. Stephen Walt's (1987) balance-of-threat theory argues that a state's relative strength is just one factor—albeit a very important one—in others' assessment of its threat. Physical proximity, regime ideology, a past history of antagonisms, and perceptions about the relative advantage of offensive or defensive capabilities are introduced as additional information in forming a net assessment of threat.

One may therefore infer that the motivation for undertaking balancing would be stronger when the potential balancers are located in proximity to a rising power, when they do not share similar regime ideologies, when they have had a history of conflict, and when military technology and geographic features make them more vulnerable to an attack launched by the rising power. Conversely, this motivation to balance would be less intense when states face a rising power that is far away, that shares a similar regime ideology, and with whom they have had a history of peaceful relations. Moreover, the urgency to undertake balancing is diminished and the temptation to pass the buck enhanced when officials perceive that the rising state's military forces face significant technological, doctrinal, and geographic impediments in projecting a threat to them, and that strategic defense enjoys an advantage over strategic offense (e.g., Christensen and Snyder 1990; Hopf 1991; Van Evera 1999). *Ceteris paribus*, countries that are physically contiguous to a powerful neighbor should be more inclined to balance against it than others that are farther away, especially when they are separated by a water barrier (Mearsheimer 2001).

Balancing should be more likely when the target is just powerful enough to cause concern but not so overwhelmingly powerful as to render this policy futile and even counterproductive. Robert Jervis (2009, 207) remarked, "while balance of power theory argues that states will unite in the face of a *potential* hegemon, it does not speak to what to expect once unipolarity is established" (emphasis in the original). In a related vein, Robert Pape (2005, 17) argued that because of the danger of being picked off by the hegemon, a balancing coalition should either form abruptly or not at all. Balancing is most likely to be directed against a target that is growing stronger, but is not yet so strong that it has become unstoppable. Naturally, the more extended the period during which this target is gathering strength, the greater the opportunity that the prospective balancers would have to develop and implement their balancing policies.

The discussion thus far has addressed plausible motivations to balance. These motivations should be coupled with an actual capacity to implement them. A significant part of the wherewithal for undertaking balancing derives from the prospective balancers' internal conditions. Do they have strong economies, competent militaries, demographic heft, and a vibrant scientific and technological base to give balancing policies a reasonable chance of success? To the extent that the prospective balancers are endowed with these attributes and, indeed, if they are able to outmatch the target in some important respects (e.g., information technology, military training), balancing becomes a more credible and feasible option.

Naturally, the available national resources have to be mobilized in balancing against another country. Elite–mass consensus, social cohesion, and the ruling elite's competence are all relevant to the efforts to rally political support for balancing. These political conditions operate in conjunction with the availability of material wherewithal for undertaking balancing policies. Balancing policies are an easier "sell" if they are aligned with popular sentiments. Conversely, when public opinion is heterogeneous, divided, and even antagonistic, a regime faces political headwinds, such as in Pakistan with its role supporting the U.S. campaign against the Taliban.

As already remarked, a small domestic resource base can be offset by external conditions. Balancing theories emphasize the role played by a powerful outsider that helps to overcome the impediments to collective action. It provides a counterpoise around which a countervailing coalition can be organized. Presenting a reverse perspective, Kaufman and colleagues (2007) showed that the emergence of a powerful newcomer (heretofore an outsider to the pertinent international system) had often been a key factor in defeating the ambitions of an aspiring hegemon in the pre-modern era.

## Contemporary East Asian Context

The impulse to balance is dampened when states form a security community, when they share common liberal norms, and when popular and elite attachment to sovereignty and nationalism is receding. Thus, one can plausibly invoke these factors to explain a lack of balancing by countries in the North Atlantic area against current U.S. primacy. These considerations, however, generally suggest an opposite effect in East Asia where, for example, ostensible nationalism, territorial disputes, and contested sovereignty should compound rather than restrain states' motivations to balance. Moreover, a history of acrimony and even wars between China and Taiwan, Korea and Japan, and China and Japan should abet these motivations. Armed conflicts have pitted China against India, Vietnam, and Russia since 1949. Like European countries, these Asian countries live in a congested neighborhood and in many cases share land borders with each other. This geographic reality should incline them to be more sensitive to the security imperative emphasized by balance-of-power theories. In contrast, North America has just three countries, with the United States dominating its two neighbors and being flanked by two oceans.

By and large, China's neighbors should present the "most likely" cases for balancing. After all, Japan and South Korea have had large-scale wars with China in the recent past, and they are located right next to China. Others—most notably India, Vietnam, and Russia—have had serious border clashes with China. Some (e.g., the Philippines, Vietnam) have contested Beijing's territorial claims in the South China Sea. Still others, such as Burma (Myanmar), Thailand, Malaysia, the Philippines, and Indonesia, at one time or another have had to fend off communist insurgencies backed by Beijing. Taiwan faces an existential threat because Beijing has always insisted on the island's reunification with China. Thus, it should be most concerned about China's rising power and should pursue armament and alignment in order to offset this development.

Some may argue that many of China's neighbors are too small to balance against it. Size, however, is not the overriding factor (but is likely to interact with other variables, such as the availability of an outside patron) in shaping a state's decision to "take on" a larger neighbor. Cuba and Georgia, for instance, have not shied away from confronting the United States and Russia respectively. Not too long ago, Taiwan and Thailand balanced against China. Their small size, being a constant, could not explain changes in their behavior. Moreover, although Laos, Mongolia, and even Taiwan may be characterized as small, Vietnam, South Korea, and Japan are hardly so. Naturally, when compared to China, these countries are smaller in population and territory. But then, by other measures, such as economic production and military spending, China is "small" when compared to the United States. Similarly, Iran, Turkey, and Pakistan were outsized by the Soviet Union, but this fact did not stop them from balancing against Moscow (Walt 1987, 1988). Even at the height of its imperial power, Britain had only a small army and population compared to its continental neighbors. Therefore, it is not persuasive to claim size, in and of itself, as a reason for the absence of balancing by China's neighbors.

Compared to those East European countries that bandwagoned with Hitler's Germany (Larson 1991), China's larger neighbors possess a greater capacity to balance against it. Japan, South Korea, Russia, India, and even Vietnam are demonstrably capable of taking on this oppositional role. The first four countries are members of the G-20, with the largest economies in the world, and Vietnam fought a protracted war ending in U.S. withdrawal from Indochina. In addition to significant physical size, all these countries have seen their economy expand rapidly in recent years. Additionally, with the possible exception of Russia in the late 1980s and early 1990s, these countries are not typically associated with attributions of administrative incompetence, elite dissension, regime illegitimacy, and lack of social cohesion. Indeed, Taiwan, Korea, and Japan were once offered as paradigmatic examples of strong developmental states (e.g., Amsden 1989; T. Gold 1986; Johnson 1982).

When a country has powerful bureaucrats, a homogeneous society, subdued class cleavages, a strong national identity, and continuous rule by a single party, balancing policies are less likely to be hampered by domestic circumstances. These descriptions apply to Japan, South Korea, and Taiwan, albeit to varying degrees and at different times. Although all three have more recently opened their political processes to competition, at one time they all have experienced one-party rule (the Liberal Democrats in Japan and the Nationalists in Taiwan) or direct or quasi-military rule (South Korea). Whereas subethnic identities have been a contentious issue in Taiwan, this situation does not apply to Japan and South Korea. Compared to most other countries, they should rank higher in social cohesion, elite consensus, and national solidarity.

These observations suggest that the larger East Asian countries should have both the material resources and the political capacity to undertake balancing policies. Some countries lack domestic resources or cohesion to mount a forceful balancing effort against a powerful neighbor. Those countries just mentioned, however, hardly fit such characterization. Their positions relative to China are surely not comparable to those of the Central American and Caribbean countries relative to the United States.

In addition to their considerable physical and economic heft as well as significant policy capacity, the prospective balancers bordering China have already established active and dense networks for undertaking policy coordination, exchanging information, and forging a united front on specific issues. These networks not only incorporate existing regional organizations such as the Association of Southeast Asian Nations (ASEAN), but also hold deep and intimate security arrangements that tie South Korea and Japan to the United States. Given the extensive physical infrastructure, policy networks, and coordination agreements that already connect Washington to its formal and informal allies in this region, it should be easier to organize a collective response to rising Chinese power. If balancing policies do not occur under these propitious conditions, they should be even less likely in other circumstances.

Finally, as already mentioned, a countervailing coalition may appear to offer a realistic chance of containing China, since it has not yet become overwhelmingly powerful. Moreover, unlike Germany's rapid reemergence after the Weimar era or revolutionary France's sudden military ascendance based on *levée en masse*, China's recent ascendance has by now stretched over three decades. Although potential balancers sometimes may not have sufficient time to react to a sudden threat, this amount of time should be long enough to assess whether balancing against China has occurred.

## Armament and Alignment

How does one know when balancing is occurring? The behaviors in question, defense efforts and alignment pursuits, are relative matters that invoke queries about "compared to when, and to whom?" In the next chapter, I will offer some statistics on military expenditures in the Middle East for comparisons with East Asia. In this chapter, I will focus on trends over time and on spatial distributions among China's neighbors.

States' military budgets do not name a specific enemy, and defense treaties do not designate an explicit target—even though one may in many instances reasonably infer the object of their attention, given available circumstantial information. This is especially so when states in an adversarial relationship find themselves having already experienced a series of militarized disputes—such as those described by the literature on enduring rivalries (e.g., Colaresi, Rasler, and Thompson 2007; Diehl 1998; Diehl and Goertz 2000; Stinnett and Diehl 2001). It is more challenging, however, to determine whether a state is the target of others' balancing efforts when their relations have not been characterized by elevated and recurrent tension.

Officials can engage in deliberate misrepresentation (Fearon 1995). They often say one thing but intend another. Therefore, one cannot rely on their public statements, even if they declare an ostensible target for their military programs and diplomatic alignment. Beijing's leaders, for example, are not oblivious to the possibility that Washington's military assets and coordination efforts that are publicly dedicated to the campaign against international terrorism may be really intended to contain China. These military assets and arrangements can in fact be useful for both purposes—and many other imaginable scenarios. Leaders are fully aware that the military hardware and diplomatic support being currently developed by their neighbors can be turned against them in the future. Although great powers are preoccupied with one another, the secondary and minor states are more concerned about relations with their immediate neighbors and historical rivals (such as Thailand for Burma, and Vietnam for Cambodia).

Realists typically insist on a material analysis of the circumstances that states find themselves in because intentions are always subject to change. Today's allies or neutrals can become tomorrow's enemies. Moreover, realists contend that there is a reciprocal relationship between capability and intention, such that one's weakness tempts others to become more aggressive. Presumably, this is what Roman military writer Flavius Vegetius Renatus had in mind when he advised, "*Si vis pacem, para bellum*"—if you wish for peace, prepare for war. This observation implies that armaments and alignments are rarely a bilateral matter. Efforts supposed to contain a professed target can have the unintended effect of alarming third parties, causing them to undertake similar action to protect their security. I will return to these concerns later in this chapter.

For those reasons just given, one can never be completely confident in asserting whether a particular country is the target of others' balancing policies—although one can be more or less certain in making such inferences. On the question of whether China's neighbors have sought to balance against its rising power, one can examine the changes over time and the spatial distribution of their military expenditures. A reasonable place to start would be to ask whether these states have increased their military expenditures during the years of China's rapid and sustained growth. If they have ratcheted up these expenditures concurrently with China's power gains, their behavior offers *prima facie* evidence that balancing may be occurring. This evidence, though necessary, is insufficient for concluding that balancing is occurring because, after all, the increases in their defense spending can be intended for another target, triggered by alternative developments (such as international terrorism and domestic insurgency), and even motivated by reasons relating to the management of domestic political economy, considerations of rent-seeking, and the pulling and hauling of bureaucratic politics. Absent a general trend of rising defense spending in the region, it is difficult to claim that balancing against China is occurring. If defense spending relative to domestic economic capacity has actually fallen over time, this information should contradict the proposition of balancing behavior. Proponents of balancing behavior would certainly not expect a relative decline in the defense spending of China's neighbors while China is growing stronger.

As for spatial distribution, one would expect defense spending to vary with physical distance from China and with the existence of water barriers. Given the "loss of strength gradient" (Boulding 1962) impinging on states' ability to project power from their home base and the "stopping power of water" (Mearsheimer 2001) that further diminishes this ability, those countries located near China should feel more threatened by its rising power than others that are farther away and protected by the ocean. China's military continues to be largely a land force, and it lacks a blue water navy and a long-range air force. Presumably, states that used to fall under China's imperial sway—such as Mongolia, Vietnam, and South Korea—are the most likely candidates for ramping up their military expenditures. Because it faces an indisputable existential threat, Taiwan should be most concerned about China's increased military capability. One may be able to explain away why Australia and New Zealand have not raised their defense budgets, but it is much more difficult to dismiss such behavior on the part of China's closest neighbors if one wants to claim that balance-of-power dynamics is operating. The non-occurrence of the expected in these cases is more devastating for balance-of-power theories.

As for alignment, membership in joint institutions, formal pledges of neutrality, and even defense pacts cannot be assumed to necessarily reflect states' true intentions. These formal declarations and treaty commitments may not always indicate actual balancing policies. Despite their treaty obligations, allies often abandon their partners when the latter are attacked. According to one estimate (Sabrosky 1980), states honor their defense commitments in only about one out of four cases (or 27% of the time). More anecdotally, ruling elites in the Middle East joined the Arab League not for the professed purpose of promoting unification and coordinating military action against Israel, but rather for precisely the opposite reason: to protect their sovereignty and advance their domestic control (Barnett 2003). Ironically, by joining the League, they sought to "*counter* this pan-Arab design" and to "reduce pressures for unification" (Solingen 2008, 285; emphasis in the original). The Nazi–Soviet Non-Aggression Pact of 1939 and the Soviet–Japanese Neutrality Pact of 1941 also come to mind as graphic examples of formal agreements whose ostensible purposes only served to disguise the signatories' true intentions.

Finally, a state may extend critical assistance even if it is not a formal ally bound by treaty obligations. Washington's relations with Tel Aviv approximate this situation. Its commitment to the defense of Taiwan is more uncertain. Having unilaterally abrogated its defense treaty with the island, Washington has expressed continued interest in peace across the Taiwan Strait. It has practiced a deliberate policy of "strategic ambiguity" (R. Bush 2005; Tucker 2005). This example cautions against categorical assertions about particular alignments being directed against China (or any other country) because it shows that officials do not necessarily have fixed or definite intentions.

Stated starkly, the formation or existence of a formal alliance does not necessarily indicate a balancing motivation, nor does its absence imply an absence of such a motivation. As I will discuss in Chapters 5 and 7, alliances can be used to restrain or control a junior partner and to promote transparency in relations with potential competitors. Alliances can even be used by adversaries to each neutralize the danger emanating from the other. The Nazi–Soviet Non-Aggression Pact and the Soviet–Japanese Neutrality Pact were undertaken so that these future belligerents would not have to fight in an additional front and could avoid having their troops tied down to prepare for such a contingency—at least for the time being.

Treaties and alliances are not always pursued for the sake of power accretion; rather, they have often been used to manage or postpone a military conflict between potential adversaries. As Patricia Weitsman (2004) showed, both the original League of the Three Emperors (the *Dreikaiserbund*) in 1873 and the subsequent reconstituted treaty in 1881 were intended by Russia and Austria-Hungary to keep a watchful eye on each other, and by Germany to hedge its security policies (thus avoiding having to choose sides in a conflict between Austria-Hungary and Russia) and prevent its partners from becoming France's allies. Similarly, Austria-Hungary and Italy subsequently joined the Triple Alliance in order to avoid the contingency of having to fight each other while confronting their other adversary, Russia and France, respectively. In these cases, the allies faced a greater threat from each other than from others outside their alliance. Such "tethering" motivation to control an ostensible ally, though not necessarily predominant, was also present in U.S. alliances with post-1945 Germany and Japan. In short, alliances need not be motivated exclusively, or even primarily, by a balancing agenda.

This observation in turn provides a possible answer to the question raised earlier: why would the two bloc leaders in a bipolar world want to seek allies if their security does not depend on these allies? The two leading powers in a bipolar world are by definition much more powerful than their allies, so the addition or subtraction of even a major ally should not jeopardize their security. Their behavior seems enigmatic if one sees alliances as intended only or even primarily for the purpose of augmenting the power of their members in order to balance against an external threat. Their behavior becomes less puzzling if one considers that a tethering motivation may be behind alliance formation. Alliances enable bloc leaders to influence their junior partners' security policy, sometimes to restrain the latter from developing their military autonomy or precipitating an unwanted confrontation with an ostensible common enemy. Indeed, the more an alliance leader guarantees to protect a junior partner (e.g., Taiwan, South Korea), the more it should be concerned about moral hazard—namely, the risk that this guarantee will encourage its partner's opportunism (e.g., to engage it in an involuntary war so as to recapture territories lost to communism). Leaders of monetary blocs have a similar motivation—called "entrapment" by Jonathan Kirshner (1995)—to shape the other members' economic incentives and financial orientations, restraining these subordinate states' behavior by limiting their options.

## Corollaries of Balancing

An exclusive focus on military spending may mislead rather than inform when attempting to discern whether balancing is occurring. For instance, states may be tempted to free-ride and thus spend less on their own defense if they are convinced that a powerful ally would step in to subsidize their security (Olson and Zeckhauser 1966). Therefore, other behavioral indicators should be consulted when making inferences and seeking convergent validation about balancing behavior.

Besides arms spending, balancing includes states' alignment policies. The formation of formal alliances, as indicated by accession to a defense treaty, is not very time-sensitive. In the years since China began its rapid and sustained growth, the United States has not formally taken on any new allies, and Japan, South Korea, and Australia, for example, have not made any new defense pacts or withdrawn from any old ones. The two major changes in U.S. alliances in the Asia Pacific region over roughly the past four decades involved Washington's unilateral cancellation of its defense treaty with Taiwan, and the end of its security ties with New Zealand after a dispute over the visiting rights of nuclear-armed U.S. naval vessels.

Although formal alliances do not show much temporal variation, a different indicator can be used to gauge changes in states' alignment on and coordination of security policies. The number of U.S. troops stationed in various Asia Pacific countries is instructive not so much because it points to the balance of military capabilities, but rather because it signals the relevant states' intentions. If a country accepts U.S. troops and bases, it broadcasts its intention to coordinate and possibly fight with Washington in a future conflict. By this action, it communicates its alignment to the world. States do not take lightly an agreement that allows foreign forces and bases on their soil, as this decision can obviously impinge on their sovereignty, arouse domestic opposition, and even get them into an unwanted conflict (South Korea and Japan, for example, have been wary of being drawn into a conflict between the United States and China over Taiwan). By assigning its troops to particular countries,

Washington is also broadcasting its intention to come to their aid should there be a conflict. The larger the U.S. troop deployment, the greater is the implied commitment. If balancing is meant to deter a potential aggressor that is gaining strength, one can infer whether it is occurring by observing changes over time in a commitment that is obviously costly to both allies.

International trade offers another corollary of balancing policies, although it does not itself represent balancing as traditionally defined. However, trade and other kinds of economic exchange, such as loans and investment, do have important security externalities, and these externalities have aroused concerns about power shifts. Some realists have emphasized that trade confers uneven economic gains that can in turn affect the balance of military capabilities. Such concerns about relative gains impede trade among prospective adversaries (e.g., Gowa 1994; Grieco 1988; Liberman 1996). States eschew trade when they believe that it will contribute to their opponents' strength. After all, this is why the United States led trade embargoes against the Soviet Union and China during the Cold War (Mastanduno 1992).

Trade and other economic relations can be exploited for political advantage. Albert Hirshman (1945) showed that Nazi Germany deliberately fostered the trade dependency of the Balkan countries in order to extract political concessions from them subsequently. Whether deliberately set up or not, extensive and especially asymmetric economic ties can cause political vulnerability, creating a basis for future political holdup by one's opponents should they decide to initiate sanctions (e.g., Baldwin 1985; Copeland 1996; Drezner 1999; Hufbauer, Schott, and Elliott 1990).

Finally, commerce changes domestic distribution of power and interests. It produces stakeholders in continuing and even expanding commerce with a potential target to be balanced, thereby making it more difficult in the future for a state to mobilize domestic support for its balancing policies and for it to convince the target of these policies about the credibility of its deterrence threats. Various countries have tried to exploit the security ramifications of commerce to their advantage. For example, pre-1939 Britain and France sought to use commercial policies to influence public opinion and private interests in Japan and Germany (e.g., Lobell 2007; Papayoanou 1999). Some Americans have supported trade with China with the professed aim of transforming Chinese society.

Below, I present data on armament (internal balancing) and alignment (external balancing). Data on China's trade with its neighbors supplement these two direct measures of balancing. Unlike armament and alignment, which can have any number of intended targets and which can be redeployed against a different target in the future, trade flows identify the parties involved in these transactions (even though trade can be rerouted, such as when Taiwan's firms tried to bypass official restrictions that were previously imposed on them by transshipping through Hong Kong when trading with China). When these multiple indicators converge, they lend greater confidence when concluding that balancing against China is, or is not, occurring.

## Blowin' in the Wind

The answer to the question whether China's neighbors are balancing against it can be straightforward and elusive at the same time. As already mentioned, armament and alignment can have multiple, often undeclared, targets that are subject to change over time. China need not be the necessary or exclusive reason for its neighbors' changing armament and alignment. Events unrelated to China—such as the U.S.-led campaign against terrorism—may be a reason for these changes. Moreover, U.S. military personnel can include combat forces but are not necessarily limited to them.

This said, it is difficult to sustain expectations about balancing against China if there is scant evidence from armament and alignment behavior to support them. Where else should one look for this evidence if it cannot be discerned from defense spending and military collaboration? Recognizing that the figures for individual countries and specific years can be fallible, one would naturally want to attend to patterns across countries and trends over time. It is one thing for Mongolia, Laos, or Bangladesh not to increase their defense spending on the grounds that they are too small, poor, or distant (either physically or figuratively) from China, but it is quite another matter to see South Korea, Japan, and Taiwan behaving similarly. It is difficult to maintain that the latter neighbors are too weak to balance, or in Taiwan's case, that it does not face an existential threat. Their behaviors should be especially informative, since evidence on balancing is most likely to come from them. Moreover, should the data over time for the latter countries contradict the trend expected by balance-of-power theorists, this evidence would be more damaging. Have they become more alarmed by China's recent power gains, disposing them to mobilize their domestic resources to a greater extent than previously in order to strengthen their defense?

China's neighbors are grouped into three categories in Tables 1 and 2. The first group consists of those countries that share a contiguous border with China. This group is most exposed to China's military, which is still primarily a land force. It includes Russia and several members of the Commonwealth of Independent States (e.g., Kazakhstan, Kyrgyzstan, and Tajikistan). These states have joined China in the Shanghai Cooperation Organization, and thus present a contrast to their European counterparts, who have sought to join NATO. The second group of countries in Tables 1 and 2 is in China's near abroad. Although they do not share a land border with China, they often have intense economic exchanges and intimate historical ties with China, especially for South Korea. The third group, labeled "maritime," refers to countries that are separated from China by water. This water barrier can be quite variable, however. Thus, Taiwan is much closer to China—both physically and culturally—than New Zealand is to China. There are obviously other ways of grouping the various countries, such as on the basis of cultural affinity, economic interdependence, or regime similarity. Tables 1 and 2 are organized instead on the basis of physical proximity and the "stopping power of water" according to balance-of-power theorists' traditional emphasis on a state's ability to project its military power.

Each group contains some especially salient and therefore informative cases. Among China's contiguous neighbors, India, Russia, and Vietnam each commands sufficient heft to undertake balancing behavior, and they all have had acrimonious relations with China. Among those in the near abroad, Thailand and especially South Korea have been close U.S. allies, and one would expect them to be strong candidates to deepen their alignment with Washington in any emergent balancing coalition against Beijing. The behavior of countries in the last group— China's maritime neighbors such as Taiwan, Japan, and Malaysia—should be especially instructive. Taiwan faces pressure from China to reunify, and it is the most likely target of Beijing's military action. Japan is China's natural competitor for influence among their mutual neighbors, and it is also a long-time close ally of the United States. With its large ethnic Chinese population and its previous experience of having to fight a communist insurgency supported largely by its citizens of Chinese descent, Malaysia should have an added domestic reason for being concerned about a rising China. The majority of the citizens of Singapore, its nearby neighbor, are of Chinese origin.

Table 1 shows a broad pattern, featuring a declining defense burden for almost all of China's neighbors. The major exception is North Korea, which has increased its military spending as a percent of gross domestic product from 21.5 in 1995 to 31.1 in 2005. Pyongyang's behavior, however, is more reasonably understood as balancing against South Korea and the United States rather than China. Two former members of the Soviet Union, Kyrgyzstan and Tajikistan, have also increased their defense burden, albeit much more modestly. These cases indicate more of a concern about possible challenges from Islamic fundamentalists than from China. Significantly, these three countries that show

TABLE I

*Defense burden (military expenditures as percent of gross domestic product)*

|  | 1990[a] | 1995 | 2000 | 2005 |
|---|---|---|---|---|
| China | 3.5 | 4.3 | 4.3 | 3.8 |
| *Contiguous* | | | | |
| Afghanistan | n.a. | n.a. | n.a. | 1.8 |
| India | 2.7 | 2.2 | 2.6 | 2.3 |
| Kazakhstan | 2.9 | 1.9 | 0.8 | 1.0 |
| Korea, North | 21.5 | 29.3 | 29.1 | 31.1 |
| Kyrgyzstan | 0.7 | 1.6 | 2.9 | 3.1 |
| Laos | 2.5 | 5.0 | 2.0 | n.a. |
| Mongolia | 8.6 | 1.8 | 2.2 | 1.3 |
| Myanmar | 7.2 | n.a. | n.a. | n.a. |
| Nepal | 1.0 | 0.9 | 1.0 | 1.8 |
| Pakistan | 7.1 | 6.0 | 4.0 | 3.4 |
| Russia (USSR in 1990) | 11.0 | 4.0 | 4.8 | 4.1 |
| Tajikistan | 0.3 | 1.0 | 1.2 | 1.4 |
| Vietnam | 7.9 | 5.1 | 5.0 | 4.9 |
| *Near Abroad* | | | | |
| Bangladesh | 1.2 | 1.4 | 1.4 | 1.1 |
| Cambodia | 3.5 | 2.6 | 2.2 | 1.1 |
| Korea, South | 4.2 | 2.8 | 2.5 | 2.3 |
| Thailand | 2.5 | 2.2 | 1.5 | 1.2 |
| Uzbekistan | 2.7 | 1.1 | 1.5 | 1.4 |
| *Maritime* | | | | |
| Australia | 2.2 | 2.3 | 2.0 | 1.9 |
| Brunei | 5.3 | 6.3 | 5.1 | 3.2 |
| Indonesia | 1.5 | 1.6 | 1.0 | 1.2 |
| Japan | 1.0 | 1.0 | 1.0 | 1.0 |
| Malaysia | 2.7 | 2.8 | 1.7 | 2.3 |
| New Zealand | 2.1 | 1.4 | 1.2 | 1.0 |
| Papua New Guinea | 2.2 | 1.2 | 1.0 | 0.6 |
| Philippines | 2.2 | 1.4 | 1.2 | 0.8 |
| Singapore | 5.0 | 4.6 | 4.8 | 4.6 |
| Taiwan | 4.7 | 3.8 | 2.4 | 2.3 |

SOURCES: http://www.state.gov/documents/organization/121777.xls and http://www.globalsecurity.org/library/report/2003/wmeat9900/19476.xls, both accessed on April 14, 2009.

[a] The figures for this column are military expenditures as a percentage of gross national product. For Kazakhstan, Tajikistan, and Uzbekistan, the figures are for the year 1992; Kyrgyzstan's figure is for 1993; and Russia's 1990 figure is for the USSR. The figures for Cambodia, Myanmar, and North Korea are for 1991, and Laos's figure is for 1989.

substantial increases in military spending happen to be the least likely to target China in their military preparations.

There is scant evidence that countries located closer to China, or those that face a greater existential threat from China, have undertaken more vigorous armament programs. Mongolia, Vietnam, Thailand, and South Korea have all reduced their defense burdens, and substantially so in the case of Mongolia.

TABLE 2

*U.S. military personnel stationed abroad*

| | 1970 | 1990 | 1995 | 2000 | 2005 |
|---|---|---|---|---|---|
| *Contiguous* | | | | | |
| Afghanistan | 7 | — | — | — | 19,500 |
| India | 39 | 43 | 27 | 20 | 31 |
| Kazakhstan | — | — | 9 | 11 | 6 |
| Korea, North | — | — | — | — | — |
| Kyrgyzstan | — | — | 1 | 9 | 5 |
| Laos | 22 | — | 3 | 2 | 3 |
| Mongolia | — | — | — | — | 5 |
| Myanmar | 13 | 10 | 9 | 7 | — |
| Nepal | 5 | 10 | 7 | 5 | 9 |
| Pakistan | 24 | 55 | 28 | 22 | 35 |
| Russia / USSR | 30 | 58 | 60 | 101 | 44 |
| Tajikistan | — | — | 1 | 1 | — |
| Vietnam | 390,278[a] | — | 4 | 16 | 13 |
| *Near Abroad* | | | | | |
| Bangladesh | — | 9 | 9 | 8 | 7 |
| Cambodia | — | — | 2 | 4 | 5 |
| Korea, South | 52,197 | 41,344 | 36,016 | 36,565 | 30,983 |
| Thailand | 39,212 | 213 | 99 | 526 | 114 |
| Uzbekistan | — | — | 1 | 3 | 1 |
| *Maritime* | | | | | |
| Australia | 559 | 713 | 314 | 175 | 196 |
| Brunei | — | — | — | — | 9 |
| Indonesia | 34 | 32 | 46 | 51 | 23 |
| Japan | 82,264 | 46,593 | 39,134 | 40,159 | 35,571 |
| Malaysia | 13 | 14 | 35 | 18 | 16 |
| New Zealand | 157 | 53 | 51 | 6 | 7 |
| Papua New Guinea | — | — | — | — | — |
| Philippines | 23,440 | 13,863 | 126 | 79 | 55 |
| Singapore | 10 | 50 | 166 | 411 | 169 |
| Taiwan | 8,813 | — | — | — | — |

SOURCES: http://www.heritage.org/Research/NationalSecurity/troopMarch2005.xls, accessed on April 14, 2009; Kane (2004).

[a] South Vietnam

Even Taiwan has cut this burden in half between 1995 and 2005, falling from 4.7% to 2.3% of its gross domestic product. Japan, India, and Russia all have an acrimonious history with China, and they show a steady or declining defense burden. Although one may argue that fiscal stringencies forced Russia to reduce its armament spending in some years during this period, the same cannot be said about the other two. China's neighbors should have become more able to bear a heavier defense burden due to their growing economies, but they did not. The data support David Kang's (2003b, 2007b) claim that East Asian countries have not balanced against China.

One may try to interpret these data in a way that is more congenial to balance-of-power theories. For example, one may argue that U.S. military superiority has reduced the incentive for East Asian countries to spend on their own defense. This rationalization, however, cannot explain why their defense spending has declined over time even though the United States has always had a military superiority. It also begs the question why these countries did not balance against a preponderant United States as balance-of-power logic would suggest. And why has this spending fallen for East Asian countries but not for those in the Middle East? Still another rationalization is the argument that East Asian defense spending did not rise because of the financial crisis of the late 1990s. This crisis, however, did not affect some (such as Taiwan) as much as others. One would therefore expect to see differences in the pertinent countries' defense expenditures rather than a general pattern of decline over time. Moreover, economic downturns may actually encourage officials to undertake countercyclical fiscal stimulation, including military Keynesianism, to increase aggregate demand. Ad hoc attempts to cast the data in Table 1 in a more favorable light for balance-of-power expectations are not very persuasive.

Turning to the deployment of U.S. military personnel, one sees in Table 2 a trend contradicting the thesis that a countervailing coalition has been forming against China. A persistent and substantial reduction has taken place in the number of U.S. military personnel stationed in Thailand, South Korea, Japan, Australia, and the Philippines—and not just in comparison to 1970, when the Vietnam War was still raging. Afghanistan presents the major exception to this trend, and this case is obviously related to Washington's campaign against the Taliban. Singapore has also seen an increase in the number of U.S. military personnel stationed there, but because it is located far from China's land-based military, it is not clear whether China is the target of this United States–Singapore security cooperation. Combating regional terrorism, boosting maritime protection, and leveraging U.S. support on nonmilitary issues relative to nearby states (e.g., Indonesia, Malaysia, and Vietnam) offer equally plausible and not necessarily mutually exclusive rationales. In general, the data presented in Table 2 can hardly sustain the claim that China is being balanced by collective military action. Taiwan again offers the most critical case. If such collaboration has been occurring, one should most likely see it in United States–Taiwan ties.

Instead of reinforcing its commitment to the island's defense, the United States has withdrawn the military personnel that were once stationed there. The broad pattern and trend over time in the deployment of U.S. military personnel supports David Kang's (2007b, 185) observation that "The United

States is [also] not balancing China." Given declining U.S. troop deployment, it also becomes more difficult to argue that East Asian countries' falling defense burdens can be explained by their reliance on American military support.

Trade between China and its neighbors has taken off both relatively and absolutely. Table 3 shows that China has taken up an increasingly large portion of its neighbors' imports and exports. There have been very large jumps in

TABLE 3

*Trade concentration*

|  | 1991 | 1996 | 2001 | 2006 |
|---|---|---|---|---|
| *Imports from China as Percent of Total Imports* | | | | |
| Australia | 3.5 | 5.2 | 10.0 | 15.3 |
| Brunei | 2.9 | 2.6 | 5.7 | 6.9 |
| Cambodia | 3.8 | 4.3 | 14.1 | 35.7 |
| Indonesia | 3.2 | 3.7 | 6.8 | 13.1 |
| Japan | 6.0 | 11.6 | 17.0 | 20.7 |
| Korea, South | 4.2 | 5.7 | 10.3 | 17.9 |
| Laos | 8.0 | 3.4 | 9.7 | 12.3 |
| Malaysia | 2.2 | 2.4 | 7.8 | 14.8 |
| Mongolia | 17.5 | 14.6 | 21.3 | 30.2 |
| Myanmar | 29.5 | 21.4 | 23.2 | 35.8 |
| New Zealand | 1.9 | 3.7 | 7.5 | 12.8 |
| Papua New Guinea | 0.7 | 1.6 | 2.7 | 6.2 |
| Philippines | 1.9 | 2.0 | 7.0 | 11.1 |
| Singapore | 3.4 | 3.4 | 8.6 | 13.1 |
| Taiwan | 0.8 | 2.6 | 4.8 | 13.0 |
| Thailand | 3.0 | 2.6 | 7.3 | 11.8 |
| Vietnam | 0.7 | 2.9 | 13.2. | 20.6 |
| *Exports to China as Percent of Total Exports* | | | | |
| Australia | 3.7 | 5.7 | 12.0 | 17.7 |
| Brunei | 0.1 | 0.0 | 4.5 | 3.3 |
| Cambodia | 0.8 | 2.3 | 3.0 | 16.2 |
| Indonesia | 4.8 | 4.6 | 9.2 | 9.9 |
| Japan | 3.2 | 7.1 | 16.4 | 23.6 |
| Korea, South | 1.5 | 9.1 | 21.9 | 31.1 |
| Laos | 2.7 | 2.3 | 2.0 | 4.5 |
| Malaysia | 2.3 | 2.9 | 11.7 | 19.7 |
| Mongolia | 29.8 | 29.8 | 47.2 | 75.3 |
| Myanmar | 20.1 | 11.6 | 6.1 | 6.9 |
| New Zealand | 1.8 | 2.8 | 7.9 | 7.5 |
| Papua New Guinea | 0.7 | 3.2 | 4.9 | 6.3 |
| Philippines | 1.5 | 1.8 | 11.0 | 45.5 |
| Singapore | 1.8 | 2.9 | 13.2 | 16.7 |
| Taiwan | 0.0 | 0.6 | 4.4 | 38.6 |
| Thailand | 1.5 | 3.3 | 12.3 | 19.3 |
| Vietnam | 0.5 | 4.1 | 8.8 | 7.7 |

SOURCES: http://www.correlatesofwar.org/COW2%20Data/Trade/Trade.html; Barbieri, Keshk, and Pollins (2008). This table appeared originally in S. Chan (2010a), © 2010 International Studies Association.

nearly all of these countries' import and export concentrations on China. For instance, the percent of Australia's total imports coming from China has risen from 3.5 in 1991 to 15.3 in 2006, and the comparable figures are 6.0 and 20.7 for Japan, and 4.2 and 17.9 for South Korea. For some small countries located close to China, such as Cambodia (35.7%), Mongolia (30.2%) and Myanmar (35.8%), their reliance on China has reached the point of accounting for about one-third of all their imports.

The export data tell an even more dramatic story. The degree to which China's neighbors have come to depend on it as a destination for their exports has risen several times over a brief period of seventeen years (1991–2006). Thus, although in 1991 Australia exported only 3.7% of its goods to China, this proportion rose to 17.7% in 2006. These figures went from 3.2% to 23.6% for Japan, 1.5% to 31.1% for South Korea, and from practically nonexistent (if one is to believe the data from some official sources) to 38.6% for Taiwan. As just implied, the exact figures for trade, as well as for defense spending and U.S. military personnel, are likely to be incorrect due to various reasons of deliberate or inadvertent errors. For example, given legal restrictions, Taiwan's trade with China has been definitely underreported. Thus, one should not put too much confidence in the precision of these data but instead ought to attend to relative magnitude and general trends.

Regarding the latter aspects, there is little doubt that a huge increase in intra-Asian trade and a reorientation of this trade toward China have taken place. One would not expect to see these developments if the pertinent states had security concerns about China's rise. Given Taiwan's historical contention and ongoing sovereignty dispute with China, its heavy export concentration is especially remarkable from the traditional realist perspective. In 2009, over 41% of its exports went to China. Those countries that should feel most threatened by China's rise—such as Mongolia, South Korea, Vietnam, and especially Taiwan—have drawn closer to China rather than farther away from it. Their behavior does not accord with balance-of-power expectations. Similarly, Japan's huge trade with, investment in, and development assistance to China are puzzling from a balance-of-power perspective since these two countries would appear to be natural competitors. In contrast, Japan has competed vigorously in its commercial relations with other democratic, developed states (Heginbotham and Samuels 1999).

Even though they may be surprising to balance-of-power theorists, phenomena such as those just noted are hardly unexpected in standard gravity models of trade based on countries' physical distance from each other and their size and factor endowments. Whereas balance-of-power theorists would predict China's closest neighbors to be most threatened by its rising power, the latter models would suggest the opposite: the closest neighbors would be best positioned to trade with China, and would incur the greatest opportunity costs for forfeiting this trade.

## Further Discussion

One sometimes hears the odd claim that realism or balance-of-power theories can account for the absence of balancing behavior by China's neighbors against its rising power, and that this phenomenon is due to ongoing commercial interests, diplomatic accords, and even physical and cultural proximity. Thus, it is said that the United States has withdrawn its military personnel from Taiwan because of Washington's agreement with Beijing dating back to the time when Richard Nixon visited China in 1972. Similarly, the substantial economic return to Taiwan from trading with and investing in China is invoked to explain why it has not pursued balancing policies. A third rationale argues that some of China's neighbors are just too small to balance against it.

These arguments are problematic for multiple reasons. To start with, it is misleading to suggest that realists or balance-of-power theorists do not expect China's neighbors to balance against it. This suggestion fails to distinguish between different variants of realism, and conflates balance-of-power theories with balancing theories. It also flies in the face of a rather substantial literature belonging to the "China threat" school, expecting and even advocating balancing policies against China (e.g., Bernstein and Munro 1997; Khoo and Smith 2005; Mosher 2001; Roy 1994; Segal 1996; Thayer 2005). Although many China and East Asian scholars do not share the view that Beijing necessarily has an aggressive or revisionist agenda (e.g., Chan 2004a; Johnston 2003a; Ross 1997), some still see the operation of balance-of-power dynamics (e.g., Ross 1999, 2004, 2006). Several prominent international relations scholars have also written about "China's unpeaceful rise" and premonitions of a more tumultuous region (e.g., Betts 1993/94; Brzezinski and Mearsheimer 2005; Friedberg 1993/94; Mearsheimer 2006).

It is true that balance-of-power theories have focused on interactions among great powers. Christopher Layne (2005, 106), for example, remarked that "balancing is a great-power phenomenon, because only great powers can prevent one among them from attaining geopolitical predominance." This observation, however, is more applicable to internal balancing than to external balancing. With respect to the latter, a large volume of literature exists on whether secondary and even minor states are generally inclined to balance against a more powerful neighbor, to align with it, or to even bandwagon with it (e.g., R. Kaufman 1992; Labs 1992; Schweller 1994; Walt 1992).

There are at least some historical examples of weaker states resisting even to the point of fighting against overwhelming odds when their sovereignty or independence was threatened. Thus, Belgium fought Germany in World War I, and Denmark fought Prussia and Austria in 1864. Although their fighting was rather limited, several minor German states sided with Austria against Prussia in 1866. It is commonly understood that a smaller state cannot hope to match a powerful neighbor's military capabilities. However, the very idea of external balancing points to a way whereby a state, unable to count on its own internal resources to thwart a larger power, can nevertheless ally itself with another great power for protection. Therefore, the claim that some of China's neighbors are too small does not in itself offer a satisfactory explanation for the lack of balancing against it.

History is replete with examples of the confrontations of smaller countries with their larger and more powerful neighbors: Greece versus Turkey, Somalia versus Ethiopia, Pakistan versus India, Ecuador versus Peru. The power asymmetries between these enduring rivals are substantial, but the discrepancies are even greater in cases involving Finland and Georgia vis-à-vis the Soviet Union and Cuba and Nicaragua vis-à-vis the United States. After all, Iraq, Serbia, Iran, and North Korea in one way or another have all been defiant when faced with overwhelming international pressure. Given these examples and possible others, invoking the argument of "too small to balance" is not analytically helpful.

Rather, it would be more useful to ask why some small states take on their larger neighbors whereas others do not. As mentioned earlier, the availability of an extra-regional supporter or patron is a critical factor. Regime ideology and survival may be additional considerations, as in the case of North Korea's military spending. Just because no one seriously believes that North Korea will ever be able to catch up with the United States militarily does not mean that Pyongyang has given up on its efforts to reduce the enormous asymmetry working against it. If so, why should one accept this logic in explaining away Taiwan's failure to undertake balancing against China? Surely, public statements by U.S. officials, urging Taiwan to spend more on its own defense, and Chinese statements, condemning the sale of U.S. weapons to Taiwan, belie the view that because Taiwan suffers from a serious strategic disadvantage, any increase in its military capabilities is a matter of irrelevance or indifference to Washington or Beijing, or a wasted effort on its part to shape cross-Strait relations.

I have emphasized as well that size is a relative matter, and that some of China's neighbors (e.g., Russia, India, Japan, and even South Korea and Vietnam) can hardly be characterized as small in the larger regional or international context. Even more importantly, physical size is a relatively constant factor. The preceding discussion on balancing concerns the changes over time in the behavior of China's neighbors. A constant cannot in itself explain why the supposedly small countries were antagonistic toward China at one time but have recently reversed their behavior. This reversal likely reflects their changing motivation because their expanding economies should have improved their ability to afford higher defense spending.

It is also unhelpful to argue that current economic gains motivate states to eschew balancing policies. This argument is unhelpful because it evades the more important question: given the security externalities of trade, why would states—especially the politically and militarily vulnerable ones such as Taiwan and South Korea—want to enter into close commercial relations with China in the first place? After all, these countries, as well as Japan and the United States, had once banned trade with and investment in China. Why did they reverse their official stance during a time when balance-of-power theorists would have expected them to become more alarmed by rising Chinese power?

Similarly, physical and cultural proximity presents a double-edged sword. This condition can promote cooperation but also stimulate competition. Conflicts recur among Arab states despite their shared culture, and territorial disputes that stem from physical proximity have been a major cause of repeated militarized disputes and even wars (Senese and Vasquez 2008; Vasquez 1993). Conversely, despite their past history of conflict, the West European states have established a security community, so that the idea of going to war against one another has become unthinkable. What are the higher-order explanations that account for these different outcomes among countries sharing similar culture and geographic contiguity?

Pointing to diplomatic accords, cultural affinity, and trade benefits to explain an absence of balancing behavior is not a customary practice of realist scholarship. In fact, realists frown on using these variables as explanations for states' policies. Moreover, these variables are more appropriately considered the hallmarks of liberal approaches to analysis. It is fair to ask what is left of realism if it appropriates these liberal explanations as its own (Legro and Moravcsik 1999).

As mentioned at the start of this chapter, cost-benefit analysis motivates a variety of research approaches, ranging from Graham Allison's (1971) rational-actor model to Anthony Downs's (1957) economic theory of voting. Realists and balance-of-power theorists admit cost-benefit analysis, but such analysis does not necessarily make one's research "realist" or vindicate balance-of-power claims. Balance-of-power theories present a particular logic of cost-benefit analysis, suggesting that states take counteractions against a dominant or rising power—even while acknowledging the substantial economic and political opportunity costs that can be entailed by these actions. Their attempts to reverse a security deficit are supposed to override secondary considerations, such as current commercial benefits and existing diplomatic accords.

Jack Levy and William Thompson (2005) looked for evidence of balancing over five centuries of European alliance formation on the grounds that Europe should provide the "most likely case" for balance-of-power theories. Europe's past should provide the "easiest test" for these theories—if these theories' expectations do not pan out in Europe, they are much less likely to be realized elsewhere. These analysts' scope conditions stipulated that balance-of-power theories should pertain only to autonomous continental multistate systems dominated by land-based military powers. This boundary requirement exempts phenomena that would have otherwise appeared anomalous for balance-of-power theories—namely, the absence of balancing against a dominant maritime state, like Britain or the United States, with the largest economy, navy, and overseas possessions. Finally, Levy and Thompson hypothesized that balancing (in this case, the formation of a countervailing alliance) should not necessarily be expected against just the more powerful continental state. Rather, this countervailing alliance should only come to pass after the leading state has reached a critical threshold, so that it has gained the capability of making a hegemonic bid (defined in this case to mean the possession of at least one-third of the land-based military capabilities in a multistate system). Even within these restrictions seemingly intended to give balance-of-power theories the most favorable circumstances for confirmation, Levy and Thompson (2005, 30) found that a balancing alliance to check the dominant land-based power formed only 55% of the time. Put differently, in slightly less than half of the time, the other great powers failed to form a blocking coalition.

I mention this study because, as a continental power possessing a large share of East Asia's land forces (exactly how large this share is would depend on one's definition of this regional system's membership), China meets some of the scope conditions stipulated by Levy and Thompson. In other words, outside of historical Europe, China's large size and its status as a continental power with a large standing army should provide quite conducive conditions for balancing behavior against it to be observed (if not by the smaller countries, then surely by the larger ones like Japan, India, and Russia). Indeed, one would be hard pressed to imagine another contemporary setting where balance-of-power theories would encounter a more receptive set of circumstances. Yet, China's neighbors have not generally pursued balancing against it. This non-occurrence of the expected is more damaging to balance-of-power theories because, as it was just mentioned, China meets the scope conditions of being a continental power with a disproportionately large share of the land-based military capabilities in East Asia. If balance-of-power dynamics are not operating here, where should one expect them to prevail?

Significantly, the one scope condition suggested by Levy and Thompson that is missing in this case is that a regional system should be autonomous—meaning that there should not be an important extra-regional power whose policies might confound the dynamics of local balancing. In East Asia, the United States assumes this role and in turn raises three questions. First, if one takes regional autonomy seriously as a scope condition for testing balance-of-power theories, then no region today can meet this requirement because the United States has now become the world's undisputed unipole. Second, should the presence of an extra-regional power be taken to be a substitute for local balancing or a facilitator for this balancing by China's neighbors? The latter alternative appears more believable because after all, it did occur roughly between 1949 and 1972—when China was much weaker than it is today. This temporal direction, however, is "wrong" for balance-of-power expectations—when China was weaker, more balancing was directed against it, but when it became stronger, this balancing declined. Third, the above discussion begs the question whether the United States itself has been balancing against China or, more accurately, taking actions to block China's rise. As David Kang (2009, 20) mentioned, it is difficult to characterize Washington's policies toward China in the past three decades or so as "balancing" in the traditional sense of the term.

Balancing policies are often presented as a hedge against an uncertain future because as a country grows stronger, it may become more aggressive. Therefore, its neighbors would also seek military strength in order to protect themselves against this growing power. Such efforts, however, would in turn cause alarm in the target of their balancing policies, thereby getting all the relevant parties into a series of actions and counteractions. The well-known arms-race model formulated by Lewis Richardson (1960) questions "what would happen if leaders do not stop to think." Leaders, however, are not mindless and myopic. They realize that their own armament behavior can trigger counter-armament by others. Thus, they adjust their policies to avoid the dangerous "mirror images" and "echo chambers" that Richardson's model warns us about.

This recognition, in turn, calls attention to the obvious fact that states do not assign all their economic resources to defense. That they eschew the allocation of their economic resources to military purposes to the fullest extent possible in turn suggests that contrary to offensive realists' expectations, states are not hell bent on maximizing their power in terms of their military capabilities. Surely, Japan's decision to maintain its defense budget at about 1% of its gross domestic product indicates its unwillingness to ramp up its armament rather than its physical or economic (though not necessarily political) inability to do so (Heginbotham and Samuels 1999). That Japan and South Korea have thus far not pursued nuclear weapons is less an indication of their technical inability than their strategic self-restraint. By not arming themselves to the full extent that their economic and technological capacity permits, their self-restraint invites reciprocal behavior from others. Departing from realism's dominant focus on material conditions, this reasoning suggests that defense spending is often less important for affecting power balances than for communicating reassurance to significant others and for conveying an intention, even a commitment, to forego arms competition, if others would cooperate.

There is yet another kind of hedging, one that relates to one's economic competitiveness relative to states other than the ostensible target of balancing. International relations are n-adic rather than dyadic. If a country eschews trade with China, would it be forfeiting prospective gains relative to others? Thus, for instance, if Taiwan were to boycott commercial relations with China, would it suffer a relative loss in its economic competition with South Korea, Hong Kong, and Singapore? If the United States restricts it imports from and exports to China, would this restriction redound to the benefit of the Europeans and the Japanese? Traditional balance-of-power theories tend to focus on bilateral relations, thus overlooking the opportunity costs that balancing policies can have in one's positional contest with significant third parties. Given first-mover advantages and large returns to scale, these are not inconsequential considerations. As already remarked, these considerations should loom especially large for those countries that are best positioned to capture the benefits of economic, political, and cultural exchanges with China. In other words, the opportunity costs are especially acute for those countries for which balance-of-power theorists have the strongest expectations.

Leaders hedge also because they are in simultaneous pursuit of multiple objectives. For instance, they want to enhance both the security and economic well-being of their country. These desiderata are often in tension, forcing leaders to make tough choices. As discussed in the next chapter, leaders face a guns-versus-butter tradeoff, and between current and future consumption.

However, states have a vote in shaping other states' decisions by acting or not acting cooperatively. Moreover, a state's own decisions can create path dependency, producing institutions and interests that constrain subsequent choices.

Hedging in international relations is therefore not the same as buying an insurance policy for protection against a natural disaster. One's actions can actually influence the probability of the unwanted event (or for that matter, the wanted event) coming to pass, suggesting the possibility of a self-fulfilling or self-negating prophecy. A policy of containment by means of internal and external balancing "front loads" the expenses. That is, one pays the costs up front in the hope of deterring a future threat. In retrospect, one never knows for certain, however, whether this threat would have materialized absent one's actions (perhaps the target of one's balancing never had any intention of committing aggression in the first place), and whether one's actions actually contributed to greater hostility from the target, producing a conflict spiral that culminated in a confrontation that one's balancing policies had intended to prevent. In contrast, a policy of engagement "back loads" the expenses—one pays far greater security costs if it turns out that one has been wrong in misplacing one's trust (that is, in mistaking an aggressive state for a peaceful one). Naturally, as proponents of engagement would argue, one's policies could also have the positive effect of converting a potentially aggressive state into a peaceful partner.

Although the United States was critical in containing the spread of Asian communism during the 1950s and 1960s, its role as a vital security provider and political stabilizer is not nearly as unambiguous today. This remark may strike many Americans as a heresy, for they tend to see their country as playing an indispensable role in underwriting Asian security and stability. Asians may very well have their own reasons to exaggerate the importance of the United States in ensuring their national security and regional stability; they also may deliberately overstate the tension in their mutual relations in order to keep the United States engaged. Continued forward U.S. military deployment contributes to their defense, and Asian countries may be wary of disabusing expansive (and expensive) American notions of the role played by the United States in addressing various real or imagined threats, including the one supposedly emerging from a rising China. These views are gratifying to many Americans, and they are therefore slow or reluctant to challenge them. As a consequence, Americans may not be sufficiently critical in asking whether East Asia will necessarily turn into a dangerous region (both for Asians themselves and for Americans) if the United States decides to adopt the more aloof role of offshore balancer—and alternatively, whether Asians will necessarily join a

U.S.-led coalition to check rising Chinese power. As Kang (2003c, 164) noted, the answers to these questions are much less obvious than usually suggested by the conventional wisdom prevalent in U.S. policy and academic circles. Hedging, of course, can be practiced by East Asian countries to protect themselves not only from rising Chinese power, but also from American abandonment—and domination.

Survey data show that Asians, even those in maritime states and traditional U.S. allies, do not necessarily have more favorable views of the United States than of China (e.g., Inoguchi et al. 2006). As Davis Bobrow (2008b, 240) observed, "among most publics [in different countries in East Asia and other parts of the world], the United States does not have the sort of policy 'credit rating' (which would be manifest in large supportive majorities) that would encourage their elites simply to bandwagon with Washington." To the extent that public attitudes in a country are ambivalent and even antagonistic toward the United States, Washington's efforts to garner its support would be more difficult (the challenges facing the United States in Pakistan come to mind). Such a situation also inclines the allied government to demand greater compensation and to engage in more "foot dragging," paying lip service without making a tangible effort to implement its public pledges. These remarks do not imply popular support in any East Asian country for bandwagoning with China or even strong sentiments to see it develop into a military peer to balance against the United States (Bobrow 2008b). Rather, they are meant to caution against overconfidence about the probability of and underestimation about the costs involved in getting a prospective or ostensible ally's support when it faces a skeptical or divided public. Prevailing mass attitudes in East Asia do not suggest that there is a strong consensus motivating incumbent elites to balance against China—or the United States for that matter.

History suggests that the public rationale given for U.S. intervention in the Vietnam War (e.g., the domino effect of spreading communism, the "Munich lesson" against appeasement) and the worst premonitions at the time of U.S. withdrawal from that conflict have turned out to be unwarranted. Relations among Southeast Asian countries and between them and China have become more cordial and less acrimonious after this withdrawal. Similarly, despite Washington's diplomatic derecognition of Taiwan and the termination of their defense treaty, war has not happened across the Taiwan Strait. As another example, South Korea has become more self-confident, so that the redeployment of U.S. troops away from the demilitarized zone and even the reduction of U.S. troops stationed on the peninsula no longer arouse acute security concerns in Seoul. Such anecdotal evidence does not invalidate the suggestion that forward U.S. military presence is an indispensable stabilizing force in East Asia. It should, however, at least suggest the need for examining this suggestion as an empirical proposition rather than accepting it as an axiomatic principle.

Finally, some proponents of balance-of-power theories may react to the evidence presented in this chapter with the comment, "I knew it all along." Their reaction may imply that one would hardly expect China's neighbors to increase their arms spending or engage in countervailing alignment in response to rising Chinese power. If so, one may ask counterfactually whether, had China's neighbors taken up such policies in recent years, this occurrence would have been counted as confirming balance-of-power theories. Conversely, would these states' behavior during the 1950s and 1960s—when many had higher defense burdens and were more closely aligned with the United States—be construed to support these theories? Proponents of these theories cannot have things both ways; that is, interpreting both the non-occurrence and the occurrence of supposed balancing behavior as supporting balance-of-power reasoning (although, in contrast, balancing theories may contribute to understanding this difference).

One may claim support for balance-of-power theories by stretching the concept of balancing to include a variety of behavior beyond just increasing armament and countervailing alignment. As already mentioned, this analytic move would in effect acknowledge that the cardinal tenets of the traditional and dominant balance-of-power perspective are not being observed in East Asian states' actual behavior. Moreover, by broadening the concept of balancing to include many other sorts of behavior, one would be stripping balance-of-power theories of their most distinctive and central features, which have engaged the attention of scholars and officials alike. This move would also make this concept so encompassing and elusive that empirical refutation would become virtually impossible. In short, one would not be arguing about how East Asian states have actually been behaving, but rather about whether balance-of-power theories should be revised retrospectively to accommodate their anomalous behavior. As John Vasquez (1997) has remarked, such attempts are theoretically degenerative in the sense that they try to salvage an existing paradigm by changing conceptual labels without adding any new analytic content.

# 4

# The Political Economy of Defense
and Regime Strategy

Evidence presented in the last chapter suggests that there has been a general trend of declining defense burden and a reduction in U.S. military personnel deployed in the Asia Pacific. Moreover, there is mounting intra-regional trade; one manifestation of this development is that the Asia Pacific countries have become more important commercial partners for China and vice versa. The overall picture presented by these data is one of rising cooperation and receding security concerns.

This chapter seeks to explain this phenomenon. Its basic thesis echoes Thomas Berger's (2003, 389) observation that the East Asian countries have arrived at "a far reaching consensus that economic development should be the overarching national objective." This broad agreement on the priority of promoting growth and development has become increasingly entrenched in domestic institutions and interests and, except in North Korea, has become the predominant basis for elite legitimacy and the underpinning for stable interstate relations in this region. In the following discussion, I first try to show how truly remarkable East Asia's recent history has been by contrasting it to that of the Middle East. I then present an econo-political account, suggesting that the ruling elites in these two regions have adopted decidedly different strategies to sustain regime survival and leadership legitimacy. Whereas East Asian elites have turned to economic performance as the *sine qua non* for their political power and popularity, their counterparts in the Middle East continue to rely on nationalism, militarization, and externalization of conflicts as the basis for political control. Third, I explain why these strategies for regime maintenance and elite legitimacy matter for international relations, focusing especially on officials' choices between "guns" and "butter." As discussed later, the ascendance of a political coalition with internationally oriented economic interests can be highly consequential in reducing regional tension and fostering cooperative interdependence. I conclude this chapter by delving briefly into a discussion of the "why of why"—that is, I try to offer some ideas about why, in contrast with Middle Eastern leaders, East Asian ones have decided to stress economic performance based on a model of export-led development as a strategy for enhancing and keeping their political legitimacy and power.

## Contrasting with the Middle East

When one observes that East Asian countries are demilitarizing and increasing their economic exchanges, one naturally begs the question "compared to whom?" In contrast to the region's own past, there has certainly been an impressive process of détente and conciliation since the end of the Vietnam War. The *Report of the ASEAN-China Eminent Persons Group* stated, "Between the inception of ASEAN in August . . . 1967 and the formal establishment of ties between ASEAN and China in 1991, relations between the two sides went through a process of evolution from confrontation and suspicion to dialogue, cooperation and strategic partnership based on equality, good neighborliness and mutual trust" (quoted in Qin and Wei 2008, 130–131). This statement is also generally applicable to China's relations with its other neighbors so that, for instance, Beijing's ties with Seoul, Moscow, and New Delhi are more cordial now than four or five decades ago. It has settled most border disputes with its neighbors, often on terms that were more favorable to its negotiation counterparts (Fravel 2005).

Despite premonitions that East Asia might be "ripe for rivalry" (Betts 1993/94; Friedberg 1993/94), no new Cold War, not to mention any actual hot wars, has broken out. Notwithstanding strong nationalist feelings, acrimonious histories, and shallow regional institutions, occasional disputes have been restrained by diplomatic efforts, and the region has managed to stay at peace during the past three decades. Etel Solingen (2007, 757) called attention to the declining defense burden for the region as a whole—falling from 2.6% in 1985 to 1.8% in 2001—compared with global averages of 5.4% and 2.5%, respectively. Concomitantly, intra-Asian exports rose from 30% in 1970 to 55% in 2004. More recent figures, reported in the last chapter, show a continuation of these trends. This phenomenon has led Solingen to envision a *"Pax Asiatica."*

This vision offers a sharp contrast to the conditions in the Middle East, where the defense burden reached 17.3% in 1985 and 7.7% in 2001—or about three times higher than the global average. Intra-Arab trade has remained low since the 1950s, accounting for only about 7%–10% of commerce among the pertinent countries. Low economic growth, high military expenditures, cross-border subversion, recurrent militarized disputes, and more recently, the emergence of domestic and international terrorism, have distinguished this region. Solingen (2007, 758) noted that "since 1965, the incidence of inter-state wars and militarized conflicts was nearly five times higher in the Middle East" compared to East Asia. She characterized the former region as "*Bella Levantina*," quoting Fred Halliday's (2005) remark that "External intervention, interstate war, political upheaval and interethnic violence are compounded by the vagaries of oil prices and the claims of military, nationalist and religious movements" (Solingen 2007, 758). The Middle Eastern countries have experienced a higher incidence of military conflicts even though, in contrast with East Asia, their region is characterized by far less diversity "regarding language, ethnicity, religion, development levels, and regime types" (ibid.)—conditions that should have promoted more peaceful relations according to conventional wisdom.

This brief regional comparison offers a point of departure for this chapter, in which I try to explain the absence of balancing policies and the emergence of regional cooperation in East Asia, as I suggested in the last chapter. Although they started from rather comparable political economies in the 1950s, East Asia and the Middle East have undertaken different development strategies and experienced different trajectories since then. In the years immediately after World War II, both regions saw the rise of authoritarian regimes dominated by conservative rulers, military officers, large landlords, and commercial interests favoring import substitution. These regimes offered domestic rents to powerful conservative interests, and generally sought legitimacy by using scapegoating tactics and by directing mass hostility against an external target. Authoritarian rule, suppression of labor and political opponents, and corruption and rent-seeking policies (including high levels of military spending) were justified in the name of national security.

From about the early 1960s on, however, the so-called newly industrializing countries (NICs) in East Asia began to turn to export-led industrialization. The ruling elites in Taiwan and South Korea, preceded by their counterparts in Japan, started a process whereby, as Solingen (2007) argued, they pivoted their political legitimacy and regime survival on economic performance rather than nationalism, militarization, and populism based on political mobilization against internal and external scapegoats. Significantly, the adoption of this strategy was followed by others in the region; in the 1970s, Thailand, Malaysia, the Philippines, Indonesia, and eventually China and Vietnam emulated, albeit to different degrees, the initial NICs (Taiwan, South Korea, Singapore, Hong Kong, and of course Japan, as the first non-Western NIC). Success begot success in the sense that the model of export-led growth became widely accepted in East Asia, and this wide acceptance in turn gave further momentum to its acceleration and entrenchment (Amsden 1989; S. Chan 1993; Clark 1989; Deyo 1981, 1987; T. Gold 1986; Haggard 1990; Hewison 1989; Johnson 1982; Jones and Sakong 1980; Wade 1990; Woo 1991).

Some have used the analogy of the flying geese formation to describe this contagion effect, first set off by Japan's "economic miracle." Others have noted that the more successful East Asian political economies have been characterized by both a strong competent state and one that is embedded in society (e.g., Evans 1995). In contrast, Middle Eastern countries continue to be mired in economic stagnation, burgeoning population, authoritarian rule, recurrent incursions and militarized disputes, and an inward-looking political economy dominated by inefficient state enterprises and a powerful military–industrial complex (Binder 1988; Luciani 1990; Owen and Pamuk 1999; Waterbury 1983). Seemingly small differences initially have compounded over time to become huge discrepancies between the two regions in terms of their economic growth, international orientation, and elite strategies for survival and legitimacy.

The contrasting strategies of ruling elites in the Middle East and East Asia are instructive about the interactions between their domestic agendas and their propensity for external conflict. The thrust of Randall Schweller's (2004, 2006) study of the "underbalancing" phenomenon is to focus on the domestic distribution of influence and incentives. Rather than assuming balancing as a natural outcome, one problematizes it and asks about those conditions that can affect its probability. What conditions, both internal and external, are likely to influence officials' willingness and ability (Most and Starr 1989) to pursue certain policies, such as balancing against a neighbor? I argue that one needs to tie international relations theories more closely to an understanding of domestic political economy. "Black boxing" the internal political dynamics of states and elite agendas overlooks an important source of variation in foreign policy and regional stability.

## Strategies of Regime Survival and Legitimacy

Obviously, leaders face the constant challenge of two-level games (Jacobson, Putnam, and Evans 1993; Putnam 1988); that is, they have to address domestic and foreign constraints and incentives concurrently. When deciding whether to pursue balancing policies, they are not unmindful of the implications that their decisions can have for their domestic political fortune—more specifically, the implications for their own political longevity and popularity. Recognizing that officials care about multiple goals draws attention to the fact that armament and alignment options can have undesirable side effects. Internal and external balancing intended to maximize national security can impinge on domestic economic performance and may cause a decrease rather than an increase in this security in the long run, such as by stimulating an arms race and exhausting one's financial capacity. Paul Kennedy (1987) warned about the danger of "imperial overstretch" that has repeatedly confronted great powers in the past.

Pervasive instability in the Middle East and increasing cooperation in East Asia can be traced to their respective elites' grand strategies to ensure their political tenure and legitimacy. Introducing the distinctive domestic models of political survival characteristic of the two regions, Solingen (2007, 758) observed, "*Leaders in most East Asian states pivoted their political control on economic performance and integration into the global economy whereas most Middle East leaders relied on inward-looking self-sufficiency, state and military entrepreneurship, and nationalism*" (emphasis in the original). Naturally, there is considerable variation among countries located in both regions. Just as Burma (Myanmar) and North Korea are "outliers" in East Asia, Lebanon, Morocco, and Turkey often present exceptions to generalizations about the Middle East. But by and large, compared to Middle Eastern countries, East Asian countries have smaller public sectors relative to their domestic economy, capture a much larger share of international investment capital, export a much higher percentage of manufactures in their overseas trade, bear much lower defense burdens, and experience fewer militarized conflicts with their neighbors.

These contrasts suggest that East Asian and Middle Eastern countries have generally followed separate paths that approximate the distinction Richard Rosecrance (1986) made between "strategic" or "territorial states" on the one hand and "trading states" on the other. Domestic interest groups forge ruling pacts and develop grand strategies that respond to their existing internal political and resource conditions and the opportunities and challenges emanating from abroad. When those preferring economic and political openness prevail, they seek international integration and cooperation. They oppose policies that would cause market closure, impede capital flows, and destabilize financial institutions. These preferences in the long run tend to embed themselves politically and institutionally, and when such incentives and practices spread to neighboring countries, they increase the prospects of regional stability.

Naturally, the reverse can also be true: distribution coalitions consisting of sprawling military–industrial complexes, large state enterprises, bloated bureaucracies, and import-substituting firms can become entrenched, making a change of regime strategy more unlikely the longer these distribution coalitions have dominated the domestic political economy. These groups have a vested interest in exaggerating foreign threats and hyping nationalism in order to sustain support for funding a large state apparatus. These proclivities in turn are likely to exacerbate and perpetuate regional tension, whether as an unintended side effect or as the direct result of deliberate policy.

How would turning to an export-led growth model and, more generally, to a regime strategy of pivoting political legitimacy and survival on economic performance influence regional relations? Such a turn would point to an overall tendency, though it would hardly always be a *fait accompli*, for those with an internationalist outlook and interests to be put in charge of domestic and foreign affairs. This internationalist orientation typically favors open access to foreign markets and the liberalization of domestic ones, stable and low currency values facilitating exports, free movement of capital and low borrowing costs, and efficient allocation of production factors according to a country's comparative advantage. There is also a general tendency to emphasize the production of consumer goods rather than the development of capital-intensive, large-scale heavy industries that are usually preferred by the military–industrial complex, and the investment in both physical infrastructure and human assets. Barriers to trade and investment—such as entrenched rent seekers, government regulations, high tariff and nontariff restrictions, and institutionalized forms of graft, corruption, and other inefficiencies—are likely to encounter objection from an internationalist coalition. Given this coalition's priorities, its policies understandably seek to lower international tension and promote economic interdependence. The ascendance of such a coalition to ruling position tends to dampen the logic of balancing and power competition and to lessen the usual impediments that hamper commerce between adversaries. Scott Kastner (2009) studied trade across the Taiwan Strait as a paradigmatic example of how economic interdependence can thrive even between ostensible adversaries when dominant coalitions on both sides have an internationalist orientation stressing economic performance.

Recent scholarship on the pacifying effects of economic liberalism provides further theoretical underpinning for my arguments. Two causal mechanisms are particularly pertinent in connecting a state's political economy to peaceful international relations, and both of these suggest that market-based exchanges rather than democratic institutions are more fundamental reasons for

international peace (McDonald 2007, 2009). These mechanisms refer respectively to the extent of state control over public properties and that of barriers to
international economic competition. With regard to the first mechanism, large
state enterprises and monopolies enhance ruling incumbents' fiscal discretion.
The funds from these sources enable them to reward political cronies (thereby
to consolidate their domestic rule) and to bypass the necessity of seeking the
consent of (or making concessions to) a larger number of constituents who
would otherwise have to be taxed to raise this money. The latter condition is
critical in many classical liberal explanations as to why public control of the
purse strings, such as that exercised by an informed electorate or a representative legislature, can restrain international bellicosity. In the words of David
Ricardo (quoted in McDonald 2009, 51), "There cannot be a greater security
for the continuance of peace, than the imposing on ministers the necessity of
applying to the people for taxes to support a war." A state's access to funding by virtue of its control of public assets removes this constraint of popular
approval, accounting in part for the phenomenon that relations among those
states with a larger public sector tend to be less peaceful.

This generalization implies two corollaries. First (as suggested later), countries with large stores of natural resources such as minerals are more likely to
have nationalized enterprises, which gives the incumbent elites a freer fiscal
hand without being compelled to seek the consent of citizens whose income
would otherwise have to be taxed for armament or foreign expansion. Second,
to the extent that a state wages war without raising taxes, it can dampen public
opposition to this conflict by concealing the conflict's short-term economic
costs. One common way to escape from the constraint of popular approval
is to finance war by borrowing rather than taxing—as the United States has
done in funding its Iraqi and Afghan campaigns. The burden of debt payment
is shifted to future generations.

The second mechanism refers to a state's trade policies, which tend to be
both a reflection of its peaceful disposition and a cause for this disposition—
both tied, yet again, to a country's domestic distribution of influence and
interests. Protectionist policies are supported by internationally uncompeti-
tive industries. These industries are beholden to the incumbent elite imposing trade barriers because they would otherwise be unprofitable undertakings
destined to fail under competitive pressure. They are inclined to curry political
favor from the state rather than to develop their economic competitiveness.
Moreover, they are more willing to pay a price in supporting belligerent or
expansionist foreign policy in the hope that they can make economic gains
abroad due to their government's political protection rather than to their own

competitiveness. Opposite tendencies prevail when a government eschews protectionism. Free trade favors those firms that are competitive internationally, which means, by definition, that they do not need to rely on their government to be profitable at home or abroad. Indeed, if they are already competitive internationally, why would they want to pay the added cost of a higher defense burden and risk being shut out of foreign markets if their government pursues belligerent or expansionist foreign policy?

To the extent that officials pivot their political tenure and regime popularity on economic performance, they will adopt grand strategies that are internationalist in orientation and that tend to have the intent and effect of curtailing armament, nationalism, and the military–industrial complex. They prefer fiscal frugality, macroeconomic stability, and open market access—conditions that would be jeopardized by armed conflict and regional tension. A strategy that hinges on economic performance to maintain regime survival and legitimacy, though initially motivated by domestic incentives and focused on internal conditions, is nonetheless consequential for regional and international relations. This is not to say that the genesis of this strategy did not have anything to do with the challenges and opportunities presented initially by the external environment. Although this strategy was surely formulated by East Asian NICs originally when the United States assumed a central role, over time they became less obsessed with the United States as a provider of credit, investment, technology, managerial expertise, and military protection, and as a destination for their exports. This diversification away from a U.S.-centric economic network is shown by the ongoing trend toward greater intra-Asian commerce.

Significantly, as the number of states pursuing a strategy of regime legitimacy that favors economic performance grows, they are drawn by their own internal political logic, rather than an external compulsion induced by balance-of-power dynamics, to enter into cooperation. "Therefore, there is a virtual built-in guarantee that like-minded internationalizing coalitions will be, *ceteris paribus*, reluctant to defect through militarized strategies or to exacerbate territorial or ethno-religious disputes. The potential for armed conflict and extensive military buildups threatens the economic and political fundamentals—fiscal conservatism; macroeconomic, political, and regional stability; global access—that an internationalizing strategy requires" (Solingen 2003, 65). This observation about the linkages between domestic and foreign policies and about "a virtual built-in guarantee" for like-minded states to cooperate is very important and germane to my thesis. It points to the associational logic of international society mentioned in Chapter 2, but these states can also be motivated in part by competitive logic, as discussed below.

When a state makes decisions about how much money to devote to consumption and how much to defense, it incorporates its anticipation of its counterparts' similar allocations. The choices states make are therefore interdependent or mutually contingent (Powell 1999, 40–81), and extend beyond bilateral ties to considerations of competitiveness relative to other relevant states. Consumption, in Powell's formulation, is the intrinsically valued end, whereas defense spending is a necessary expenditure to guard against being attacked. The more a state spends on one item, the less it is able to spend on the other. I will return to discussing guns-versus-butter tradeoffs in the next section.

When one multilateralizes the context of these tradeoff decisions among many states in a region, the contagion of a strategy of pivoting regime and elite legitimacy on economic performance tends to foster a sense of generalized reciprocity. Reduced defense spending by one state, when reciprocated by others, not only lowers tension and builds confidence generally, but also permits more resources to go to consumption—and even more importantly, to investment, which can in turn produce more resources in the future. The prospects of these future resources provide positive reinforcement for further cooperation and tension-lowering policies, including a renunciation of internal and external balancing.

The survival and legitimacy strategy of East Asian leaders inclines them to make an intertemporal tradeoff that favors reducing defense spending and indeed, foregoing current consumption in general, in favor of more investment to grow resources for future consumption and still more investment. The larger domestic resource bases created by these decisions and the experience of economic cooperation promoted by them, in turn, give these leaders' states bigger stakes in the status quo, making balancing policies less necessary and more counterproductive. In Chapter 7, I will return to this idea, arguing that this dynamic produces self-enforcing agreements which do not need to depend on external authorities for cooperation to occur. The benefits of current cooperation—and the forfeiture of these benefits in the event of noncooperation—serve in themselves as a bond or credible commitment to refrain from conduct that can undermine cooperation. Moreover, these returns create vested interests that have a stake in furthering cooperation, and entrench and legitimate successful strategies as "winning ideas"—thus fostering, again, a self-sustaining process.

I have just mentioned the effects of path dependency, suggesting that policies and institutions tend to become entrenched over time. It is germane to add that with respect to commerce, it is much more politically challenging to terminate or reduce ongoing ties than to eschew these ties when they have never existed. In other words, commerce creates stakeholders who will lobby for the continuation and expansion of economic relations (Long 1996). Therefore, once begun, it takes considerable political effort and capital to roll back these relations. In contrast, it is easier for a state to stop its firms from trading with an adversary when they have never done so before (Mastanduno 1992). Thus, the default tendency is for commerce to expand in the absence of states acting to reverse it. This, in turn, means that the more natural course is for regional economic exchanges to intensify. Significantly, these expanding economic exchanges increase the opportunity costs to those states that decline to join.

States that pursue import substitution, subsidize inefficient public enterprises, and support large military establishments have trouble keeping up with competitors that follow an alternative model of export expansion, market liberalization, and global integration. Because of its chronically poor economic performance, the Soviet Union found itself falling further and further behind the United States during the Cold War. The Soviet economy reached only half the size of the United States, even when it was at its height. Due to the sharp and steady decline in Soviet economic capacity throughout the 1970s and 1980s, it became increasingly difficult for Moscow to sustain its military expenditures, which were consuming about 40% of its budget and 15%–20% of its gross domestic product (Brooks and Wohlforth 2000/2001, 22–23). Mikhail Gorbachev was disposed to undertake reform and retrenchment in light of his country's severe economic deterioration. He faced serious difficulties in continuing Moscow's competition with the West because the Soviet Union's defense burden threatened to collapse the economy. He remarked forthrightly "our goal is to prevent the next round of the arms race. If we do not accomplish it, the threat to us will only grow. We will be pulled into another round of the arms race that is beyond our capabilities, and we will lose it, because we are already at the limit of our capabilities. Moreover, we can expect that Japan and the FRG [West Germany] could very soon join the American potential . . . If the new round begins, the pressure on our economy will be unbelievable" (ibid., 29).

Gorbachev's statement makes an important point, namely that the influence of external pressure can force a regime to initiate fundamental policy change. This influence stems, to a large measure, from the competitive logic of the interstate system. That is, the motivation to reform comes largely from the realization that one's country is falling further behind strategically and economically, and in order to catch up, a basic change in policy has to take place.

*Perestroika* and *glasnost*—as well as Vietnam's economic renovation (*doi moi*) and China's economic reforms launched in the late 1970s—stemmed from the realization that continuing "business as usual" would jeopardize both elite survival and national security.

Another point to be underscored from this example of Soviet decline and reform is the influence of ideas—collective beliefs about which policies work, or do not work, in contributing to national security, economic capacity, and elite authority. Old ideas, such as those propagating central planning, state enterprises, and an inward-looking economy become discredited when they fail consistently to deliver the promised results. They become susceptible to being dislodged by replacement ideas when the latter's advantages are demonstrated successfully by neighboring countries.

Just like interests and institutions tend to become entrenched, ideas about how a country should go about managing its security and economic well-being are "sticky" (Legro 2005, 2007). Existing grand strategies and elite models of control tend to be perpetuated unless and until they lose their credibility and when an alternative set of ideas gains widespread support. The other implication of this discussion is that ideas can have a contagion effect. The successful ones tend to be emulated by neighboring countries, in part because of the logic of competition—that is, the defensive motivation to replicate successful models, lest one fall behind strategically and economically.

Furthermore, the above account of the Soviet predicament draws attention to an important distinction between capability and motivation as competing plausible reasons for downsizing a country's military. Low defense spending may be due to either economic decay and financial exhaustion, or policy incentives and programmatic preferences. The declining defense burdens of East Asian countries reflect the latter situation. With their expanding economies, many of them could have spent more on their military, but they have not. That they have eschewed higher military expenditures because of their policy choices rather than their dire circumstances is significant. If dire circumstances were the reason for their restraint, they would have returned to armament pursuits when their economies improved.

Although not nearly as dire, China faced a situation similar to the Soviet Union's before Deng Xiaoping's enactment of economic reforms (Harding 1987). It was lagging seriously behind the economic performance of its neighbors, such as Taiwan and South Korea, not to mention Japan. Persistent economic underperformance has serious security consequences. Some realists see or advise that security concerns should always trump economic interests, whereas others are willing to make an intertemporal exchange in favor of expanding current economic capacity for the sake of improving long-term security prospects (Brooks 1997; Kirshner 2003).

The examples just offered about Russia's and China's turn to economic liberalization and political reorientation suggest that another powerful force is at work. States are sometimes influenced to make basic policy adjustments simply because their economic incapacity will not permit them to continue business as usual. In order to compete more effectively in the international system, regimes have to emulate their more successful counterparts abroad (Huntley 1996). Thus, good practices tend to drive out bad ones, forcing regimes to alter their survival strategy for the sake of improving or simply avoiding a loss in their international and, more importantly for them, domestic position. They may temporize (as the Soviets did long after their serious economic decline had become evident), but they cannot put off the necessary changes indefinitely.

This proposition in turn raises the question of why East Asian states were able to switch to a strategy relying on export-led growth after an initial period of following import substitution whereas, in contrast, Middle Eastern countries have by and large persisted in their alternative model of regime survival stressing nationalism, a large public sector, and mobilization against internal and especially external enemies. As discussed later, oil revenue or foreign remittances, and the massive and continuing infusion of U.S. aid contributed to disguising the reality of economic stagnation, and encouraged procrastination to put off tough decisions in the Middle East. Additionally, Middle Eastern proponents of the existing regime strategy have been in a stronger political position to resist reform because they did not experience the devastation or the threat of destruction that supporters of some *anciens régimes* faced in East Asia from communist revolutionaries and insurgents.

As suggested above, current or former communist countries such as Russia, China, and Vietnam have switched from relying on nationalism, central planning, large public enterprises, collectivist ideology, and political and military competition with the West as strategic pillars for their regime survival and legitimacy. They finally came to accept the logic of "if you cannot beat them, then join them." This change reinforces the contagion, or diffusion, in East Asia of a regime strategy that gives priority to economic performance. This is a significant development because, again, it has dampened incentives to undertake balancing policies by resorting to armament and alliance. East Asian states have actually downsized their military establishment and pursued open regionalism—the reverse of what one would have expected if they were seeking to balance against rising Chinese power. The available evidence suggests that a virtuous cycle of demilitarization and economic interdependence may have taken hold. As Solingen (2003, 66) remarked, "Reciprocal incentives to cooperate are highest where internationalizing strategies are more fully in place and their political agents more strongly entrenched, conditions that are, of course, interrelated. Thus, internationalizing coalitions beget the conditions of self-sustained, rather than externally imposed, regional cooperation."

This discussion contributes to the broader debate about whether trade promotes peace (e.g., Barbieri 2002; Russett and Oneal 2001). It also raises the reverse possibility: states that are peacefully inclined choose to trade and enter into other forms of commercial relations in the first place. Trade is endogenously determined, and as I have tried to show in the last chapter, "trade itself reflects interstate cooperation and conflict" (Stein 2003, 112). Peaceful disposition and economic interdependence are characterized by Granger causality. They have a reciprocal and positive effect on each other. The point about endogeneity is worth repeating; it is a reminder that states "select" themselves into what they expect to be rewarding interactions. This selection is highly significant because it discloses their assessments of situations and signals their future intentions. Thus, for instance, when states become involved in extensive trade and make asset-specific investments in each other, their behavior communicates their preferences and intentions (a point that will be taken up again in Chapters 5 and 7). They would not take these steps if they expect imminent or even probable conflict.

These remarks are also germane to the debate about the role of international organizations and treaties in promoting regional cooperation. Various institutions, such as APEC, ASEAN, ARF, and ASEAN-Plus-3, have forged networks of "omni-enmeshment" and multilateral diplomacy (these acronyms refer to Asia Pacific Economic Cooperation, Association of Southeast Asian Nations, ASEAN Regional Forum, and ASEAN plus China, Japan, and South Korea). There is substantial statistical evidence supporting the view that common membership in intergovernmental organizations is correlated with dyadic peace between states (e.g., Russett and Oneal 2001; Russett, Oneal, and Davis 1998). Nevertheless, there is also strong evidence of a reverse causality, which suggests that peaceful states are inclined to join multilateral institutions in the first place, thus confirming the logic of self-selection.

The formation of these multilateral institutions in East Asia and the Asia Pacific more broadly followed rather than preceded the pertinent states' switch to economic performance as a basis for their regime and elite maintenance, and has therefore been more a consequence than a cause of this strategy. This observation again underscores the point that when states join multilateral institutions, their decision to join broadcasts their preferences and future intentions. It also relates to the debate about whether treaties tend to only "screen" states which have ratified them, or whether they also constrain these states' behavior (Simmons and Hopkins 2005; Von Stein 2005). The proponents of the former (screening) claim that only states that have already paid the adjustment costs and that have already made a commitment to discharge their treaty obligations would join these formal accords in the first place. That is, their behavior has been predetermined and is not affected by their act of joining or ratifying the treaties. Joining treaties or multilateral institutions only serves the purpose, albeit a very important one, of publicly separating (that is, distinguishing) these norm-abiding states from others that have yet to decide whether to abide by the relevant norms.

The proponents of the latter (constraint) argue that joining treaties can actually change states' behavior, influencing them to act in a manner that they would not have in the absence of their treaty obligations. This latter argument coincides with the logic used to explain why engagement or omni-enmeshment can pay peace dividends. This claim can certainly be true. This discussion, however, suggests that the volume of cross-border trade and the number of regional institutions are in and of themselves indicative and predic-tive of the level of cooperation among states. They provide a gauge to assess the extent to which balance-of-power dynamics is operating and are a harbin-ger of how likely it is to emerge in the future.

## Guns–Versus–Butter Tradeoffs

To suggest that East Asian elites have increasingly stressed a strategy of regime survival and leadership legitimacy based on economic performance offers only an incomplete explanation of why they have not gone full bore in attempt-ing to balance against rising Chinese power. As already mentioned, leaders are not myopic. They are cautious about not setting off chain reactions that would cause counter-armament or a countervailing alignment. Given finite resources, military and civilian consumption have to involve zero-sum (even negative-sum) choices at some point. What is spent on guns cannot be spent again on butter. Moreover, public policies inevitably face choices between current consumption (both public and private) and future consumption. Re-sources consumed by current spending (whether for defense or other purposes) will not be available for investment, thus reducing the potential resources that future economic growth would provide. Although rising consumption can fuel additional investment, the general distinction between money spent and money saved or invested is clear, and the tradeoff is more acute if consumers spend on imported goods manufactured abroad. These remarks echo Bruce Russett's (1970) inquiry, "what [is the] price [of] vigilance?"

The tradeoffs presented by defense spending come in direct and indirect forms. In the direct form, when the share of defense spending in a fixed overall budget goes up, the share of nondefense spending necessarily has to go down. Therefore, by definition, higher defense spending means lower nondefense spending in this direct form. Government support for health, education, and welfare (broadly defined to include a variety of civilian programs such as those intended to assist needy citizens, subsidize energy, housing, and transportation costs, and fund investment to develop or improve public infrastructure) declines in this scenario. Such broadly defined social spending naturally has large constituencies, and officials are usually wary about cutting it because they worry about alienating voters and losing popular support. Consequently, the available evidence often does not show a strong relationship associating increases in the absolute amount of defense spending with decreases in the absolute amount of social spending (e.g., Dabelko and McCormick 1977; D. Davis and Chan 1990; Peroff and Podolak-Warren 1979).

The tendency is instead for both to trend upward over time (e.g., Clayton 1976). Except for Reagan's and the senior Bush's administrations, higher U.S. defense spending in the recent decades has not necessarily come at the expense of lower social spending (e.g., Kamlet, Mowery, and Su 1988; Russett 1982; Russett, Starr, and Kinsella 2009). Weak support for this direct form of tradeoff between defense and social spending is not surprising because caring about their own political tenure, elected officials typically refuse to choose between guns and butter. They want to increase spending for both—and at the same time, avoid raising taxes in order to fund these programs. They therefore often resort to running a budget deficit and issuing public debt to cover it. This political maneuver transfers to future generations (voters who are too young to vote or who have not been born) the costs of repaying the debt (as well as the other opportunity costs), while appeasing demands from current voters for more government programs. The tradeoff between guns and butter thus takes on an indirect form—increasing current consumption at the expense of future consumption.

There is a large literature on the consequences of this tradeoff, pitting government spending on defense against the prospects of future economic growth (see S. Chan 1993, and Hartley and Sandler 1990, for reviews of the pertinent literature; and Mintz and Huang 1990, 1991, for exemplary studies on this topic). The relevant research seeks to determine the opportunity costs of defense spending, asking the implicit counterfactual question of how much faster the economy would have grown if less money had been allocated to military purposes. As mentioned earlier in this chapter, this allocation has consumed a much higher proportion of the economies of Middle Eastern countries than of those of East Asian countries. The defense burden for Saudi Arabia, Oman, and Qatar has exceeded 10% of their respective gross domestic product, and North Korea's has been estimated at 20% (Russett, Starr, and Kinsella 2009, 349) and even at over 30% (Table 1, Chapter 3). In 2008, the U.S. Defense Department employed 670,000 civilians and another 3.6 million were working for defense-related industries, accounting for about 3% of the total civilian workforce (ibid.). In the same year, the United States spent over $600 billion on national defense and related space and energy programs, amounting to 4.2% of its economy compared to a global average of 2.5%.

The 2008–2009 recession required massive government spending to bail out failing financial institutions, stimulate the economy, and extend assistance to the unemployed (with the official unemployment rate at about 10%, and the real but unofficial rate, counting those who have given up looking for jobs, at about 15%). This massive spending, accompanied by sharply reduced tax revenues, resulted in a federal budget deficit of $1.9 trillion in 2009 (*Denver Post*, January 21, 2010, 7A). This deficit has been financed in part by borrowing from foreigners, including the Chinese, who have been estimated to hold more than $800 billion in U.S. public debt in mid 2009 (a figure that has risen to $1.154 trillion by February 2011). The extent to which this foreign indebtedness is a cause for security concern will be discussed in Chapter 5. Parenthetically, in the absence of more tax revenues, a mounting debt implies that a larger portion of the government's budget will have to be allocated to future interest payments, leaving less fiscal maneuver room for making adjustments to the rest of the budget. Discretionary spending now takes up only about one-third of the U.S. federal budget, with defense programs consuming about half of that portion.

Modern militaries are capital-intensive and technology-intensive and for that reason defense expenditures can influence growth prospects by affecting the supply and costs of credit and expertise. These expenditures, like other kinds of public spending, have to be financed either by government taxation or borrowing, both of which take money from the private sector. In either case, this spending has the effect of pitting the state against the private sector in competing for capital. This competition makes credit more expensive for the private sector, which has to pay a premium in order to secure funds for investment. Large, chronic budget deficits abet inflation, which encourages consumption and discourages saving. A persistently low savings rate in turn has an adverse effect on capital formation, reducing the availability and increasing the cost of credit, thus depriving private enterprises of the necessary funds to finance expansion and innovation. These are the long-term financial consequences when fiscal policies try to "get a quart out of a pint pot," as exemplified by the "imperious economy" of the United States (Calleo 1982). Statistical evidence from a cross-national analysis (e.g., Deger and Smith 1983) and from time-series analyses of individual countries such as Taiwan (e.g., S. Chan 1988; Ward, Davis, and Chan 1993) shows a pattern whereby, absent offsetting factors, a high defense burden curtails capital formation.

Some cross-national studies indicate a rough one-to-one negative relationship between military expenditures and total investment (R. Smith 1977, 1980). Other studies on developing and developed countries alike also report an adverse impact of the defense burden on investment, albeit sometimes in an indirect fashion and with a time lag (Cappelen, Gleditsch, and Bjerkholt 1992; Deger 1986; DeGrasse, McGuiness, and Ragen 1983; Huang and Mintz 1991). Britain's and America's primacy as global hegemons, however, has helped them to lessen the tension between defense burden and private investment. Some studies have questioned whether such a tradeoff has adversely affected them (e.g., D. Gold 1990; Rasler and Thompson 1988). They hint instead at a reverse causality, whereby declining investment and a sagging economy have dampened consumption, both public and private. Thus, these variables may have reciprocal effects—effects that can also be mediated by other factors. For instance, the interactions between physical capital and human capital may be more important for economic growth than their independent effects (notwithstanding their large cash reserves, oil-producing states have not generally succeeded in initiating autonomous, self-sustaining growth because of the relative scarcity of indigenous expertise). Moreover, the persistent "crowding out" of private investment by public consumption—whether for defense or nondefense purposes—over many years can have a cumulative effect in lowering future growth (R. Smith and Georgiou 1983). Statistical correlations between annual observations of the levels of or changes in defense spending and economic growth are unable to capture this cumulative and perhaps accelerating effect over time.

Massive government programs on defense, space, and energy also compete with the private sector for talent and expertise. Some have estimated that about half the scientists and engineers in the United States were at one time employed by these programs. If so, these programs can deprive private industries of the best brains for product innovation and cause a relative shortage and intense wage competition for human resources in research and development at different times in the most dynamic industries of their day—such as automobiles, electronics, machine tools, information-processing, and communication systems. These industries have been involved in the fiercest competition for exports and overseas market shares, and have served as the engine for domestic growth in Japan's and Germany's post-1960 experiences. These industries also happen to require massive capital investment to capture economies of scale and to respond to rapid product cycles.

Military spending has the greatest effect of "squeezing out" both capital and talent from these leading and most innovative industries—and also from those dominating the export sector and engaging in intense international competition. Export competitiveness in manufactured products has in turn fueled the economic dynamism of some countries, such as East Asia's NICs. Historical evidence suggests that a high defense burden has tended to impair export competitiveness, causing persistent trade deficits, currency devaluation, and eventual industrial hollowing. The tendency for high military expenditures to be statistically associated with declining export competitiveness among the advanced industrialized countries is significant (Rothschild 1973). It is highlighted by Japan and Germany, with their low defense burden and high volume of manufactured exports at one end of the distribution, and the United States with the opposite attributes at the other end. It underscores the claim advanced earlier that regimes emphasizing economic performance as a basis for their popularity and legitimacy, especially those that pursue a model of export-led growth, are likely to eschew militarization and armament rivalry.

The statistical evidence associating defense burden negatively with export competitiveness points to a long-term tradeoff and does not deny salient exceptions to the rule. One should not therefore expect one year's military expenditures to cause a decline in exports the following year. Rather, a chronically heavy defense burden is likely to sap a country's export of manufactured products. Thus, it matters whether the exports in question are manufactures, natural resources, or services. One would not expect military expenditures to affect adversely a country's competitiveness in the latter sectors and, as argued below, a concentration on exporting natural resources is actually likely to encourage higher military expenditures.

Moreover, mitigating factors can ameliorate the deleterious effects that the defense burden has on manufactured exports. Foreign assistance, including subsidized credit and easy market access, can ease the defense–exports tradeoff. Thus, for a long time, Taiwan and South Korea featured high growth rates in exporting to other countries even though both had rather heavy defense burdens (S. Chan 1988; Moon and Hyun 1992). These "outliers" point to another consideration, namely, a cross-sectional analysis that takes a snapshot of the pertinent relationship between defense burden and the growth of manufactured exports is sensitive to sample size and composition (the countries or years that are included in or excluded from the sample). This cross-sectional evidence is less reliable than time-series analysis, which at least allows a more valid basis for inferring cause and effect.

Furthermore, the defense burden need not have an immediate or uniform impact on export competitiveness—that is, the adverse impact can be delayed and then suddenly accelerate. This effect is likely to be nonlinear, cumulative, and progressive. It can become visible and acute only after a long period during which the evidence showing a tradeoff may be weak or even absent. This may apply especially when a powerful country, such as the United States (D. Gold 1990; Huang and Mintz 1991; Mintz 1992), can resort to offsetting policies to ward off, even if only for a time, the negative consequences of large military expenditures. In the short and even medium term, military expenditures on research and development may actually boost the competitiveness of those civilian high-technology sectors benefiting indirectly from this funding.

The defense burden is not the only or even the most important determinant of economic performance. Its effects can be ameliorated or exacerbated when they interact with other germane policies and conditions, producing a long-term cumulative impact that is difficult to reverse once those interests and institutions favoring large military expenditures have had a chance to entrench themselves. The development models and regime strategies attributed to East Asian and Middle Eastern countries embed military spending in a nexus of other institutional and policy proclivities, and suggest strong "stickiness" because these proclivities are mutually reinforcing.

These remarks raise another important implication that pertains to the marginal product of capital—that is, the productivity gain to be made from each additional increment of capital, such as that which may be forthcoming from a switch from defense spending to investment in civilian production. Without undertaking major reforms in the other institutions, policies, or conditions that impinge on economic performance, even a fairly large reallocation of resources from defense to investment can only make a relatively small contribution to economic gain. Thus, the old Soviet economy was estimated to have a marginal product of capital as low as 0.1—suggesting that a shift of 5% of gross national product from defense to net investment increases economic growth by only 0.5% (Hildebrandt 1992, 222). This illustration shows how defense spending and its consequences are tied in with other institutions, policies, or conditions, such as those dispositions favoring state enterprises, import-substituting firms, military–industrial complexes, large-scale public patronage, and a powerful organized "labor aristocracy." Defense spending is just one piece, albeit an important one, in this large framework of interlocking interests and influences operating on the domestic political economy. Of course, there is no guarantee that any resource savings from defense cutbacks, even if they should occur, would go to investment rather than consumption—raising the demand for manufactured imports from other countries and thereby contributing to an income shift across borders, furthering differences in trade competitiveness, and even increasing domestic inflationary pressure.

Significantly, although reducing the defense burden may promote the prospects of economic growth in the long run, military retrenchment can cause economic dislocation and political backlash in the short run. There is a long tradition of neo-Marxist analysis, claiming that advanced capitalist economies require heavy military expenditures to offset chronic underconsumption and that they use these expenditures as a countercyclical fiscal tool (e.g., Baran and Sweezy 1966; Melman 1974). Without taking on the motivations being attributed by this literature to the phenomenon of a persistently high defense burden that sometimes seems insufficiently sensitive to changes in the international environment (such as the end of the Cold War), military retrenchment can indeed produce short-term adverse consequences for local communities, specific industries, and the general employment prospects of discharged personnel (not to mention the profit margins of those firms that have become dependent on defense contracts). These short-term costs, both economic and political, can discourage incumbent officials from accepting draconian austerity measures, even though military retrenchment may have long-term benefits for the overall economy. They typically have short time horizons and are therefore reluctant to pay the price of political unpopularity and adjustment traumas currently, leaving their successors to claim credit for a healthier economy in the future.

## The Why of Why

The tendency for massive public spending, including military expenditures, to have a dampening effect on future economic growth can be mitigated or exacerbated. One obvious factor is the extent to which an economy is already operating at full capacity. When there is little slack, adding government spending to the existing money in circulation can only elevate inflationary pressure.

Another factor pertains to extraordinary revenues or savings rates that can relax fiscal constraints (e.g., Frederiksen and Looney 1983; Lebovic and Ishaq 1987; Looney and Frederiksen 1988; Ward, Davis, and Chan 1993). Massive income from oil exports and, for those countries that do not themselves produce energy, remittances abroad stemming from these revenues provide the financial wherewithal for some Middle Eastern countries to pursue increasing defense and social spending concurrently. In contrast, East Asia is generally a resource-poor region. Even though many countries in this region started the 1950s and 1960s with regimes dominated by conservative elites, powerful generals, and economic interests favoring import substitution, they subsequently parted company with Middle Eastern and Latin American countries.

They turned to export-led growth and emphasized economic performance as a basis for regime survival and legitimacy. In some ways, they made a virtue out of necessity in that their resource poverty did not provide other more attractive ways out for their regimes after the easy phase of import substitution had run its course. They could not be complacent and rely on the export of natural resources to "coast." The only major resource that the Northeast Asian countries had to speak of was their human capital—a relatively cheap, trained, and disciplined workforce—which gave them a competitive advantage in their initial drive to expand manufactures with low technology but high labor content.

In contrast to East Asia, the Middle East and Latin America have more abundant natural resources. Different countries in Latin America and the Caribbean have relied on the export of sugar, coffee, banana, tobacco, beef, grain and, of course, minerals such as bauxite, copper, and oil. These resource endowments oriented Middle Eastern and Latin American countries in a direction whereby they continued to favor import substitution, large state enterprises, and mass consumption at the expense of mass savings (S. Chan 2001a; Fajnzylber 1990), and their belated turn to market liberalization and export expansion was impeded by greater domestic opposition and was delayed for a longer time than in East Asia. Rich national endowments in natural resources are often described as a disguised curse—the so-called Dutch disease—which promotes complacency and postpones the tough choices that a regime needs to make. This discussion points to one reason for the different strategies of regime survival and legitimacy noted earlier.

There are other reasons. Generally speaking, U.S. policies have supported conservative political stalwarts and economic oligarchs in Latin America and the Middle East, and have helped to sustain the existing political and economic system in these regions. In contrast and in large part due to its efforts to fight Asian communists and contain Chinese influence, Washington promoted political and economic reform by its East Asian allies during the 1950s and 1960s. It encouraged change versus stasis in Taiwan, South Korea, Japan, and Southeast Asia. The massive inflow of U.S. assistance provided a source of extraordinary income for some countries and had the same practical effect as oil revenues, providing funds that could enable friendly regimes to relax guns-versus-butter tradeoffs. Except for South Vietnam, South Korea and Taiwan had received most U.S. aid in East Asia. The prospect of this assistance coming to an end, however, gave their regimes a nudge to initiate important policy adjustments away from import substitution starting at different times in the 1960s (e.g., T. Gold 1986; Jacoby 1966). American financial aid came also in forms other than direct grants that benefitted others in the region. The Korean War and later, the Vietnam War, fostered U.S. spending and demand for various goods and services. In this way, some have argued, Japan's economy got its jump start from the Korean War. Hong Kong, Singapore, Thailand, and Taiwan also benefited from U.S. spending related to the Vietnam War. But again, as these conflicts wound down, East Asian regimes were energized to develop new strategies for economic growth and political control.

In contrast, Middle Eastern countries still continue to receive massive amounts of foreign aid. Solingen (2007, 762) noted that five countries (Israel, Egypt, Jordan, Turkey, and Iraq) received cumulative foreign assistance in an amount that exceeded $8 billion compared to only two in East Asia (South Vietnam and South Korea). Sudan received more aid than Taiwan ($4.4 billion compared to $4 billion). When factoring in Russian aid, Egypt received more foreign assistance between 1956 and 1965 than Israel, and of course, both (plus Iraq after the U.S. invasion) continue to be the leading recipients of American largesse. In addition, Saudi Arabia, Kuwait, and the United Arab Emirates have provided funds to other Middle Eastern countries. This "financial lifeline" lessens incentives to turn to export-led growth, to downsize the state's role in the economy, or to cut back on military spending. Indeed, recurrent military and political conflicts in the region have the effect of ratcheting up and keeping up the latter spending, thereby perpetuating the so-called backlash strategy of elite survival (Solingen 2003)—one that relies on nationalism, state patronage, and mobilization against external foes as a source for regime power and legitimacy. The longer this strategy lasts and its supporters have a chance to entrench themselves, the more difficult it becomes institutionally and politically to alter the existing policy course.

One can imagine another historical difference accounting for the relative reluctance and tardy response of Middle Eastern and even Latin American countries to adjust or abandon their model of economic development and elite survival. Japanese colonialism and Chinese and Korean civil wars have had a greater effect in upsetting and uprooting traditional interest groups—

distribution coalitions in Mancur Olson's (1965) well-known phraseology—in East Asia than in the Middle East and Latin America (Barrett and Whyte 1982; S. Chan 1993; S. Chan and Clark 1992; Cumings 1981, 1984, 1990; Haggard 1990). Landlords, organized labor, and even nascent capitalists suffered terribly under colonial occupiers, as a result of internecine civil war, and during the subsequent period of authoritarian rule. Precisely because these war-related shocks had weakened civil society, the states in Japan, Taiwan, and South Korea became stronger and were able to override the objections of various vested interests that could or would have otherwise obstructed necessary reforms. If they were not physically eliminated by political enemies (e.g., landlords at the hands of communists), many compradors and corrupt officials literally abandoned the *anciens régimes* and fled to Hong Kong, Canada, and especially the United States.

Thus, earlier political traumas and the departure of some powerful interests opposed to reform created the necessary political space for policy change. Having suffered a terrible beating administered by their communist opponents, Taipei and Seoul were finally motivated to initiate necessary reforms—simply out of fear of losing out to these opponents again. Land reforms to appease the peasants and macroeconomic stabilization to avert a repeat of hyperinflation exemplified these initiatives. Defeat in World War II and occupation by U.S. forces also enabled reforms to proceed in Japan. One sees here a fortuitous combination of circumstances and incentives (or what Most and Starr, 1989, described as "opportunity" and "willingness") that produced a new policy orientation.

Precisely because of the perceived strategic importance of Japan, South Korea, and Taiwan, Washington was self-motivated to come to their assistance and to include them in a grand alliance to contain Chinese and Soviet communism. Rivalry with the Soviet Union, desire to secure energy supply, and recurrent Arab-Israeli conflicts had a similar effect in engaging Washington's attention in the Middle East. In contrast, because it enjoys unrivaled primacy in the Western Hemisphere, the United States has not been nearly as interested in urging and promoting social and economic reforms there—or to provide the necessary assistance to facilitate these changes. Whereas it has stood on the side of reform in East Asia, Washington has consistently sided with conservative interests in Latin America and the Middle East. Even though there have been figures such as Fidel Castro and Gamal Abdul Nasser, no one equivalent in stature to Mao Tsetung or Ho Chi-Minh has threatened to bring about region-wide revolutionary change. Notwithstanding the challenges mounted by Castro and Ernesto (Ché) Guevara, the Alliance for Progress did not provide nearly as much foreign assistance to states in the Western Hemisphere as that received by U.S. allies in East Asia and the Middle East (of course, oil-rich Middle Eastern states did not need U.S. financial assistance).

This remark implies that the threat of a communist revolution and the actual experience of suffering a setback from the communists had a therapeutic effect on various East Asian regimes—even those that did not directly experience large-scale communist insurrections (e.g., Japan, Thailand) and those that successfully met these challenges (e.g., Malaysia, Singapore, Indonesia, the Philippines). Certainly, complacency is not a characterization that comes to mind in reference to Taipei or Seoul. At the same time, despite public rhetoric that might have at one time suggested otherwise, today Taipei and Seoul have little interest in resuming armed conflict to "settle the score" with their respective communist adversary. In contrast, the idea of *Nakba*—or cataclysm—still pervades the Arab world, motivating repeated attempts to challenge Israel. This sense of seeking a historical reversal was certainly palpable before the Camp David Accord, which eventually produced the Egyptian-Israeli peace treaty. And it continues to thrive in parts of the Middle East, thus providing continuous justification for an emphasis on nationalism and militarization. Nowadays, one never hears of an intention to roll back communism or recover the mainland in East Asia.

There is an even deeper historical origin to East Asia's—or at least Northeast Asia's—emphasis on economic performance. Ever since the times when Western powers came knocking on the doors of these countries, seeking to open them to foreign commerce, national economic revitalization has been quite literally a matter of national security and even national survival. The distinction, prevalent in Anglo-American discourse, between security as a matter of confronting military threats and economics as a matter of maximizing consumption has not been characteristic of strategic thinking in these Asian countries. Rather, the call for "rich country, strong army"—starting with Japan's Meiji Restoration—has been the hallmark of their national security agenda (e.g., Samuels 1994). Economic development has been seen as an inseparable part of and an essential basis for national security. Surely, Chinese and Japanese nationalism in the late 1800s and early 1900s was animated by a burning desire to catch up with the West economically and technologically. Since World War II Japan has given priority to the pursuit of technological and economic capabilities rather than military capabilities (Heginbotham and Samuels 1999). This orientation later also permeated South Korea's and Taiwan's strategic culture and, with Deng Xiaoping's economic reforms, it has also become evident in China's policy agenda. There is a gradual but unmistakable shift in the strategic thinking of officials in almost all countries in East Asia (again, with the notable exception of North Korea) whereby economic power is displacing the importance of political and military power (Berger 2003). In one analyst's words (Wan 2003, 302), "economic performance has become a cornerstone of legitimacy for countries in the region," including those in Southeast Asia (Alagappa 1995).

One final set of comments about those policies or conditions that can lessen the tension between guns and butter, and between current and future consumption, is in order. It pertains to the United States rather than countries in East Asia or the Middle East. Given the dominance of the U.S. dollar as an international currency, Washington has been in a privileged position to control global finance and credit. It has managed to run chronic and heavy deficits in its government budget and trade account by issuing debt denominated in the dollar. This policy has been tantamount to exporting domestic inflation and forcing U.S. trade partners and debtors to subsidize Washington's fiscal extravagance. When it unilaterally decided in 1971 to abandon its commitment to convert dollars into gold, it brought about a massive devaluation of the dollar assets held by foreigners. In the words of Susan Strange (1987, 568–569),

> In most countries, whether the balance-of-payments is in surplus or deficit indicates the strength or weakness of its financial position. With the United States, the exact converse can be true. Indeed, to run a persistent deficit for a quarter of a century with impunity indicates not American weakness, but rather American power in the system. To decide one August [1971] morning that dollars can no longer be converted into gold was a progression from exorbitant privilege to super-exorbitant privilege; the U.S. government was exercising the unconstrained right to print money that others could not (save at unacceptable cost) refuse to accept in payment.

This remark was made over twenty years ago. In the wake of the most recent financial crisis that pushed the global economy to the brink of another great depression, Washington's trade partners and debtors are expressing increasing concerns about the future value of their dollar-denominated assets. The Chinese, Japanese, Taiwanese, and Saudis are among the largest creditors to whom the United States owes money. They, the other oil producers, and the European countries are making noises about moving away from the U.S. dollar as the principal medium for settling their international accounts. Whether various proposals to develop a basket of currencies to replace the dollar are practicable or even desirable may be debatable, and in the short term there still appears to be no alternative to the dollar as the world's premier currency. It does seem, however, that the super-exorbitant privilege enjoyed by the United States in getting "a quart out of a pint pot" is not guaranteed to last forever. Huge budget deficits would cause long-term dollar depreciation

against other currencies, and the weakening dollar would in turn drive commodity prices higher. The price of gold exceeded $1,900 per ounce in August
2011, a huge increase from the days when it was fixed at $35 per ounce. In
the six years before 2008, the U.S. dollar lost cumulative averages of 25%–30%
against other major currencies (Bergsten et al. 2008, 18). This decline has been
further exacerbated in the wake of massive federal deficit spending undertaken
to stimulate an ailing economy.

In November 2010, to stimulate a lethargic economy, the U.S. Federal
Reserve announced "quantitative easing" to add $600 billion to circulation.
This policy had the effect, whether intended or not, of causing dollar devaluation and hurting other countries' trade competitiveness. The infusion of this
enormous amount of liquidity also led "hot" money to flow to developing
countries, increasing the danger of asset bubbles there. The Fed's announcement was criticized by other countries, with Germany's Finance Minister
Wolfgang Schäuble saying, "It doesn't add up when the Americans accuse the
Chinese of currency manipulation and then, with the help of their central
bank's printing presses, artificially lower the value of the dollar" (*Wall Street
Journal*, November 9, 2010, A15). The dollar's decline was more pronounced
among Asia Pacific countries, sliding 11.4% against the Japanese yen during
the period between January 1 and November 12, 2010; 10.6% against the Thai
baht; 9.1% against the Malaysian ringgit; 9.0% against the Australian dollar;
and 7.7% against the Singapore dollar (*Wall Street Journal*, November 15, 2010,
C6). It fell by 5.5% against the Taiwan dollar, 3.3% against the South Korean
won, and 2.8% against the Chinese yuan. By tying its currency to the dollar,
China has built a dam diverting the impact of dollar depreciation to other
countries.

Americans have commented, sometimes derisively, on China's so-called
socialism with Chinese characteristics. With Washington's massive bailout of
private financial institutions and automobile firms (including the "cash for
clunkers" program), one begins to hear snickers from the other side of the
Pacific about capitalism with American characteristics. That Washington supported the International Monetary Fund's demanding conditionality imposed
on Asian countries after their economies were devastated by financial crises
in the late 1990s, and that it did little else to alleviate their economic predicament, caused widespread resentment. That the United States refused to take
its own medicine after the 2008 financial crisis caused by subprime mortgages
aroused additional skepticism and even hostility. The Fed's unilateral resort to
"quantitative easing" further undermined credible commitment by a hegemon
to refrain from abusing its power (e.g., Ikenberry 2001; Lake 2009).

China's political economy and its leaders' policies offer a sharp contrast to those of the United States. China's very high savings rate helped to finance its economic growth. Its savings rate reached an astonishing level of more than half of China's gross domestic product in 2006 (Bergsten et al. 2008, 106). Although at 36% of gross domestic product, China's investment was in the initial decade of its economic reform roughly comparable to that of its East Asian counterparts. This amount exceeded 40% between 2004 and 2007, and its massive anticyclical stimulus program introduced between 2008 and 2009 augured a further surge in this rate. In 2008, China's capital investment reached 44% of its economy, with consumption taking up only 35% (Reich 2009, A25). In contrast to the situation in the United States, China's high savings rate and huge foreign reserves (at an estimated $2.13 trillion in June 2009, and reaching above an estimated $3 trillion in April 2011) meant that Beijing did not have to resort to debt financing in order to pay for its stimulus program of about $600 billion. Whereas about two-thirds of the U.S. economy is estimated to be dependent on consumer spending, this figure has been about half as much for China. Fundamentally, China's economy has focused on investment and production, whereas the U.S. economy has been oriented toward consumption—both public and private. The structural differences between these two economies, and their shifting competitiveness in international trade, account for the fact that the Chinese currency, the rembinbi, appreciated about 18% relative to the U.S. dollar between 2005 and 2008 in nominal terms, and about 11% in real terms.

Fiscal capacity can ease or constrain policy choices with respect to a government's management of the macro economy and its conduct of foreign relations. This capacity, however, is itself the result of prior choices about the relative priorities to be assigned to spending on guns or butter—and more generally, to current consumption or future consumption. The Soviet Union's demise and the decline of other empires preceding it underscore the danger of imperial overstretch (Kennedy 1987)—when a country's economy becomes overextended and decreasingly capable of supporting its expansive and expensive interests abroad.

In November 2009, an intense debate took place within the U.S. administration about whether to authorize deploying an additional 30,000 to 40,000 troops to Afghanistan—a course of action that Barack Obama decided to support in the end. The cost of the Afghan war reached $6.7 billion in June 2009 alone, doubling the previous year's level. The White House's Office of Management and Budget estimated that each additional soldier sent to Afghanistan would cost about $1 million (Entous 2009), thus calling attention to

DEFENSE AND REGIME STRATEGY

the fiscal considerations emphasized in this chapter. On its seventh anniversary (reached on March 19, 2010), the direct cost of the Iraq War had reached $712 billion according to the National Priorities Project. The total direct and indirect long-term cost of this conflict could reach $3 trillion (Stiglitz and Bilmes 2008). Both conflicts (in Iraq and Afghanistan) have been funded by borrowing rather than taxation. They have been supported largely by supplemental appropriation—that is, via the mechanism of special or off-budget funding, outside regular fiscal processes.

## Further Discussion

A country's external relations are inevitably influenced by its domestic politics, most particularly by its elite's strategy for survival and legitimacy. In this chapter I have argued that a turn to emphasizing economic performance as the cornerstone of this strategy has promoted political cooperation and economic integration in East Asia, contrasting this region with the Middle East. Thus, the absence of overt and energetic balancing behavior noted in the last chapter has its origin in a country's domestic political economy and in the choices its leaders have made about feasible and desirable policies for economic development and political maintenance.

Timing, in the sense of concurrent events (such as the Korean and Vietnam wars), the advantages conferred on the "first mover" (in this instance, the first countries to turn to export-led growth), shortened periods of pursuing import substitution, and the recency of traumatic shocks caused by communist victories (or in Japan's case, defeat in World War II) all contributed to the greater willingness of East Asian regimes to switch to, again albeit at different times and to different extent, an export-led model of economic development. This model's popularity spread as its success compelled even the more reluctant inward-looking countries to make changes, though in some cases belatedly and slowly. In contrast, the "resource curse" produced by both oil revenues and U.S. assistance has had the general effect of retarding or impeding a switch away from nationalism, militarization, and state enterprises as a means of maintaining the ruling elites' political control and economic interests in the Middle East.

The probability of balancing policies occurring is affected by the ruling elites' attitudes toward the guns-versus-butter tradeoffs in their direct and indirect forms. The severity of these tradeoffs is influenced by internal and external circumstances, and different elites have varying propensities to accept or decline these tradeoffs given their policy priorities, strategic inclinations, and feasible alternatives available to them to lessen the impact of these tradeoffs.

The basic point about tradeoffs, however, is that they force leaders to make choices. Leaders cannot have both guns and butter and maximize both current and future consumption without having to face some constraints at some point. The fact that these constraints exist, albeit to different degrees for different countries, provides an important insight about why balancing policies do not occur even when balance-of-power theorists expect states to undertake them under seemingly propitious circumstances.

Mass political attitudes also have a role in buttressing and affecting regime strategies. They influence economic development and democratization and are in turn influenced by the latter (Inglehart 1977, 1990, 1997). In East Asian countries, "survival" values dominate, expressing concerns about economic insecurity and competitive achievement that are typical of transitional societies in the process of industrializing (Inglehart et al. 2004). Such emphasis motivates economic performance as a national priority. In contrast, in mature industrialized societies, postmaterialist values of self-expression are more prevalent, promoting tolerance for diversity and respect for human rights. Because economic development is likely to produce a culture shift toward postmaterialist values, popular attitudes in East Asia should gradually become more similar to those in postindustrial societies, as already seen in Japan.

To repeat the central point of this discussion, states' external relations are embedded in their governing elites' dominant strategy for regime survival and leadership legitimacy, and to the extent that this strategy emphasizes economic performance based on export expansion, global access, private entrepreneurship, and conservative fiscal and monetary policies, they tend to eschew moves in line with balance-of-power expectations. If a region is populated by many like-minded regimes with such an internationalist outlook emphasizing economic growth as a source of political legitimacy, we are likely to observe regional interactions approximating a situation of complex interdependence (Keohane and Nye 1977). Faced with their declining competitiveness, laggards are often motivated to join the winners, as exemplified by Mikhail Gorbachev's *perestroika* and *glasnost*, and Deng Xiaoping's liberalization and opening of the Chinese economy.

It is an ironic but underanalyzed phenomenon that authoritarian regimes may be in a stronger political position to undertake such volte-face than democracies with their entrenched distribution coalitions (Olson 1965). Scholars such as Samuel Huntington (1968) and S. Martin Lipset (1963) have written extensively about political institutionalization and the importance of timing and sequencing in a country's mass mobilization and economic development. The recent history of Northeast Asia's political economies points to authoritarian regimes' emphasis on development before economic distribution and political participation. In contrast, in Latin America mass mobilization has preceded economic development, thereby contributing to more intense political conflicts over distribution and producing the earlier phenomenon of military intervention and soft authoritarianism intended to suppress a population that has already been mobilized (Collier 1979; O'Donnell 1979).

It is also worth noting that once a contagion emphasizing economic development has taken effect, a virtuous cycle tends to gather further momentum. Immersion in a fast-growing and expanded free(r)-trade zone provides a stimulus for faster economic growth and further integration (Olson 1982). Thus, we have the seeds of self-sustaining and self-reinforcing regional forces promoting further economic and political cooperation, moving away from Hobbesian dynamics characteristic of a world of anarchy and self-help. At the same time, the Soviet Union's demise serves as a dire warning against imperial overstretch and as a strong reminder to those who pay attention: "by the end of the twentieth century the increased significance of science and rapidly changing technology as determinants of relative power, including military clout, mean that security is better served by a strategy that facilitates economic development rather than one that seeks to accumulate foreign territory, resources, and population" (Goldstein 2003a, 62).

In contrast to the prevailing East Asian strategic conception emphasizing economic growth and power, the United States has followed a more *realpolitik* approach, giving primacy to political influence and military capabilities. According to the Stockholm International Peace Research Institute, the United States accounted for 46% of defense expenditures made by all the countries in the world in 2006, an amount that was almost eleven times larger than China's defense expenditures (Brooks and Wohlforth 2008, 29). It is odd and even ironic that having accounted for nearly half of the world's defense expenditures, the United States continues to be concerned about national security defined primarily in terms of military power. When Americans speak of keeping a balance of power, they probably have in mind the maintenance of an actual *imbalance* of power in America's favor. As Christopher Layne (2009a, 129) remarked, "Because of geography, and military capabilities, [the United States] has enjoyed—and even after 9/11 still does (or could) enjoy—something close to absolute security. To put it a bit differently, even if, as a general proposition, security in the international system often is scarce, for the United States it has been abundant." Layne (2009a, 130) continued, "From an *objective* standpoint the American homeland essentially has been unthreatened existentially" (emphasis in the original).

Reflecting an opposite obsession, even after they have compiled huge foreign reserves, East Asian countries continue to be obsessed with savings and exports. This divergence can be easily noticed in U.S. policy and academic discourse on balance of power, with a focus on armament or alignment to deter or contain other countries (including China)—without any sense of inconsistency, especially for those American realists who insist on intention-free analysis, that it is the United States that should be the source of others' balancing concerns if military capabilities are what is important. At the same time, East Asian governments and firms defend their market shares and currency pegs as if that is the most important thing for their national security, even if objectively speaking their industries and currencies have already become very competitive by global standards. East Asian economic conduct has caused a backlash in other countries, including the United States, because of perceptions of their mercantilist agenda. Conversely, U.S. application of "muscular" policies in places such as Iraq, Afghanistan, and Kosovo has aroused objections and concerns due to foreigners' misgivings about Washington's hegemonic ambitions. Robert Pape (2005, 9) remarked, "the Bush strategy of aggressive unilateralism is changing the United States' long-enjoyed reputation for benign intent and giving other major powers reason to fear its power." The United States has become more unpopular abroad and more isolated in multilateral forums such as the United Nations (e.g., Bobrow 2008a; Katzenstein and Keohane 2007; Kohut and Stokes 2006; Voeten 2004).

The tension between the two strategic conceptions operating on opposite sides of the Pacific Ocean is a concern because it increasingly erodes the basis of the historical bargain struck previously by the United States and its Asian allies. Since the end of World War II, the latter have accepted political deference to the United States and its military dominance in exchange for easy access to the U.S. market and a chronic U.S. trade imbalance. The security agendas of countries on both sides of this relationship have been predicated on this linkage (Gilpin 2000). With the end of the Cold War and growth of massive U.S. trade and budget deficits, continued dollar depreciation, and such heavy indebtedness that American consumers are much less able to buy foreign imports, this link is being severely tested by the recession of 2008–2009. John Ikenberry and Michael Mastanduno (2003, 431) remarked that "the incentives for Asian trading states to embrace a U.S.-centered security order are increased to the extent U.S. officials tolerate [trade] deficits." Naturally, the reverse can also be true. Asian states' incentives are decreased to the extent that the United States becomes more protectionist and their dollar-denominated assets become increasingly devalued—and if China displaces the United States, as it has already done for some East Asian countries, as their most important export market and investment destination.

One may anticipate an argument being made to the effect that precisely because the United States protected them militarily, East Asian countries were able to give priority to their economic performance. A more extended form of this argument was given by former U.S. Secretary of Defense William Perry:

> Some critics argue that our military presence and security alliances are relics of the Cold War. The most extreme among them say that we should pull back our forces from the region, terminate our agreements that provide security for our allies and allow normal balance-of-power politics to fill the vacuum. This is a seductive line of thought, but it has dangerous consequences. For years, the U.S. provided a secure environment which allowed the Asian Pacific nations to build their economies rather than their national defense structures . . . If we were to withdraw our military forces from the region, this would all change. Countries would be forced to rethink their needs, with building up defense structures at or near the top of the list. Rapid growth of military structures, plus historical animosities, would be a volatile mix that could quickly destabilize the region . . . dramatically increasing the risk of regional conflict (quoted in Layne 2009a, 130).

There is merit to this argument when applied to the initial turn by Japan, Taiwan, and South Korea to emphasizing economic performance and pursuing an export-led growth model. Surely, these countries' defense burdens would have been much heavier, even to the point of crushing their economies, had it not been for the subsidies they received from Washington, both directly and indirectly. Moreover, the U.S. market was certainly critical for these countries' export-based growth strategy. U.S. military protection did not have a similar salutary effect in changing Middle Eastern countries' model of political economy, however. Moreover, even though Latin American countries have faced a more benign external security environment, they did not turn to a strategy of elite legitimacy pivoting on economic development and to an export-led growth model until considerably after East Asian countries had made these choices. Finally, as a general empirical proposition, the argument that U.S. military protection enabled East Asians to give economic performance top priority needs to be tempered because this emphasis became contagious only after the height of U.S. military involvement in the 1960s. China's economic liberalization followed a period of U.S. military retrenchment after the Vietnam War, and the region-wide embrace of economic growth and interdependence really took off after the end of the Cold War. These remarks do not deny that the U.S. connection was vital for the initial switch to export-led growth by East Asia's earlier NICs. While not insignificant, this U.S. role has become less important over time.

The U.S. security blanket provided a military protection that lessened the impact of guns-versus-butter tradeoffs for many East Asian countries, and Washington's economic assistance and ideological prodding helped to pave the way for Japan's, South Korea's and Taiwan's initial turn to an export-led approach to economic development. Sino-American rapprochement was also not irrelevant to China's changing perceptions of the Soviet threat and Deng Xiaoping's market reforms. Since these countries' initial turn to pivot regime legitimacy on economic performance, considerable power shifts in the region and occasional U.S. military retrenchment have not altered East Asian elites' fundamental policy agenda and orientation. Once this pivoting on economic performance has had a chance to embed itself in their domestic political economies, it becomes more difficult to reverse this emphasis due to the effects of distribution coalitions and institutional "stickiness." This entrenchment signifies a domestic pact that favors external cooperation and thus sends a reassuring signal to other states. When these pacts become pervasive across countries in the region, they communicate credible commitment (even if unwritten) all around to eschew balance-of-power dynamics. Significantly, in the situation just described, foreigners can be more reassured than otherwise that balancing policies (emphasizing, as they traditionally do, armament and alliances) are less necessary, because domestic interest groups would be more effectively restraining their respective states from aggression and aggrandizement.

That Taiwan has continued its outward economic orientation and its process of political liberalization despite Washington's decision to terminate its defense treaty with the island offers a powerful indication that once an internationally oriented coalition favoring economic performance has gained power and has had a chance to consolidate itself, a reversal of policy course favoring a garrison state or military–industrial complex becomes much less likely to occur. Similarly, as will be discussed in Chapter 5, Seoul's basic policy emphasizing economic and political opening has not wavered despite fluctuations in Pyongyang's bellicosity and despite its tendency to resort to occasional saber rattling. However, institutional stasis and policy inertia can also work in the opposite direction. As demonstrated by the Soviet Union's experience, a state can continue to pursue its ostensible security imperatives, favoring guns over butter, for a long time, even after the limitations and costs of such a course of action have become quite evident. The political gridlock characterizing Washington's debate on increasing the national debt ceiling in August 2011 and the subsequent downgrading of the U.S. credit rating by Standard and Poor's again attest to the difficulty of reversing policies even in the face of a looming crisis.

# 5

## Balance-of-Power Expectations Versus Credible Commitment

Balancing power means exactly what it says: the pursuit of policies—armament or alignment—that are intended to restore some equilibrium in the distribution of national power, especially in military capabilities. The problem with these policies, however, is that they only offer a transient solution, treating the symptoms rather than the basic causes of a changing power distribution. This is so because, in the final analysis, national power originates from a state's internal capacity, especially its economic health, which in turn is the ultimate source for its military capabilities. Balancing policies are unlikely in the long run to bend states' growth trajectories, which tend to reflect whether they undertake self-defeating or self-strengthening policies.

In her analysis of the Warring States period of Chinese history, Victoria Hui (2005) demonstrated that the Kingdom of Qin adopted important military, political, and administrative reforms that enabled it to defeat its rivals and unify China, thereby overcoming other states' efforts to balance against its power. Contrasting ancient China with early modern Europe, Hui showed that European states pursued several self-defeating policies—most notably their reliance on mercenary soldiers, tax farming, and venality of office and title—which stymied the development of strong states, thereby enabling balance-of-power dynamics to prevail in European interstate relations.

Even states that approached near-hegemonic positions stumbled and descended into decrepitude because they followed self-defeating policies. The Spanish Habsburgs' counterproductive policies are legendary. The diversion of productive economic activities to religious and other nonproductive estates, the protection of powerful interests (e.g., the Mesta) opposed to entrepreneurship, the repeated foreign military campaigns that strained and eventually exceeded available military and fiscal resources, the excessive reliance on windfall revenue (silver from South America), a predilection for luxurious imports, and finally the government's fiscal extravagances, loan defaults, and currency debasement can all be counted among the causes contributing to the Spanish Empire's decline.

Self-defeating policies have been committed by other would-be hegemons, such as when Napoleon's France, Hitler's Germany, and Tojo's Japan fought repeatedly and even concurrently against other countries, thereby forcing the victims of their aggression to join hands to defeat them. Self-defeating policies have also been committed by ostensible defenders of the international status quo such as Philip V's Spain, which took a hard line against all perceived challengers to its authority or power. Its bellicosity against "all comers" eventually exhausted its military and fiscal capacity, accelerating its process of decline (Treisman 2004).

Researchers sometimes select the dependent variable of war occurrence and are therefore prone to overemphasize the danger of underreacting to an emergent danger. An example of this is when states failed to respond forcefully and quickly to Napoleon and Hitler, and when this failure was followed by war. However, researchers often do not pay enough attention to the opposite situation—an inability and/or unwillingness to confront a rising power—such as when Britain decided to concede to U.S. primacy in the Western Hemisphere and when it allied itself with Japan in the late 1800s and early 1900s (Bourne 1967; Friedberg 1988; Rock 2000). War did not happen in the former case. In the latter case, it did, albeit in an indirect fashion, by encouraging Japanese audacity to attack Russia in 1905 (Nish 1986; Paul 1994). Tokyo had counted on British support to induce the Russians to accept a *fait accompli*, and thus to settle for peace with it after a short conflict (a protracted war would have put Japan at a serious disadvantage).

More recently, the Soviet Union's failure to balance against the United States did not produce war, and is not typically considered a failure of balance-of-power theories. Few U.S. scholars point to the Soviet Union's demise as evidence undermining these theories or suggesting world peace would henceforth be endangered by U.S. predominance. Significantly, Moscow's belated turn to *perestroika* was hardly uncontroversial; it was resisted by military and party hardliners. Therefore, its eventual policy of retrenchment and accommodation was not a foregone conclusion. "Faced with a hostile external environment and severe internal economic constraints, states do not always choose appeasement: they sometimes choose war" (Evangelista 1993, 165).

The upshot of these comparative anecdotes is that policy errors can result both from underreacting and overreacting to a supposed threat. Moreover, what turned out in retrospect to be a clear threat were ambiguous signs at the time when decisions had to be made. As both Stephen Walt (1992, 453) and Randall Schweller (1999, 20–21) have remarked, it was not until Hitler's invasion of Prague in 1939 that his aggressive agenda became clear. Germany's prior demands to revise the Versailles Treaty's harsh terms (including war reparations), reclaim sovereignty in Danzig and the Rhineland, and represent ethnic Germans in Czechoslovakia, could hardly be construed to indicate revisionist or expansionist intentions. They were in fact perceived as legitimate and reasonable by many in Britain (e.g., R. Kaufman 1992; Walt 1992). The certainty of hindsight results only from our post hoc knowledge about the occurrence of wars and their outcomes (Kahneman, Slovic, and Tversky 1982).

Moreover, there is a tendency for people to imagine that they are just reacting to others' provocations without considering that their own supposed balancing actions could have contributed to the eventual hostility (Jervis 1968). Yet, Washington's assistance to Britain (including the Lend-Lease program) surely contributed to Germany's animosity (Stein 1993), and the U.S. strategic embargo against Japan was the proximate cause for Tokyo's launch of the Pearl Harbor attack (Barnhart 1987; Ike 1967). In history, causes and effects are inevitably interwoven in a less straightforward manner than they are in theory.

Nevertheless, the "fog" preceding the outbreak of war has more to do with uncertainties about the pertinent states' intentions than their capabilities. States would presumably want to maximize their consumption rather than spend their money on military projects if they could make a credible commitment to each other not to attack (Powell 1999). The inability to provide persuasive mutual assurance of peaceful intentions underlies the well-known paradox of the security dilemma (Jervis 1978). In this chapter, I first introduce briefly the so-called rationalist explanations of war (Fearon 1995; Gartzke 1999; Wagner 2000). I attend especially to states' efforts to communicate reassurance and commitment so that war, or balancing policies, may be averted. From this perspective, the credible communication of intentions—rather than the balancing of power—helps to preserve international peace and stability.

I then turn to Robert Axelrod's (1984) seminal work on the evolution of cooperation. In particular, I show that instead of getting caught in a game of matching one another's military and diplomatic assets, states can follow the tit-for-tat model to signal their intentions. This discussion is followed by four brief "case studies," or rather, extended illustrations, each of which introduces one or more significant puzzles from the dominant balance-of-power perspective. These cases illuminate interstate signaling intended to both deter and reassure.

Attention to both deterrence and reassurance is important because of the chief insight of prospect theory (Kahneman, Slovic, and Tversky 1982; Kahneman and Tversky 1979, 2000). Based on extensive experimental data, prospect theory shows that people have a strong aversion to suffering losses and that they are much more disposed to taking risks to avoid these losses than to seek gains. This common tendency has been used to explain foreign policy (e.g., Boettcher 2005; Farnham 1994, 1997; Levy 1996, 1997; McDermott 1998; Taliaferro 2004).

Research on prospect theory offers three implications supported by Germany's historical interactions with its European neighbors (J. Davis 2000). First, states may undertake aggressive policies as a result of its insecurity (a fear of incurring losses or experiencing relative decline) or its greed (a desire to obtain gains at others' expense). Thus, aggressive policies can have very different motivation sources.

Second, attempts to influence aggression that is motivated by insecurity are more likely to succeed through a strategy of reassurances and even promises. Conversely, deterrence threats should be more appropriate for dealing with aggression that is motivated by greed. When officials fail to make this distinction in addressing these two types of aggression that have different motivations, they are apt to produce counterproductive results, abetting greater bellicosity from the target state in both cases.

Third, policies attempting to deter a target state that perceives itself to be in the domain of loss will require greater resources and effort than those seeking to discourage a target state that sees itself in the domain of gain. In other words, a target that is trying to recover from a loss or to reverse its decline will be more difficult to deter, as it is with North Korea today and as it was with imperial Germany in 1914. An insecure state motivated by a desire to avoid losses will be more willing to take risks than a confident one seeking to make gains. Conversely, because "people's utility functions are generally steeper in the domain of loss than in the domain of gain, prospect theory leads us to expect that promised rewards can be modest and yet achieve significant return in terms of increased target utility" (J. Davis 2000, 37).

This observation in turn offers two hypotheses contrary to balance-of-power reasoning: a rising state such as China will be more reluctant to get into conflicts than a declining state, and engagement and cooperation will be more effective in shaping its incentives than containment and coercion. A strictly adversarial view emphasizing deterrence overlooks the role of promises

and reassurances that may be undertaken concurrently with threats in dealing with potential adversaries. Moreover, states often seek not only to deter
adversaries but also to restrain their own allies. Before turning to elaborate on
these themes, I want to explain why I chose some cases for my analysis but
not others.

## Rationale for Case Selection

Recently, Japan's disputes with China over the Senkaku/Diaoyutai islands and
with Russia over the Northern Territories/Southern Kurils have been in the
news. Japan also has an ongoing territorial dispute with South Korea over the
Takeshima/Dokdo islands. Similarly, China and its Southeast Asian neighbors
have contested sovereignty in the South China Sea, such as over the Spratly
islands. Other analysts have accorded considerable attention to these frictions.
Why do I not give them more significance?

Recurrent recriminations and disputes are not unusual. For example,
Anglo-American relations have been rather acrimonious at times, such as
when the United States and Britain clashed over border demarcation with
Canada, both in Alaska and Maine (the so-called Aroostook War), and when
the United States lent assistance to Canadian rebels (most famously in 1838,
in the controversy over Britain's seizure of the U.S. steamship *Caroline*, which
was transporting men and materiel to support insurgency against British rule).
Thus, frictions such as these are not unique to China's relations with others,
and should not be stressed over more important macro developments. The
trend in China's relations with its neighbors has been moving toward conciliation, with China having settled most of its border disputes and on terms
generally more favorable to its counterparts (e.g., Fravel 2005). I tend to see
the glass more than half full.

Reasoning counterfactually, China's disputes with its neighbors would have
been more serious had it not been for Beijing's efforts to restrain popular
sentiments. My hunch is that this is also true of Japanese and Vietnamese governments when they have faced popular domestic sentiments in their disputes
with China. I am inclined to argue that crises are what states want to make of
them. This view echoes Walt Rostow's reaction to the Viet Cong's attack on
Pleiku, commenting that such attacks are like "streetcars"—implying that they
happen rather routinely and offer officials regular opportunities to escalate if
they wish. The more remarkable feature about such incidents is not that they
happen but rather that they are capped at low levels. Thus, these recurrent
recriminations are "trumped" by other considerations. Moreover, that these
incidents recur is not too surprising because leaders may wish to remind their

foreign counterparts about the prospects of mutual restraint (i.e., setting off balance-of-power dynamics) if the other side does not restrain itself. Finally, when leaders are more certain that their relations are on solid ground, they are more willing to enter into disputes—knowing that there is only a small danger that these disputes will spiral out of control. As I will explain later, whether a particular dispute needs to be taken seriously depends on whether one thinks officials are just posturing or are truly resolved. One can make this distinction by watching to see whether they are willing to accept heavy self-imposed costs and "rock the boat" of bilateral and even multilateral relations. So far, I have not seen evidence of this kind.

My logic for case selection and analysis differs from the typical research approach that seeks to confirm some hypothesized behavior such as balancing. I stress, instead, the non-occurrence of the expected (such as when a powerful state restrains itself) or the occurrence of the unexpected (such as when a rising state's neighbors refrain from balancing against it). These phenomena are instructive because, after all, realists would not expect the world's second largest economy (Japan, at least until very recently) to disavow nuclear weapons and accept foreign soldiers on its soil, nor potential adversaries (such as China and Taiwan, and China and the United States) to enter into intense commercial relations. Thus, I focus deliberately on a few strategic points, either because they provide the crucial linchpins for interlocking international and domestic bargains (i.e., the United States, China, and Japan), or because they represent especially informative cases (e.g., if Taiwan, facing an existential threat, fails to balance against China, it would be more devastating for balance-of-power reasoning than, say, if New Zealand fails to do so). Indeed, given the logic of most likely case, if balance-of-power dynamics is not operating in East Asia (or only weakly so), where China, as a rising continental power, should especially produce such reaction, where else should one expect it to prevail?

Stasis can present empirical puzzles and can be as theoretically informative as change. The security environment for East Asian leaders has surely undergone significant transformation in the wake of major developments such as China's rise, the Soviet Union's collapse, the end of the Vietnam War, and the region's economic growth. There have also been government turnovers, shifts in public opinion, and occasional tensions—such as the sinking of the South Korean naval vessel *Cheonan*. Yet, remarkably, internal and external bargains have largely stuck. Japan and South Korea, for example, have remained "tethered" to the United States. The persistence of their alliances—in view of major changes in these countries' security environments—is what needs to be explained. As Kenneth Waltz (1993, 66) averred, "For a country to choose not to become a great power is a structural anomaly." Japan's continued reliance on the United States for its security is thus contrary to balance-of-power reasoning. Similarly, the continuation of the U.S.–South Korea alliance—even though Seoul has gained an overwhelming advantage over Pyongyang, both economically and militarily—contradicts this reasoning. Moreover, if Soviet or Chinese power presented a common threat to Japan and South Korea, these countries should have collaborated. "Explaining this seemingly irrational behavior [South Korea and Japan remaining averse to a bilateral defense treaty] is a difficult task for the Realist school of thought in international relations, according to which states with common allies and common enemies should be friendly" (Cha 1999, 2).

The many "dogs that did not bark" are important to my emphasis on credible commitment. Some of the cases discussed below pose enigmas not only to realism or balance-of-power logic but also to liberalism. For instance, liberals would argue that in the absence of important institutions such as those that protect property rights or enforce contractual obligations, even mutually profitable exchanges do not occur (e.g., North 1990). Yet, Taiwan's trade with and investment in China have thrived without such legal institutions, at least until very recently. Similarly, regime similarity and mutual trust, reinforced by compatible political markets, should enhance commerce. But these conditions cannot account for the "super-economic fusion" between the United States and China. Credible commitment, however, offers an explanation where these other perspectives fail to do so.

## Rationalist Explanations and Credible Communication

Leaders misrepresent. In making public statements, they often deliberately hide or exaggerate their capabilities, bluff their resolve, and stake out negotiation positions that they are actually willing to concede. Conflicts escalate and wars occur because leaders are unable to discern one another's true capabilities and intentions. Rationalist theorists argue that "war is in the error term" in the sense that if belligerents had perfect information about each other's capabilities and intentions before starting a conflict, they would surely prefer to reach a negotiated settlement (Blainey 1973; Fearon 1995, 1998a; Gartzke 1999; Wagner 2000). Because war is inefficient (i.e., costly), belligerents would spare themselves the costs of fighting it if they could foresee how a conflict will turn out. They would negotiate a settlement to avoid war if they had this foresight, but this foresight is hampered by officials' tendency to misrepresent and to keep vital information (or private information) to themselves.

Moreover, deals are difficult to reach because of the commitment problem. How can a state be sure that its counterpart will not renege in the future if circumstances become more favorable to it? Concerns about an inability to enforce the terms of a contract prevent an agreement from being reached in the first place. For this reason, the involvement by powerful third parties is often sought to guarantee the terms of a ceasefire or peace settlement in both civil and interstate wars (e.g., Fortna 2004; Walter 2002; Werner and Yuen 2005). Other possibilities, such as the indivisibility of the contesting parties' objectives, may also impede the pursuit of peace. I will, however, focus in this chapter on the credible disclosure of intentions, including the commitment to stand by a deal, in the context of East Asian relations.

How can a state tell when another is being sincere and distinguish this sincere counterpart from others who are insincere (but pretend to be sincere)? Conversely, how can a state try to assure another that it is being sincere, that it will not renege on a deal at an opportune time in the future? These questions pertain to the security dilemma underlying realist formulations of international relations and many balance-of-power theories. These formulations warn about the dire consequences that can ensue should a state misplace its confidence, mistaking an unreliable counterpart for a dependable one—thereby setting itself up for a serious disappointment and even a fatal error due to the other side's opportunism, such as when a state disarms but its counterpart surreptitiously retains or develops powerful weapons.

Proponents of the security dilemma argue that absent effective enforcement to punish rule breakers or deal violators, states engage in self-help. They seek to improve their security through unilateral actions. Their actions, however, alarm their counterparts because when one state gains strength, its neighbors necessarily have a weaker security position (Jervis 1978). These other states may therefore feel compelled to react, causing a "vicious circle of security and power accumulation" (Herz 1950, 157). This negative spiral has catastrophic consequences for regime strategies that pivot on economic performance, as explained in Chapter 4.

This unwanted negative spiral can be avoided if states can communicate effectively their intention to refrain from harming one another. The commitment problem stems from a state's inability to convince its counterpart(s) that it will refrain from opportunistic behavior in the future, when circumstances change. This is a pervasive problem in interstate relations (Fearon 1995, 1998a, 1998b; Powell 2006). For instance, expected adverse power shifts may dispose a declining state to start a preventive war before it becomes even weaker—

because it is suspicious about a rising power's future intentions (Copeland 2000; Layne 2009a; Levy 1987).

There is a large literature on how states may try to overcome the commitment problem standing in the way of their cooperation. For example, Barbara Walter (2002) showed that guarantees by neutral and powerful third parties can help end civil wars. Elkins, Guzman, and Simmons (2006) argued that the spread of bilateral investment treaties have enabled states to compete for capital when prospective host countries committed themselves to protect foreign direct investors by guaranteeing their contractual rights and entitling them to international arbitration. As a third example, states deliberately "tie their hands" by guaranteeing the political independence of their central banks and pegging their currency to fixed exchange rates. They undertake these commitments to alleviate investors' concerns about inflation (e.g., Broz 2002). To offer yet another example, leaders of transitional regimes join international organizations to communicate their commitment to reform policies and their resolve to oppose any backsliding (Mansfield and Pevehouse 2006). By pledging to follow the charters of international organizations, these leaders hope to "lock in" not only themselves but also their successors to pursue democratization and economic liberalization.

Although not usually presented as a credible commitment, the interlocking nature of contemporary liberal democracies' defense industries provides a strong guarantee that they are unlikely to go to war against one another (Brooks 2005). Modern weapons industries involve large multinational corporations that have joint research and development programs, shared asset ownership, cross-licensing, and extensive cross-border coproduction of critical components and subcontracting relations. This interpenetration and integration of defense industries makes it more difficult for the most advanced industrial countries to fight a major war against one another. I will argue in the next chapter that interlocking economic and financial networks in the Asia Pacific have had the effect of committing the relevant countries to cooperation.

Finally, the inability to commit can also have consequences. This happens when governments are divided, and when there are frequent turnovers among officials and constant policy shifts. The consequent inability to make credible commitment causes speculative attacks against a country's currency and produces recurrent exchange-rate crises (e.g., Leblang and Satyanath 2006). The precipitous drop in the value of the euro in May 2010, brought on by Greece's severe financial crisis and investors' skepticism about the fiscal soundness of some other members of the euro zone (e.g., Portugal, Ireland, Spain), reflected general concerns about the European Union's inability to make a credible commitment to stabilize and reverse the serious budgetary imbalance afflicting its member states.

How can states credibly signal their intention not to increase their armament or join exclusive clubs in return for others' commitment to peaceful relations? Robert Axelrod's (1984) classic study on the evolution of cooperation offers the most authoritative and informative analysis germane to this question. His tit-for-tat program has emerged time and again as a superior strategy for playing the game of the prisoner's dilemma (Axelrod 1980a, 1980b). When faced with the risk of opportunistic or exploitative behavior by other players in this game, a tit-for-tat player follows these tenets: it is always optimistic and nice but provokable; its responses are proportionate to others' behavior; and it is always willing to forgive. This means, in practice, that the tit-for-tat strategy requires a player never to initiate the first hostile move to take advantage of another player, to always retaliate when another player behaves opportunistically, to be measured in one's retaliation so that it does not start a chain reaction of recriminations, and to always be willing to let bygones be bygones and take a chance to reinitiate cooperation after an acrimonious interlude. Taking into account the "shadow of the future"—the recognition that states are engaged in continuous and repeated encounters over the long haul—a strategy embodying these tenets is more efficacious than any other in resolving the security dilemma. It should be obvious that this tit-for-tat strategy incorporates elements of both deterrence and reassurance—threats to retaliate against defection and promises to cooperate conditioned upon others' cooperation.

I argue that East Asian countries have by and large followed these tenets, thereby enabling them to avoid balance-of-power dynamics. They have generally tried to communicate credible signals indicating that they will eschew intense armament and exclusive alignment if others reciprocate, that they will refrain from unilateral actions to alter the status quo, and that they will bind themselves to mutual or multilateral projects of interest that present huge opportunity costs should anyone decide to defect. I make these attributions based on inferences from the observed behaviors by Taiwan, North and South Korea, Japan, and China—behaviors that appear in one way or another quite puzzling from standard balance-of-power expectations.

## Commerce Across the Taiwan Strait

Enemies or potential enemies are not supposed to trade with each other because commerce has security externalities, conferring economic benefits to an adversary, and these benefits can contribute to its military capabilities (Gowa

1994; Grieco 1988; Liberman 1996). The security implications are especially severe when commercial relations are highly asymmetric. Moreover, when commerce increases the interests and influence of certain domestic groups, such as those with an internationalist economic outlook, it makes future attempts to balance or deter one's commercial partner more difficult because of potential opposition from these groups (e.g., Lobell 2007; Papayoanou 1999). As suggested by proponents of dependency theory and students of economic statecraft (e.g., Hirschman 1945), the stronger side can exploit its commercial advantage for political gain. Its leverage depends in part on how easily the weaker side can endure or replace the lost trade or investment. Interest groups inside the weaker or more dependent country often lobby their government to refrain from policies that can destabilize the current commercial relationship or limit its future prospects.

Therefore, Taiwan's burgeoning and highly unequal commerce with China is incongruous with balance-of-power logic. After all, it faces an existential threat from Beijing which has not tried to hide its agenda, seeking the island's reunification with China. Yet, over 40% of Taiwan's total exports and 60%–70% of its foreign direct investment have gone to China in recent years. Of its total 23 million in population, 1.5 to 2 million people are long-term residents of China. Why would Taiwan's businesspeople run the obviously high risk of being subject to political holdup? Why would their government allow this commerce to proceed and even expand, given its political ramifications and security externalities? In contrast to the figures just reported for Taiwan, China's investments in Taiwan have thus far been practically nonexistent, and its trade with the island has reached only the low single digits as a percentage of its overall trade.

Remarkably, the greatest expansion of cross-Strait trade and investment occurred during the two recent Taipei administrations that had professed an ostensible pro-independence agenda—those of Lee Teng-hui and, especially, Chen Shui-bian. Why did these politicians not act more decisively to stop, or at least to limit, the speed and scope of Taiwan's trade with and investment in China? With the passage of time, deepening and widening commercial relations would only compound Taiwan's economic, political, and military costs in the future, should there be a rupture in cross-Strait relations, or even war. Balance-of-power realists would expect a true advocate of Taiwan's independence to oppose increasing economic integration with China, a development that would lock the island more tightly in the latter's economic and, possibly in the future, political orbit. Whatever may be the current costs of limiting or stopping cross-Strait commerce, the future costs would surely be much higher if ongoing trends are allowed to continue and should Taipei declare independence one day. This remark in turn raises this question: If Taiwan's politicians and businesspeople are unwilling to tolerate these current costs, why would Beijing believe that they would accept even heavier costs in the event of commercial termination in the future?

An alternative interpretation to the standard balance-of-power logic emphasizes that Taiwan has the greatest comparative advantages in language, culture, geography, history, and economic complementarities to trade with and invest in China. If Taiwan were to eschew commerce with China, it would incur the largest opportunity costs and, by default, concede to its peer competitors, such as Singapore and South Korea, which would surely not forfeit their chance to do business with China. Thus, competitive relations are multilateral rather than bilateral, as are often portrayed in balance-of-power accounts. Taiwan's government and firms were anxious to work out the Economic Cooperation Framework Agreement (ECFA) with China, lest their products lose out to competitors from Southeast Asia when, on January 1, 2010, petroleum products, textiles, automobiles parts, and machinery exports from the ASEAN member countries began to receive tariff-free treatment from China.

In light of my earlier discussion on credible commitment, that Taiwan's government has permitted cross-Strait commerce to reach current levels is highly significant. Its acquiescence, even approval, of this development is tantamount to "hostage giving"—that is, wittingly exposing the island's economic health and stability to the severely destabilizing consequences of political turmoil, should Taiwan declare independence one day. Because both sides can easily anticipate these possible consequences—Taiwan's stock, currency, and real estate prices would crash in that event, insurance for air and shipping freight would skyrocket, and there would be a massive exodus of foreign companies and capital located on the island—Taiwan has in fact made a huge de facto commitment to forego independence. This action speaks louder than partisan rhetoric intended by Chen Shui-bian and his Democratic Progressive Party to mobilize their core constituents. Thus, commerce offers a highly credible medium for signaling one's intentions and preferences, and it enables outside observers to distinguish "cheap talk" intended for domestic consumption from tangible reassurance intended to be taken seriously (S. Chan 2009).

Because cross-Strait commerce took off during the administration of Chen Shui-bian, an ostensible pro-independence president, this timing is highly significant. Chen's action—or rather inaction to stop or limit this commerce—disclosed whether he truly cared more about the island's political independence or its economic performance. When faced with a tough choice, he turned out to be an "economics first" rather than "security first" type (Benson and Niou 2007). His inaction contradicts the neorealist position, which makes worst-case assumptions about the security threats facing states, contending that concerns for military security will and should always trump the pursuit of economic benefits, whether in the short or long term (Brooks 1997). The converse of this observation is also highly relevant. The Taiwan case is particularly germane to the argument advanced in Chapter 4 that East Asian elites have generally turned to a regime strategy emphasizing economic performance rather than security competition. Commerce across the Taiwan Strait demonstrates especially clearly that economic considerations are over-riding security considerations.

Significantly, Taiwan's commercial assets in China are integrated into the market and production chains there and are therefore not easily extricated. Given their relative immobility and asset specificity, and given their huge and asymmetric size, these commercial ties represent a credible commitment to avoid political rupture. This commitment is highly credible because Taiwan's economy would be seriously hurt in that event. At the same time, the very exis-tence of these commercial ties gives leaders on both sides of the Taiwan Strait an alternative to military mobilization, or other saber rattling or war scare tactics, in order to communicate their intentions, preferences, and resolve (verbal state-ments, absent tangible consequences, are likely to be dismissed as cheap talk). As several scholars have pointed out (Gartzke and Li 2003a, 2003b; Gartzke, Li, and Boehmer 2001), these dense commercial ties enable leaders to use financial markets to signal their resolve and disclose the intensity of their preferences. As will be discussed in Chapter 7, they can deliberately provoke a market panic in order to communicate the gravity of a situation. The more serious the market turmoil and thus the more severe the self-imposed costs stemming from this turmoil, the more credible are these leaders' professed intentions.

Cross-Strait relations have thus far not deteriorated to the point of causing a market panic. Although one can never be absolutely sure, such deterioration is unlikely because of the logic of selection. Taiwan's government leaders and businesspeople are not myopic. Had they expected a political rupture or war, they would not have entered into these dense commercial relations in the first place. This observation does not deny the possibility that their expectations may turn out to be wrong; after all, states that had significant, interlocking business interests did go to war in 1914 and 1939. Nevertheless, trade can increase due to reasons such as declining transport costs rather than easing po-litical tensions, such as before World War I. Indeed, the absolute size of trade may be less important than its direction of change and the extent to which it

represents *free* trade—tariffs had actually been rising among the future belligerents in the decades before the two world wars (e.g., McDonald and Sweeney
2007) whereas, in contrast, political, economic, and communication barriers
have actually been falling across the Taiwan Strait.

Moreover, a strictly bilateral view is inadequate for inferring the extent
to which international commerce can affect the probability of conflict or the
prospects of its resolution (Bohmelt 2010). To the extent that the disputants in
a bilateral conflict can easily turn to third parties (e.g., if the United States or
Japan would make up for Taiwan's trade shortfall with China), the opportunity
costs of a confrontation would be reduced and, other things being equal, the
less effective their bilateral trade would be in restraining a conflict in the first
place. Conversely, the greater the prospective adjustment or replacement costs,
the stronger would be the deterrent effect of trade in discouraging conflict
between these partners. To the extent that two economies become closely
integrated—such as due to linked currencies or large sunk investments that
lock one partner to the other's monetary policy, domestic market, or production chains—these self-binding arrangements increase the opportunity costs
of having to find alternative markets or suppliers.

This reasoning introduces a further implication. To the extent that third
parties to a bilateral dispute stand to gain scarcity rents and extra profits arising
from one of the disputant's desire to diversify its economic relations (or offset
trade shortfalls), they have an incentive to see this dispute endure rather than
conclude. What is true for Japan and the United States in the case of Taiwan
should also apply to China and Russia vis-à-vis Iran—that is, the more effective Washington's economic embargo against Tehran, the greater the commercial leverage Beijing and Moscow can gain over the latter and the more profit
they can derive from their business deals with it.

This discussion on cross-Strait commerce also suggests that deterrence
threats need not be explicitly stated; given the context, they can be understood by all concerned. Moreover, as with nuclear deterrence, when a threat is
actually executed, it means that the deterrence policy has failed (e.g., when the
West had to actually impose economic sanctions against Iran or bomb Serbia,
it became clear that the latter countries had been undeterred by its threats to
undertake these actions). Thus, the issuance of public threats and especially
the actual harming of economic hostages are in and of themselves informative
acts, suggesting failed deterrence. In contrast, China's ongoing and expanding
commerce with Taiwan and other countries communicates reassurance. These
relations are premised on an expectation of greater returns (Axelrod's shadow
of the future), and this expectation restrains opportunism and sustains con-

tinued cooperation. In the language of "tit for tat," both sides of the Taiwan Strait have pursued policies that are optimistic, nice, and forgiving after Ma Ying-jeou succeeded Chen Shui-bian as Taiwan's president in 2008.

## Security Politics on the Korean Peninsula

Balance-of-power reasoning can explain why Pyongyang has sustained a persistently high defense burden, maintained a program of nuclear armament despite international pressure, and undertaken missile tests on various occasions. These actions may be construed as internal balancing to compensate for North Korea's increasingly perilous position—its international isolation, domestic decrepitude, and lopsided disadvantage when facing Seoul's economic and military capabilities. It is more challenging to explain why given its increasingly dire circumstances Pyongyang has not been able or willing to pursue more effective external balancing. During its steady and sharp decline, it has moved farther away from rather than closer to Beijing and Moscow, its two historic foreign patrons. Thus, North Korea's alignment behavior is puzzling. Given the power shift in Seoul's favor over time, balance-of-power reasoning would also lead one to expect Beijing and Moscow to align themselves more closely with Pyongyang rather than distancing themselves from it. Finally, considering its advantages over North Korea, Seoul should have less need for an alliance with the United States. Concomitantly, Washington should also see less need to act against a weaker North Korea. The continued presence of U.S. troops in South Korea is puzzling when viewed in contrast with China's withdrawal of its troops from North Korea quite some time ago—even though North Korea is closer to China and should therefore be more important to China's security.

Pyongyang's bellicose rhetoric, saber rattling, and much publicized nuclear and missile tests are attempts to communicate the regime's internal solidarity and its strong resolve, rather than to demonstrate its military might. Although one may be unsure about North Korea's military capabilities, few would be persuaded by Pyongyang's public posturing that it is stronger than Seoul, not to mention Washington. Rather, its behavior indicates its policy priorities and political resolve. Pyongyang's actions communicate that national autonomy and regime survival are at the very top of its priorities, so that it is willing to accept the price of alienating its traditional allies in Beijing and Moscow if closer alignment with them requires compromising these goals. Seen in the light of prospect theory, North Korea's risk-taking behavior reflects a sense of acute vulnerability. By exacerbating its loss aversion, foreign pressure and threats are likely to be ineffective and could even arouse further bellicosity.

Conversely, prospect theory implies that foreign reassurances would be a more effective strategy.

Diplomatic conduct before and during the Six-Party Talks also belied balance-of-power logic, suggesting that South Korea should be alarmed by North Korea's armament and China's rising power. Seoul has instead become more closely aligned with Beijing and Moscow, and has moved farther away from Washington and Tokyo (Rozman 2007). Roh Moo-hyun's government disagreed with the George W. Bush administration's emphasis on hard coercion and pressure, rather than soft persuasion and inducement, to convince Pyongyang to give up its nuclear weapons program. It extended economic assistance and political gestures to Pyongyang in a continuation of the sunshine policy adopted by the previous administration of Kim Dae-jung, and it shared Beijing's and Moscow's concerns that Washington was more interested in regime change than a political compromise exchanging Pyongyang's renunciation of nuclear weapons for Washington's political recognition and security guarantees. It suspected that Washington's policy was really intended to perpetuate South Korea's dependence on the United States, to contain China, and to legitimize Japan's armament (Rozman 2007, 80). Roh even said publicly that it was "understandable" for Pyongyang to develop nuclear weapons given its security environment in a veiled reference to Bush's doctrine of waging preventive war (ibid., 62).

Lee Myung-bak's election as South Korea's new president produced a change in policy emphasis away from reassuring North Korea to confronting it. This switch became even more pronounced after the sinking of the *Cheonan* on March 26, 2010. In response to this alleged attack by North Korea, Lee suspended trade relations and demanded that the United Nations act to sanction Pyongyang. South Korean forces also participated in joint military exercises with the United States to demonstrate readiness. Seoul therefore communicated its "provokability"—even while ruling out direct military retaliation.

What can explain Pyongyang's pursuit of nuclear weapons? Three propositions come to mind. First, a fear of being abandoned by its chief allies may have caused Pyongyang's desperation to develop these weapons as a last resort to ensure its regime survival. There may be an inverse relationship between internal balancing and external balancing, so that international de-alignment encourages more intense armament efforts. The theory of collective action and public goods (Olson and Zeckhauser 1966) would have predicted this much—as junior partners of an alliance become less confident about the bloc leader's ability or willingness to provide for their defense, they become less inclined to free-ride on this leader's military capabilities. In other words, free-riding actually indicates that a junior partner has confidence in the alliance leader's military to provide a public good by protecting, say, not only China's or Russia's homeland but also North Korea's. Given Pyongyang's rudimentary nuclear arsenal, these weapons would hardly change the prevailing military balance. Instead of signaling a capability for assured destruction, their acquisition communicates an intention of assured resistance.

Second, alliance and armament can be substitutable (Most and Siverson 1987). Discussions on balancing policies often treat internal and external balancing efforts as complementary policies. Alliance with a foreign power, however, can serve to dampen internal pressure for and external suspicions about arming oneself. Such reasoning contends that alliance with the United States contributes to restraining South Korea's and Japan's indigenous armament and military autonomy. Conversely, Seoul's and Tokyo's continued alliances with Washington communicate to other countries a message of reassurance—indicating that they will not fully arm themselves for independent military operations. These examples suggest that alliances can have multiple declared and undeclared targets, including both friends and foes. Parenthetically, substitutability also characterizes several East and Central European countries' policies on nuclear weapons. Poland, Hungary, and Czechoslovakia (later the Czech Republic) demanded NATO membership in exchange for their agreement not to develop indigenous nuclear arms, and the Ukraine gave up the nuclear weapons that the Russians had left on its soil in return for security pledges from the United States, Britain, and Russia (Kramer 1999).

Third, the problem of commitment has stalled negotiations to end North Korea's nuclear program. States find it difficult to reach an agreement because they suspect that their counterpart will cheat and defect. They are wary that the other side will renege after having discharged their part of the deal. Washington insisted on sequencing such that North Korea has to dismantle its weapons program before the United States would extend economic assistance and security guarantees. This attempt by Washington to guard against Pyongyang's opportunism is perceived by the latter as "a U.S. ploy to disarm the country before invasion" (Joo 2007, 183). Pyongyang wanted an arrangement whereby these exchanges would be carried out simultaneously. Worse than Washington's failure to deliver on its part of a deal, would Pyongyang's effective nuclear disarmament actually encourage Washington to attack once it could be sure that Pyongyang was denuclearized? Ironically, the U.S. invasion of Iraq has had the effect of encouraging Pyongyang (and Tehran) to develop nuclear weapons in the belief that only a nuclear deterrent could prevent a similar attack (Mueller et al. 2006).

Given their concerns about others' opportunism, states often try to multi-lateralize their negotiations by getting important third parties involved in the process so that they might help enforce compliance. The third parties may very well have their own reasons for wanting to see a settlement and to guard against defection by the other participants. Thus, negotiations about Pyong-yang's nuclear weapons have been conducted as Six-Party Talks in Beijing, consisting of North and South Korea, Japan, Russia, China, and the United States. In an interesting twist, Pyongyang wanted to have bilateral talks with Washington in order to avoid becoming the target of multilateral pressure from the other significant states.

In addition to Taiwan, South Korea offers an example *par excellence* of a country which has switched its regime legitimacy from one that focused on external threat to one that pivots on economic performance. Even in its rela-tions with its supposed nemesis, North Korea, there has been an enormous amount of change such that "the current belief in South Korea [is] that mili-tary issues are secondary to economic issues," and that "[t]hough strategic mo-tivations are important, economic motivations for engagement [with North Korea] have become more crucial, especially since the 2000 summit [between Kin Jong-il and Kim Dae-jung]" (Kang 2007a, 54–55). With respect to poli-cies toward North Korea, Seoul's attitudes have generally been more similar to Beijing's and Moscow's than to Washington's ( Joo 2007; Kang 2007a; Yoon 2007). Like the Chinese, South Koreans were worried that the Bush admin-istration was intent on bringing about a "hard crash" in North Korea. This development would have presented huge political and economic problems for both Seoul and Beijing, including the prospect of a massive flow of refugees from North Korea and possibly a last-ditch effort by Pyongyang to save itself through military brinksmanship. From the perspectives of Seoul, Beijing, and Moscow, the latter's nuclear and missile tests were not unrelated to the Bush administration's not-so-subtle agenda for regime change in Pyongyang, its as-sertion of a unilateral right to wage preventive war, and the precedent set by its invasion of Iraq (e.g., G. Bush 2002; Levy 1987, 2008b; Mueller et al. 2006; Silverstone 2007). They were all opposed to military action against Pyongyang.

That South Korea has maintained its alliance with the United States also demands explanation. Over time, Seoul has gained an enormous advantage in its rivalry with Pyongyang. By the mid 1990s, South Korea's economy was twenty-seven times, perhaps even forty times, larger than North Korea's, and its military spending was seven times higher (Kang 2003a, 357; Suh 2004, 137). When this much disparity is involved, it simply distorts the common language to invoke balance of power (as opposed to possibly balance of threat) as a justification for U.S. policies to support South Korea against North Korea. This linguistic device distracts attention from pursuing the puzzle, from a balance-of-power perspective, of Seoul's continued alliance with the United States. Why would Seoul want to retain its alliance with the United States after it had acquired more than enough capabilities to go it alone? After all, an alliance implies a loss of national autonomy, reduced policy discretion, and even domestic unpopularity due to the presence of foreign bases and military personnel on one's soil. If a military disadvantage should encourage a state to seek foreign partners, then a reversal indicating the acquisition of a lopsided advantage should have the opposite effect. The persistence of the U.S.–South Korea security treaty is therefore puzzling from the realist view (Suh 2004). Various reasons may be invoked to explain this persistence, such as embedded domestic interest groups, institutional "stickiness," and a convergent value outlook. These reasons, however, originate from liberalism rather than realism.

Given this discussion's emphasis on interstate signaling of intentions and preferences, what would a reversal of the status quo—meaning the termination of the U.S.–South Korea security treaty—communicate to the other states? It would mean that South Korea would henceforth be an independent operator "playing the field." The substitution effect between armament and alliance, noted earlier, would be reversed. Indeed, the abrogation of this treaty would mean that Seoul would be free to develop an autonomous military. This development could in turn unleash the very balance-of-power dynamic that the alliance has ironically helped to restrain. It could thus threaten to undermine the heretofore emphatic focus on economic performance adopted by almost all countries in the region. These remarks about South Korea are even more pertinent to Japan, a discussion to be taken up in the next section. As noted already, economic interdependence is increasingly overtaking this "tethering" effect in being allied with the United States as a contributor to regional peace.

The U.S.–South Korea treaty is not germane to reasons of balance of power with North Korea as its target—South Korea already has a commanding economic and military lead over North Korea. Rather, the treaty serves as a signal to reassure other states that Seoul has no intention of going down a path of autonomous militarization. Whereas the persistence of the U.S.–South Korea security treaty points to business as usual, its cancellation would introduce huge uncertainties about the future intentions of all the pertinent states. This treaty is important not so much because the current power balance on the Korean peninsula depends on it—rather, it discloses Seoul's future intentions not just or even primarily with respect to Pyongyang but also with respect to Beijing, Tokyo, Moscow, and Washington.

One further puzzle from a "straight-up" balance-of-power perspective deserves recognition. It pertains to Seoul's allocation of resources to develop its military assets. If North Korea or, for that matter, China were its primary security concern, one would surmise that South Korea's ground forces would receive most of this investment. Yet, Seoul has been investing in force-projection capabilities, such as building a blue-water navy and developing its satellite technologies (Cha 1999, 213; Kang 2009, 11). These capabilities prepare Seoul for a variety of possible conflicts, including those involving Tokyo over their territorial dispute. This remark reiterates the caveat mentioned in Chapter 3, cautioning against jumping to the conclusion that a country's armament spending or its alignment behavior is necessarily aimed at a particular adversary, such as China or North Korea.

In view of Axelrod's tit-for-tat strategy previously discussed, North Korea's policy stance is pessimistic and provokable. Pyongyang is acutely sensitive to the commitment problem, and is deeply suspicious about the enforceability of any disarmament deal. It has charged that the previous agreement framework has failed because an exchange of foreign assistance and fuel for North Korea's deactivation of its nuclear reactors has not been followed through by the West. Pyongyang has demonstrated that it is easily provoked to retaliate against such a perceived defection. Naturally, the United States and its allies have made opposite allegations, and have been no less skeptical about Pyongyang's motivations and reliability.

In contrast to Pyongyang, Seoul's strategy has by and large been nice, in the sense that it has refrained from any opportunistic actions that could contribute to initiating new rounds of military escalation. During the period of Kim Dae-jung's sunshine policy, it was even optimistic and forgiving in undertaking conciliatory initiatives in the hope of initiating reciprocal cooperation. Seoul's economic assistance to Pyongyang and its political overtures were reassuring in that they communicated a general disposition not to "pile on"—that is, not to exploit Pyongyang's dire circumstances for relative gain.

## Japan's Nuclear "Allergy," Its Self-Imposed Defense Cap, and the Missing Korean Link

U.S. Secretary of State John Foster Dulles remarked in 1952, "suicide was not an illogical step for anyone concerned about Japan's economic future" (quoted in Nitta 2002, 74). In response to his country's dire conditions, Japan's postwar Prime Minister Shigeru Yoshida adopted a policy that exemplified the pursuit of regime survival—indeed national survival—pivoting on economic performance. The Yoshida Doctrine emphasized Japan's economic recovery as the country's most important goal, and accepted its subordination to the United States in security and political matters as a necessary condition for achieving this goal.

A disavowal of a heavy defense burden and an abstention from foreign security entanglement are corollary pillars of this doctrine (Pyle 1996). Tokyo has resisted persistent U.S. pressure, starting with John Foster Dulles's attempts in 1950 following the outbreak of the Korean War, to boost its armament and military profile in the name of burden sharing (Nitta 2002). It has kept its military expenditures at about 1% of its gross domestic product since Eisaku Sato's administration in the 1960s. This low defense burden has been maintained even though there have been substantial changes in Japan's security environment in the years since then. Although Tokyo has undertaken some quasi-military activities abroad, such as those in Cambodia, Iraq, and Afghanistan, these activities have been largely confined to U.N. peacekeeping missions or limited logistical support for U.S. operations. Article 9 of Japan's constitution, renouncing war as a legitimate means for settling international disputes and eschewing the development of the country's war potential, has provided the legal basis for limiting armament and foreign military involvement. Japanese public opinion continues to reflect a strong strain of antimilitarism (Berger 1993, 1998, 2003). The most prominent feature of Japan's strategic policy has been its disavowal of nuclear weapons, in addition to its voluntary capping of its defense burden and the continuation of its defense treaty with the United States.

Few would argue that Japan's failure to develop nuclear weapons reflects its technological or economic inability. This non-occurrence offers, instead, a powerful signal about Tokyo's intentions and preferences. Its decision to eschew nuclear weapons may be reversed in the future, but it has already persisted for some time and is unlikely to change under current circumstances. A country in Japan's situation could gain bargaining leverage by not pursuing nuclear weapons; if it acquired these weapons, this development could set in motion balance-of-power dynamics that could work to its own and its neighbors' collective detriment. This line of reasoning is alien to balance-of-power realists, who cannot imagine that a country such as Japan would, on its own, decide not to become a "normal" country. After all, "The default position of states, especially when it comes to military matters, is not dependence, but autonomy and independence, if they can achieve it" (Art 2005/06, 185).

Tokyo's alliance with the United States has been presented or viewed by some Japanese and Americans as an alternative to Japan going after its own nuclear weapons (Samuels 2007), with the converse that "A Japan bereft of the United States is ultimately a Japan with nuclear weapons" (Art 2008, 279). The American suggestion that a Japan tethered to the United States is preferable to one that is detached from it should not have come as a surprise to Chinese ears or those of other East Asians. Such a suggestion, of course, implies that the U.S.-Japanese alliance is not exclusively aimed at balancing against China; it has also been intended to restrain Japanese rearmament. Given the fact that this treaty was signed long before China's recent power gains—indeed, at a time when China did not have nuclear weapons and did not have any means of threatening Japan militarily—the possibility that Washington's restraining motivation has always overshadowed its balancing motivation would not have escaped Chinese and Japanese attention. Kenneth Pyle (2010, 5) has described this motivation forthrightly: "The [San Francisco] peace treaty [signed in 1951] nominally returned Japanese sovereignty, but the bilateral security pact compromised it. John Foster Dulles, who negotiated the treaty, privately told British officials that the arrangements 'amounted to a voluntary continuation of the Occupation.'" He remarked that to describe such arrangements "as an alliance is a stretch so far as the way alliances are most often understood . . . Historically, alliances sometimes are motivated less by a desire to influence the balance of power than by an intention to manage and control the weaker country" (ibid.).

The continued presence of U.S. troops and military bases in Japan has become more unpopular over time (Johnson 2000), with Yukio Hatoyama's administration promising to relocate or reduce this presence, especially in Okinawa. Hatoyama subsequently reversed his campaign pledge to relocate U.S. bases outside of Okinawa, choosing instead to abide by an earlier agreement with the United States to relocate within the island itself, despite intense domestic opposition (this decision caused a further drop in his already low popularity, and contributed to his decision to resign as prime minister after having served in that capacity for less than one year). Prior to his resignation announcement, his administration had reportedly initiated a review of the past practice of U.S. vessels carrying nuclear weapons while visiting Japan, thus violating Japanese laws banning such weapons. It is therefore far from clear that Tokyo has been aligning more closely with Washington in response to China's recent rise. Parenthetically, a 1984 controversy over the visiting rights of U.S. vessels with nuclear weapons on board roiled U.S. relations with New Zealand and stymied these countries' bilateral part in the ANZUS alliance (the Australia, New Zealand, and United States Security Treaty).

Due to divergent identities and racial prejudices, the United States built very different alliance structures in Europe and Asia after World War II (Hemmer and Katzenstein 2002). The Southeast Asian Treaty Organization (SEATO) was hardly multilateral in the same sense as the North Atlantic Treaty Organization (NATO). The former's membership consisted of more European or European-populated states than indigenous Asian states (most notably, Thailand and the Philippines). Washington eschewed multilateralism in East Asia, preferring instead a hub-and-spokes design, managing security affairs bilaterally with each of its Asian partners. Equally significant, Taiwan, South Korea, and Japan were not invited to join SEATO. Even more strikingly, even though these three have been formal allies or, in the case of Taiwan after the United States abrogated their mutual defense treaty, Washington's tacit protégé for many years, they are not tied together among themselves by bilateral or multilateral security agreements. This absence of formal security arrangements among these U.S. allies is enigmatic from a balance-of-power perspective.

To a large extent, this phenomenon has been due to U.S. incentives. In the 1950s, Washington had multiple goals that called for not only containing China but also controlling its East Asian allies. In contrast to the European situation, U.S. allies in East Asia were less militarily crucial to Washington's containment effort and, should containment fail, less consequential to contributing to the actual fighting. Therefore, the latter countries' collective contribution to military deterrence and engagement in war would be less important than that from Washington's European allies, whereas the coordination and autonomy costs to the United States for sponsoring and underwriting a multilateral alliance would have been more substantial. Washington would lose discretionary power in an East Asian multilateral security organization without enough benefits to compensate for the loss (Cha 2007). This discretion would be undermined in multilateral settings, where the smaller allies may use their numerical advantage to offset predominant U.S. power. Conversely, Washington would enjoy much stronger bargaining leverage in a one-on-one setting, and could forge a series of bilateral deals that would be less constraining on it.

Even more important, whereas Britain, France, and the other NATO countries were interested in maintaining the military and political status quo in post-1945 Europe, the same cannot be said about Chiang Kai-shek and Syngman Rhee, who had threatened repeatedly to launch military campaigns against their communist foes with the aim of reunifying China and Korea under their respective control. These junior partners therefore threatened to embroil the United States in an unwanted war against the Chinese and perhaps

Soviet communists. Alliances enable power aggregation with partners but also help the leading partner to control and restrain its allies. For Washington, the former rationale was more important in Europe and the latter more so in Asia. Bilateralism in the latter region maximized U.S. discretion and control, and minimized its risk of entrapment by its allies (Cha 2007; G. Snyder 1997).

In conjunction with its security commitment to Taipei, Washington demanded that the latter's use of force should be subject to "joint agreement" and sought assurances that equipment provided by the United States would not be used against China without Washington's "prior consent" (Cha 2007, 112–113). As for South Korea, Article 3 of the U.S.-ROK Mutual Defense Treaty addressed the contingency of "an armed attack in the Pacific area on either of the parties in territories now under their respective administrative control, or hereafter recognized by one of the parties as lawfully brought under the administrative control of the other." This formulation "implies that the United States has no treaty obligation to help South Korea if the South should attack the North" (Murata 2007, 142).

Because Taiwan, South Korea, and the Southeast Asian countries were much weaker than Japan, multilateralism would not have worked effectively in East Asia as it did in Western Europe, where fears of German rearmament were managed by embedding and enmeshing Bonn in a wide range of multilateral economic, political, and military institutions. Bilateralism turned out to be Washington's preferred way to control its East Asian allies in order to avoid being dragged involuntarily into armed conflicts started by them (Cha 2007). Seen in this light, alliances are not employed for the sole purpose of balancing against an ostensible adversary. They have the double purpose of restraining one's allies from unwanted rearmament and curbing their bellicosity. This latter purpose has been described by Paul Schroeder (1976) as a *pactum de contrahendo*, or a pact of restraint.

This dual characteristic cautions us, yet again, against jumping to the conclusion that an alliance or alignment is necessarily or only aimed at a particular country, such as China. Lord Hastings Ismay, the first secretary general of NATO, has often been quoted as saying that this alliance was intended to keep "the Americans in, the Russians out, and the Germans down" (quoted in Mastanduno 2007, 33). In an earlier era, the Quadruple Alliance (1814) and the subsequent Congress of Vienna (1815) were as much intended to thwart France's bid for hegemony as to check the ambitions of the coalition's partners (Ikenberry 2001, 101). Similarly, the two Leagues of the Three Emperors, the Triple Alliance, and the Triple Entente served a "tethering" purpose, at least for some of their members. Sometimes such agreements are intended to restrain the signatories *against each other*—posing a greater threat to each other than to third parties, this perceived threat could possibly be the motivation for them to enter into an agreement in the first place (Weitsman 2004). Pacts reached by the Soviet Union with Germany and Japan before World War II offer the most obvious examples.

Although subtler than U.S. relations with Taipei and Seoul, Washington's security commitment to Tokyo has also been motivated by a strategy to "to create deep and robust ties and thereby create a Japanese reliance on the [U.S.-Japanese] alliance to channel growth and development in a controlled direction beneficial to U.S. interests" (Cha 2007, 116). Victor Cha described this strategy as a "grand soft binding rationale," quoting U.S. Secretary of State John Foster Dulles saying: "the thing that is designed to be inhibited is not [Japan's] participation in collective security, but [its] recreation of a distinctive national force." In Dulles's words, "We have got to use delicate methods, a light tackle. We are absolutely confident that if Japan is basically committed to the free world and accepts U.S. troops in and about its territories we will have complete control over any rearmament plans Japan may adopt" (quoted in Cha 2007, 117).

This U.S. strategy has left a strong legacy such that "When examining the Japanese tradition of the use of institutions in international relations, bilateralism stands out" (Inoguchi 2007, 51). Noting that security matters have never been on Japan's agenda in a multilateral forum, Takashi Inoguchi (2007) described Tokyo's policy orientation as "bilateralism *über alles*." Japan's bilateral relationship with the United States has been the basic pillar of its security and foreign policies. The defense treaty with the United States offers protection to Japan while at the same time it reassures its neighbors who worry about a possible renewed Japanese militarism (Kawasaki 2007). Another legacy of this special relationship has been that, unlike Germany—which has become much more deeply and broadly embedded in European multilateral institutions—Tokyo has been spared the incentive to more vigorously seek reconciliation with those neighbors that it had invaded and conquered during or prior to World War II (Cha 2007, 122).

Despite Washington's evident preference for bilateralism in East Asia, Tokyo's concerns about entanglement and even entrapment are relevant. Glenn Snyder (1991, 105) defined alignment as "a set of mutual *expectations* between two or more states that they will have each other's support in disputes or wars with particular other states" (emphasis in the original). Tokyo has hedged on the extent to which it will allow U.S. military bases in Japan to be used in a possible conflict on the Korean peninsula or across the Taiwan Strait. It is clearly concerned about the danger of being dragged into a war that it would rather avoid (Cha 1999; Green 2002).

The so-called Korea clause in statements issued by Japan's leaders and the possibility of waiving prior consultation for the United States to use military facilities on Okinawa have been constant sources of creative ambiguity. The former refers to whether South Korea's security is "essential" to Japan's own security, and the latter touches on whether Tokyo would tacitly allow unhampered U.S. use of Japanese territory for military operations in contingencies such as those involving the Korean peninsula and the Taiwan Strait. The 1978 U.S.-Japan Defense Cooperation Guidelines went through revisions in 1997, with its core provision stating that "the two Governments will take appropriate measures . . . in response to situations in areas surrounding Japan" (Murata 2007, 140)—an elastic clause designed to satisfy Washington's desire for greater contribution by Japan and Tokyo's wish to avoid an outright commitment to assist the United States in an unwanted war.

Subsequent Japanese statements have been contradictory about whether Taiwan would be included in the "areas surrounding Japan," contributing to a deliberate confusion by suggesting that this idea is situational rather than geographic (Green 2001, 90–92). Tokyo "refused to stipulate the contingencies under which it would provide rear area support for U.S. force" (Heginbotham and Samuels 1999, 194), while professing support for the U.S. objective to "encourage the peaceful resolution of issues concerning the Taiwan Strait through dialogue" (Wan 2007, 160). Japanese officials have resorted to such evasive language in order to hedge their country's policy, and have not joined in any formal defense arrangement with Taiwan or South Korea.

The legacies of colonialism and war continue to affect Japan's relations with its other neighbors, especially South Korea and China (e.g., Cha 1999; Christensen 1999; Whiting 1989). They have contributed to the missing formal security link between Tokyo and Seoul. Taiwan's continual limbo status subjects Tokyo to cross-pressure but also gives it a bargaining chip in its relations with Beijing and Washington. It presents a "potential thorn" to China that is not unappealing to Japan (Pempel 2007, 127). Parenthetically, strategic hedging, policy ambiguity, and even public coyness are not unique to the Japanese. When initially approached about U.S. support in a hypothetical Chinese-Japanese confrontation over the Diaoyutai/Senkaku islands, the U.S. State Department "responded that the U.S.-Japan treaty did *not* apply in this case" (emphasis in the original)—only to reverse its position subsequently (Green 2001, 87).

As just noted, concerns about entrapment are not limited to the stronger partner in an alliance. Former South Korean President Roh Moo-hyun stated publicly on March 25, 2005, that "we will not be embroiled in any conflict in Northeast Asia against our will. This is an absolutely firm principle we cannot yield under any circumstance" (quoted in S. Snyder 2007, 249). This explicitness went beyond Tokyo's deliberately vague statements. Elite as well as public opinion in South Korea has shifted in favor of China (e.g., Kang 2009; Shin 2007). Therefore, compared to Tokyo, it seems even more doubtful that Seoul would offer military support to the United States in a possible Sino-American confrontation over Taiwan.

There is a debate about whether democracies are more reliable allies than non-democracies (Gartzke and Gleditsch 2004; Gaubatz 1996), but the very fact that Japan does not have a defense treaty with South Korea and Taiwan, and that the United States has itself abrogated its defense treaty with Taiwan, speaks volumes. Like Tokyo, Washington has pursued a strategy of deliberate ambiguity in dealing with the Taiwan issue (R. Bush 2005; Tucker 2005). One encounters in this case an absence of credible commitment to deter a potential adversary and, if deterrence should fail, to fight. This posture of deliberate ambiguity is telling because balance-of-power realists would have expected the United States and its ally, Japan, to say "we will definitely fight you" instead of "we *may* fight you" if China invades Taiwan (Fearon 1997). Taiwan's reunification with China would increase the latter's accumulation of power considerably. Beijing knows how a truly resolved state would act—it would commit itself to fight in the event of a Chinese invasion in a highly public manner, and it would state its intention to intervene repeatedly in order to deliberately engage its reputation. It would also make credible commitment in the form of investing tangible resources, such as stationing troops in and creating a joint military command with the country that it is seeking to protect by extended deterrence (Huth 1988). If Japan—or for that matter, the United States itself—were engaged in checking China, one would expect a much more vigorous policy from both Tokyo and Washington in support of Taiwan's independence. Washington has instead tried to reassure Beijing that it opposes Taiwan's independence.

## China's Ownership of U.S. Debts

Since the late 1970s, China's grand strategy has been to focus on economic performance, following Deng Xiaoping's injunction that "except in the situation of an all-out war, China should always firmly adhere to this central task" (quoted in Horowitz and Ye 2007, 36). In its foreign relations, Deng enjoined that China should always "observe calmly; secure our position; cope with affairs calmly; hide our capacities and bide our time; be good at manipulating a low profile; never claim leadership" (*Ching Pao*, November 5, 1991, 84–86). With this policy outlook, Beijing joined the other East Asian countries which had earlier pivoted their regime survival and leadership legitimacy on economic performance. This strategy requires a stable international environment and avoidance of actions that would put China in "America's strategic headlights" (Pollack 2005). Displaying self-restraint in not raising military expenditures as much as it could have given its increasing economic capacity is one way for Beijing to reassure Washington. The purchase of massive amounts of U.S. debt offers another. Although there has been considerable American concern about China trying to use its ownership of U.S. debt to influence Washington, preliminary analysis shows that even in the midst of the severe financial crisis of 2008–2009, there were limits to attempting such influence (Drezner 2009).

With foreign exchange reserves estimated at about $3 trillion in mid 2011, China has accumulated the world's largest reserve account to finance a variety of plausible programs. That it has so far not used this money for military expansion to the extent that it could have is highly significant. The question is not so much whether China's defense spending has risen or whether Beijing has modernized its armed forces in recent years. It has. Rather, the question is whether it could have ratcheted up its armament even more than it has. It could have, but it has not. This non-occurrence is significant. China, Japan, and other East Asian countries have kept their defense burdens at relatively low levels because they lack the interest in ramping up armament, not because they lack the capability to finance it. Their self-restraint reflects their judgments about their security environment, about the relative importance of economic performance for their domestic agenda, and about the danger of triggering armament races and competing alliances that would worsen rather than improve their lot.

Instead of deploying its considerable funds to finance weapons purchases and military expansion, Beijing has chosen to invest an estimated 60%–75% of its foreign reserves in dollar assets (Bergsten et al. 2008, 18). By early 2011, China has bought over $1.154 trillion in U.S. government debt. Why would Beijing want to extend this massive loan to finance America's spending deficit? Does not this loan subsidize, at least in part, Washington's defense programs, which, in the eyes of some balance-of-power realists, ought to focus on China as their intended target? Invoking the explanation that Beijing is interested in keeping the value of the renminbi low, thereby keeping its exports competitive, would be implausible from the dominant balance-of-power perspective. After all, for most realists, security considerations are supposed to trump commercial interests.

There is, of course, a flip side to this question. Why would Americans submit themselves to the risk of being held up politically, given their heavy indebtedness? After all, currency and credit vulnerabilities can be used by other states to coerce political concessions. Washington itself practiced this coercion against its ally, Britain, during the Suez Canal Crisis of 1956. Massive sales of the pound in New York weakened the British currency, depleting London's already precarious foreign reserves. Moreover, the United States blocked Britain's access to funds from the International Monetary Fund and refused to guarantee export–import loans unless Britain agreed to withdraw its troops from Egypt. This economic coercion succeeded in forcing Britain to end its conflict with Egypt on U.S. terms (Kirshner 1995; Kunz 1991). With that said, it is also important to recognize that Washington combined its coercive policy with promises of monetary assistance if London complied. Moreover, U.S. demands in this case were specific rather than "transcendental" (meaning that they addressed clear, observable, and finite policy changes rather than more general and fundamental challenges to a regime's core agenda). It is also easier for a longtime ally such as Britain to yield to U.S. pressure. In contrast, when facing an adversary, any other country would worry that its reputational loss would invite further coercive attempts (Drezner 1999).

Some Americans worry that Beijing may "dump" the dollars it owns, thereby raising U.S. interest rates and causing a sharp contraction of the American economy. This worry reflects a concern that China will use its dollar holdings to extract political concessions from the United States. It is difficult, however, for Beijing to "dump" dollars without causing severe repercussions for itself. This action—even mere rumors that it is being considered—would drive up the price of other currencies such as the euro, the yen, and the renminbi itself. The consequent appreciation of these currencies would impair other countries' (including China's) trade competitiveness and produce severe dislocation for their economies. Moreover, a massive sale of China's dollar holdings would reduce their value, thus forcing Beijing to take a huge "haircut." As Bergsten and colleagues (2008, 19) remarked, "the only plausible circumstance under which China might 'dump' its dollars is if it thought the United States might be about to freeze those holdings itself, as it did with Iran's dollar assets in 1979 after the revolution in that country and its takeover of the US embassy."

This observation suggests that a "dumping" of U.S. dollars by Beijing is likely to be a *response* to bilateral relations after having already deteriorated to a very serious point. This chapter, however, emphasizes the question of why Beijing would want to *initiate* its extension of huge loans to the United States. Surely, Chinese leaders are not unaware of the risk that their assets could be frozen or repudiated. Moreover, they are not oblivious to the fact that their dollar assets have suffered large losses recently. Prior to 2008, the value of the U.S. dollar had declined 25%–30% relative to other major currencies, and considerably more so compared to "real" assets, such as oil and many other commodities (Bergsten et al. 2008, 18). According to Gregory Chin and Eric Helleiner (2008, 92), a 10% drop in the value of the dollar translates to about a 3% reduction in China's gross domestic product. Thus, why would Beijing wittingly submit itself to such political and economic vulnerability? If Chinese leaders were truly the "security first" type, obsessed with accumulating military capabilities in a zero-sum competition with the United States, they would not have acted in this manner.

Rather, Beijing's purchase and holding of vast amounts of U.S. dollars signify nonverbal assurance of and commitment to stable Sino-American relations. It is a form of binding—not balancing—behavior whereby the economic and political costs of a rupture would be enormous for both sides. Just as the United States would not want to become financially dependent on a potentially hostile power, China would not want to loan money on such a large scale to a similar power. The behavior of both sides becomes understandable if it is seen as a bilateral investment in good future relations. Their respective sale and purchase of dollar assets is both an indicator of current expectations of these future relations and a harbinger and determinant of these future relations. After all, people are strategic. They formulate their policies in anticipation of others' likely reactions to their policies.

The logic of selection argues that they would not enter into particular relations were it not for their judgment that these encounters would be rewarding for them (Danilovic 2001; Fearon 2000; Gartner and Siverson 1996; A. Smith 1996). This remark does not mean that people's judgments are infallible or that states with a large stake in ongoing commercial interests have not gone to war. People are fallible, and economically interdependent states have engaged in conflict. The point, however, is that such conflict occurred *despite* rather than because of their earlier intentions, and it happened contrary to their best though still fallible judgments. It should also be noted that people's actions can influence their future relations. Statistical evidence supports strongly the general proposition that states with a large volume of bilateral trade are likely to avoid war (e.g., Oneal and Russett 1997).

States' future relations are subject to strategic choice (including effective re-assurance), and are not structurally determined. By deliberately exposing itself to the possibility of severe repercussions, a state makes a credible commitment to cooperate. This commitment is credible precisely because the repercussions of upsetting the ongoing relationship would be so costly. Policies that are nice, optimistic, and forgiving—as in Axelrod's tit-for-tat model—as well as those that entail great potential self-imposed costs, contribute to building confidence. They mitigate suspicions about opportunistic behavior that can impair mutually beneficial cooperation from being launched in the first place, and they help to consolidate and expand ties that promise greater mutual benefits in the future.

Sovereign debts involve mixed-motive games with a strong cooperative component. The creditor country naturally wants to charge a high interest rate—but only if it is consistent with its basic objectives of protecting its investment and advancing stable relations. The debtor country would obvi-ously want to reduce and even eliminate its debt burden, but it is cognizant that self-serving actions, such as loan default and currency devaluation, would hurt its long-term reputation, which, in turn, would hurt its future borrowing prospects. Thus, Axelrod's "shadow of the future" encourages mutual parti-san adjustment and the avoidance of myopic behavior. The promotion and enforcement of credible commitment need not rely on "gunboat diplomacy" or other coercive measures because the parties are aware of their shared stake in preserving long-term relations (Tomz 2007). This phenomenon is highly significant and provides an example of the type of self-enforcing agreements that will be discussed in Chapter 7. Prospective returns from future coopera-tion provide a surety against defection, such as debt repudiation or political manipulation.

Wars have happened between countries with large loan exposures, such as between Britain and Russia in the Crimean War, and Germany and Russia in World War I. My discussion only suggests that both sides have a mutual vested interest, albeit one that may be overridden by other more important objectives, in maintaining their ongoing relationship. Moreover, the creditor country has a vested interest in the debtor country having peaceful foreign relations. The reason is not difficult to understand: costly wars and excessive defense spending would undermine the debtor country's ability to repay its loans. They would also cause the creditor country's loan holdings to depreciate as a result of inflationary pressures or market uncertainties due to international tension involving the debtor country. Similarly, the debtor country has an interest in seeing its creditors continue to offer cheap and abundant sources of loans; this money would otherwise become less available or more expensive should it be diverted to these countries' military projects as international tensions rise.

Reputation in one arena can affect reputation in another. Reliability in international finance can boost the credibility of a country's military deterrence and its promise to comply with treaties to protect the environment. Moreover, the reputational stake is not limited to bilateral relations. Others involved in the credit market can observe the pertinent states' behavior and draw conclusions about their trustworthiness, which in turn affects their long-term ability to make loans or borrow money. During the American Civil War, the Confederacy encountered great difficulties in issuing bonds in Europe because Mississippi, Arkansas, and Florida had previously repudiated their debts (Sexton 2005). Similarly, those countries that had defaulted on their loans in the 1930s subsequently had a much tougher time trying to borrow when investors became highly risk-averse (Tomz 2007).

As just noted, a country's credibility has security implications beyond the financial markets. Its ability to borrow from foreign sources can contribute to its ability to win wars or outcompete the opposition in protracted rivalries such as the Cold War and earlier contests that pitted the Netherlands and Britain against Spain and France, respectively. Stronger institutions for debt financing and greater creditworthiness enabled the former countries to offset their physical disadvantage in prevailing over their larger opponents (Rasler and Thompson 1983).

More generally, democracies have a financing edge in international competition (Schultz and Weingast 2003). They are better able to make a credible commitment to repay their debts, and this credible commitment in turn facilitates their access to foreign loans and contributes to their victories in protracted contests. The advantage that democracies enjoy enables them to tap into a much larger resource pool than their domestic tax base, and to stretch their funding of consumption over a long period without having to impose a severe tax burden on their economy (this latter situation is known as "tax smoothing," and is akin to mortgage loans helping individuals to buy houses). Thus, for instance, whereas imperial Germany had to resort primarily to domestic funds to finance its war efforts in 1914, imperial Britain could borrow from abroad. Similarly, the Netherlands, Britain, and the United States enjoyed an advantage over their illiberal rivals, Spain, France, and the Soviet Union, respectively, in their competition for international funding. "This is not to suggest that government deficits are good for economic health" (ibid., 9), only that when states decide to compete internationally, those with greater access to public finance have an advantage. A stronger ability to borrow foreign capital enables them to mitigate the guns-versus-butter tradeoff, though not to avoid its consequences forever.

As already mentioned, a state's domestic institutions are relevant to its credibility. Democratic leaders are more subject to punishment by their constituents, who have a long-term interest in sustaining economic growth, limiting taxes, and lowering the costs of borrowing. The more leaders are influenced by these political constraints, the less incentive they have to default and the more credible is their commitment to repay their loans, which in turn means they can borrow money more easily and at lower interest rates. This form of credible commitment is inherent in the nature of a political system, giving democracies an advantage over autocracies. Democratic leaders are perceived to be more prudent in their domestic and foreign policies because their larger "selectorate" is in a more powerful position to punish them at the polls for failed policies (e.g., Bueno de Mesquita et al. 1999, 2003). They are also restrained from arbitrary action by the institution of checks and balances.

The United States offers a paradigmatic case. Congress has the constitutional power to authorize government borrowing. This legal provision denies the executive branch unilateral discretion in managing public debts (including a possible decision to repudiate these debts, which would require congressional approval). Moreover, because many groups have direct or indirect interests in U.S. treasury bills (e.g., the people whose retirement pensions and savings accounts have invested in these instruments), a representative institution such as the U.S. Congress is very unlikely to cancel debts or alter their terms retrospectively. Consequently, compared to autocracies, which lack political checks and representative bodies, creditors do not demand nearly as much of a risk premium when making loans to a democracy like the United States. With that said, democracies sometimes act arbitrarily and selfishly. The Federal Reserve's announcement in November 2010 to introduce $600 billion of "quantitative easing" caused the dollar to fall against other currencies, including the yuan (thus devaluing China's dollar assets), and was criticized by other countries as an obvious abuse of power and retreat from credible commitment.

Do foreign creditors enjoy the same protection as domestic bond holders? Washington can freeze a foreign government's assets held in the United States or in accounts it has opened with U.S. financial institutions. Nevertheless, although both foreigners and U.S. citizens purchase U.S. government bonds, domestic creditors typically represent a majority interest in any given series of these bonds. The mixture of foreign and domestic bond holders in each series of bonds makes it difficult to discriminate against the former without also hurting the latter (Schultz and Weingast 2003, 30). This difficulty presents a credible commitment not to engage in opportunistic behavior. This credibility is reinforced by the fact that government bonds are traded constantly on secondary markets worldwide, thus truly diversifying their ownership. The government cannot initiate policies, or can only do so with great difficulty, to hurt foreign bond holders (including allies) without also hurting a far larger number of domestic bond holders. The shadow of the future restrains impulses to repudiate debts because this action would make future borrowing more difficult and expensive. At the same time, a creditor country's decision to extend loans reflects its judgment about the borrower's creditworthiness and trustworthiness. This decision is also a credible commitment to maintain cordial relations in the future. It would not want to fund a potential adversary's financial needs. Thus, credible commitment is operating on both sides when states make and accept large sums of sovereign loans. Naturally, as implied by my earlier reference to U.S. "quantitative easing," such credible commitment requires continuous confirmation.

In his recent book, Zachary Karabell (2009) used "Chimerica" to describe the "superfusion" between the U.S. and Chinese economies. The massive U.S. economic stimulus program in 2008–2009 relied on borrowing from the Chinese, who have acquired their large foreign reserves by exporting to overseas markets, including the American market. This phenomenon is not new; during the 1970s and 1980s, Japan's large trade surplus and savings helped to fund chronic U.S. deficits. Karabell's terms may appear exaggerated, but these descriptions of Sino-American relations are more accurate than the balance-of-power perspective. His basic idea of emphasizing binding is more sound than the alternative characterization of balancing, which would suggest a zero-sum view of clashing national units of us-versus-them. This statement, again, does not deny that efforts to manage a country's foreign relations can involve a variety of approaches, including those often described as soft balancing. Elements of cooperation and competition can coexist. But such mixed-motive, multiple-sum games paint a very different picture of international relations than the characterization given by balance-of-power realists.

Further Discussion

Competing perspectives on international relations and political economy involve more than idle academic debate, as they impinge directly on the conduct, choice, and perception of foreign policies—such as binding versus balancing. They can contribute to self-fulfilling prophecies and self-defeating policies. Henry Kissinger was right when he said that "even a paranoid has real enemies." However, by acting as a paranoid, one may turn non-enemies into enemies. North Korea comes to mind in both respects.

Ironically, the one case that *seems* to support balance-of-power reasoning happens to be North Korea—at least with respect to its pursuit of armament, especially nuclear weapons—in view of the sharp and steady decline which has put Pyongyang in a serious disadvantage relative to Seoul. Balance-of-power reasoning, however, cannot account for North Korea's policy of external balancing (or rather, its lack thereof). Despite a steady, unfavorable power shift, Pyongyang has moved farther away from Moscow and Beijing, its traditional patrons. Beijing and Moscow have also become more reluctant to support Pyongyang, whose sagging economy has become increasingly unable to support its heavy defense burden. High military expenditures, in turn, have had a huge deleterious effect on its economic performance. North Korea is the exception among East Asian countries because it continues to follow a strategy of regime survival relying on state control, national autonomy (*juche*), military mobilization, and foreign scapegoating. This strategy has caused economic and political decay, and will bring about an inevitable policy change or regime collapse when it reaches its final point of exhaustion.

North Korea's pursuit of military capabilities—especially nuclear weapons and missile technologies—to the point of consuming an estimated 30% of its gross domestic product, reflects less an attempt to balance power than to signal resolve. Pyongyang faces a huge economic and military disadvantage with respect to Seoul—not to mention the United States. Although it could conceivably devastate Seoul in a conventional attack and even threaten to strike Japan with some of its missiles, these are last-resort actions that would surely trigger massive retaliation and cause its regime's demise. Pyongyang has practiced brinksmanship diplomacy with the intent to communicate its willingness to cause unacceptable damage to America's close allies rather than to even the power balance that currently operates to its huge disadvantage. It is signaling its determination to strike back if it is backed into a corner, professing a strategy of assured retaliation rather than assured destruction.

Why should Washington and indeed Beijing and Moscow care whether Pyongyang develops nuclear weapons? These rudimentary devices do not pose a direct threat of upsetting the power balance in Northeast Asia as much as they raise doubts about the resolve that the United States and other countries have to enforce nuclear nonproliferation (e.g., Cha and Kang 2003). The effects that Pyongyang's nuclear program can have on the region's power balance tend rather to be indirect. It threatens to provoke balance-of-power dynamics by setting off a possible chain reaction whereby other countries (e.g., South

Korea, Taiwan, even Japan) may be motivated to also develop nuclear weapons. This appears to be one of the very few remaining cards that Pyongyang can play. The evidence presented thus far suggests that East Asian countries have generally not practiced internal or external balancing. They have especially refrained from undertaking expensive armament programs. The United States, China, Japan, Russia, and South Korea—participants in the Six-Party Talks held in Beijing to negotiate an end to North Korea's nuclear-weapons program—have professed a common interest in preventing the logic of balance of power from gaining traction in East Asia.

Those who disagree with me may argue that, except for North Korea, one has not seen internal or external balancing in East Asia because leaders in this region have made an intertemporal tradeoff, whereby they seek to maximize short-term economic gains for the sake of improving their long-term security position. This inclination captures the rationale of the so-called postclassical realists described by Brooks (1997). Skeptics may also argue that internal balancing, or armament, has not been ratcheted up by East Asian countries because they have been behaving like free-riders, relying on the United States to protect their country.

Note, however, that both claims acknowledge that balancing behavior has not actually occurred and try to explain away this non-occurrence, which should present an anomaly to balance-of-power theories. Additionally, the former rationalization accepts that states do not always assign priority to security concerns, and that these concerns can be trumped by economic interests. The latter argument concedes that states are actually willing to trust others to protect them, a very dubious premise for those realists who are deeply skeptical about dependence on others' goodwill for one's safety. Why should one count on an ally's good intentions if these intentions are always subject to change? And, if Japan is willing to subcontract the provision of its national security despite its financial wherewithal to go it alone, which other country would be disqualified from behaving similarly? Finally, the proposition that states are engaging in an intertemporal tradeoff that favors current economic benefits to pursue future security gains more effectively (i.e., that countries are just biding their time) is practically unfalsifiable. The predicted future is left deliberately vague and open-ended, and if the expected behavior does not occur, one could always ask for more time. This proposition also leaves out higher-order variables because, presumably, one would not claim that Canada is making such an intertemporal tradeoff in its relations with the United States, nor Italy in its relations with France. So what factors would distinguish these relations from, say, China's relations with the United States or Japan? Those realists who insist on intention-free analysis and a material basis for national policies would be hard-pressed to come up with these factors.

Leaders can commit huge blunders. By their own aggressive actions, Napoleon, Hitler, and Tojo left no option for their victims but to join forces and fight back for survival. They repeatedly lashed out against their neighbors, whose attempts to accommodate, appease, and hide from them were dashed time and again. These aggressors' own self-defeating policies were the primary reason for mobilizing others' counteractions against them. This argument suggests that it is not so much the possession of preponderant power that threatens the neighbors of an aspiring or existing hegemon, but rather the manner in which this country uses its power. Significantly, not all rising states are similar to Napoleon's France, Hitler's Germany, or Tojo's Japan. Moreover, even when states engage in aggressive or bellicose policies—as is the case with North Korea—they are not necessarily motivated by an expansionist or revisionist agenda. Their policies may in fact be driven by a sense of insecurity, vulnerability, and fear of losses.

A concern with the manner in which power is used rather than the possession of power per se motivated warnings about George W. Bush's brand of assertive unilateralism (e.g., Bacevich 2002; Craig 2004; Daalder and Lindsay 2005; Jervis 2005; Layne 2006a, 2006b; Walt 2002, 2005) and the "blowback effects" of maintaining an expansive and expensive imperial presence abroad (e.g., Johnson 2000; Kennedy 1982). It is ironic that while American scholars studying China have paid much attention to how other states have tried to manage China's rise, including their supposed pursuit of balancing policies against Beijing, these same scholars have not paid the same degree of attention to the concurrent U.S. ascendance to unrivaled primacy and the relatively unbridled exercise of U.S. power by the Bush administration. It is a further irony that whereas East Asian states have increasingly turned to economic performance as their policy priority, the United States has been slower to adapt to the changing global political economy and has held on to a more ideological, even "realist" (labels that are more often attributed to other countries rather than to one's own), view of international relations. As I have tried to show, China, Japan, Taiwan, and South Korea have all stressed economic performance as a policy priority and have de-emphasized military capabilities, even when dealing with their traditional nemeses.

There are signs that under Barack Obama's administration, Washington's domestic and foreign policy priorities are changing. On his November 2009 trip to the summit meeting of the Asia Pacific Economic Cooperation countries in Singapore, the U.S. president raised hopes for the creation of a free-

trade area in this region. He announced that the United States would participate in the Trans-Pacific Partnership with Chile, New Zealand, Singapore,
and Brunei. This announcement, among other policy indications, signaled an
intention to give more emphasis to America's economic relations compared to
the Bush administration's prior emphasis on military capabilities. In addressing
an audience of Chinese university students, President Obama stated that "the
U.S. and China don't have to be rivals." Moreover, he stated explicitly that
power in international relations is "no longer a zero-sum game" (CNN live
video, November 16, 2009).

Thus, President Obama's speech challenged directly the dominant realist perspective on balance of power. Those who subscribe to this perspective contend that states balance against others' military capabilities regardless
of their perceptions of others' current or likely future intentions (S. Chan
2010a). Their logic would suggest that the United States would be a prime
candidate for others' balancing policies because it has been spending nearly
as much on the military as the rest of the world *combined*. Although the Bush
administration's policies were counterproductive in many respects and aroused
anti-American sentiments abroad, there is little evidence that other countries
are balancing against the United States. This phenomenon is not happening
against the United States just as it is not occurring against China.

States are not always myopic in pursuing their objectives. They often undertake actions seeking to reassure others that may be suspicious about their
intentions, and to invest in credible commitment intended to defuse the dynamics of power competition. Leaders are certainly not unaware that their
attempts to balance against others, ostensibly from a defensive motivation,
can induce adverse reactions from the intended targets and even from those
who are not the immediate targets but who nevertheless may feel threatened
because these attempts may be interpreted to portend, rightly or wrongly,
future intentions. Others can push back, thereby causing one's policies to become self-defeating. When a state has to implement its deterrence or sanction
threat, it means that its policy seeking to alter another's behavior has failed.
After all, had its threat worked, it would have been unnecessary to implement
it. Similarly, if states have to actually carry out armament and alliance policies
to balance against another, it means that the threat to balance against power
has failed.

The converse is also true. The logic of selection argues that states would
not initiate relations or enter into commercial deals were it not for their prior
expectation that these interactions would turn out to be productive or at
least more rewarding than feasible alternatives. Accordingly, while trade can

promote peace among states, peacefully disposed states will trade with one another from the outset. Similarly, the presence or absence of balancing policies is in itself indicative of states' evaluations of their current and prospective relations, and their awareness of how their own actions can influence others' subsequent behavior. This logic and evidence, presented here, suggest that states are not hardwired to balance against rising powers but tend to be conditional cooperators.

# 6

## Growth, Trust, and Historical Comparisons

In this chapter, I take up four topics germane to theories of power balance and balancing theories. First, are countervailing policies of increasing armament and joining alliances an effective long-term solution to checking a rising power, or are the sources of power shifts among states located primarily inside them? If domestic factors and policies are the more influential determinants of changing interstate power balance, then efforts focusing on armament and alliances are of limited usefulness in the long run and indeed, excesses in undertaking these balancing policies can be self-weakening.

Second, balance-of-threat theory—which offers one example of balancing theories—argues that states balance against the one that poses the greatest menace to them rather than the one with the most capabilities. If so, it matters whether the dominant or rising power is perceived by others to have a status-quo or revisionist agenda. The existing literature typically posits that as the world's hegemon, Britain and later the United States are status-quo powers whereas latecomers that seek to replace them are necessarily revisionist states. This treatment rests more on assumption than analysis, and I address this issue, albeit relatively briefly, with respect to the United States both in its initial rise to the status of a regional hegemon and more recently as a global hegemon.

Third, when faced with unfavorable power shifts, should a declining state take up balancing against all comers or should it resort to a more multifaceted approach in dealing with multiple upstarts? I offer a brief discussion of Britain's management of its relative decline. When faced with several rising powers impinging on its interests in different parts of the world, London undertook a variety of policies aimed at accommodating, aligning with, and even appeasing some of its potential rivals. In contrast, imperial Spain adopted an indiscriminate policy of confronting and fighting all challengers, a policy that exacerbated its decline. This discussion underscores the proposition that rather than being structurally determined, balancing policies involve important strategic choices. Moreover, balancing is not a bilateral matter but needs to be considered in a multilateral context.

Fourth, if armament and alliances may end up being self-defeating, then what can be done to avoid needless and even dangerous competition? As with power-transition theory and balance-of-threat theory, defensive realism suggests that some states are aggressive but others are not. If so, what can peaceful states do to reassure others about their benign intentions? This question impinges on balance-of-power theories, which are premised on the claim that one cannot rely on others' good intentions and must instead respond to the reality of their capabilities. I compare U.S. policies toward Russia and China after the Cold War's end in order to draw some implications from theories about fostering trust and balancing against power or threat. In particular, I address the issue of how increased power affects a state's disposition to trust others, and how its own actions are likely to affect others' disposition to trust it. Before discussing this and the other topics just mentioned, I turn to differentiating balance-of-power theories from their chief competitor, the power-transition theory. Confusion about the logic of these theories has often characterized discussions on China's rise.

## Which Theory Is It?

Although scholars often invoke balance-of-power theories when framing their discourse on China's recent ascendance, their analyses sometimes insinuate the power-transition theory's premise (Organski 1958; Organski and Kugler 1980). The latter theory basically contends that the persistence of U.S. predominance—a decisive imbalance of power—is conducive to international peace and stability. Conversely, China's rise heightens the danger of destabilizing the existing regional and perhaps even world order. It is this latter supposition that fosters a concern for balancing against a rising China—while overlooking the same logic for other states' response to Washington's achievement of a historically unprecedented unipolar status globally. Kenneth Waltz (2000, 36) warned, "When Americans speak of preserving the balance of power in East Asia through their military presence, the Chinese understandably take this to mean that they intend to maintain the strategic hegemony they now enjoy in the *absence* of such a balance" (emphasis in the original). This analytic tension or incongruity often goes unrecognized; few Americans have argued on the grounds of balance of power that China's rise can contribute to regional stability or even peace or, conversely, that an imbalance of power favoring the United States in East Asia or elsewhere has had a reverse effect. As Jack Levy (2002) observed, British writers often commented on the balance of power on the European continent without at the same time attending to the implications of their analyses for Britain's primacy at the global level. The proper names of states rather than the actual distribution of national capabilities drove their conclusions.

There are at least six areas of incompatible views between balance-of-power and power-transition theories. First, balance-of-power theories suggest that a parity, or equilibrium, of national capabilities is conducive to international stability and sometimes even peace (notwithstanding the occasional view that it is necessary to go to war in order to preserve a particular power balance). In contrast, and as mentioned above, power-transition theorists make the opposite argument—that a situation of capability parity (or one that is approaching such parity) is likely to augur instability and even war (e.g., Kim 1989, 1991, 1992, 2002; Kim and Morrow 1992; Kugler 2006; Kugler and Lemke 1996, 2000; Lemke 2002, 2004; Lemke and Tammen 2003; Lemke and Werner 1996; Organski and Kugler 1980; Tammen et al. 2000). Power-transition theorists claim that this risk is the greatest when a fast-growing great power approaches or overtakes an erstwhile leading state. A rapidly rising China is a source of concern for power-transition theorists but, because this development will reduce U.S. preponderance and bring about a more balanced distribution of power, it should presumably contribute to greater regional stability according to balance-of-power theories.

This should at least be the conclusion reached by those who stress intention-free analysis based solely on states' material capabilities (especially if they focus on the distribution of such capabilities among the so-called great powers, such as in the Sino-American relationship). Waltz's (1979) seminal work sought to move away from motivational attributions, choosing to focus instead on systemic influences when distinguishing his neorealist theory from its classical predecessors. Attention to states' intentions—or alleged or perceived intentions—as a crucial independent variable would open the door to formulations such as Stephen Walt's (1987) balance-of-threat theory, and would introduce a distinction between supposed power-seeking and security-seeking states. Randall Schweller's (1994, 1996) analysis on "bandwagoning for profit" also pointed to greed as a motivation for some secondary states to join a dominant power in the hope of sharing the spoils of the latter's aggression. When power-transition theorists speak about some states as revisionist and others as status-quo powers, they are of course engaging in motivational attribution, and their analyses emphasize the interaction effects brought about by a state's increased power and ambition that can make it dangerous to others.

Second, according to at least those balance-of-power theories that are based on offensive realism's premise, all states are potentially power seekers. That is, when given an opportunity, all states will try to maximize their power. This view implies that other states should be most concerned about a concentration of power in American hands, and that Washington's current unipolar status would incline it to seek even more power. The leading scholar on offensive realism, John Mearsheimer (2001), has of course argued that after achieving regional hegemony in the Western Hemisphere, Washington's chief foreign policy objective has been to prevent other great powers from attaining a similar status in other regions of the world. That is, the United States is supposed to have become a satisfied power and to have assumed a defensive role as an offshore balancer.

This view reflects in part the so-called stopping power of water, which limits the projection of U.S. power. This consideration is supposed to have somehow overridden the general tendency claimed by offensive realists that all states want to expand their power until they are stopped by others' counterpower, or until they become the undisputed hegemon. In Mearsheimer's (2001, 34, 35) words, "Even when a great power achieves a distinct military advantage over its rivals, it continues looking for chances to gain more power. The pursuit of power only stops when hegemony is achieved;" and "States do not become status quo powers until they completely dominate the system." If so, the United States should be the poster child for offensive realism as Christopher Layne (2003) argued.

There is some ambiguity about whether the word "system" in the above quotation refers to the interstate system as a whole or just a regional system. Mearsheimer's analysis implies the latter meaning. His suggestion that the United States is the only status-quo great power assuming the role of an offshore balancer in a world populated by power seekers, however, runs into two problems. Empirically, it does not correspond with Washington's actual post-1945 grand strategy of pursuing forward military deployment and energetic diplomacy in an attempt to prevent the emergence of a multipolar world, as Christopher Layne has observed (2009a, 2006b). Moreover, the United States is far more than just a regional hegemon because, especially after the Cold War, it has attained a degree of global preponderance unprecedented in the past 500 years (Brooks and Wohlforth 2008). Theoretically, Mearsheimer's

contention does not answer why the "stopping power of water" would encourage Washington to exercise self-denial in expanding its power globally
while at the same time, motivate it to fight two world wars, because it evidently did not have confidence in Germany's and Japan's self-restraint if they
were to become predominant in Europe and Asia, or in their power expansion
being stopped by the oceans separating them from America.

In contrast to offensive realists, who see all states being motivated by power
maximization, power-transition theorists do not see all states as potentially aggressive and place instead a distinctive emphasis on differentiating the so-called
status-quo states from the revisionist ones. Only the latter type of states, when
approaching the capability of the leading state, will challenge the international
order and spark a war for world domination. In other words, power-transition
theory sees some states as security seekers—fundamentally content with the
existing international order—and other states as dissatisfied and seeking to
overthrow it. It is alleged that when a satisfied latecomer overtakes the leading
state, the risk of war is mitigated, such as when the United States surpassed
Britain. Conversely, when a dissatisfied or revisionist power displaces the leading state, or threatens to do so, as when Germany overtook Britain, the risk
of war is heightened.

As originally formulated, power-transition theory does not explain why a
declining hegemon might not be tempted to wage a preventive war against a
rising latecomer, or why this latecomer would remain dissatisfied and precipitate a major war even though the passage of time should permit it to secure
further gains (S. Chan 2004b, 2008a). Indeed, as just remarked, what did Germany have to gain by starting a war if it had already overtaken Britain by the
time of World War I? Additionally, whether a state is revisionist or committed
to the status quo is either simply asserted or defined in terms of its support for
the leading state, which in turn assumes by default that the leading state is necessarily committed to the international status quo and rules out the possibility
that it may be interested in changing the international order.

One can also be troubled by the possible circularity in labeling a particular
country as revisionist retrospectively, after learning that it has fought a war
against an erstwhile hegemon. That is, instead of being an analytic antecedent
to the outbreak of a hegemonic war, revisionism becomes a post hoc attribution assigned to one side of this belligerence by virtue of its having fought
this war.

Third, power-transition theorists see domestic factors as the primary determinants of national power. States are seen to move ahead or fall behind one
another mainly because of their domestic conditions and policies. Having a

large population base is a necessary though clearly insufficient basis for aspiring to great-power status. As for policies, a government's ability to mobilize and extract national resources, including human effort, is seen to give an advantage to some countries over others. Therefore, a smaller state in terms of asset endowment can still prevail militarily over larger adversaries due to its superior mobilization and extraction capability (Organski and Kugler 1978). Past wars between Israel and its Arab neighbors, and between Vietnam and the United States, testify to the importance of this consideration in addition to other less tangible factors, such as greater domestic consensus, better military training, and a stronger dedication to the national cause.

Because it emphasizes domestic assets and capabilities, power-transition theory assigns a less critical role to international relations, including the extent to which foreign containment or engagement can influence states' power trajectories. Indeed, in pointing out the Phoenix factor, the original authors of power-transition theory suggested that even a disastrous defeat in interstate war does not prevent the vanquished states from reinitiating their prewar pattern of growth in about two decades (Organski and Kugler 1980). Thus, war devastation and even foreign occupation cannot in the long run deflect a state's growth curve that was already evident before the war's start.

Fourth, power-transition theory is explicitly concerned with the bilateral relationship between the two leading powers in the international system. This statement does not deny that the designation of these two countries can be questionable, such as when its proponents argued that Germany's overtaking of Britain led to World War I. This argument is questionable because the United States had overtaken Britain as the world's premier power long before 1914, and Germany never even approached the United States in its national power. In contrast to power-transition theory's bilateral focus, balance-of-power theories take a more multilateral approach. After all, the very idea of external balancing, or alliances and alignment, directs attention to how states conduct diplomatic maneuvers to improve their strategic position or negotiation leverage.

Fifth and related to the above distinction, balance-of-power theories and certainly balancing theories can address how secondary and even minor powers try to manage their international relations, whereas by focusing on the two leading states, power-transition theory is by definition concerned with this relationship between great powers. It is not so much concerned with the behavior of the secondary or minor powers, as far as the danger of hegemonic war is concerned. At the same time, this theory only addresses a situation whereby a rough parity has come to pass between the extant hegemon and the challenger—typically defined operationally to mean a situation where the latter has attained at least 80% of the former's capabilities. This threshold condition questions whether power-transition theory is at all applicable to analyzing contemporary Sino-American relations. Few analysts applying this theory to study current Sino-American relations would argue that China has already reached, or is even remotely close to reaching, this capability threshold. Moreover, assertions about these countries representing *regional* bipolarity cannot be reconciled with power-transition theory's traditional focus on contest for *global* hegemony.

Finally, whereas the currently dominant formulations of balance-of-power theorists emphasize the anarchic nature of interstate relations, power-transition theorists see these relations as basically hierarchical (e.g., Lebow and Valentino 2009). According to the latter perspective, the two leading powers are after all fighting about alternative international orders. Without this linchpin of international order, it hardly makes sense to characterize some states as status-quo oriented and others as revisionist. In an anarchic world, states engage in self-help without being constrained by common rules, shared principles, or hierarchical authority. It is odd for some balance-of-power theorists, who stress structural anarchy, to attribute status-quo or revisionist orientations to states at the same time. Structural anarchy would suggest an absence of international order—without which there can be no status-quo power. Although couched in balance-of-power argot, American discourse on China's rise often advances the view that the United States should maintain its preponderance in Asia because it is the only country capable of holding anarchy at bay and because one cannot be sure of China's future intentions when it becomes more powerful.

## Sources of Power Shifts

Power shifts can be traced to domestic or foreign sources. In Chapter 4, I emphasized that a strategy of regime survival and elite legitimacy pivoted on economic performance has been the principal reason for East Asia's faster economic growth and its general stability and peace compared to the Middle East. This strategy has promoted economic growth by pursuing export expansion, macroeconomic stability, and investment in human resources. Realists tend to define national power primarily in terms of military capabilities, but a state's military capabilities may not correspond with its economic vigor at any given moment. Over the long run, it is the latter that ultimately determines the former. When a state's expenditures on perceived security needs persistently outstrip its economic capacity, it risks imperial overstretch—a common cause for the decline of great powers (Kennedy 1987), with the Soviet Union providing the latest example. Domestic decay usually precedes the fall of empires such as those of the Habsburgs and Romans (e.g., Elliot 1984; Gibbon 1993; Kagan 1962; Kirby 1920; Vicens Vives 1969), rendering them vulnerable to foreign challenges.

There is a general consensus that a state's sheer bulk in terms of its demographic and territorial size is not enough for achieving great-power status. Size indicates a potential for this status but is not a requirement for it. Historically, Britain, the Netherlands, and Portugal attained global primacy despite their relatively small size. Their entrepreneurial dynamism, efficient capital formation, social cohesion and adaptability, and capacity for technological and institutional innovation gave them a competitive advantage over their much larger rivals in expanding and applying their resource base.

Richard Rosecrance (1986) emphasized this advantage when distinguishing states that pursue a "strategic vision" in contrast to others that are "trading states." If physical size were the sole or even the most important source of national power, the Soviet Union should have prevailed in the Cold War, and China and India should have ranked high on the interstate pecking order. Even though these states could boast a large population, territorial expanse, and even high volumes of steel production and energy consumption, they have lagged behind the West European states, the United States, and Japan in interstate competitiveness in the past century. Such traditional measures of national power tend to be especially misleading in the information age with its short product cycles and rapid technological change (S. Chan 2005; Porter 1990; Tellis et al. 2000).

The theory of long cycles in international relations offers another example of theories of power balance. It agrees with power-transition theory and the discussion above that a leading state's ability to foster innovative technologies is the key determinant of its global status. According to this theory, a state's ability to attain global leadership historically comes from and is sustained by its status as a technological pioneer (Modelski 1987; Modelski and Thompson 1996; Reuveny and Thompson 2004). This asset is far more important than the possession of a large military or population—or even a large economy, which requires the constant stimulation of new innovations and scientific breakthroughs, especially in the leading sectors, to sustain its expansion.

Four implications follow from this discussion. First and most obviously, an overemphasis on balancing against another country's military capabilities is questionable and even risky to the extent that these policies overlook or undermine a state's economic performance and technological competitiveness. Second, balancing policies in the form of increasing armament or alliances are less effective and important in comparison to domestic reform to encourage productivity and innovation.

Third, although balance-of-power theorists have been traditionally preoccupied with the military exploits of an ambitious and expanding state, this approach to acquiring national power has become increasingly obsolescent. Military conquest might have paid off in the past and under special conditions, but these circumstances are increasingly irrelevant to today's international relations. Peter Liberman (1998) argued that invaders could exploit modern societies by using coercion and repression to extract resources from industries in the occupied countries. His examples came primarily from Germany's seizure of Belgium and Luxembourg in World War I, France's occupation of the Ruhr during the interwar years, and the Soviet Union's exploitation of its East and Central European allies (although he included Japan's conquest of Korea and Taiwan, the latter societies were neither industrial nor modern at that time). These cases point to intense exploitation of a conqueror's industrialized neighbors populated by co-ethnics, requiring ruthless policies to intimidate the local population and to manipulate the existing communication infrastructure and administrative capacity of a captive society.

By implication, when the victim of aggression is preindustrial and far away, it is less likely that conquest will pay; and when, in addition, it is culturally alien, the occupying force is also more likely to encounter fierce nationalist resistance and cultural backlash. Moreover, when the conquering state is a democracy, it is more inhibited in adopting ruthless policies of coercion and repression, and is therefore again less able to profit from its conquest. Recent U.S. experiences in Iraq, Afghanistan, and Vietnam are congruent with these generalizations.

Significantly, to the extent that an aggressor state is more effective in augmenting its power by military conquest, its success will arouse other states' security concerns and incline them to join a countervailing coalition to oppose it. Therefore, Germany, Japan, and the Soviet Union, which were the subjects of Liberman's study, all encountered increasing opposition from other states, who were energized to act as a result of the aggressors' ruthless policies and their gains to scale (Powell 1999). Accordingly, whether military conquest will pay off is at least a contingent outcome dependent in part on the victims' and third parties' responses to it. Under contemporary conditions, it is likely to be unprofitable and even self-defeating due to the invader becoming bogged down and encountering resistance from other states.

This discussion has a fourth implication. Although size does not necessarily confer great-power status, it can affect relative growth rates. As an economy gets bigger, it becomes increasingly difficult to maintain, not to mention accelerate, its rate of growth. A larger economy's share of the aggregate capabilities of all the great powers inevitably suffers when a more backward and smaller economy starts to take off. The latter enjoys the advantage of backwardness, benefitting from the lessons that its predecessors have acquired from trials and errors. It is also easier, mathematically, to make larger percentage gains when one has a smaller base. This larger relative gain by a smaller economy, however, can bend the growth trajectories of its more advanced and bigger counterparts, and the consequent ripple effects can be quite traumatic for the latter countries and destabilizing for relations among them. These are the fundamental insights of the power-cycle theory, which offers yet a third example of theories of power balance.

More specifically, power-cycle theory (Doran 1989, 1991, 2003; Doran and Parsons 1980) attends to the security implications of the expansion and contraction of relative power among a small number of major states. Even when a state is making absolute gains in its capabilities, it may still be losing power relative to other fast-growing states. As mentioned above, a larger leading state's relative position in the great-power system can be adversely affected by the rise of its lesser counterparts. The interactions among the pertinent states' growth rates can influence their relative power cycles in surprising and drastic ways.

In particular, relatively small absolute gains by one of the lesser great powers can tip a leading great power's growth trajectory, causing its rate of growth to decelerate and even reversing the direction of this change from positive to negative in relation to the other great powers in the system. This was the situation prior to 1914 when Russia's faster growth, albeit from a smaller base, set Germany on a course of relative decline (even while it was still growing in absolute terms). Power-cycle theorists argue that when states experience critical inflection points at which the velocity or direction affecting changes in their relative power shows a reversal, their leaders are especially likely to succumb to anxiety or arrogance, which in turn increases the probability of their miscalculation. They are more likely to act impulsively and opportunistically at these junctures. The odds of conflict escalation rise with the number of great powers simultaneously experiencing these critical inflection points (Tessman and Chan 2004). For those great powers experiencing or anticipating relative decline, such as Germany prior to World War I, there is also a stronger temptation to wage preventive war before their adversary catches up (Copeland 2000; Lemke 2003; Levy 1987).

In addition to helping to locate especially tumultuous and dangerous times when great powers are likely to clash, power-cycle theory calls attention to three issues. First, cognitive and institutional rigidities contribute to international tension and instability. This tendency stems from a failure by states to adjust their perceived interests and their international role conception in a timely and sufficient manner to reflect their changing capabilities. Resistance to scaling back one's interests and role abroad characterizes states experiencing downward mobility. The failure of a declining power to downsize its foreign commitments and missions in accordance with its diminished resources in turn has the effect of further exacerbating its decline. Conversely, states experiencing upward mobility are more likely to avoid rash behavior because they hope to make additional gains (absolutely and relatively) with the passage of time. They are likely to demand full compensation for what they regard their relative power entitles them to only when they sense that their power growth has already peaked (Powell 1999)—that is, when they feel that waiting will not give them additional gains.

With that said, rising powers are not immune to errors of arrogance and overconfidence. In contrast to balance-of-power theories, power-cycle theory suggests that aggressor states (e.g., Napoleon's France, the Kaiser's and Hitler's Germany, Tojo's Japan) are more likely acting out of a sense of panic and desperation rather than cockiness and confidence. They precipitate wars of conquest against their victims because the "window of opportunity" is closing on them—that is, because they feel time is working against them. Their potential adversaries are gaining on them. According to this reasoning and contrary to power-transition theory, wars are more likely to be started by states whose advantage is diminishing rather than by those that are catching up (thus Germany rather than Russia/the Soviet Union in the two world wars). Preventive wars are by definition launched by those states that have a power advantage currently but worry about this advantage slipping away in the future. They feel that it is better to wage war now than later. Contesting the usual American discourse on China's rise, this perspective suggests that "if destabilizing policies are to be initiated, the perpetrator will likely be a declining United States" (Copeland 2000, 243).

Second, power-cycle theory agrees with power-transition theory and long-cycle theory in emphasizing the domestic sources of changing power balances among states. Accordingly, one cannot effectively manage the security implications of power shifts by focusing just on armament or alliances. When the target of such balancing efforts happens to have a large population, resource base, and technological capacity, engagement and containment are likely to have only marginal effects. Far more consequential is the policy agenda pursued by the target itself, such as whether it pivots its strategy of regime survival and elite legitimacy on economic performance, nationalism and militarism, or imperial expansion. A state's own self-defeating policies, such as those adopted by the Soviet Union and North Korea, are more important causes for their relative decline or stagnation.

Third, power-cycle theory puts the relative rise and decline of great powers in an explicitly multilateral and dynamic context. This deliberate focus in turn has several implications. Some states are inevitably moving ahead and others failing behind in relation to each other, and the security implications are far from clear when one broadens one's perspective beyond a bilateral zero-sum view. When seen in a multilateral context, another state's gain may or may not be to one's detriment, as it is more uncertain whether this rising power will turn out to be an ally or adversary. A more dynamic view also suggests that a state's growth inevitably slows down and its relative power suffers as other states accelerate their growth. Just as China's recent gain has caused the United States and Japan to experience a relative positional loss, it will also eventually face the same situation as Brazil and India enter into their fast-growth phase.

Significantly, history has recorded many instances of peaceful power transition, such as when the United States overtook Britain, Japan overtook the Soviet Union, and China overtook Germany. Indeed, until the 1880s, the Composite Index of National Capability (Singer 1987; Singer, Bremer, and Stuckey 1968) gave China a higher score than the United States. Because we often select war occurrence as the dependent variable, we do not give enough analytic weight to occasions when the (war) dog did not bark. Moreover, when one pays attention to the multilateral context of great-power relations, one is reminded that a dominant power often faces several challengers. In the late 1800s, the United States, Germany, Russia, and Japan were all gaining on Britain. That London finally ended up fighting Germany and not the others reflected its strategic choice rather than historical inevitability. Regime or cultural similarity alone hardly explains Britain's decision to form alliances with Russia and Japan, to accommodate and appease the United States, and to confront Germany.

Finally, power-cycle theory points to the regular and even natural processes governing the rise and decline of great powers. Smaller upstart states have an easier time making relative gains at the expense of their larger counterparts, who have dominated the world system. It is more difficult for dominant powers to sustain, not to mention accelerate, their rate of growth. The consequent power shifts have the effect of producing a more balanced distribution of power. This effect accords with Waltz's clarification, quoted earlier, that a balance of power does not necessarily have to result from balancing policies. It can recur regardless of officials' intentions.

## Revisionism and Selective "Balancing"

As Karen A. Rasler and William R. Thompson (2000, 310) remarked, "declining incumbents select, to some extent, which challengers they will fight and with whom they will ally to meet the intensive challenge." Therefore, structure is not destiny. Although ongoing or prospective power shifts are important in shaping the context of decision making, officials still have the capacity to exercise strategic choice. Declining hegemons often face several rising powers. Which of them should be balanced against, and which ones should be conciliated? Balancing theories speak in part to the motivations influencing these choices. For example, physical distance, regime similarity, and cultural affinity may be among the pertinent factors (Schweller 1992).

It is too simplistic to assign categorical labels such as revisionist or status-quo orientation to explain international relations. In reality, "most states have a mixed bag of preferences: They play defense and offense at the same time, seeking to preserve the status quo in some situations and to upend it in others" (Crawford 2003, 203). Thus, for instance, the United States is interested in preventing nuclear proliferation (a status-quo objective) and, at the same time, promoting democratization and market reform abroad (revisionist goals). Similarly, China has both status-quo and revisionist objectives so that, for example, it is more interested in stabilizing the military and political situation on the Korean peninsula while seeking to effect a change in Taiwan's relations with it.

Some have argued that since the end of the Cold War and especially during the George W. Bush administration, American officials have behaved as "assertive nationalists" (e.g., Daalder and Lindsay 2005; Jervis 2003, 2005; Walt 2005). In Stephen Walt's (2005, 23) words, "the United States is in a position that is historically unprecedented, and . . . it has used its power to mold a world that would be compatible with U.S. interests and values. The United States has not acted as a 'status quo' power: rather, it has used its position of primacy to increase its influence, to enhance its position vis-à-vis potential rivals, and to deal with specific security threats."

Commenting on a more distant past, John Mearsheimer (2001, 238) observed, "the United States was bent on establishing regional hegemony, and it was an expansionist power of the first order in the Americas." He quoted Henry Cabot Lodge saying that the United States had "a record of conquest, colonization, and territorial expansion unequaled by any people in the nineteenth century." It had expanded its territory fourfold during the first half of the nineteenth century and, by the century's end, it had realized its re-gional hegemony in the Western Hemisphere. From 1898 to 1913, it gained seven times more colonial territory than imperial Germany (Copeland 1996, 28–29). Whether defined in terms of actual conduct (such as territorial ag-grandizement on the North American continent and colonial war in the Phil-ippines) or adherence to existing international norms (such as Washington's unilateral declaration of the Monroe Doctrine), the United States was not a status-quo power in the nineteenth century. It is therefore problematic to claim that it was a "satisfied power," thus accounting for the peaceful power transition between it and Britain.

Until about the end of the nineteenth century, Anglo-American relations were competitive and even acrimonious. The two countries had fought a war in 1812 and came close to another military confrontation in the Oregon dispute in 1845–1846. In order to stop rising U.S. power, Britain considered intervening on the Confederacy's behalf in the American Civil War (Little 2007b; P. Thompson 2007). Kenneth Bourne (1967, 408) wrote, "the United States remained an enemy of Britain's calculations . . . until 1895–96. Until after the Venezuelan affair any increase in the territory and strength of the United States was regarded as a direct threat to the British possessions and British power and influence in the western hemisphere." The British were suspicious of American intentions and wary of American designs on Canada (Owens 1997). The two countries competed for political and commercial in-fluence in the Western Hemisphere and in East Asia. Hindsight bias, knowing that the United States and Britain were allies in World War I, makes Anglo-American relations before that conflict appear much more cordial than was actually the case.

Britain did eventually come to terms with the inexorable expansion of American power. By the end of the nineteenth century, it had conceded to U.S. hegemony of the Western Hemisphere. Britain made a series of unilat-eral concessions to accommodate the United States (Rock 2000). The bound-ary dispute between Venezuela and British Guyana and that between Alaska and the Canadian Northwest were settled in favor of Washington. Moreover, London was powerless to stop the construction of the Panama Canal, which further boosted U.S. naval power.

Britain yielded in the face of mounting resource constraints, forcing it to make hard choices in coping with challenges from multiple fronts (Friedberg 1988). It appeased the United States in the Western Hemisphere, took on Ja-pan as a junior partner in East Asia, and patched up its differences with France and Russia (W. Thompson 1999; Vasquez 1996). These policies of alignment and accommodation were accompanied by the recall of the royal navy to waters closer to the home islands—all with the intent of focusing on the more nearby threat coming from Germany. Geographical proximity inclined London to be more mindful of rising German power, but Berlin's bellicose policies also contributed to British anxieties and fears.

Britain's strategy of coping with its relative decline suggests that balancing policies are hardly a matter of all or nothing. Rather, they involve compromises with and even appeasement of some rising powers in order to better concentrate the available resources on others. It contrasts with Spain's policy under Philip IV of responding with bellicosity to all perceived challengers in the hope of establishing a reputation for resolve. Madrid hoped that this reputation would in turn deter future challenges. This policy, however, exhausted the Habsburgs in a long series of wars in the Netherlands, Italy, and Germany, with the setbacks and weakness caused by each successive conflict encouraging rather than discouraging further challenges to Spanish primacy. Spain's policy was self-defeating and accelerated its decline. As Daniel Treisman (2004) argued, selective appeasement is probably a rational strategy when the stakes of a contest are either very high or low, or when the costs of fighting are very high. When one of these conditions exists, even a highly resolved hegemon should rationally appease a challenger in order to conserve its resources to more effectively deter other challengers in the future. This being the optimal strategy for a strong incumbent, a weaker one will not be able to improve its reputation for resolve by adopting a different strategy.

Britain pursued a strategy of selective and anticipatory appeasement in the years leading up to World War I (Kennedy 1981). If scholars focused their attention just on Britain's bilateral relations with the United States, France, Russia, and Japan, they would see a series of concessions and efforts attempting to reach accommodation and conciliation. The strategic rationale behind these moves of appeasement becomes more understandable, however, when they are given a multilateral context in which London faced severe resource constraints to take on all rising powers. It chose to focus on Germany. With that said, British policies aimed at balancing against Germany's rising power also exacerbated anxieties and fears in Berlin, thereby creating an echo chamber of rising Anglo-German antagonism (Kennedy 1982; Kydd 1997a). Armament (such as the Anglo-German naval race) and alignment (such as Britain's rapprochement with France and Russia) heightened rather than eased tensions, contributing to self-fulfilling predictions of another country's hostility. With mutual suspicion and hostility feeding upon each other, a spiral of conflict ensued until war broke out (Jervis 1976).

In the mid 1930s, London and Paris did not readily and fully pursue balancing policies against a resurgent Germany in part because of their domestic politics and in part because, as mentioned above, Germany's intentions had not yet clarified. Moreover, as Walt (1992, 464) pointed out, they were distracted by their desire to maintain their respective overseas empires: "Britain and France had difficulty balancing Hitler precisely because they were overcommitted in other regions!" Thus, an inability to set clear priorities contributed to a diversion of their resources and attention. Given their resource constraints and attention limitations, states do not have the luxury of being everywhere at the same time. The contemporary relevance of these remarks for the United States should be obvious, as Washington is currently fighting two wars in Iraq and Afghanistan (as well as military attacks against Libya), engaging in coercive diplomacy against Iran and North Korea, waging a global campaign against terrorism, and facing high unemployment and serious budget deficits in its domestic economy.

My discussion also underscores the need to attend to multiple rising powers and the inherent uncertainty in judging which ones are likely to become more menacing (Edelstein 2002). There is the danger of both false negatives (the error of mistaking an expansionist power as a peaceful one) and false positives (treating a peaceful power as an expansionist one, thereby turning it into an enemy). This difficulty suggests the importance of reassurance policies that states can adopt to signal their "type"—that is, communication by peaceful states to distinguish themselves from expansionist ones.

## Power, Trust, and Costly Signals

Effective communication of one's policy intentions and preferences is at the core of recent rationalist theories explaining why wars start and end (e.g., Fearon 1995, 1998a, 2004; Fortna 2004; Gartzke 1999; Powell 1996, 1999; Wagner 2000; Walter 2002; Werner 1999; Werner and Yuen 2005). Reassurance policies seek to establish one's trustworthiness in others' eyes.

They should have a goldilocks quality (Kydd 2005). If they are too weak, they are not credible because less trustworthy (or more aggressive or expansionist) states would also be willing to undertake them in an effort to disguise their true character. Conversely, if reassurance signals are too strong, states risk being exploited, because uncooperative counterparts will not reciprocate their conciliatory gestures. Their counterparts may even misinterpret these gestures as concessions made out of weakness rather than niceness. Experimental research has shown that when people learn that their counterpart is either unable or unwilling to retaliate, they are likely to exploit this perceived weakness and escalate their demands (Reychler 1979; Shure, Meeker, and Hansford 1965).

In the mid 1950s, Joseph Stalin recalled Soviet occupation forces from Austria and demobilized about one million of his armed forces. Were these moves intended by him as signals to reassure the West and to invite reciprocity? One can only guess. John Foster Dulles, the U.S. Secretary of State at the time, saw these moves as stemming from Moscow's economic difficulties rather than its changed political agenda. He interpreted them to suggest Soviet weakness rather than niceness, and responded by strengthening the Western alliance against Moscow (Holsti 1962).

One may argue that Stalin's actions in this case were not sufficiently costly to Moscow and therefore inadequate in changing Dulles's beliefs about Soviet intentions. It is more difficult to dismiss Mikhail Gorbachev's decisions (e.g., Checkel 1993; Kydd 2005; Risse-Kappen 1991, 1994; Wohlforth 2003). He conceded to U.S. demands in concluding the Intermediate-Range Nuclear Forces Treaty in 1987, withdrew Soviet troops from Afghanistan in 1988, and disavowed any intention to intervene militarily when fellow communist regimes in East and Central Europe were toppled in 1988 and 1989. He dismantled communism and introduced multiparty elections in Russia, and dissolved the Soviet Union by allowing the secession and independence of the non-Russian republics. Moreover, he consented to Germany's reunification and accepted the NATO membership of a reunified Germany—in other words, he did not seek to balance against a stronger Germany, one that became part of the Western alliance. Massive military retrenchment and fundamental economic liberalization ensued. His policies and those of his successor, Boris Yeltsin, were thus anomalous for balance-of-power expectations. Richard Ned Lebow (1994, 268) remarked, "Soviet foreign policy under Gorbachev is outside the realist paradigm."

From Moscow's perspective, subsequent U.S. actions must have appeared quite disturbing. The United States extended NATO to include Russia's former allies, and even started to collaborate with Poland and the Czech Republic to build a missile defense system aimed ostensibly at Iran. It abrogated the Anti-Ballistic Missile Treaty, refused to ratify the Comprehensive Test Ban Treaty, and initiated National Missile Defense. Moreover, it introduced military personnel and bases on Russia's borders, including parts of Central Asia that used to belong to the Soviet Union. It attacked Russia's erstwhile allies, Serbia, Iraq, and Afghanistan. In one way or another, these events arguably challenge the tacit understanding that Moscow had for ending the Cold War. Each of them could be perhaps explained in isolation by factors peculiar to it, but collectively they present a general pattern that must be highly disconcerting to Moscow. From the perspective of balance-of-power and balance-of-threat theories, these U.S. actions are incongruous. Whether Russia was seen as becoming weaker or nicer, these theories would have led one to expect more conciliatory or accommodating U.S. policies.

Russia's relative decline occurred at about the same time that China started to make relative gains. These two cases offer a nearly ideal comparison for balance-of-power theories. One former nemesis of the United States was becoming weaker (setting aside intentionality), and the other was becoming stronger. How did Washington respond to these divergent situations? It appears that it behaved in a manner exactly contrary to balance-of-power theories. Whereas U.S. policies toward Russia had become more aggressive, its policies toward China had become more conciliatory.

Washington has worked more closely with Beijing in dealing with the two possible hot spots in East Asia—the Taiwan Strait and the Korean peninsula. American leaders, including President George W. Bush, strongly rebuked former Taiwanese President Chen Shui-bian for his pro-independence schemes. Former U.S. Secretary of State Colin Powell even declared, "There is only one China. Taiwan is not independent. It does not enjoy sovereignty as a nation" (quoted in Chu 2007, 247). On December 21, 2007, former U.S. Secretary of State Condoleezza Rice publicly castigated Chen's introduction of a referendum initiative to apply for United Nations membership (as "Taiwan" rather than "Republic of China"), describing it as a "provocative policy." On the matter of North Korea's nuclear program, Washington has collaborated with Beijing in the Six-Party Talks held in China.

Significantly, closer cooperation between China and the United States cannot be easily attributed to Beijing adopting more conciliatory or accommodating policies compared to Russia. After all, Sino-American relations experienced repeated tensions such as China's Tiananmen crackdown in 1989, its missile tests in Taiwan's vicinity in 1995, the U.S. bombing of the Chinese embassy in Belgrade in 1999, and the collision between a U.S. EP-3E surveillance aircraft and a Chinese interceptor fighter near Hainan Island in 2001. These events suggest China's and Russia's changing relative strength rather than their respective policies as a more important determinant of U.S. policies. Contrary to balance-of-power theories, however, U.S. policies appear to have pushed harder against a weaker Russia than a stronger China.

According to this interpretation, reassurances made in the context of deteriorating power do not have the desired effect in changing the other side's policies regardless of the latter's changing perceptions of the reassuring state's intentions. My earlier claim that a state can affect others' policies toward it needs to be qualified; it applies more appropriately to reassurances coming from a rising state, one that chooses to communicate self-restraint in the exercise of its power even though it has gained a greater capacity to act on its interests. This contextual consideration, as I will argue in the next chapter, is important in influencing the effectiveness of interstate signals.

Reciprocated cooperation is the aim of reassurance policies. The above discussion questioned whether the United States has felt that it does not have to make major concessions to the Soviet Union/Russia given its overwhelming strength. American behavior is more suggestive of responding to Russia's capabilities rather than its intentions but in a way that is contrary to both balance-of-power and balance-of-threat theories. The end of the Cold War and subsequent developments appear to raise a double challenge to these theories: Moscow decided not to balance against Washington's stronger power, and Washington did not respond to Moscow's reduced threat and diminished capabilities by lowering its armament significantly and initiating de-alignment (or disengagement from Europe and Asia in order to assume the role of an offshore balancer, as expected by some realists such as John Mearsheimer).

China and other states pay attention to what the United States does. They draw conclusions from U.S. behavior toward not just Russia but also smaller states, such as Cuba, Venezuela, Iraq, Iran, Afghanistan, and North Korea. One way for states to demonstrate that they are interested in seeking security rather than maximizing power is a general disposition to tolerate dissidence from and accept the autonomy of their weaker neighbors, ones that clearly cannot threaten their security (Kydd 1997b). Military intervention and covert subversion against these states are likely to be taken as evidence of a revisionist rather than status-quo agenda.

Another way to signal an intention to seek security rather than maximize power is to promote and accept agreements on arms control, forsake opportunities to increase one's strategic advantage, and adopt a pattern of military deployment indicating a basic defensive posture. Still another way to communicate benign intention is to bind oneself to multilateral institutions and refrain from encroaching on another great power's traditional sphere of influence. Moreover, the manner in which a country (or government) treats its domestic dissidents, minorities and, by extension, others who are in comparable situations, and the ideology it espouses in justifying its foreign policy offer clues about whether it seeks to improve its security or expand its power. Finally, it has been argued that to the extent offensive and defensive military capabilities are distinguishable, a state's investment in its force structure and weapons development can be informative about its type as a security seeker or power maximizer (Glaser 1994/95; Jervis 1978; Levy 1984; Montgomery 2006; Van Evera 1998).

In all these respects, U.S. conduct since the Soviet Union's demise has been disconcerting to other states precisely because the Soviet Union/Russia, its Cold War adversary, had invested in costly concessions. The pertinent conduct is not limited to policies toward Russia, but includes other manifestations, such as the Bush doctrine of waging preventive war, the treatment of enemy combatants, and the rejection of international accords or institutions such as the Kyoto Protocol and the International Criminal Court. Land mines may be construed as defensive instruments, but "star war" initiatives, missile defense systems, and aircraft carriers and long-range stealth bombers are more likely to lend themselves to offensive power projection (that an aircraft carrier projects a state's offensive power is no less true for China if it decides to deploy one; Ross 2009a, 78).

Washington's efforts to upgrade warheads designed for ground bursts (with the obvious purpose of destroying hardened silos housing enemy missiles), to improve further the accuracy of its submarine-launched ballistic missiles, and to engage in aggressive tracking of Russian submarines would make little sense except for enhancing a capability to launch a disarming first strike (Lieber and Press 2006). These steps were undertaken even after it has attained unquestioned nuclear primacy to such an extent that these authors concluded "Russian (and Chinese) leaders can no longer count on having a survivable nuclear deterrent" (ibid., 9). They are significant because they offer meaningful clues to other states about whether Washington is motivated to seek security or maximize power. Actions that have the intent or effect of improving one's ability to nullify the other side's nuclear retaliation exacerbate the commitment problem discussed in the last and again the next chapter. They do so by obviously increasing the value of defection. Similarly, self-restraint—choosing not to act in certain ways even when one clearly has the capacity to do so (such as Japan and South Korea eschewing nuclear weapons and going "independent" militarily)—can also be highly revealing about one's policy agenda as a security seeker or power maximizer.

More recently, the Obama administration has announced a willingness to abandon a missile defense system based in Poland and the Czech Republic but continued to pursue a less costly system announced at a meeting with its NATO partners in Lisbon on November 19, 2010. It has previously declined to reconsider its rejection of an international ban on antipersonnel mines. After the 2010 midyear election, some Republican Senators tried to hold up the ratification of the Strategic Arms Reduction Treaty (START) negotiated with Moscow. Although this effort failed, the ratification process (entailing strong administration lobbying and presidential promise to continue the missile defense program) and the accompanying debate aroused concerns about U.S. credibility (including the president's ability to "deliver" deals reached with other countries and to commit to arms reduction). Washington's actions or inaction in such cases are not as important in further affecting power balances that already favor the United States heavily as they communicate its current preferences and future intentions. They undermine U.S. credibility in advocating nuclear nonproliferation for other states, and discourage costly concessions by them. For those that are predisposed to question U.S. motives, such as Iran and North Korea, these signals tend to reinforce their suspicions.

## Further Discussion

In essence, the logic behind the dominant balance-of-power perspective is "better safe than sorry." It shares the basic premise of offensive realism that all states are aggressive or potentially so (Mearsheimer 2001). Because other states' intentions are assumed to be invariant, one must take steps to balance against their power. Defensive realism, in contrast, accepts that some states are not aggressive but are only interested in seeking security rather than expanding their power. The problem, however, is that states are unable to tell confidently which ones among them are security seekers and which ones are power seekers. This inability to distinguish the two types causes even the security seekers to act as power seekers lest they be exploited by the latter type. A tragic security dilemma stems from this difficulty of making an accurate recognition, and mutual suspicion (the desire not to be exploited as the "sucker") produces a suboptimal outcome for some states that would have otherwise liked to cooperate ( Jervis 1978).

When balance-of-power theorists undertake intention-free analysis, they are accepting the offensive realists' premise that in effect assumes all states' intentions are the same (i.e., as a constant) rather than trying to analyze them as a variable. This position, however, makes an assumption into a conclusion. As Andrew Kydd (1997a, 1997b, 2000, 2005) has shown, some states are clearly more interested in security than power; moreover, security seekers can engage in effective signaling to disclose their type to other states. That is, with respect to defensive realism, there are things states can do — or choose not to do — to reduce their uncertainties about each other's intentions. To the extent that they are reassured that another state has peaceful intentions — even if it has more power and is getting stronger—they will not balance against it. This is after all the most important conclusion from Stephen Walt's (1987, 1988) balance-of-threat theory, explaining why almost all major states and many minor ones allied with the United States against a weaker but more threatening Soviet Union during the Cold War.

Accordingly, balancing policies in the form of arms races and competitive alliances are not the inevitable results of power shifts if states can communicate effectively their benign intentions. Reassurance policies are costly signals sent with the aim of establishing trust. These signals are intended to influence other states' perceptions and shape their behavior. If the recipients of these signals are the security-seeking type, they are likely to respond by reciprocating one's concessions, and their reciprocity will in turn bring about more subsequent rounds of accommodation, conciliation, and cooperation. This is the basic rationale behind Charles Osgood's (1962) famous GRIT proposal (Gradual and Reciprocated Initiatives in Tension-Reduction). Conversely, a power-seeking type would be more reluctant to reciprocate because it is wary of giving up its advantages or potential gains even if it becomes persuaded that its counterpart is only interested in security. If it senses that the other side's concessions are a result of weakness, it is likely to respond by "piling on" even though these concessions have already improved its security.

Whether another state is trustworthy or untrustworthy, and whether it is a security seeker or power seeker, is never a categorical decision to be made once and for all, but is rather an evolving assessment requiring constant feedback and adjustment. In addition to current information, historical experience matters. David Kang's (2007b) analysis of China's historical ties with its neighbors is pertinent. It shows that although China had insisted on formal political subordination from its neighbors, it had generally refrained from undermining the authority or autonomy of its nominal vassal states. Moreover, Beijing's influence had been historically based more on its cultural hegemony than direct economic or political control. This tendency had contributed to East Asia's experience with long-standing Chinese hegemony rather than balance-of-power dynamics.

This observation does not imply that in today's world, China's neighbors would consent to, much less welcome, a return to their traditional relations with China, only that their historical experience with China would have an influence on their perceptions of and approaches to managing a rising China. The point about history making a difference is also pertinent to the absence of balancing behavior opposing current U.S. primacy. As I will discuss in Chapter 7, Washington's earlier institution-building efforts to foster quasi-constitutional arrangements involving mostly its West European allies have produced a reservoir of trust and a sense of legitimacy accorded to its use of power.

Besides current behavior and historical relations, a state's policy processes can be informative about its intentions. The critical variable is the transparency of these processes. When these processes are transparent, others are more able to discern a state's intentions because information is more available and reliable. Authoritarian regimes with obscure policy processes are more likely to be distrusted, not necessarily because they are inherently more aggressive, but rather because there is simply less information to base judgments on. This reasoning, as Kydd (1997a) pointed out, is distinct from the proposition that democracies are better able to make credible commitment due to their higher audience costs, a proposition that has in turn been used to suggest that democracies should be more successful in resolving interstate conflicts in their favor. Rather, the current argument claims that due to their openness, democracies provide more information for other states to judge their intentions—and to the extent that this openness enables them to disclose more persuasively that they are seeking security rather than power, they are more likely to reassure others. "If a democracy is really a security seeker, the openness of its policy processes will reveal this to the world" (Kydd 1997a, 119). There is, however, a corollary to this proposition. "Of course, if the democracy is greedy, this will be revealed as well, producing justified distrust on the part of other states and a lack of cooperation" (ibid., 129). Thus, although democratic transparency contributes to reducing uncertainty, it has a double-edged quality, disclosing whether a state offering this transparency is being motivated by a security or power agenda.

Andrew Kydd (1997a) illustrated his argument about democratic transparency with a discussion of the political debates in Germany and Japan about whether to contribute to U.N. peacekeeping forces in the wake of the first Gulf War. The domestic controversies surrounding their eventual decisions to join these missions in Iraq, and the intense opposition mobilized against these decisions and the stringent restrictions placed on them, demonstrated to outside observers that these former World War II belligerent states were not about to revive militarism. As in the case of U.S. ratification of START, the processes that produce policy decisions—and not just these decisions themselves—can be highly informative.

The circumstances surrounding the U.S. initiation of the second Gulf War in 2003, however, offers a compelling contrast. There was little legislative oversight or public scrutiny preceding the Bush administration's rush to war. As aptly characterized by Chaim Kaufman (2004, 2005), the lead-up to this war was infused with "threat inflation" and "a failure of the marketplace of ideas." Neither institutional checks and balances, nor a skeptical public, prevented the launching of this war of choice (Mearsheimer and Walt 2003) without the legitimating authority of the United Nations and over the objections of important U.S. allies such as Germany and France. This war has aroused particular skepticism about U.S. motives after claims about Saddam Hussein's links with Al Qaeda and his development of weapons of mass destruction turned out to be untrue. *Ex post* information revealed by democracies' openness in this and other cases of actual or possible preventive war shed light on whether their decisions were motivated primarily by security or power considerations (Levy 2008b; Levy and Gochal 2001; Ripsman and Levy 2008; Trachtenberg 2007).

The preceding discussion has dwelled much more on the United States than China for the simple reason that China's power and policies are not unrelated to U.S. power and policies—and to other states' reactions to their respective power and policies. To the extent that many studies on China's rise focus only on China's power and policies without taking into account those of the United States, as well as other states' evaluations and perceptions of both, they have serious shortcomings. The United States is, for all countries in the world, including China, the "elephant in the room." Accounting for almost half of the world's military expenditures, it has on objective grounds far less to worry about its security than all others—if security, as typically presented in realist discourse, is taken to mean a state's survival if it should be defeated in war. No other major state enjoys nearly as favorable a geographic position, being flanked by two oceans and sharing land borders with just two much weaker and friendly neighbors. Far more than any state in the world, the United States is safer from the catastrophic contingency of having its survival endangered but has pursued policies seeking to increase further its safety margin.

At what point will this demand for extra safety, or security, be satisfied, and can this quest become so expansive that it is tantamount to power maximization? This effort can be expensive in both tangible resources and intangible goodwill (including trust). It compounds a tendency remarked upon by Colin Elman (2003, 16): "It is possible that, when states are approaching capabilities of hegemonic proportions, those resources alone are so threatening that they 'drown out' distance, offense–defense, and intentions as potential negative threat modifiers."

This logic also holds an important implication for China's policy toward Taiwan. When the United States had troops and weapons on Taiwan, Beijing could legitimately claim a security concern—no less than Washington's

assertions about the threat posed by Soviet military presence in Cuba. A belligerent Chinese posture would be more understandable and may even ironically appear to be more reassuring in this context because such a posture would
be in line with what one would expect from a security seeker. However, as
Beijing's power grows (and its security position improves) and as Taiwan no
longer poses the threat that it did when it was formally allied with the United
States and served as an "unsinkable aircraft carrier," Beijing's bellicosity can
now be more suggestive of a power-seeking motive.

It is possible, as some scholars (e.g., Kang 2007b) have argued, that other
East Asian states do not necessarily see China's treatment of the Taiwan issue
in the same light as other issues—that is, they do not necessarily think this
treatment can be generalized to China's other foreign policies. Assuming this
to be the case, China's self-restraint should enable it to send an even more
powerful signal about its benign intentions (because in this case, Beijing should
have less to worry about the adverse fallout resulting from its taking a more
bellicose course of action). Conversely, if China's treatment of Taiwan can
affect other states' perceptions of its general disposition, it should be more
concerned about how it proceeds because the stakes involve not only its relations with Taiwan and the United States, but also its long-term relations with
its other neighbors. Whether the reunification of Taiwan is motivated more
by concerns about national sovereignty and popular legitimacy than geostrategic calculations (Wachman 2007) is therefore pertinent to inference about
Beijing's general intentions.

Parenthetically, this discussion is also pertinent to U.S. policies toward
Cuba—which shares a comparable geostrategic position relative to the United
States as Taiwan's to China. One may debate about whether Cuba's alliance
with the Soviet Union had once posed a security threat to the United States,
but this threat has clearly vanished since the Cold War's end. Washington's
continued economic and political boycott of the island, however, suggests
other motives are at work, including possibly the influence of domestic political partisanship. Even setting aside the more contentious and therefore intrac-
table issues of nationalism and contested sovereignty impinging on relations
across the Taiwan Strait, one cannot but notice that there has been far greater
progress in relaxing tension, opening political dialogue, and fostering economic intercourse in this case than in U.S.-Cuban relations. These differences
in relating to a smaller nonthreatening neighbor are observable by other states,
which draw inferences about the powerful state's motivations. Stasis—in this
case, the absence of major change in U.S. policies toward Cuba despite other

transformative events such as the Soviet Union's collapse and Barack Obama's election—can be highly instructive.

Balance-of-power theorists (in contrast to balancing theorists) make worst-case assumptions about states' motivations and therefore do not incorporate this variable in their explanation. Trust and the challenges standing in the way of establishing it, however, are not independent of power balances. The greater a country's relative power—and concomitantly, the less its costs for fighting and the greater the potential gains from fighting—the higher the threshold it requires for trusting another country (Kydd 2005). That is, it is more difficult for others to establish their trustworthiness in its eyes or alternatively, the more concessions it will demand from others in order for them to establish their trustworthiness in its eyes.

Given its higher threshold for trusting others, a more powerful country is also more prone to defect—to pursue noncooperative, even aggressive, policies, even while others offer concessions and restraint. This tendency accounts in part for Washington's policies in the wake of the Soviet Union's disintegration, brought up earlier in this chapter. As another implication of this proposition, being less powerful than the United States, other major states such as France, Germany, and Russia are more willing to accept a higher level of uncertainty about Iraq's, Iran's, and North Korea's weapons intentions and less inclined to support a preventive war against these countries.

Thus, paradoxically, a country usually becomes less trusting even while it becomes stronger. "Greater power and lower costs for fighting raise the minimum trust threshold, so that even small doubts that another country is untrustworthy may be enough to tip the United States over the edge into conflict. When a country is extremely good at fighting, the incentive to trust the other side to keep their word diminishes, and the incentive to take matters into one's own hands grows" (Kydd 2005, 249). But when a state successfully resists these impulses by actually investing in mutual trust, its behavior becomes an especially powerful and credible commitment to cooperation. I will return to this point in the next chapter in discussing post-1945 U.S. efforts to institutionalize cooperation among the Western powers.

Some realists expect a more imbalanced situation after the Soviet Union's demise to cause other states to balance against the United States, whether by hard or soft means, and regardless of actual U.S. conduct. The above line of argument, however, contends that other states are likely to distrust the United States more because of its conduct than its power. Since China has also been gaining power, similar expectations should apply to it. Has increased power made Beijing more distrusting? Has this increased power made others also to distrust it more? The evidence presented in Chapter 3 shows that China's neighbors have thus far undertaken little overt arming or alignment against it.

It is relatively easy to discern power shifts measured in tangible national assets such as foreign reserves, economic production, and weapons procurement. For China's neighbors, the more elusive question is the extent to which China can be trusted—relative to other major states, such as the United States and Japan. Public opinion surveys indicate that in many countries around the world, including those in the Asia Pacific, such as South Korea, Thailand, Malaysia, and even Australia, trust in or affection for China are not necessarily lower than those for the United States (e.g., Bobrow 2008b; S. Chan 2010a; Katzenstein and Keohane 2007; Kohut and Stokes 2006). Seen in this light, these countries' general rapprochement and conciliation with China do not have to reflect their accommodation to rising Chinese power—their behavior may instead indicate at least in part their becoming more reassured by China's peaceful disposition, that is, by their assessment of how Beijing may use its increased power rather than its acquisition of this increased power.

# 7

## Preferences, Intentions, and Multilateralism

Balance-of-power theorists claim that military capabilities provide the ultimate protection for states' survival because discerning others' preferences and predicting their future intentions is difficult. One ought to therefore be safe rather than sorry and rely on one's own military capabilities to check those of others. By following this line of reasoning, one presumes that states cannot communicate effectively their preferences and intentions or make credible commitments to bind their future actions.

If the above characterization seems extreme, then one would want to inquire about how states can effectively communicate their preferences and intentions, offering persuasive assurances to others that they will pursue their interests and exercise their power with restraint (e.g., Elman 2009, 70). Presumably, others' perceptions of a state's trustworthiness can be influenced by its behavior. This behavior can reassure others or frighten them. Whether a state is perceived to have a revisionist or status-quo agenda depends on more than its self-characterization. Other states are likely to emphasize deeds rather than words, with due consideration given to the context in which the observed behavior occurs.

Officials often disguise and misrepresent their true preferences, intentions, and capabilities in order to gain a strategic advantage by deception or to increase their domestic popularity through political posturing. Because insincere states try to mimic sincere ones, the resulting "pooling" makes it difficult to determine their real motivations and true character. How can an observer separate the "good" from the "bad," dismissing some statements and behavior as deliberate misrepresentation (as hot air or a "head fake") but taking other communications seriously? When a state's actions entail significant self-imposed costs, they are especially informative about its true preferences and intentions.

Several examples should help to illuminate this point. If a sovereign debtor continues to make full and prompt loan repayments even during hard economic times, bondholders should be more confident of its creditworthiness. This behavior distinguishes it from other "fair weather" debtors that would only honor their loan obligations when their economy is thriving (Tomz 2007). For another illustration, it is easy to imagine a country eschewing protectionism when it is running a trade surplus. If, however, a state resists protectionist temptations during a balance-of-payment crisis, especially when it could have invoked "escape clauses," this behavior communicates a more credible commitment to free trade. As a third example, when a democracy offers a substantial concession to an autocracy, its overture is *ipso facto* more credible than if the roles were reversed because it is taking a greater risk of being exploited (i.e., it is taking more of a leap of faith), as information about the autocracy's preferences and intentions is inherently less available and reliable (Kydd 2005). Conversely, if an autocracy declines to reciprocate a democracy's conciliatory move—even given the latter's more transparent policy processes and more believable commitment stemming from the nature of its political institutions (e.g., Schultz 2001), this behavior should also be highly revealing about its preferences and intentions. This is so because, given the information-rich environment in which a democracy operates, the autocracy should be less worried about being exploited by democratic duplicity. Therefore, its failure to reciprocate lends credence to its designation as an uncooperative type.

As yet another example, when offensive and defensive military capabilities can be distinguished and when neither has an advantage over the other, states' armament procurement can be informative about whether they have an offensive or defensive motivation (Montgomery 2006). This motivation can be even more confidently established if a state's arms acquisitions "go against the grain"—that is, when it invests heavily in obviously defensive capabilities (e.g., mines, trenches, fortifications) when the offense is popularly believed to have an edge, or when it develops offensive capabilities (e.g., panzer divisions, long-range bombers) in a world supposedly dominated by defense.

As a final illustration, accommodation by a major albeit secondary state is, *ceteris paribus*, more meaningful than a similar move by either a superpower or a minor power. A superpower can afford to be accommodating without compromising its huge advantages, whereas a minor power is likely to lack other choices. Yet, when a hegemon plays by the rules and recognizes others states' interests even when it could have overpowered any opposition, this self-restraint establishes a reputation for moderation and commitment to multilateralism. As will be argued shortly, this self-restraint or self-binding makes its exercise of power more legitimate and efficient. Significantly, this practice highlights the associational or societal view of balance of power mentioned in Chapter 2. As I noted there, writers such as Hans Morgenthau (1948) and Hedley Bull (1977) considered not only the competitive dynamic among states but also the cooperative dynamic. States often exercise self-restraint while at the same time trying to restrain others (Little 2009, 40).

It is not difficult to offer real-world instances of states acting out of character when the advocates of at least some versions of realism or balance-of-power theories would have expected them to behave in a self-regarding and even myopic fashion. Thus, West Germany—and subsequently, a reunited Germany—deliberately embedded itself politically, economically, and militarily in various multilateral institutions in order to reassure its neighbors that it would not and could not pursue assertive unilateral policies, and that alarm bells would go off to warn its neighbors long before such policies were to become a realistic prospect. Additionally, despite their much vaunted historical animosity, Japan's official development assistance has given priority to China—something that would have been inexplicable if Tokyo were obsessed with limiting the latter's development potential. Similarly, China kept its promise not to devalue the renminbi in the midst of the Asian financial crisis in the late 1990s, when its neighbors were using currency depreciation to stimulate their exports. And, as discussed below, after World War II the United States chose to forge self-binding institutions, especially with its West European allies, rather than opt to exercise its overwhelming power without being hampered by these institutional constraints (Martin 2003). This is not how a greedy, shortsighted hegemon would have acted.

Six points should be emphasized. First, when states act in a way that contradicts situational expectations, their behavior is more telling about their preferences and intentions. Put differently, when states behave in a self-denying and even seemingly other-regarding way, this behavior offers more compelling information about their character. Naturally, such inferences are subject to constant updating, incremental revision, and confirmation from multiple occasions and sources of information. Second, the more their behavior involves self-imposed costs, the more credible are their disclosed preferences and intentions, because those who would have otherwise tried to misrepresent themselves are more likely to be deterred by the high costs of undertaking such deception. Third, inaction or the non-occurrence of the expected can be highly informative. That China did not devalue its currency during the Asian financial crisis and that its neighbors did not undertake internal and external balancing offer germane examples of "dogs that did not bark." Similarly, Japan's disavowal of nuclear weapons is significant—a decision stemming presumably from its unwillingness rather than inability to produce such weapons. Accordingly, rather than focusing only on what has happened, analysts should attend to those nonevents that communicate important information about states' self-restraint.

Fourth, a reputation for reliability and good faith can be generalized in such a way that the trust and cooperation that were established in one situation can affect another situation. Of course, the reverse also applies. A state's reputation for untrustworthiness in one relationship can infect its other relationships and other issues areas (e.g., Brooks and Wohlforth 2008; Ikenberry 2003; Martin 2003). This is a somewhat different rendition of the idea of audience costs (Fearon 1994), pointing to the fact that there are always foreign onlookers watching and seeking to discern a state's character from its behavior toward others.

Fifth, balance-of-power theorists have things easy because they assume away the most difficult analytic and policy challenge of discerning states' preferences and intentions. By comparison, states' relative power capabilities and the trends influencing their ongoing power shifts are generally matters of common knowledge. Indeed, when scholars rely on routinely available information—such as a country's demographic size, economic growth rate, export volume and debt level, and possession of nuclear weapons and aircraft carriers—they can hardly claim any knowledge advantage over officials (or even some journalists) with access to much more timely, accurate, and sensitive data.

Sixth and as already mentioned, whether other states choose to balance against a powerful or rising country is influenced not just by the latter's capabilities but, more importantly, by how others perceive its preferences and intentions. Therefore, this potential target of balancing can influence others' polices through its own conduct. The following discussion suggests that such a state can try to reassure others and build others' confidence in its peaceful intentions and preference for cooperation by embedding itself in multilateral relations and institutions.

When a state invests in these multilateral relations and institutions, it is not necessarily motivated by a desire for power accretion. Thus, for instance, Washington's efforts to forge a multinational coalition to sanction a recalcitrant state are less important for aggregating its capabilities with those of its partners and more important as a signal demonstrating its resolve to follow through with its policy (Martin 1993a, 1992). Coordination with others entails transaction and reputation costs, and a willingness to incur these costs communicates a strong preference and a serious intention. A less determined state would just "talk the talk" without, however, putting up with the trouble and costs of developing a multinational coalition. The following discussion turns first to the U.S. role in fostering a new world order after World War II, and then to recent regional developments in East Asia.

## U.S. Institution-Building After 1945

Leading states have rare opportunities to reshape the international order after decisive victories in major wars. To varying degrees and with different success, in 1815, 1919, and 1945 Britain and the United States were inclined to and capable of enmeshing other states in a network of reciprocity whereby the dominant power agreed to restrain itself from unbridled and indiscriminate exercise of power in exchange for more compliant and cooperative behavior from the rest. The Congress of Vienna, the League of Nations, the United Nations system, the Bretton Woods regime, and the North Atlantic Treaty Organization exemplify such efforts at institution building to promote coordination, albeit with varying degrees of effectiveness and longevity. These institutions feature the associational or cooperative aspects of international relations, with states considered as participating members of an international society rather than as interacting units of an interstate system.

John Ikenberry (2001) showed that states are not myopic. They often enter into agreements that enable them to cooperate despite their power asymmetries and mutual concerns about opportunistic behavior. Both the strong and the weak make an intertemporal tradeoff. After World War II, the United States decided not to pursue its momentary advantages by applying its raw power to the fullest extent, and instead sought to engage its potential competitors in the future and to invite them to join institutions that could sustain and legitimize its power in the longer term. Conversely, the weaker European states agreed to participate in these institutions in order to curtail the U.S. impulse to either dominate or abandon them. Being in a weaker position, those exhausted by war accepted the immediate and tangible returns from cooperating with the hegemon, even though this acceptance meant that they would forfeit some of the autonomy and discretion to be possibly gained in the future when they would be in a stronger bargaining position.

By exercising self-restraint and constructing mechanisms for positive gains, a hegemonic or rising state can dampen other states' fears of its preponderant or increasing power and encourage them to support rather than oppose its primacy or ascent. Lisa Martin (1993b) argued "multilateralism makes sense from the perspective of a farsighted hegemon. It requires short-term sacrifices of control of decision making but can result in more stable arrangements over the long term . . . Overall, multilateralism provides a relatively cheap, stable organizational form. In exchange for a loss of some power over decision making and probably some decrease in distributional benefits, the hegemon gains a stable decision-making forum."

Thus, power and institutions are not independent, presenting separate or opposite domains in theory or practice. By forging institutions of cooperation such as NATO and the Bretton Woods regime, the United States did not foreswear its power advantages, but by binding itself to these institutions' rules, it did make the pursuit of these advantages more predictable, acceptable, and even legitimate to other states. Multilateralism in this institutional form, as John Ruggie (1993) explained, involves the coordination of interstate relations based on a set of generalized principles such as nondiscrimination, diffuse reciprocity, equal and open membership, and the indivisibility of members' well-being. Importantly, an international order, regime, or organization may involve three or more members and thus be multilateral but still not begin to approach these criteria for multilateralism as an institutional form.

Three points come to mind immediately. First, U.S. policies after World War II promoted multilateralism much more than did other victors in previous wars. Second, Washington pursued multilateralism to a far greater extent in its relations with its West European allies than with its East Asian allies. And third, even though, as discussed later, East Asian countries have developed a large number of multilateral institutions in recent years, these institutions still lack a high degree of multilateralism in Ruggie's sense of generalized principles.

Instead, interstate cooperation or collaboration in East Asia has followed more closely an alternative approach of relying on self-enforcing arrangements (based mostly on bilateral deals but also increasingly taking on multilateral forms), as explained below. With that said, both approaches—multilateralism and self-enforcing arrangements—have the intent and effect of dampening power plays and building confidence. They do not enable states to aggregate power in the traditional sense of external balancing, but rather help to defuse power and restrain its use by a policy of deliberate entanglement. The basic tenet of Bismarckian diplomacy is deliberate entanglement by shaping a rising power such as China into an indispensable partner, or as Avery Goldstein (2003a, 58) noted, at least a very attractive one. This type of diplomacy was used to divert and manage a countervailing power that might otherwise have been mobilized against the Second Reich (Joffe 1995), although, as just implied, it was based on a series of bilateral deals rather than multilateralism.

Washington's post-1945 institutional investment necessarily meant binding itself to those rules that it wanted to foster, but at the same time had the offsetting advantage of reducing other states' incentives to obstruct U.S. policies and even to balance against preponderant American power should they become stronger in the future. Thus, international cooperation and the stability of international order do not necessarily depend exclusively or even primarily on a hegemon's power but can also be advanced by the practice of self-restraint, the norms of mutual adjustment, and credible reassurance and commitment to cooperate with other states. Concomitantly, power disparities do not have to be incompatible with a stable order or continued cooperation, and can in fact serve as a catalyst to create and sustain them.

In this discussion, I do not imply that China's rapid ascent is comparable to the American and/or British victories of 1945, 1919, and 1815. Clearly, China does not enjoy nearly the same extent of asymmetric power advantage that characterized America's and even Britain's postwar position—and of course, there has not been a major war such as those that exhausted or at least seriously weakened America's or Britain's adversaries and allies alike. Furthermore, unlike the United States and even Britain, China does not have democratic institutions to lend transparency to its decision processes and give its policy commitments more credibility. These democratic advantages are important to reassure other states that a dominant or rising power will indeed play by the rules. Finally and most importantly, China has not undertaken self-binding through multilateralism as a generalized principle in its relations with other East Asian states, even though it has assumed a more active role in many multilateral institutions.

According to Ikenberry (2001), the period immediately following a major war provides a window of opportunity for creating a new international order, as the old one has just been destroyed or discredited, and as both the victors and the vanquished may be most interested in developing new institutions to stabilize their relations. Such an opportunity, however, can also exist without the immense destruction of a major war and the lopsided power asymmetries that result from it. The years immediately after the Soviet Union's dissolution presented such an opportunity for the United States to launch new initiatives to institutionalize multilateral cooperation among the major states. Power shifts, such as those that are transforming East Asia's regional structure, may also motivate both the rising power and its neighbors to seek ways to stabilize their relations and consolidate the basis for their long-term cooperation.

A rising power clearly has an incentive to sustain the ongoing processes that have enabled it to move up the international hierarchy and that should enable it to continue its ascent. It should want to demonstrate its credible commitment to stable relations, signaling its peaceful intentions and reasonable goals to other states. It cannot throw its weight around like a preponderant power that has just emerged victorious from a major war. Indeed, bellicose assertiveness would exacerbate other states' fears, causing them to join a countervailing coalition to check this country's rising power and inclining the currently dominant country to even consider launching a preventive war against it (Copeland 2000; Layne 2009a; Lemke 2003; Levy 1987, 2008b; Thayer 2005; Van Evera 1999). A rising power's neighbors have an incentive to lock it into a more predictable future relationship while they still enjoy a relatively favorable bargaining position. They can thus avoid the opportunity costs associated with balancing through armament and alliances, including triggering a conflict spiral that would convert the rising power into a permanent adversary. These mutual incentives suggest that a balance-of-power dynamic need not be the inevitable result of power shifts. Indeed, the balance-of-power dynamic failed to materialize in the wake of power transitions such as when Japan, Germany, and China overtook Britain, France, and Russia/the Soviet Union economically in the recent past.

An extant or aspiring hegemon can do something about others' perceptions of its motivations and possible actions. Evelyn Goh (2007/08) introduced the ideas of "omni-enmeshment" and "complex balancing" to suggest that Southeast Asian countries have undertaken a multidirectional and subtler form of diplomacy to engage and influence China. Significantly, this is an approach that China, as well as other states, could also adopt. It is, in some ways, reminiscent of Otto von Bismarck's complicated diplomatic maneuvers that sought to ensure that other European states would not gang up on a rising Prussia and that all would be beholden to Berlin in some important ways (Hamerow 1972; Medlicott 1965; Williamson 1986). Joseph Joffe (1995) suggested that the United States should follow this strategy after the Cold War, and Avery Goldstein (2003a) argued that, since the 1990s, China has followed it in its broad outlines by pursuing a series of "strategic partnerships" with other major states. Importantly, other states need little persuasion by Beijing (or Washington) to realize that strategic disengagement, domestic disarray, or a precipitous decline on the part of either China or the United States would work to their own severe detriment.

I have just argued that the manner in which a rising power conducts itself will influence whether others balance against it. It is also important to consider whether the existing international order is sufficiently open to admit new entrants. Although there has been much discussion about whether a rising state is inclined to challenge or accept the existing international order, less attention has gone to the fact that this order is rigged to favor the interests of dominant powers. There is, of course, a general recognition that, in Robert Gilpin's (1981, 29) words, "in international society the distribution of power among coalitions [of states] determines who governs the international system and whose interests are principally promoted by the functioning of the system," and that "dominant states have sought to exert control over the system in order to advance their self-interests." In a similar vein, Kenneth Organski (1958, 327–328) noted that the dominant nation "always benefits disproportionately" from the existing international order at the expense of weaker states and that "the dominant nation and its supporters are not usually willing to grant the newcomers more than a small part of the advantages they receive." Randall Schweller (1998, 84) also observed that "after all, states that find the status quo most agreeable are usually the ones that created the existing order; as the principal beneficiaries of the status quo, they more than anyone else have a vested interest in preserving it." The powerful may even be motivated to revise this order so that their interests can be further advanced.

These remarks naturally lead to the question of whether the existing international order, and especially the hegemon that has played a critical role in fostering and propagating it, are capable of integrating rising newcomers. As I have suggested earlier, Japan was a clear exception to the generalization that powerful maritime states do not encounter balancing reactions. Japan's expansionist policies met stiff opposition from other imperialist powers even though its conduct was not more nefarious or aggressive than that of those other states. Japanese leaders during and after the Meiji Restoration were anxious to introduce and adopt Western practices and institutions in an effort to gain national strength and international respectability. In fact, as Yuen Foong Khong (2001, 40) suggested, Japan "proved an example *par excellence* in conforming its government institutions, legal system, and general international practices to the interests, rules, and values of 'civilized' international society, as prescribed by Western nations." Imperial Japan engaged in colonial conquest and territorial aggrandizement according to the political and military norms prevailing at the time. Its ambitions were thwarted by other imperialist powers and indeed, Japanese delegates could not even get their allies in World War I to support the principles of racial equality and national sovereignty at the Versailles Conference.

Therefore, it is not just a matter of whether a rising power is revisionist or committed to the status quo. Whether this country decides to challenge the existing international order also depends on whether this order can accommodate its interests. The quasi-constitutional arrangements fostered by the United States after 1945 are important in this context. The nature of international order itself influences a rising state's choice to challenge it or to integrate within it (Ikenberry 2008a, 27). Washington has urged China to become a "responsible stakeholder." As Christopher Layne(2009a, 120) has noted, "responsibility" has been largely defined in terms of Chinese integration into the U.S.-led order on American terms. Both these American terms and Washington's actual conduct will matter greatly in how the Chinese, and indeed people in other countries, perceive the legitimacy of U.S. power and of international institutions currently dominated by it.

When Washington acts in a manner that is perceived to break existing agreements, apply double standards, and assert special prerogatives, these actions tend to undermine this legitimacy (e.g., when it waged preventive war against Iraq without United Nations approval, opposed the International Criminal Court unless Americans were given special treatment even while demanding the prosecution of war crimes committed in Serbia and Sudan, sold weapons to Taiwan despite a previous agreement with Beijing to reduce such sales, overlooked Israel's nuclear weapons while focusing on Iran's and North Korea's programs, and invoked self-exempting reasons or engaged in unilateral actions such as resorting to the so-called Super 301 provision to sanction what it perceives to be others' unfair trade). The key point about a hegemon's self-binding behavior in strengthening multilateralism is that it assumes a "responsibility" to "play by the rules" (Ikenberry 2001; Martin 2003). To the extent that contemporary multilateral institutions provide open and equal access to all countries and to the extent that their mechanisms for resolving disputes are based on rules that are generally agreed upon, these qualities make "Today's Western order . . . hard to overturn and easy to join" (Ikenberry 2008a, 23). If, as suggested by most proponents of theories of power balance, the rise and decline of national power are determined primarily by factors internal to a country, then there is generally little that the United States can do to thwart China's rise. Ikenberry argued that even if that is so, the United States can and should try to integrate China into the extensive, rule-based system of institutions that Washington's leadership has helped to establish, thereby protecting its own long-term interests and perpetuating the Western order.

## The Puzzle of Different "Regionalisms"

Regionalism has developed in various forms and proceeded at varying paces in different regions (Bhalla and Bhalla 1997; Grieco 1997). Intergovernmental and nongovernmental institutions have created a dense web among the West European states for which multilateralism has advanced the furthest in the world. Conversely, sub-Saharan Africa, the Middle East, and Latin America have lagged in the development of multilateral arrangements, which have turned out to be less institutionalized and effective in these regions. Multilateralism in the Asia Pacific has followed the principle of "open regionalism." The Asia Pacific Economic Cooperation (APEC) forum, founded in 1989, has exemplified this principle. Professing the nonexclusive nature of their relations, its members have sought to strengthen ties with all states and have denied any discriminatory intent against nonmembers. APEC has admitted a large and heterogeneous group of states (but also Hong Kong and Chinese Taipei). Its membership encompasses a huge geographic area and features significant diversity in physical size, economic development, regime character, and cultural heritage.

The Association of Southeast Asian Nations (ASEAN) has arguably served as the core and spur for APEC development. Established in 1967, it was originally motivated, at least to a substantial extent, by its founding members' concerns about Vietnamese expansion, even though they had publicly disavowed any security agenda when their organization was first launched. These original members (Indonesia, Malaysia, the Philippines, Singapore, and Thailand) were subsequently joined by Brunei Darussalam, Cambodia, Laos, Vietnam and most recently, Burma (Myanmar). ASEAN has played a leading role—and in some respects, even a pivotal role—in initiatives to organize subsequent regional forums or organizations such as APEC, the ASEAN Regional Forum (ARF), ASEAN Plus Three, and the East Asian Summit (EAS). Respect for its members' sovereignty and noninterference in their domestic affairs were emphasized in ASEAN's founding philosophy.

Conventional wisdom has it that due to these distinctive features of the "Asian" or ASEAN outlook, multilateralism in the Asia Pacific has assumed a very different form and orientation from those in Western Europe and North America. APEC members are seen to favor an ad hoc, discreet, and informal approach to managing their collective affairs. In contrast to their West European and North American counterparts, they have been seemingly more wary of and less enamored with efforts to formulate explicit rules, negotiate legal agreements, and build formal organizations. They have instead preferred private consultation aimed at facilitating informal understanding and consensus building, with an emphasis on establishing dialogues rather than on necessarily achieving tangible results from these processes. When accords are reached, they tend to reflect the least common denominator, deliberate obfuscation to paper over differences, and informal accommodation. APEC members are said to be especially resistant to any infringement, real or imagined, on their sovereignty. This sensitivity has in turn engendered the idea of "concerted unilateralism" and contributed to observations such as those just mentioned (e.g., Deng 1997; Green and Gill 2009; Higgott, Leaver, and Ravenhill 1993; Mack and Ravenhill 1995; Simon 1993). These observations have buttressed Robert Scalapino's (1987) characterization of "soft regionalism." APEC's annual summit meetings have routinely produced declarations that are the products of creative ambiguity. "Pledges to promote regional cooperation usually are couched in highly contingent terms, lack any enforcement mechanisms or penalty provisions, and will not come due until well into the future" (S. Chan 2001b, 7).

Upon further reflection, however, such observations may be overstated to the extent that they imply some distinctive, even unique, quality about APEC or its East Asian members. After all, similar descriptions can be extended to, for example, the outcome of the 2009 Copenhagen conference to reduce global carbon emissions. Significantly, APEC's membership includes more than just East Asian countries, with the United States playing a major role (Australia, Canada, Chile, Mexico, New Zealand, Peru, and Russia are among the other non-Asian members). Additionally, although APEC clearly lags behind the European Union in institutionalization, it does not compare unfavorably with multilateralism in North America, Latin America, or the Middle East. National character and political culture—such as "Asian values"—are likely to be only part of the explanation and are in themselves insufficient to account for the variations in multilateral institutionalization across the different regions.

Countries in Latin America and the Middle East share far greater cultural homogeneity than those located in the Asia Pacific, and they also have more similar economic outlooks and political regimes. Yet multilateralism has not advanced farther in those regions. Moreover, if fewer members and larger power asymmetries among them should make it easier to build multilateral institutions (as one would expect from theories of collective action and hegemonic stability; e.g., Kindleberger 1973; Olson 1965), it is difficult to explain the situation in North America. The North American Free Trade Agreement has seen little institutionalization and has remained mainly as two sets of bilateral relations connecting the United States to Canada and to Mexico separately and with only weak connections between the latter two countries.

This observation in turn calls attention to important historical differences between U.S. policies and attitudes toward Western Europe, East Asia, and the Western Hemisphere. Washington's varying motivations have been consequential for the different degrees and orientations of regionalism. These U.S. motivations can be contrasted with China's and for both countries, policies and attitudes toward East Asian regionalism have undergone changes over time. These differences illuminate impulses tending to abet, confirm, or reinforce the logic of balance of power, in both its adversarial and associational senses.

## Alternative Impulses for Regionalism

The last section's closing remarks call attention to the tendency to judge the Asia Pacific with Western Europe's experience (a successful outlier in regional cooperation) rather than with that of Latin America, Eastern Europe, and the Middle East—regions that are more homogeneous than the Asia Pacific culturally, economically, and politically and that should therefore be better positioned for integration and institutionalization. Moreover, there is a tendency to overlook historical progress, that is, the extent to which multilateral institutions and confidence-building measures have developed in East Asia in recent decades, making it a far more stable and less dangerous area than previously (Alagappa 2003a). As a consequence, diagnoses and prognoses of East Asia's security circumstances have often turned out to be more pessimistic than warranted. Finally, there is a tendency to assume that Washington's policies toward Western Europe, where most of its major allies were located and where it was most concerned about the Soviet Union during the Cold War, were similarly applied in East Asia. As already pointed out, however, whereas the United States pursued multilateralism in Western Europe—adopting those quasi-constitutional and multilateral arrangements described by Ikenberry (2001) to integrate and "lock in" its allies—its policies in East Asia were distinctly bilateral in nature, with a special emphasis on the U.S.-Japan alliance.

Significantly, neither Washington nor Tokyo have promoted or accepted multilateralism in East Asia. Both have been ambivalent and even opposed to multilateral initiatives (Cha 2003). They have preferred looser, more informal, and less exclusive membership (notwithstanding efforts to boycott Burma) in order to dilute institutional initiatives, check perceived Chinese influence, and include the participation of non–East Asian states such as Australia, India, New Zealand, and the United States itself. Both the United States and Japan would rather emphasize their bilateral security alliance and even ad hoc coalitions (sometimes described as "minilateralism") in pursuing their priorities. Thus, that regionalism appears to have taken on features of informality and ad-hocracy, often becoming "talk shops" and offering little more than photo opportunities at summitries, has been due to more than just Asian values. These features also reflect U.S. preferences, which have coincided with Japanese and, until rather recently, Chinese preferences. By making these remarks, I do not mean to claim that cultural identities and norms have been irrelevant to the development of "soft institutionalism" in East Asia (Acharya 2001, 2003). Rather, this historical outcome has been overdetermined, with different material and nonmaterial factors converging on the same expectation (e.g., Crone 1993).

Beijing was initially skeptical of multilateral institutions such as ASEAN, being concerned that it could become the target of others' collective containment and that such forums would interfere with its domestic affairs. Since the 1990s, however, it has taken an increasingly active role in multilateral diplomacy in East Asia and in international organizations more generally (e.g., Johnston 2003b; Kent 2007; Wu 2009). It has favored APT, with its membership limited to Southeast Asian countries and China, South Korea, and Japan, as the chief mechanism for promoting regionalism. In contrast, Japan has promoted the EAS which also includes Australia, India, and New Zealand.

The U.S. preference is more closely aligned with Japan's, but with an emphasis on an even more inclusive membership that is trans-Pacific (such as APEC and ARF) rather than strictly East Asian (such as APT). Washington objected to multilateral institutions that would exclude it. It continues to assign primacy to its bilateral alliances such as those with South Korea, Australia, and especially Japan, and subordinates multilateral institutions to these bilateral security ties (Cossa 2009). Moreover, it supports ad hoc multilateral approaches (in contrast to institutionalized ones) to address issues such as North Korea's nuclear weapons. The Korean Energy Development Group (KEDO), the Six-Party Talks, and the Proliferation Security Initiative (PSI) exemplify such "coalitions of the willing." These proclivities distinguish Washington's investment in building strong, binding multilateral institutions in partnership with its West European allies. The multiplicity and overlapping agendas of regional institutions in the Asia Pacific reflect in part (but only in part) efforts at enmeshment and containment by multiple states—efforts sometimes described as soft balancing.

Although, as Ikenberry has argued, power and institutions need not be incompatible, it is also understandable that when a powerful country becomes even more powerful, its natural inclination is to act unfettered and to prefer ad hoc arrangements (Walt 2009, 116–117). The invasion of Iraq by a U.S.-led "coalition of the willing" comes to mind. The same reasoning, however, suggests that when a hegemon behaves out of character by promoting multilateralism and accepting self-binding rules, it conveys credible information about its intentions to limit the practice of self-aggrandizement and the indiscriminate use of its power.

Historically, large power asymmetries—that is, an imbalance of power—can either empower a hegemon to pursue policies unencumbered by multilateral institutions (as in the case of George W. Bush's policies of "assertive nationalism;" Daalder and Lindsay 2005; Walt 2005) or enable it to foster quasi-constitutional arrangements (as in the case of Harry Truman's policies of offering institutional assurance and commitment to major U.S. allies; Ikenberry 2001; Kydd 2005; Martin 2003). Which approach it adopts illuminates its confidence in the relative efficacy of power and institutions.

The power asymmetries between the United States and its East Asian allies have been historically more lopsided than those between the United States and its West European allies. For this reason and also cultural/racial differences, Washington's policies in East Asia have tilted more toward power as emphasized by traditional realism than multilateral institutions as promoted by liberalism. These paradigms offer relatively distinct injunctions and predictions about state behavior. Realists would expect a dominant power in highly asymmetric relations to stress bilateral relations, in the fashion of U.S. hub-and-spokes alliances in East Asia, lest its discretion and freedom be hampered by the secondary and minor states in multilateral forums. This power would prefer to make separate deals with each weaker partner to maximize its own control. Furthermore, it would attempt to link issues so that its advantages in one arena can be used to gain concessions in another arena. Naturally, weaker states would have the opposite preference, disposing them to separate issues in negotiations to protect their vulnerability in one arena from being exploited in another. They would also favor rules and institutions that would constrain a dominant state's use of its overwhelming power.

To the extent that regional politics takes on the competitive logic of relative gains and reflects deep skepticisms about the enforceability of international agreements as described by realists, states should/would avoid locking themselves into arrangements that could produce greater and more lasting relative benefits for their neighbors. They are instead likely to favor informal, ad hoc, nonbinding agreements with low exit costs. Conversely, to the extent that states already share fundamental values and long-standing ties, they should have fewer reservations about entering into formal binding agreements.

Their "political markets"—based on common social conventions, shared political cultures, stable policy institutions, and a generalized sense of diffuse reciprocity—should increase confidence that commitments would be kept (Deutsch et al. 1957). The adoption of formal rules and acceptance of binding obligations is indicative of the level of existing trust that disposes states to cooperate in the first place. The above empirical propositions are stated as bivariate relationships although, clearly, actual observed behaviors tend to be more complicated and they result from the interactions among multiple causes (such as those just hypothesized).

The extent to which a state is motivated by liberal or realist impulses can be inferred from the above propositions. What is its stance on the size and heterogeneity of membership in international institutions, the linking or decoupling of issues to be negotiated, and the acceptance or rejection of binding institutions based on majority (rather than unanimity) rules (e.g., S. Chan 2001b; Grieco 1988)? Standard liberal expectations suggest that a smaller and more homogeneous membership promotes cooperation for reasons of selective incentives, greater trust, and the relative ease of detecting and punishing opportunistic behavior. Among parties with relatively equal power, a broader agenda with multiple issues should facilitate cooperation because negotiators can offer side payments and engage in logrolling. Proponents of functionalist logic even argue that successful cooperation in relatively technical matters can spill over to more politicized issues impinging on national sovereignty (e.g., Haas 1958; Mitrany 1976, 1966). This rationale points to integrating rather than compartmentalizing multilateral discussions on economic and security cooperation. Finally, binding commitments—especially those that are backed up by a serious and credible penalty for nonperformance—should promote trust and discourage defection.

As already mentioned, the United States has pursued distinctly different policies in East Asia and Western Europe, preferring bilateralism rather than multilateralism in the former region. It has been also acutely sensitive to any East Asian institution—such as Malaysia's proposal for an East Asian Economic Group—that would exclude it, and has lobbied strongly for Japan to also oppose such proposals, to the extent of threatening to reexamine its security commitments if the United States were to be excluded from East Asian, as distinct from Asia Pacific, regional organizations (Grieco 1999). On the one hand, Washington has preferred to restrict Asia Pacific forums to discussion of economic matters, leaving security coordination or negotiation to either its bilateral alliances or ad hoc groups such as the Six-Party Talks to address North Korea's nuclear program. On the other hand, it has not shied away from issue linkages, as when it attempted to couple the extension of most-favored-nation trading status (despite its label, this treatment actually means normal trading status) with China's record on human rights. Asian countries have generally been sensitive to any perceived attempts to use economic sanctions to challenge their sovereignty or to interfere in their domestic affairs (Moon and Chun 2003). As the weaker side in its relationship with the United States, China has also opposed issue linkages. Its former foreign minister, Qian Qichen, declared that "we do not approve of the practice of linking things which have nothing to do with trade issues" (quoted in Aggarwal 1995, 53).

These remarks caution against the assumption that just because Washington's policies have supported institutionalized multilateralism in Western Europe, it has followed similar policies in East Asia. In contrast to China, which only has an alliance with North Korea, the U.S. emphasis on its hub-and-spokes bilateral relations in East Asia offers a closer parallel to Bismarck's alliances "which did not so much aggregate as immobilize power, playing out in manifold variation a single theme: link everybody to the center so that they remain both tied down and beholden to Berlin" (Joffe 1995, 110). At the same time and in contrast to the United States, China's objective position is more similar to the Second Reich's, which faced the predicament of being "too weak to hold its own, too strong to be left alone" (ibid., 108). This predicament does not apply to the United States, as it is clearly capable of holding its own militarily against all comers.

Moreover and significantly, whereas the United States tried to resolve permanently, not just postpone temporarily, the so-called German problem by helping to integrate and embed Berlin securely in various economic, political, and military institutions of multilateralism (most notably NATO and the European Union), its "hegemonic project in Asia Pacific is more a holding action than a progressive strategy for resolving security problems" (Mastanduno 2003, 156). Specifically, although U.S. policies restrained tension on the Korean peninsula, across the Taiwan Strait, and in Sino-Japanese, Korean-Japanese, and Russo-Japanese relations, Washington has been satisfied with a temporary abatement rather than conclusive settlement of these antagonisms. Indeed, as Michael Mastanduno (ibid., 157) acknowledged forthrightly, "for the United States, an uneasy stalemate is preferable in current circumstances to any attempt at resolution." Rather than acting as a force for cohesion and reconciliation, U.S. policies in East Asia continue to be based on hub-and-spokes and divide-and-rule principles. This phenomenon accounts at least in part for Washington's legitimacy deficit in East Asia as noted by Muthiah Alagappa (2003b, 93): "Though America's preponderant power is widely acknowledged and the United States plays a critical role in almost every major Asian conflict (Taiwan, Korea, Kashmir), such preponderance and role have not translated into authority."

Such policy proclivities associated traditionally with the practice of Bismarckian diplomacy do not necessarily distinguish the United States from China. For instance, just prior to visiting Malaysia and Indonesia in April 2011, Chinese Premier Wen Jiabao reiterated Beijing's preference for resolving its maritime disputes bilaterally rather than multilaterally, stating that "We disapprove of referring bilateral disputes to multilateral forums because it will only make the disputes bigger and more complicated" (quoted in *South China Morning Post*, April 27, 2011, A5). Recognizing such shared proclivities should curtail the impulse to present the United States as a force for liberal institutionalism and to exaggerate the differences between Beijing and Washington. To the extent that other states are not entirely reassured by their perceptions of both Chinese and American motives, it is not a foregone conclusion that they will automatically join one to balance against the other. In a potential conflict between the United States and China over Taiwan, it is not clear that Southeast Asian countries, and even traditional U.S. allies like Australia, Japan, and South Korea, would necessarily join the fray on the U.S. side (Carpenter 2005; Kang 2003b, 2003c, 2003/04, 2007b; Layne 2009a).

Open regionalism means that there are low barriers to entry but also an easy and low-cost exit option. Fewer and less powerful restraints—such as heavy institutional investment, collateral impact on other relations, reputational damage, and so on—work to bind the relevant countries to each other. This implication is in turn important for the problem of commitment. In the absence of these "ties that bind," what is there to discourage defection and cheating—opportunistic behavior that would be more inhibited when a small, select group of like-minded states interacts across a wide range of issues and over a long period of time?

In contrast to countries in the North Atlantic area adopting multilateralism as an institutional form, those in East Asia have followed a different approach to building trust and discouraging opportunism. This approach reflects the ideas behind self-enforcing arrangements, reflecting and based primarily on strong, interlocking commercial interests that have emerged among these countries. The development and consolidation of these self-enforcing arrangements are inseparable from the widespread adoption of a regime strategy that assigns priority to national economic development, one that is based on an internationalist outlook of integration with the regional and global economy.

## Self-Enforcing Agreements

The discussion thus far has addressed formal institutions, or at least regular multilateral forums, such as ASEAN, APT, APEC, and ARF. Existing studies on regionalism in East Asia or the Asia Pacific have documented how such institutions or forums have opened channels for dialogue and contributed to building some mutual confidence. There can, however, be a more subtle and important form of regionalism occurring that does not necessarily involve direct and overt government intervention and diplomatic coordination, as featured typically in the existing literature, including this chapter's discussion thus far.

Regionalism can develop among civil societies buttressed by cultural and economic exchanges such as tourism, trade, and investment. There is a long tradition of this "communication" approach to regionalism, starting with the classic work by Deutsch and colleagues (1957) on the North Atlantic security community. Others (e.g., Frankel 1993; Petri 1993) have studied East Asia's historic merchandise trade forming an interlocking network of commercial interests. The development of multinational production chains, cross-holdings of currencies and debt instruments, intricate and extensive subcontracting and coproduction arrangements, and massive foreign direct investment involving China, however, are relatively recent phenomena. China's relative exposure and importance to the global and regional economy can be gauged roughly by two statistics. Gary Hufbauer and Yee Wong (2004, 2–3) reported that China's trade as a percentage of its gross domestic product (GDP) was 56 in 2002. By comparison, this ratio (imports plus exports divided by GDP) was about 22% for both Japan and the United States. China's openness to foreign direct investment (FDI) was also higher. The stock of FDI stood at 35% of its GDP in that year—compared to 2% for Japan and 13% for the United States. Therefore, China has been much more open to foreign trade and investment, and it has been more important to its commercial partners given its economic size.

These linkages take different forms and routes such that, for example, China has become the largest destination of Taiwan's and South Korea's outbound investment capital. Chinese original-equipment manufacturers have developed deep relationships with large U.S. retailers such as Walmart, and large U.S.-based multinationals such as General Motors and MacDonald's have acquired an important stake in the Chinese consumer market. China is also a major assembler of parts and components imported from Hong Kong, Taiwan, and South Korea, and the final assembled products are shipped to the United States and Europe. Overseas Chinese communities in Hong Kong,

Taiwan, and Southeast Asia have historically financed much of the smaller and more labor-intensive manufacturing in China, but these collaborations, such as those involving petrochemical plants and semiconductor manufacturing, have increased in capital scale and technology content. With China's heavy investments in its physical infrastructure and basic industries comes a rising demand for raw materials from abroad. It has become a major importer of crude oil from the Middle East and minerals from Australia and Africa. China has taken a leading role in the currency swap arrangement launched by the Chiang Mai Initiative, and it has accumulated the world's largest amount of U.S. debt, as already discussed in Chapter 5. As a final example, an estimated 400,000 Koreans and nearly two million Taiwanese, mostly businesspeople and their families, have taken up residence in China.

Some of these linkages (e.g., currency swaps) directly involve official action or sponsorship. For most other linkages, governments are more of a background factor. Whatever may be the sources for these increasingly strong cross-border linkages, they are consequential for developing and consolidating regionalism. They forge interconnections that ensure that damages done to one pair of bilateral relations would inevitably have negative ripple effects on third parties. Therefore, for example, U.S. trade sanctions against China would also hurt Washington's formal or informal allies (e.g., Taiwan, South Korea, Australia) as well as U.S. companies doing business with or in China. Similarly, Chinese military action against Taiwan would have negative economic and financial reverberations beyond their bilateral ties. Such action would likely scare away foreign investors, drive up the price of commodities, and cause currency, equity, and real estate values to fall—not just across the Strait, but regionally and even globally. Economic and financial interdependence therefore expands the number of parties interested in regional stability.

The interdependent relationships just described do not fit the standard meaning of multilateralism in terms of building intergovernmental institutions. They refer mainly to promoting economic and financial ties that enhance shared interests and mutual stakes, as well as the implied opportunity costs of disrupting these ties. The expansion and deepening of these ties, however, are not inconsequential for building confidence among the pertinent states and even in promoting a common outlook among their elites, or in influencing mass attitudes toward important commercial partners. Several lines of argument from the literature on international political economy are germane to this claim. I discuss in this section why credible commitment is important and how self-enforcing arrangements can contribute to credible commitment.

Even though they may benefit from cooperation, states often fail to cooperate because they do not trust each other to actually execute an agreement. Suspicion that the other side will renege or behave opportunistically after an agreement has been reached prevents cooperation from being achieved in the first place. Thus, an inability to offer *ex ante* assurance for compliance with agreements stands in the way of cooperation (Fearon 1995). This issue of credible commitment is especially serious in a dynamic environment involving power shifts. One or more of the contracting parties may abandon it or revise the terms unilaterally in the future, when they may have improved their relative power.

In domestic transactions, conventions such as money deposits in an escrow account and the threat of lawsuits for breach of contract provide protection against cheating, defection, and other kinds of opportunistic behavior. Lacking a supranational authority capable of catching and punishing states that renege, international relations depend on other mechanisms for enforcement and indeed, for conveying a serious intention to abide by agreements so that such disclosure of commitment would enable agreements to be reached in the first place. Self-enforcing agreements provide such a mechanism. Contracts or arrangements are self-enforcing when the punishment for noncompliance is simply the termination of the exchange or cooperation itself. Each party to such an agreement can abrogate it unilaterally, and the threat of ending an otherwise rewarding relationship serves as a deterrent against opportunistic behavior. Thus, a tacit understanding not to raise armament is self-enforcing when each side can increase its defense spending in retaliation against the other side's aggression. Self-enforcing agreements overcome the problems of commitment and enforcement by "making the expected future benefits of continued compliance to serve as the bond" (Yarbrough and Yarbrough 1986, 18).

The commitments offered and the expectations of future benefits need not be explicit or written into formal documents. All that is needed is that the parties involved are aware of the relevant context, including gestures intended to signal trust and assurances against future breaches of contract—even those that are based on merely informal understanding or implicit bargains. In international trade, investing in specialized manufacturing facilities intended for a particular foreign market offers a parallel to escrow accounts or earnest-money deposits in the domestic context. Beth and Robert Yarbrough (1992) gave the example of Japanese automobile manufacturers' investment in machines and equipment dedicated to meeting U.S. safety and environmental standards. To the extent that these machines and equipment were developed to serve uniquely the U.S. market, Japanese producers would have forfeited this sunk cost if they should be banned from making U.S. sales in the future. That this investment would then become unsalvageable offers a compelling gesture of credible commitment not to cheat on trade agreements. Canada's regulations on the size of various merchandise containers offer another albeit less expensive stipulation for what is tantamount to a good-faith requirement for selling to its consumers.

Seen in this light, Taiwan's investment in China, the long-term contracts signed between China and its trade partners, and China's accumulation of U.S. debts also suggest important instances of making a major commitment to cordial relations. They suggest various forms of "hostage giving" and "hostage taking"—that is, voluntary submission to costly penalties should bilateral relations deteriorate. Thus, for instance, to the extent that Taiwan-owned operations in China have become embedded in the production chains and retail networks there, these investments represent sunk costs that are practically unsalvageable should there be a political rupture across the Strait. To the extent that third parties would also suffer serious consequences in the event of a breakdown, they provide additional assurances against the risk of these relations becoming unhinged. These third parties include firms operating in Taiwan that have become tied to businesses in China as parts or equipment suppliers, importers of finished products assembled in China, and institutions that made loans to and investments in those companies with a large financial exposure in China. They encompass both sovereign and nonsovereign entities, such as those states and overseas Chinese communities in Southeast Asia that have a vested stake as suppliers, consumers, co-owners, or lenders and investors in these joint operations. They also include large U.S. institutional investors and multinational firms that have acquired a direct or indirect stake in cross-Strait commerce.

It bears repeating that the linkages just described do not entail a written *quid pro quo* or even a formal declaration of intent, as in a trade agreement or defense treaty. When huge commercial stakes involving large power asymmetries occur and when the pertinent states condone or at least do not act decisively to limit such enmeshment, their action or inaction sends a strong message that suggests their commitment to keep good relations. There is a large literature debating whether international economic interdependence, especially trade, actually causes peace among states (e.g., Barbieri 2002; Mansfield and Pollins 2003; Oneal and Russett 1997; Pollins 1989; Russett and Oneal 2001). As several scholars have suggested (Gartzke 2003; Morrow 2003; Reed 2003; Stein 2003), commerce should be "endogenized"—that is, it should be analyzed not just as an influence on political relations but also as a reflection, consequence, and even harbinger of these relations.

States that are inclined to maintain peaceful relations are more likely to trade with or invest in each other in the first place. Their decision to trade and to get into deep and wide commercial interactions is itself strong evidence that they do not expect future conflict. States and businesspeople would surely not run this risk if they saw conflict looming on the horizon. My argument goes further by claiming that intense and especially asymmetric commercial ties signify a serious and credible commitment to maintain good relations, and that the existence and enlargement of these ties provide a strong enabling condition for political and even security cooperation to proceed. They render defection and opportunism costlier than they would be otherwise, and this very costliness serves as a warrant or bond for forging and even expanding cooperation.

This discussion accords with a more nuanced view of balancing policies. Niou, Ordeshook, and Rose (1989, 316) remarked that these policies are reflected not just in overt observable behavior, but that "the underlying dynamics of the balance of power are driven also by a complex set of potential threats and counterthreats of alliance." Officials and businesspeople are strategic and anticipatory, so that "threats and counters need not be explicitly embodied in formally signed agreements . . . " Consequently, "we can understand the operation of balance of power not merely in terms of the alliances we observe, but also in terms of all feasible alliances." The possibilities for alliances and, in the above discussion, commercial arrangements to be formed and dissolved, are implied by circumstances even though they may not actually materialize. Moreover, the intensity of commercial linkages and the severity of the implied costs should there be a rupture are harbingers for closer collaboration in political and even security matters. These commercial linkages can therefore communicate the potential for future alignment.

The imagery of taking and giving hostages may be graphic but is not much different from the nuclear deterrence strategy of mutual assured destruction. The Anti-Ballistic Missile Treaty between the United States and the Soviet Union deliberately left all but one of their respective population centers unprotected from the other side's nuclear retaliation. By deliberately exposing these unprotected civilian targets to the other side's countervalue strike in the event of a nuclear war, they contribute to their counterpart's deterrence threat and, in so doing, demonstrate a credible commitment not to precipitate a nuclear confrontation. In this case, there is a bilateral exchange of "hostages."

Rising economic interdependence in the Asia Pacific multilateralizes these hostage exchanges. An American boycott of Chinese-made products would also hurt Taiwan's and South Korea's business interests.

Current and ongoing trends in the Asia Pacific point to deepening and widening financial and economic linkages. When combined with China's rapidly growing economy, they foster self-enforcing regional arrangements. The cooperative relationships in this form of regionalism are self-enforcing because they do not require some external or higher authority to adjudicate disputes or punish opportunistic behavior. The forfeiture of sunk investments (in both tangible assets and intangible goodwill) and of prospective gains from future cooperation encourages self-restraint and fosters mutual confidence. Self-enforcing arrangements enable cooperation to develop in the first place by communicating credible commitment in the form of giving or taking expensive hostages, and they sustain subsequent cooperation by offering the prospects of even greater returns from future cooperation. To the extent that states' current discounted value of these future benefits from continued cooperation exceeds their expected benefits from opportunistic behavior, they are self-motivated to refrain from upsetting bilateral and regional stability.

Contrary to realists' emphasis on relative gains, such concerns should not prevent cooperation. Robert Powell (1999) showed persuasively that even in the unlikely event that all the gains go to one side of an exchange, the disadvantaged side could still benefit indirectly because, as a result of its counterpart acquiring a greater stake in maintaining the status quo, it could spend less on its military and more on consumption. Furthermore, although many realists are concerned that uneven economic gains can have security externalities, James Morrow (1997) argued persuasively that such externalities are relatively minor and should therefore be easy to offset because states typically spend less than 5% of their economic product on their military during peacetime. Most importantly, however, the credibility and effectiveness of self-enforcing arrangements based on economic interdependence depend on the priority assigned by the pertinent regimes to economic performance. These self-enforcing arrangements are credible and effective precisely because this policy emphasis has become entrenched across the region and in the pertinent countries' domestic political economy. Backsliding would jeopardize both international and domestic bargains—threatening those vested economic interests that would suffer from market closure, a shift from civilian to defense spending, and higher taxes and inflation.

Processes that incline states to assign greater importance to the shadow of the future, mentioned in discussing Axelrod's (1984) tit-for-tat model in

Chapter 5, tend to sustain cooperation and discourage defection. Moreover, the greater the contagion of these processes among those countries involved in multilateral interactions (such as in adopting and even internalizing a model of elite legitimacy pivoted on economic performance as discussed in Chapter 4), the more likely, deeply, and pervasively are such processes to embed themselves in regional processes. In a world populated largely by those who practice tit for tat—that is, by those who are nice, optimistic, forgiving, and yet provokable—cooperation and stability prevail and benefit all.

This tendency becomes stronger as it attracts more and more adherents. Moreover, the more inclined officials are to assign a large value to future returns—that is, the less they discount these prospective returns—the greater their inclination to cooperate. These prospective gains give all concerned parties a greater stake in the existing order, thereby relaxing the security effects of power shifts. Stated alternatively, the security dangers associated with power shifts are mitigated by increasing the incentives for all concerned, but especially for the rising power, to stand by existing arrangements or at least to modify these arrangements by peaceful means rather than military confrontation. A rising power's relative gain in capabilities—a variable singled out by balance-of-power theorists to suggest a state's ability to change the current system—may be accompanied by changes in its motivation because it is drawing greater benefits from the current system. These greater benefits give it a greater stake and hence a stronger incentive in perpetuating rather than challenging this system. This latter supposition is, after all, the rationale behind the standard assumption that the hegemon is committed to the status quo.

## Communicating Through Market Signals

Rising financial and economic linkages can contribute to effective communication and thus regional peace and stability in another way. Effective communication is important because states often misjudge each other's resolve and stake in a dispute. This misjudgment can cause military confrontations as, for example, when Washington dismissed Beijing's warnings that it would intervene in the Korean War. In order to convince the other side that it is highly resolved and has a large stake in a dispute, a state often undertakes military action to distinguish itself from those that only pretend to be highly resolved and to have a large stake. It undertakes costly and risky actions, such as military mobilization and display of force, because those that are just bluffing would not have been willing to pay the same costs and run the same risks. Yet taking costly and risky actions to demonstrate one's high resolve and strong preference can be dangerous. As spiral models of conflict escalation warn, military actions intended to serve this purpose can trigger countermobilization and reciprocal display. The ensuing situation could end in a game of chicken, setting the disputants on a collision course.

Rising financial and economic interdependence among states offers them an alternate and less dangerous way to signal their resolve and felt stake in a dispute (Gartzke and Li 2003a, 2003b; Gartzke, Li, and Boehmer 2001). Instead of resorting to military means, they can take actions that they know have market-destabilizing effects. They can take such costly actions in order to demonstrate their resolve and commitment so that they can separate or distinguish themselves from others that are less resolved and committed to their goal. The latter type would be hesitant to take actions that would roil the financial markets, thereby causing severe economic costs to themselves by precipitating the panicked selling of stocks, raising interest rates and commodity prices, reducing consumer confidence, and causing job losses.

Thus, as a result of rising financial and economic interdependence, officials can now deliberately trigger these economic costs to communicate their intentions and preferences in a conflict situation. The more they are willing to scare investors and jeopardize existing financial and commercial ties, the more credible are their professed intentions and preferences. The credibility of their actions also derives from the fact that economic costs are often imposed by self-regarding third parties (such as stock and bond traders) whose primary and perhaps only interest is in making money and preserving capital. Unlike government officials, these other actors do not have anything to gain by engaging in political posturing. Their expected reaction to officials' actions is "bound to carry the most credibility with observers" because all that is required is for these third parties to follow their own egoist incentives in responding to the political information made available by officials (Gartzke and Li 2003b, 567).

Naturally, when leaders avoid actions that can cause adverse market reactions, their self-restraint can also be informative. Such behavior may contradict their professed preferences or declared intentions, making them just "talk the talk, but not walk the walk." Whether due to its unwillingness or its inability, Taiwan's government under the former administration of Chen Shui-bian did not act to limit the island's increasing commercial ties with and economic dependence on China. As discussed in Chapter 5, this behavior in turn suggests that this government has subordinated its ostensible goal of political independence to the priority of Taiwan's economic growth and stability (Benson and Niou 2007; S. Chan 2009).

Such non-occurrence of the expected is significant. It is also worth noting that despite its unhappiness with Lee Teng-hui and Chen Shui-bian, who are widely perceived to favor Taiwan's independence, Beijing has by and large refrained from retaliating against Taiwan's business interests in China (Kastner 2009). Any such retaliation would scare away future investors, and hurt those interest groups in Taiwan most disposed to support reunification. This treatment of "hostages" by Beijing and, as discussed in the previous paragraph, hostage giving by Taipei, are significant in communicating credible commitment. Additionally, government inaction in these cases—what they have not done to impede or harm cross-Strait commerce—is as significant as what they have actually said or done.

Whether a government goes against interest groups representing its important constituents can disclose the intensity of its preferences or resolve. To the extent that the Democratic Progressive Party (DPP) headed by Chen Shui-bian drew its electoral support disproportionately from farmers, employers of labor-intensive operations, and small and medium-sized enterprises in the domestic service industry, it should have a powerful incentive to restrict cross-Strait commerce and to undertake protectionism to shield these supporters from Chinese competition. One would not have been surprised if it had limited cross-Strait commerce in the context of its partisan base and its professed political agenda. But, as mentioned at the outset of this chapter, the fact that it did not do so is significant given the relevant context. This inaction implies that the DPP's pro-independence statements are more likely rhetoric intended for domestic consumption or political "hot air" designed to energize partisan mobilization (S. Chan 2009). A highly resolved pro-independence government would not have subjected itself to the increasing vulnerability of being politically set up—that is, to have submitted itself to the risk of being held up politically as a result of Taiwan's increasing economic dependence on China. If it were truly serious about advancing its pro-independence agenda, it would have preferred to pay the economic costs of terminating this dependence now rather than incur a heavier penalty later.

To offer another example that is related to the discussion in Chapter 5, if Beijing were to behave in such a way that its statements or actions seriously roiled the financial markets, causing the value of the U.S. dollar to drop and interest rates to rise, this behavior would communicate important information about China's preferences, resolve, and intentions—even without engaging in any military action. The more China's economy and its ownership of dollar-denominated assets would suffer as a result of this behavior, the more these self-imposed costs would suggest that Beijing is not bluffing.

Parenthetically, this discussion should not be taken to suggest that governments refrain from administering occasional shocks to ongoing commercial relations. They do. It is, however, important to once again take context into consideration. It is one thing for Washington to limit the import of Chinese steel or tires, and another for it to ban the export of U.S. aircraft or satellite technology to China. The former actions are more likely intended to advance domestic protectionist interests, whereas, by imposing self-denying costs, the latter are more likely to be motivated by national security concerns. Given their political bases, it would be more noteworthy if a Republican administration were to impose limits on the import of Chinese garments and the export of American grain than if similar actions were to be taken by a Democratic administration. A willingness to suffer not just economic costs but also a serious loss of partisan support and political popularity helps to separate the sincere types from those who are engaging in public posturing or rent-seeking.

## Further Discussion

An inability to make credible commitments and to effectively communicate one's intentions and preferences hampers cooperation or the settlement of disputes, even when the relevant parties can gain from an improvement in their relationship. I have argued in this chapter that although intergovernmental institutions appear to have made only slow and limited progress in fostering multilateral coordination and promoting norms of mutual adjustment in East Asia, less noticed but more important progress has been made in constructing regionalism based on burgeoning financial and economic interactions among the countries in this region and, more broadly, in the Asia Pacific.

These interactions entail large and tangible sunk costs that project a commitment to good and stable relations, and they also provide a basis for further cooperation by offering the prospect for even more mutual gains in the future. The expected benefits from continued cooperation provide an effective self-enforcing mechanism against opportunistic behavior. The U.S. experience with free trade is instructive because domestic rent-seeking behavior, partisan politics, and special distribution coalitions should have worked against it. Bailey, Goldstein, and Weingast (1997) showed that the 1934 Reciprocal Trade Agreement Act strengthened the interests of exporters and that the benefits of exports, in turn, strengthened these interest groups' and their political representatives' support for and commitment to free trade. The history of U.S. trade policy therefore exemplifies a self-sustaining and self-reinforcing process. Earlier, I mentioned that in an era of globalization, the multilateralization of defense industries makes it practically difficult for advanced democracies to go to war against one another. Cross-border production arrangements, subcontracting relations, and shared ownership of assets that stem from burgeoning trade and investment in the Asia Pacific region do not have a similar direct effect on national security. Nevertheless, they serve as an important basis and impetus for cooperation.

In the absence of financial and economic linkages, such as in the case of U.S.–North Korean relations, officials have to resort to political or military actions to demonstrate their intentions and preferences. However, as I remarked earlier, political statements can be discounted and even dismissed as empty talk, and military displays and mobilization can be dangerous in that they can trigger an unwanted escalation. Financial and economic linkages present another way to communicate. They help to distinguish those statements and actions that are intended for domestic consumption or partisan gains from others that reflect a sincere and serious commitment to a particular foreign policy course. As Erik Gartzke and Quan Li (2003a, 131) remarked, "the interdependence of state and market makes leaders' talk costly and hence, more credible. Leaders engaged in political competition must choose between making competitive political claims and appeasing market concerns about stability and profitability."

In a world of mobile capital, flexible production, and hypersensitive currency and bond markets, officials cannot make idle political or military threats without at the same time causing adverse market reactions. This *ex ante* cost imposed by the market presents a disincentive for leaders who would otherwise try to misrepresent themselves. By making this misrepresentation costlier, market forces put pressure on officials to reveal their true preferences and intentions. Thus, as a consequence of the very large commercial stake that Taiwan has acquired in trading with and investing in China, outside observers— including officials in Beijing—are now in a better position to discern the extent to which Taipei is truly committed to the objective of political independence. They can discern Taiwan officials' motivation and resolve by watching the extent to which they are willing to antagonize their investors and hurt the island's economic performance, which has become closely linked to China.

Although cross-Strait relations offer the most salient example, my general argument applies also to other members of the Asia Pacific region. Chapter 3 showed that intra-Asia trade is rising, and Asia Pacific countries are turning increasingly to China as the hub of a powerful regional economy. Notwithstanding the common perception of slow and even stunted institutional development, deepening and widening financial and economic relations have increasingly tied these countries in a network of intertwined interests and shared stakes. Regionalism is advancing beyond the context of official forums and summit meetings, and it is taking shape in a manner distinct from

Washington's institution-building efforts immediately after World War II. Yet, the self-enforcing financial and economic arrangements developing in today's Asia Pacific are having similar effects in encouraging self-restraint and mutual restraint, promoting the associational and cooperative dynamic of international relations. They are inseparable from and critically dependent on the region-wide emphasis on economic growth as a policy priority, and on an internationalist strategy of development that has distinguished East Asian countries from those in the Middle East. In these relations we see the interlocking nature of international and domestic bargains that buttress and sustain regional stability and cooperation.

# 8

# Conclusion

It has been remarked that international relations theories, including balance-of-power theories, have been heavily influenced by Western historical experiences and perspectives. It has also been said that ideas do not flow freely (Risse-Kappen 1994). These two observations combined point to the phenomenon that scholars also act as idea entrepreneurs and cultural ambassadors. Their theories not only seek to explain empirically but also construct meaning for that which is to be explained, reminding one of Alexander Wendt's (1992) much-quoted remark that anarchy is what states make of it. Popular theories moreover help to frame policy discourse, giving some ideas greater legitimacy and even "obviousness" than others. Accordingly, people's analyses are not always objective, as the social sciences aspire to be. Indeed, as mentioned in Chapter 2, ideas like balance of power have been used as a symbol or justification to advance or defend policies. Such usage is not independent of a country's history or its international position. As Ido Oren (2003) observed, national origin and historical context matter in the evolution of scholarship and scholarly disciplines.

Balance-of-power theories have presented an important, perhaps even the dominant, perspective on international relations. Few proponents of this perspective would contest these observations: that states balance against the most powerful among them, especially the one that threatens to gain hegemony over them; that power is primarily a matter of possessing tangible (or material) assets, especially military capabilities; and that the United States is by far the most powerful country in the contemporary world, having indeed attained the position of a unipole. Balance-of-power theorists tend to accept these observations as the central tenets or incontrovertible facts defining the reality of international relations. When writing about China's recent relative power gains, U.S. analysts often do not apply the same analytic logic to Washington's own power and its actions toward other states, including China. Their tendency to compartmentalize international relations and to treat China as an isolated entity is troubling because it slices reality into congenial portions, thus avoiding possible contradictions to their conclusions presented by a larger empirical or historical picture.

Why should states be more concerned about rising Chinese power than extant American preponderance? This question is often not raised, or is only implied by variables outside the realist tradition, such as the democratic-peace theory (e.g., S. Chan 1997, 2010b; Doyle 1983a, 1983b; Russett and Oneal 2001). My criticism does not deny plausible material explanations for why states may react differently to Chinese and American power, such as those mentioned previously about an overwhelming preponderance discouraging balancing attempts (e.g., Brooks and Wohlforth 2008; Jervis 2009), maritime powers being less threatening than continental powers (e.g., Levy and Thompson 2005, 2010; Ross 1999, 2009b), and regional and global systems being characterized by different power dynamics (e.g., Lemke 2002; Levy 2008a; Ross 2004). These plausible explanations should be more fully developed.

They have to confront some seeming historical departures, such as the repeated military challenges to Chinese hegemony mounted by the *Xiongnu*, other states' reactions to Portuguese, Dutch, Venetian, and Japanese maritime power, and the absence of collective blocking action directed against the United States in its bid for continental hegemony in North America and subsequently regional hegemony in the Western Hemisphere. Moreover, if the United States has become too preponderant for other states to balance against it now, why did they not act earlier? Those variables just mentioned, even when considered in combination with others such as bipolarity, cannot quite explain international peace or stability in a larger historical context. For instance, the analytic combination of bipolarity and sea/land power cannot account for the relations between Athens and Sparta, between Carthage and Rome, or Japan's relations with its continental neighbors Korea, China, and Russia/the Soviet Union from the late 1800s until the end of World War II. These relations between a sea power and a land power, under conditions of approximate local bipolarity, ended in major wars.

Nor is it so obvious how bipolarity or maritime status should be determined empirically. Why should one consider the Cold War a bipolar period if the United States—not to mention the Western coalition led by it—had always enjoyed an overwhelming capability edge over the Soviet Union and its allies? The Soviet economy only came close to being half the size that of the United States, and the combined NATO countries were three to five times stronger than their Warsaw Pact counterparts. The Soviets could only claim a rough parity with the Americans in military capabilities. But if military parity is what defines bipolarity, why should one consider the current East Asian system to be characterized by bipolarity since the United States clearly has an overwhelming military advantage over China? According to the power-transition theory, a rising power must have at least 80% of the leading country's capabilities in order to be considered a potential challenger. China's current military capability is much less than that level when compared to that of the United States, and it is not likely to approach that level in the near future. As to distinguishing between a maritime and continental power, how should imperial Spain with its possessions in the New World or Japan with its "East Asia Co-Prosperity Sphere" be labeled? Or France's pursuit of both land and sea power in the eighteenth century? Should the United States be considered a continental power in its rivalry with Britain during the nineteenth century?

In the discourse on balance-of-power theories, ideas and concepts can be used in confusing and inconsistent ways so that words such as "balance" can mean their opposite, adjectives such as "status-quo" or "revisionist" are sometimes treated as fixed national characters rather than varying motivations, and different labels can be applied to the same behavior (and the same label can sometimes be applied to different behaviors) depending on the proper name of the country being discussed.

For example, Neville Chamberlain's policies have been commonly described as appeasement, but few in the West have labeled Mikhail Gorbachev's policies as such—contrary to popular opinion in Russia. Given its precarious security, North Korea's nuclear armament represents a *prima facie* instance of internal balancing, but few U.S. analysts have used the balance-of-power logic to explain Pyongyang's behavior. Some states are said to have accommodated and even bandwagoned with a rising China when their foreign policies have become more closely aligned with Beijing. Accommodation and bandwagoning, however, are not typically the vocabulary used by the same analysts when describing states that have become more closely aligned with the United States. They are described instead as joining the United States in "balancing" against China (or the Soviet Union previously), even though China (or the former Soviet Union) is (was) weaker than the United States. Because they sided with the stronger side (the United States), these states' behavior should have been seen as bandwagoning with the United States rather than balancing "with" the United States—as far as the logic of balance-of-power theories is concerned. Their behavior should have been counted as a contradiction of these theorists' expectations. The leading scholar on offensive realism can write about China's "unpeaceful rise" (Mearsheimer 2006), when this theory should have pointed to the United States as its "poster child" (Layne 2003), and being the unrivalled hegemon, "its ambitions [should have] expanded as its relative power increased" (Layne 2009b, 149).

As already mentioned, balance-of-power theories are sometimes invoked in addressing China's recent reemergence as a major regional power without, however, at the same time scrutinizing the logic for the concurrent U.S. rise to unprecedented global primacy and Washington's earlier mastery of regional hegemony in the Western Hemisphere (S. Chan 2008a). These parallel developments are often overlooked. Moreover, although packaged as balance-of-power theories, many who write about China's rise are really interested in power-transition theory, which hypothesizes that, contrary to balance-of-power theories, war is more likely to occur between two leading states when the power balance between them becomes *more* equalized, with their respective power trajectories being determined endogenously due primarily to domestic factors rather than exogenously due to other states' balancing policies (e.g., Levy 2008a).

This book makes broad claims about theory as well as policy. On theory, it argues that neither historical outcomes nor historical processes have generally conformed to balance-of-power theories. Hierarchy has repeatedly asserted itself over anarchy so that, for example, Rome, the Qin Dynasty, the Inca Empire, imperial China, Britain, and the United States have at one time or another successfully established regional or global hegemony. As for historical processes, evidence of internal and/or external balancing tends to be limited or needs to be heavily qualified in various episodes such as with respect to attempts by states to block or undermine the rise of the Persian empire, the Spanish conquest of the New World, China's traditional hegemony in East Asia, collective action against Napoleon's France and Hitler's Germany, and the primacy of the United States in the Western Hemisphere and its current global preponderance. On policy, this book claims that balancing policies emphasizing armament and alliances entail significant opportunity costs and can trigger a spiral of competition and recrimination that works to the detriment of all those caught in this process.

Thus, balancing policies can be both self-fulfilling in predicting a negative state of affairs and self-defeating in bringing about this state of affairs. East

Asian states have generally turned away from balancing policies as traditionally prescribed by balance-of-power theories, and have instead pursued a policy emphasizing economic performance based on expanding and deepening their economic relations. In contrast, Washington has given more emphasis to armament and alliances, and yet, because the United States is by far the world's strongest power, it is difficult to describe its policies as "balancing." It would be more accurate to say that they have the intent and effect of maintaining and even furthering the large *imbalance* that favors it currently, especially in terms of military assets and alliance networking.

Among the conclusions and conjectures offered by the preceding chapters, four claims bear repeating. First, balance-of-power expectations are not supported by the behavior of China's neighbors over time and by their physical location. One of the most elementary procedures for making causal inferences is to discern whether a change in the outcome variable has occurred after a putative cause (the experimental variable) has been introduced. Have China's neighbors increased their observable efforts at internal or external balancing after China's economy started to take off? They have not. In fact, their armament and alignment behavior has generally changed in the opposite direction, declining (or holding steady) during the years when China has been making relative power gains. Moreover, contrary to the expectation that states located closer to China should be more threatened by rising Chinese power and should therefore feel more compelled to take up balancing against it, they have not done so. If anything, Taiwan and South Korea have become more closely aligned with China despite their proximity to it.

The analytic weight of these observations comes from broad patterns rather than anecdotal evidence, and reflects convergence from multiple indicators of attitudes and behavior. Because one should always be wary of premature rejection of a general hypothesis based on data from a single country (China), historical comparisons with other countries' experiences would be warranted. Has the concomitant rise to global preponderance by the United States produced balancing reactions from the other states and conversely, has the precipitous decline of the Soviet Union/Russia caused its neighbors and the United States to relax their search for armament and alliances? That the answers to these questions tend to be negative should again be disappointing to balance-of-power theorists.

Second, China's relative power gains have stemmed from its economic expansion. China's recent ascent in the international power hierarchy occurred in a wider regional context, and has reflected a broader phenomenon whereby most East Asian countries have been on the economic fast track (Japan in recent years and North Korea for some time now are two prominent exceptions). The fundamental reason for this phenomenon has been a pervasive acceptance of economic performance as the most important national priority by these countries' elites. This basic policy orientation, pivoting regime legitimacy and even national security on sustaining economic growth based on interdependence, has lowered regional tension and fostered cooperation and prosperity.

The success of this orientation has inclined even those that were once skeptical to join this widening and deepening network of interlocking commercial and financial interests. The longer this process continues and the more time various national and regional institutions have to entrench themselves, the more difficult it is to revert to a world of competitive armament and rival blocs. Again, significantly, the ongoing power shifts—involving not just China, but the East Asian region as a whole—are driven by economic forces and policies. To the extent that balance-of-power theorists have traditionally focused on military capabilities as a source or measure of national power and to the extent that they continue to do so, they are likely to misjudge the evolving nature of national competitiveness in a globalized world.

Third, balance-of-threat theorists would counsel states to practice self-restraint lest their ambitions arouse other states' opposition. Moreover, there are limits to even what a preponderant hegemon can achieve (Bacevich 2008). Because the exercise of power is more effective and efficient in the long run when it is perceived to be legitimate by others, a powerful state can influence others' perceptions by reassuring them about its benign intentions and cooperative disposition. It can communicate to others that it will "play by the rules," even while not foreswearing the advantages of its superior power.

The associational logic of balance of power points to the importance of self-restraint by the powerful. It is after all the powerful that can really hurt the other states. Paradoxically, as a country becomes more powerful, it tends to become less trusting of others—as it is more able to get what it wants by fighting or threatening to do so. Yet self-restraint by a powerful state, when it could have its way but chooses not to do so by flexing its muscle, is most telling about its true character as the peaceful or cooperative type, or its opposite. It also stands to reason that the more powerful a state is, the more it can afford to be generous with others because its concessions and compromises are less likely to jeopardize its security or undermine its hegemonic status. Conversely, the more demanding and begrudging it is perceived by others, the less goodwill and trust it is likely to engender. A disposition to be other-regarding, to reassure others, and to build their trust is no less compelling for China than it is for the United States. Both can do more by, among other things, embedding themselves institutionally and economically in multilateral arrangements. When the strong resort to the rhetoric of balancing or undertake coercive action against the weak—such as when China threatens Taiwan or when the United States talks about containing China—their behavior conveys the opposite impression, and belies the logic of balance-of-power theories because the strong should already feel more secure as a result of their preponderant power.

Fourth and related to the above three observations, intra-Asian commerce has taken off. Deepening economic interdependence has offered both a bond and a harbinger for regional cooperation and stable relations. There has been a significant and ongoing shift of economic orientation among states in the region so that they are now more important to each other and, concomitantly, less dependent on the United States as a source of capital or as a market for their exports. China has displaced the United States as the leading trade partner for Japan, South Korea, and Taiwan. This trend, as I have argued earlier, provides motivation for continued cooperation by promising even greater returns in the future. By raising the opportunity costs of armament and alliances, it has concomitantly dampened incentives to engage in balancing. Interlocking economic interests and stakes constitute an effective and multilateral arrangement for self-enforcing cooperation.

Although this book is supposed to be about China's reemergence as a major regional power, the Soviet Union's demise is instructive for two reasons. First, this event stemmed not from Moscow's military incapacity or submission to foreign conquest but rather from its domestic economic decay and loss of regime popularity. In other words, the fall of the Soviet empire resulted not from the failure to undertake balancing policies but rather because the excessive pursuit of armament and alliances sapped its economic capacity, bankrupted its treasury, and caused a severe loss of mass legitimacy and confidence. This fact underscores this book's basic premise that domestic politics and calculations, especially the East Asian countries' model of elite legitimacy and regime survival pivoting on economic performance, have important consequences for foreign relations, specifically the relative absence of behavior predicted and prescribed traditionally by balance-of-power theories in these countries' response to a rising China. Naturally, a regime's choice of foreign policies, such as whether it decides to pursue armament and alliances, will also have domestic political and economic consequences.

Second, Russia's neighbors have not become more reassured by its reduced power. After the Soviet Union's demise, East and Central European states joined NATO and became more closely aligned with the United States, a behavior that can only be described as bandwagoning and not balancing. It should count as a disconfirmation of balance-of-power theories. Stephen Walt (1988, 277) wrote, "states form alliances primarily to *balance* against other states, and . . . 'bandwagoning' behavior—that is, alignment *with* the dominant state or coalition—was relatively rare" (emphasis in the original). Richard Rosecrance (2003, 157) also averred, "For the balance of power to exist, a state must balance against the stronger side and in favor of the weaker. Any other response is bandwagoning, shirking, or free-riding."

The Soviet Union's demise offers a contrast to China's recent ascent, and gives warrant to be cautious about general conclusions drawn from analyses based on just one country. The power balance between the United States and China prior to the latter's recent growth was even more imbalanced in favor of the United States than it is now. For analysts who insist on intention-free study of foreign policy conduct based on material conditions only, the East Asian countries' traditional alignment behavior can only be described as bandwagoning with the United States rather than balancing against China. China did not and still does not have the requisite capability to project its military forces and to sustain long-range conventional campaigns against most of the traditional U.S. allies in East Asia, including the physical conquest of Taiwan.

Many of these countries, including South Korea, Thailand, and even Australia, have now developed friendlier ties with Beijing. These countries were previously more dependent on the United States, being more dominated by the overwhelming influence of U.S. hegemony from a balance-of-power perspective. The logic of this perspective indicates that a stronger China would now introduce an alternative pole, albeit still a much weaker one, to counteract U.S. preponderance. Applying the logic of balance-of-power theories (as distinct from that of balance of threat), the actions of China's immediate neighbors may be interpreted to suggest that rather than succumbing to the influence of greater Chinese capability, they are freer to balance against the United States now that they have become less subject to its overwhelming influence.

For the minor and even not-so-minor states, opposing a hegemon without an alternative source of support is a risky business because one can be easily picked off and made into an example to warn others (e.g., Panama, the Dominican Republic, Serbia, Iraq, and, most recently, Libya). It would have been more straightforward for balance-of-power theorists to claim support for their position by pointing to the possibility that these countries' closer relations with China suggest the beginning signs of balancing against the United States instead of construing this development as their becoming more accommodating to a rising but still much weaker China (Ross 2006). Concomitantly, as suggested by Walt's and Rosecrance's statements quoted above, their traditional alignment with the United States indicates bandwagoning, not balancing.

Whether states are more likely to bandwagon with a rising power has policy implications. If their natural instinct is to balance against rather than to bandwagon with (or accommodate) it, especially if it is also located close to them or shares a land border with them, then another great power can count on their own predisposition to oppose this aspiring hegemon. An extra-regional power can avail itself of the option of offshore balancing, passing the buck to the frontline states to contain this rising power (e.g., Walt 1988). As an offshore balancer, it would involve itself only when the frontline states fail to take up balancing.

Today, China faces a vastly different set of circumstances than those that enabled the United States to achieve its regional hegemony in the Western Hemisphere. The two European great powers that could have tried to block the United States were engaged in their own rivalry. Britain and France were therefore distracted, and even at various times imagined leveraging the United States to weaken the other side. Moreover, no other state in the Western Hemisphere was sufficiently powerful to oppose U.S. expansion. Therefore, the inability by its neighbors to balance against it and a disinclination by Britain and France to intervene against it enabled the United States to emerge as the undisputed master of the Western Hemisphere. After the American Civil War, the United States was too powerful to be stopped from attaining regional hegemony.

Those fortuitous circumstances provided the necessary permissive conditions for the United States to become the only regional hegemon in modern world history thus far (Elman 2004). In contrast, China faces potential opposition from large local powers (Russia, Japan, India, Indonesia, and South Korea) as well as the United States as the preponderant global power. China's geostrategic position, like that of Germany, Japan, and the Soviet Union, would cause any possible bid by it for regional hegemony to encounter countervailing actions, as balance-of-power theorists would predict. Given these would-be hegemons' utter failures, Jonathan Kirshner (2010, 12) concluded, "there is no good reason to believe that if China is a rational actor motivated primarily to survive, it would embark upon a bid for hegemony." This predisposition in turn mitigates the need for its neighbors to balance against it in the first place.

As just mentioned, China's geostrategic position is similar to Germany's and even Japan's and the Soviet Union's in the sense that they all live in a congested neighborhood and in close proximity to other great powers. This geostrategic circumstance should have encouraged the United States to adopt a policy of offshore balancing as it did prior to the two world wars. Since the early 1950s, however, Washington has instead chosen forward deployment of its military forces in a ring of bases around the Soviet Union/Russia and China, and has more recently extended this posture toward the Middle East and South Asia. Thus, contrary to the expectations and even advice of leading realists such as Kenneth Waltz and John Mearsheimer that it would and should adopt the role of an offshore balancer, the United States has in fact pursued extra-regional intervention and hegemony, as Christopher Layne (2006a) has explained.

This latter policy can imply three alternatives. First, perhaps in Washington's view, the frontline states are unable to take up effective balancing against the Soviet Union/Russia or China because of their limited capabilities to do so. If so, these states should have been quite inconsequential in affecting the bilateral power balance between the United States and the Soviet Union during the Cold War, which, in turn, implies that Washington should not have really cared about them insofar as balance-of-power reasons are concerned. The relevance of these states to U.S. security, again insofar as balance-of-power considerations pertaining to another country such as China are concerned, is diminished even further during the current era of unquestioned U.S. primacy.

Second, Washington can eschew an offshore posture because it believes that without its involvement, the frontline states would not be willing to take up balancing, even if they were capable of doing so. Washington's involvement, according to this interpretation, is necessary to overcome the problem of collective action. If so, this interpretation does not provide a strong endorsement of balance-of-power theories, but actually points to Washington's lack of confidence in these theories' prediction of ubiquitous and even automatic balancing behavior by those states located near a powerful, or increasingly powerful, state.

Third, forward military deployment and extensive formal or informal alliances can be intended to actually restrain other states from developing full defense autonomy or potential countervailing armament. These arrangements then serve the purpose of *pactum de contrahendo*, and their intent is not so much to balance power as to perpetuate imbalance. It does not seem quite right to describe policies intended to sustain and expand U.S. hegemony as seeking a balance of power. By the balance-of-power theories' own logic, an important consequence of Washington's pursuit of extra-regional hegemony would be to make other states more fearful of its power and at the same time, less inclined to take up their own balancing against China.

The combined implications of several points introduced in the preceding discussion should be emphasized. The United States was able to gain regional hegemony because of a very unusual set of circumstances, resulting from "an improbable absence of either local or extraregional balancers" (Elman 2004, 563). These circumstances, due to Europe's exigencies and the weakness of America's neighbors, clearly do not correspond to East Asia's reality today, and are unlikely to be repeated in any imaginable future. Thus, it is highly unlikely that China will be able to succeed in making a similar bid for regional hegemony—not to mention repeating the mistakes of Napoleon, Hitler, or Tojo by lashing out against their respective neighbors in a serial campaign of military conquest. The latter leaders' aggression was the most important factor in causing their victims to fight back and to unite in defeating them. Any similar action by China would certainly be frustrated by countervailing policies by its neighbors and the United States, undermining its goal of survival. This recognition in turn means that it is highly unlikely that Beijing would engage in such self-defeating conduct in the first place (Kirshner 2010).

Aggressive actions would also contradict a strategy of emphasizing economic growth and securing regime legitimacy by reducing international tension and promoting integration. Another recurrent argument presented in the previous discussion is that states react not so much to another power's capabilities as to its perceived intentions (most major states aligned with the United States rather than the Soviet Union during the Cold War, even though the former was much more powerful than the latter). Thus, a country's own actions influence whether other states will balance against it.

Both Elman's (2004) analysis, which asked why France consented to the Louisiana Purchase, thereby enabling the United States to further expand its already considerable power in 1803, and the discussion by Levy and Thompson (2005), which emphasized competition among continental powers with land-based military capabilities, point to a tendency for a continental power like China to be drawn to the political dynamics of its own region. Although a continental power will have concerns about extra-regional powers, it typically gives priority to attending to developments closer to home. The Louisiana Purchase can be understood in this light. Being primarily a continental power, France's response to possible U.S. hegemony in the Western Hemisphere was muted, and it was "dictated by what [was] happening in its own region" (Little 2007a, 242).

It is reasonable to argue that unlike France, China is much more attentive to and preoccupied with the United States because the latter country, by virtue of its status as the global hegemon, is so much more powerful today than it was for France in 1803. With that said, unlike the United States, Beijing still has to be concerned about multiple large states and potential great powers located on its border or within close physical proximity to it. By contrast, the United States does not face this situation (e.g., Walt 2009, 97) and can count on most, if not all, of the larger states and potential great powers among its allies or partners. Moreover, it has enjoyed an unprecedented concentration of power, both hard and soft, as attested by Paul Kennedy's statement introduced in Chapter 1.

This latter set of circumstances highlights Washington's pursuit of extra-regional hegemony (Layne 2006a) even after having established a position of unquestionable primacy and a level of security that no other country could even hope to approach. Balance-of-power theorists have tried to address the apparent enigma presented by other states' failure to balance against preponderant U.S. power. From these theorists' perspective, it is equally puzzling that the United States has pursued extra-regional hegemony when the risk is low that any other country, China included, would succeed in establishing a regional hegemony (in contrast with the large amount of influence due to size that Germany, Brazil, India, and China have in their respective regions), a consideration that should have made offshore balancing more attractive.

There is an important irony here that is usually overlooked in discussions on China's rise. It is that while the path for China to become the world's second regional hegemon is unrealistic and indeed dangerous for Beijing, the United States has pursued a policy of global primacy and extra-regional hegemony — considering that a situation of dominance and hierarchy has actually occurred quite frequently in historical systems (S. Kaufman, Little, and Wohlforth 2007), and considering that Washington's huge preponderance has made any serious effort to balance against it much costlier and riskier for other states to undertake compared to resistance against Britain and would-be hegemons such as Germany, Japan, and the Soviet Union in recent history. For this reason, Brooks and Wohlforth (2008) argued that one should not expect to see balancing against the United States. Still, the pursuit of extra-regional hegemony is not without costs for the United States to the extent that it exacerbates the guns-versus-butter tradeoff due to overextension and to the extent that it undermines the institutions of multilateralism that Washington has taken a leading role in constructing since 1945.

Naturally, pacts of restraint can work both ways. They can be used by a dominant power to control its junior partners, but they can also be used by the weaker allies to engage the hegemon, seeking to induce and commit the latter to do their bidding and thereby engendering the latter's traditional fear of entrapment. This recognition in turn suggests that verbal support and even tangible demonstration of a willingness to contribute to Washington's efforts to "balance" against another power, whether China or some other country, may not actually serve U.S. interests. The actions and agendas of Washington's allies in Afghanistan, Iraq, and Pakistan, and some members of the "coalition of the willing" come to mind. Conversely, as Davis Bobrow (2008c, 2) observed, "efforts to modify, evade, or resist what official Washington wants do not necessarily run counter to American national interests, whatever U.S. policy makers may claim. Not all U.S. government policy preferences really advance American interests even if intended to do so." These observations recall the Chinese aphorism that "good medicine is bitter to swallow; candid advice is painful to hear."

Restraining or balancing against a hegemon by definition entails countervailing efforts. Attempts to thwart U.S. dominance and to frustrate U.S. policies, however, can also involve efforts that "go with the grain," as just implied, by means of efforts that abet existing American proclivities (S. Chan 2008b). They can take the form of inflating U.S. hubris, encouraging Washington's ambitions and overconfidence, and promoting policies that have the effect of causing American overextension. As the ancient Chinese strategist Sun Tzu remarked, "If the enemy must prepare to defend many positions, then its forces facing us must be few" (Sawyer 1994). These are methods available to the relatively weak, and do not entail outright opposition or even indirect obstruction or noncooperation as suggested by the idea of soft balancing.

Given the overwhelming capabilities possessed by the United States, one can hardly imagine any country, China included, to take up internal or external balancing against it. The utter failure of such efforts by the Soviet Union offers a compelling warning to others not to repeat the same mistake. Even a large and growing country like China cannot hope to succeed in competing with the United States in building up armaments or coalitions—a competition that would have conferred huge advantages to the United States and entailed enormous opportunity costs for China. Better to manage Gulliver by tying it down, entangling it, dissipating its energy, distracting it on multiple fronts, and even encouraging it to undertake policies that are likely to be ultimately self-weakening than to challenge it in a frontal confrontation. This reasoning suggests that balancing policies as traditionally understood in balance-of-power theories are not just impractical but downright dangerous and self-defeating. Conversely, political deference to and even selective support of Washington's agenda, such as in its war against international terrorism, does not necessarily mean acceptance of U.S. dominance or even leadership.

The general rationale just described should also apply to China's neighbors in response to its rise as a major regional power. Contrary to the logic of balance-of-power theories, the last thing they would want to trigger by their action is an arms race or the development of exclusive blocs that would have the effect of wasting their resources, closing off their options, deepening their security dependency, and jeopardizing their domestic legitimacy and regime control. Indeed, to the extent that East Asian elites have increasingly staked their political standing on economic performance based on an open economy, balancing efforts that threaten to undermine this orientation would be difficult to undertake because of the increasingly strong domestic interests that would be hurt by them. Instead of seeing a more powerful China as a security threat, most East Asian countries are reaching the opposite conclusion that it offers an enormous commercial opportunity.

To the extent that modern nationalism and weapons have made foreign conquest increasingly unrewarding, and to the extent that economic interdependence has had a similar effect, it is quite remarkable that traditional balance-of-power reasoning continues to have such a strong grip on contemporary international relations discourse. Indeed, after surveying European diplomatic history, where balance-of-power theories are most likely to receive their confirmation, Paul Schroeder concluded that even in this context balancing tended to be the last resort rather than the first choice of states responding to perceived threats. A much more common and even successful way to manage possible threats is what he described as "grouping," referring to attempts to draw a potentially threatening state "into a larger group so that group suasion and group norms, pressure, and incentives will control its actions and possibly turn the threat into cooperation" (Schroeder 2003, 119).

There is a popular Chinese adage that can be loosely translated as "turning another's spear against his shield." One version of this adage tells of an arms vendor's boast that he had the most effective spear and shield. A prospective customer was supposed to have tried to expose the inherent contradiction in this sales pitch by testing the merchant's spear against his shield. Besides the meaning of exposing a contradiction in another person's argument (in fact, the Chinese characters for spear and shield combine to form the word "contradiction"), this aphorism also has the connotation of exploiting a tension existing between two positions, reversing the roles of two parties, and turning the tables on an adversary.

There is a large body of U.S. scholarship that endorses the idea of engaging China in order to foster domestic groups there that share American ideals or that would develop vested commercial interests in trading with the United

States. Moreover, membership and participation in international organizations are supposed to socialize the Chinese into becoming more "responsible stakeholders." Less attention, however, has gone to discussing how such policies, in principle, are also available to the Chinese, such as when they try to mobilize American business interests, the voting majority of developing countries in international organizations, and popular nationalist sentiments in China to sway, promote, or justify policies that are more congenial to Beijing. That is, Beijing can try to appeal to norms, practices, and arguments that Washington itself has propagated in order to finesse, delegitimize, or question policies favored by the United States.

The opposition mounted by the U.S. Congress (by a vote of 398–15) in June 2005 against a bid by the CNOOC (China National Offshore Oil Corporation) to buy UNOCAL, the ninth largest U.S. energy company, provides one example of inconsistencies in U.S. policies on foreign investment. The proposed sale of $6.4 billion of U.S. arms to Taiwan, announced in January 2010, offers Beijing with another opportunity to highlight the concurrent U.S. demand for Chinese cooperation in sanctioning Tehran's and Pyongyang's armament programs, and to mobilize domestic American opposition to this sale by threatening to boycott those U.S. companies involved in this transaction. The U.S. Federal Reserve's massive "quantitative easing" announced in November 2010, a move that depreciated the dollar assets held by foreigners and reduced their export competitiveness, presented Beijing with an effective rebuttal to Washington's charges of currency manipulation. To the extent that the norms, practices, and arguments invoked by Beijing resonate with important U.S. allies or public opinion and interest groups in the United States, they offer a more effective and less dangerous way to influence Washington's policies than pursuing traditional balancing through armament or alliances. Beijing's leverage to influence Washington's policies tends to be the greatest when the United States is internally conflicted, whether due to tension between competing interests or avowed principles.

This last remark returns us to two earlier arguments. First, it may be recalled that according to John Ikenberry (2001, 2008a, 2008b), American power becomes more predictable and legitimate in others' eyes to the extent that the United States provides (or accepts) a more information-rich environment about its decision processes, a more open and easier access for foreigners to influence these processes, and institutionalized constraints on its own exercise of power. This being the case, one should hardly be surprised that China would, as any other country, avail itself these opportunities to inform and advance its policies. What should be surprising is the tendency for much of American discourse to be focused on changing the nature of Chinese civil society, transforming China into a "responsible stakeholder," or constraining the growth or application of Chinese power without a concomitant recognition that these influence attempts are a two-way street.

Second, my remark calls attention to the role of ideas in formulating foreign policy and to those times when these ideas are subject to intense debate and contest. Jeffrey Legro (2005, 2007, 2008) has argued that neither power gains nor increased interdependence alone can explain changes in Chinese foreign policy or for that matter, any other country's foreign policy. This argument corresponds with this book's thesis that material changes—specifically, power shifts affecting the capability balances among countries—do not necessarily produce concomitant policy changes such as balancing against a rising neighbor. Whether they do depends critically on the prevailing ideas guiding a policy elite's understanding about the most rewarding way to achieve its regime and national goals and indeed, on those ideas shaping its definition of these goals. These ideas serve as an important intervening variable that connects power shifts and fluctuating levels of interdependence to the formulation and choice of a policy approach that is not only seen to be effective for achieving the chosen regime and national goals but is also perceived as politically acceptable and legitimate. I have argued that in East Asia, elites have generally turned away from an emphasis on armament and alliances to achieve these goals, preferring instead to give priority to the pursuit of economic performance.

To further clarify and elaborate on my remark that China's (or any other country's) attempt to influence the United States (or vice versa) tends to be the greatest when the United States is internally conflicted, such an attempt can enhance or discredit the reigning ideas of a ruling elite or faction in a way that is more complicated than typically suggested by labels such as engagement or containment, or balancing or accommodating. As an example, it is not at all clear that President Ronald Reagan's "get tough" policy toward the Soviet Union contributed to Soviet concessions rather than undermining those moderates in the Kremlin espousing "new thinking," thus delaying the Cold War's eventual end (Evangelista 1993). In a similar vein, what Beijing and Washington do, or fail to do, can affect the credibility of "nationalist" and "internationalist" ideas in the eyes of the other side's elite and mass public. Resistance to revaluing the renminbi or continued arms sales to Taiwan, for example, can give a boost to the other side's nationalist ideas at the expense of internationalist ideas—and the domestic proponents of the former ideas.

Significantly and as stressed earlier, the effects of such action or inaction can be exacerbated by circumstances. Concerns about Chinese currency manipulation are heightened in the midst of a U.S. economic recession, and worries about U.S. arms sales to Taiwan are more pronounced when pro-independence forces are becoming more vocal on the island. When an "internationalist" elite faction favoring economic integration and political accommodation is in charge in the other country, one's "get tough" policies—or more generally, armament or alliance policies that fall under the rubric of balancing—are likely to undermine its credibility and ironically, give credence to its domestic opponents waiting in the wings, those espousing *realpolitik* thinking that such policies are supposed to deter or discourage in the first place.

To expand briefly on the above reference to renminbi revaluation as an illustration, Beijing's resistance to this currency adjustment is likely to lend support to those in Washington who favor a more protectionist policy. There is wide recognition that Beijing wants to keep its currency value low in order to sustain its export competitiveness and, in turn, maintain domestic employment. The story, however, can be more complicated. Washington's demand for renminbi revaluation can play into the hands of those in Beijing who want to see China's economy emphasize more indigenous sources of growth, provide more immediate material improvement for citizens' lives, and move up the ladder of global production chains by abandoning the manufacturing of goods with low technology content and high labor content. It is not hard to imagine that there are Chinese leaders who want to wean China away from a dependence on exporting cheap consumer goods, whether to the United States or elsewhere.

The advocates of these policies, sensing rising protectionist sentiments in the United States and diminished financial wherewithal by American consumers to sustain ever-increasing Chinese exports, may be interested in scaling back the "superfusion" between the two countries for political as well as economic reasons. On a relative and absolute basis, China has already deepened its trade and investment relations with its other Asian Pacific partners. The main point of the current discussion, however, is that Washington's push for renminbi revaluation can advance the cause of those Chinese leaders who would actually welcome an appreciation of the Chinese currency for reasons such as those just given. These advocates may be joined by others who want to see the yuan appreciate to dampen inflationary pressure.

Labels such as "moderates," "conservatives," "hardliners," and even "integrationists" or "protectionists" cannot fully capture the policy nuances of those involved in the pertinent debates and relations. For instance, an appreciation of the renminbi may hurt other East Asian economies as much as China's with respect to exports to the United States—since many of these exports are really reexported goods that have been assembled in China but whose parts and components have come from the other East Asian economies (the average value added attributable to the Chinese assembly has been estimated to amount to only about 20% of the final product). Moreover, an appreciated yuan can further accelerate the process of intra-Asian economic integration, reducing the region's economic dependence on the United States.

None of my arguments should be taken to imply that China has not tried to modernize its military or has not sought friendly ties with other countries. But then, hardly all efforts to modernize one's military or promote friendly foreign ties can or should be construed as evidence that balance-of-power politics is operating. Assertions to the contrary in effect try to appropriate all such data for the benefit of confirming balance-of-power theories while dismissing alternative interpretations for the observed behavior (such as armaments may be motivated by domestic rent-seeking, and foreign ties may be sought due to cultural affinity). In this book I argue that competitive armament and countervailing alliances tend to exacerbate rather than ameliorate states' security problems.

Even balance-of-power theorists would acknowledge that states try to maximize their security and economic welfare simultaneously, and that at some level and at some point the pursuit of these desiderata entails important tradeoffs. I have pushed the latter argument further by suggesting that shared economic interests can provide a more viable and acceptable alternative to the traditional balance-of-power ways of securing peace and stability. Burgeoning commercial exchanges in East Asia provide an incentive to cooperate and a credible commitment against opportunistic behavior that would jeopardize future returns. The credibility of such reassurance stems not just from states' reduced motivation to initiate military aggrandizement, but also from their diminished ability to do so, because this aggrandizement would be constrained by existing domestic coalitions and agreements (e.g., political pacts regarding defense versus welfare consumption, tax versus spending, and free trade versus protectionism). Thus, external and internal bargains can be mutually reinforcing in promoting cooperation even in the midst of large power shifts.

The dynamics I have described does not entail the argument that a potential target of others' balancing policy can make selective side payments to prospective balancers in order to induce them to refrain from joining a countervailing coalition (although this proposition can certainly be true). Rather, I argue that the very prospect of China's continued economic growth and the rewards to be gained from continued cooperation with it provides this incentive, an incentive that is enhanced by the much less attractive alternative offered by a policy of balancing against it. This cooperation becomes contagious over time as more states turn to emphasize their economic performance and reduce their defense burden, and the consequent gains in elite legitimacy and regime popularity in turn have a self-reinforcing effect that makes a return to balance-of-power politics less likely.

Beyond the influence of vested interests in sustaining and expanding regional cooperation, there is the influence of entrenched ideas—views about how a state can most effectively achieve its goals of security and welfare. When particular ideas stressing the fruitfulness of integration, engagement, and cooperation produce indisputably positive results, they receive legitimacy and can more easily turn back other challenging ideas. As Jeffrey Legro (2005, 2007) has explained, ideas provide the "meshing gear" that mediates the influence of power shifts and changing economic interdependence on a state's external strategy, and winning ideas have staying power. That is to say, contrary to a perspective that attends to only material conditions, China's foreign policy reflects not only changes in its power and economic interdependence, but also its views on how these changes will advance or hinder its interests. Ideas that have so far produced rewarding results are less likely to be dislodged by alternatives, notwithstanding changes in other variables. Prevailing ideas—collective beliefs about how a state should conduct itself in world affairs—become vulnerable when they are discredited by consistently poor, even disastrous, policy results, shattering a previous consensus and rallying support for a replacement candidate. Ideas, however, may not catch up quickly to changing interests. This is another way of saying that there can be a long lag and protracted resistance to replacing obsolescent and even counterproductive ideas in the face of declining power, diminished resources, and mounting competing demands.

The interlocking interests, stakes, and ideas motivating and sustaining growing multilateral cooperation do not necessarily banish power politics, but they do have the effect of taming its practice. This perspective therefore acknowledges the coexistence of adversarial and associational elements in international relations, with the latter elements pointing to the cooperation and "regulated intercourse" among states under the notion of an international society, featured most prominently in Hedley Bull's (1977) work. As I argued earlier, the dynamics invoked by these dual aspects of international relations involves both restraining others and restraining oneself (Little 2007a, 147).

East Asia's and especially China's policy turn to emphasizing economic performance raises yet another final set of implications for traditional balance-of-power reasoning. Throughout the Cold War Era, Washington derived a significant leverage in its relations with its European and Asian allies from three elements: its security commitment to defend these allies, the indispensability of the dollar as a medium for international commerce and as a store of value, and the critical importance of its domestic market as a destination for its allies' exports (Mastanduno 2009). In return for U.S. military protection, supply of financial liquidity, and access to the U.S. market, America's allies offered political deference, revalued their currencies, and financed Washington's chronic fiscal deficits so that it could skirt and postpone the tough tradeoffs between guns and butter, and between investment and consumption. There was, in effect, a grand bargain: U.S. military protection and the centrality of the U.S. dollar and market enabled Washington to demand political compliance from its allies and to impose the costs of financial adjustment on the latter countries. Indeed, there is a mutual recognition that Washington's fiscal challenges and pressures on the dollar have stemmed to a not insignificant extent from its overseas military presence. Although it has worked reasonably well in the past, the international bargain consisting of these deals will likely face serious challenges in the future.

This book questions whether U.S. extra-regional hegemony can be sustained in the future—now that the Soviet threat has disappeared or at least has greatly diminished (thus depreciating the value of U.S. military protection), that the largest owners of dollar-denominated foreign reserves are no longer Washington's traditional allies (and these asset holders increasingly have reason to question the future value of this currency), and that China has displaced the United States as the most important export market and investment destination for many East Asian countries. In other words, the linkages underpinning the traditional grand bargain have been seriously strained, if not yet entirely broken. Suggestions to the effect that a rising China presents a threat to be balanced sound suspicious to other states in part because these remarks can be construed as an attempt to resurrect these linkages by increasing the premium demanded for U.S. military protection and decreasing the appeal of commercial relations with China. These suggestions are also misplaced because they overlook the transformative changes that have occurred in the Asia Pacific and betray a misunderstanding of the challenge coming from a rising China. This challenge is much more economic in nature than military as the United States continues to hold an unassailable advantage in the instruments of war.

REFERENCE MATTER

# References

Acharya, Amitav. 2001. *Constructing a Security Community: ASEAN and the Problem of Regional Order*. London: Routledge.

———. 2003. Regional Institutions and Asian Security Order. In *Asian Security Order: Instrumental and Normative Features*, ed. Muthiah Alagappa, 1–30. Stanford, CA: Stanford University Press.

———. 2003/04. Will Asia's Past Be Its Future? *International Security* 28 (3): 149–64.

Adler, Emanuel, and Michael Barnett, eds. 1998. *Security Communities*. Cambridge: Cambridge University Press.

Aggarwal, Vinod K. 1995. Comparing Regional Cooperation Efforts in the Asia-Pacific and North America. In *Pacific Cooperation: Building Economic and Security Regimes in the Asia-Pacific Region*, ed. Andrew Mack and John Ravenhill, 40–65. Boulder, CO: Westview.

Alagappa, Muthiah, ed. 1995. *Political Legitimacy in Southeast Asia: The Quest for Moral Authority*. Stanford, CA: Stanford University Press.

———. 2003a. Introduction. In *Asian Security Order: Instrumental and Normative Features*, ed. Muthiah Alagappa, 1–30. Stanford, CA: Stanford University Press.

———. 2003b. Constructing Security Order in Asia: Conceptions and Issues. In *Asian Security Order: Instrumental and Normative Features*, ed. Muthiah Alagappa, 70–105. Stanford, CA: Stanford University Press.

Albertini, Luigi. 1952–57. *The Origins of the War of 1914*. 3 vols. London: Oxford University Press.

Allison, Graham T. 1971. *Essence of Decision: Explaining the Cuban Missile Crisis*. Boston: Little Brown.

Amsden, Alice H. 1989. *Asia's Next Giant: South Korea and Late Industrialization*. New York: Columbia University Press.

Art, Robert J. 2005/06. Correspondence: Striking the Balance. *International Security* 30 (3): 177–85.

———. 2008. The United States and the Rise of China: Implications for the Long Haul. In *China's Ascent: Power, Security, and the Future of International Politics*, ed. Robert Ross and Feng Zhu, 260–90. Ithaca, NY: Cornell University Press.

Axelrod, Robert. 1980a. Effective Choice in the Prisoner's Dilemma. *Journal of Conflict Resolution* 24 (1): 3–25.

———. 1980b. More Effective Choice in the Prisoner's Dilemma. *Journal of Conflict Resolution* 24 (3): 379–403.

———. 1984. *The Evolution of Cooperation*. New York: Basic Books.

Ba, Alice D. 2009. *(Re)Negotiating East and Southeast Asia*. Stanford, CA: Stanford University Press.

Bacevich, Andrew J. 2002. *American Empire: The Realities and Consequences of U.S. Diplomacy*. Cambridge, MA: Harvard University Press.

———. 2008. *Limits of Power: The End of American Exceptionalism*. New York: Metropolitan Books.

Bailey, Michael A., Judith Goldstein, and Barry R. Weingast. 1997. The Institutional Roots of American Trade Policy: Politics, Coalitions and International Trade. *World Politics* 49 (3): 309–38.

Baldwin, James A. 1985. *Economic Statecraft*. Princeton, NJ: Princeton University Press.

Baran, Paul A., and Paul M. Sweezy. 1966. *Monopoly Capital: An Essay on the American Economic and Social Order*. New York: Monthly Review Press.

Barbieri, Katherine. 2002. *The Liberal Illusion: Does Trade Promote Peace?* Ann Arbor: University of Michigan Press.

Barbieri, Katherine, Omar M. G. Keshk, and Brian Pollins. 2008. *Correlates of War Project Trade Data Set Codebook*. Version 2.0.

Barnett, Michael. 2003. Alliances, Balances of Threats, and Neorealism. In *Neorealism and the Balance of Power: A New Debate*, ed. John A. Vasquez and Colin Elman, 222–49. Upper Saddle River, NJ: Prentice Hall.

Barnhart, Michael A. 1987. *Japan Prepares for Total War: The Search for Economic Security, 1919–1945*. Ithaca, NY: Cornell University Press.

Barrett, Richard E., and Martin K. Whyte. 1982. Dependency Theory and Taiwan: An Analysis of a Deviant Case. *American Journal of Sociology* 87 (5): 1064–89.

Beard, Charles A. 1936. *The Devil Theory of War*. New York: Vanguard.

Benson, Brett V., and Emerson M. S. Niou. 2007. Economic Interdependence and Peace: A Game-Theoretic Analysis. *Journal of East Asian Studies* 7 (1): 35–59.

Berger, Thomas U. 1993. From Sword to Chrysanthemum: Japan's Cultures of Antimilitarism. *International Security* 17 (4): 119–50.

———. 1998. *Cultures of Antimilitarism: National Security in Germany and Japan*. Baltimore: Johns Hopkins University Press.

———. 2003. Power and Purpose in Pacific East Asia: A Constructivist Interpretation. In *International Relations Theory and the Asia-Pacific*, ed. G. John Ikenberry and Michael Mastanduno, 387–419. New York: Columbia University Press.

Bergsten, C. Fred, Charles Freeman, Nicholas R. Lardy, and Derek J. Mitchell. 2008. *China's Rise: Challenges and Opportunities*. Washington, DC: Peterson Institute for International Economics.

Bernstein, Richard, and Ross H. Munro. 1997. The Coming Conflict with America. *Foreign Affairs* 76 (March/April): 18–32.

Betts, Richard K. 1993/94. Wealth, Power and Instability: East Asia and the United States After the Cold War. *International Security* 18 (3): 34–77.

Bhalla, A. S., and P. Bhalla. 1997. *Regional Blocs: Building Blocks or Stumbling Blocks?* New York: St. Martin's Press.

Binder, Leonard. 1988. *Islamic Liberalism: A Critique of Development Ideologies.* Chicago: University of Chicago Press.

Blainey, Geoffrey. 1973. *The Causes of War.* New York: Free Press.

Bobrow, Davis B. 1965. Peking's Military Calculus. In *Components of Defense Policy*, ed. David B. Bobrow, 39–52. Chicago: Rand McNally.

———. 1969. Chinese Communist Response to Alternative U.S. Continental Defense Postures. In *Weapons System Decisions: Political and Psychological Perspectives on Continental Defense*, ed. Davis B. Bobrow, 151–213. New York: Praeger.

———, ed. 2008a. *Hegemony Constrained: Evasion, Modification, and Resistance to American Foreign Policy.* Pittsburgh: University of Pittsburgh Press.

———. 2008b. International Public Opinion: Incentives and Options to Comply and Challenge. In *Hegemony Constrained: Evasion, Modification, and Resistance to American Foreign Policy*, ed. Davis B. Bobrow, 222–60. Pittsburgh: University of Pittsburgh Press.

———. 2008c. Strategies Beyond Followership. In *Hegemony Constrained: Evasion, Modification, and Resistance to American Foreign Policy*, ed. Davis B. Bobrow, 1–19. Pittsburgh: University of Pittsburgh Press.

Bobrow, Davis B., Steve Chan, and John A. Kringen. 1979. *Understanding Foreign Policy Decisions: The Chinese Case.* New York: Free Press.

Boettcher, William A. 2005. *Presidential Risk Behavior in Foreign Policy: Prudence or Peril.* New York: Palgrave Macmillan.

Bohmelt, Tobias. 2010. The Impact of Trade on International Mediation. *Journal of Conflict Resolution* 54 (4): 566–92.

Boulding, Kenneth E. 1962. *Conflict and Defense: A General Theory.* New York: Harper & Row.

Bourne, Kenneth. 1967. *Britain and the Balance of Power in North America, 1815–1908.* Berkeley: University of California Press.

Brooks, Stephen G. 1997. Dueling Realisms. *International Organization* 51 (3): 445–77.

———. 2005. *Producing Security: Multinational Corporations, Globalization, and the Changing Calculus of Conflict.* Princeton, NJ: Princeton University Press.

Brooks, Stephen G., and William C. Wohlforth. 2000/2001. Power, Globalization, and the End of the Cold War: Reevaluating a Landmark Case for Ideas. *International Security* 25 (3): 5–53.

———. 2005. Hard Times for Soft Balancing. *International Security* 30 (1): 72–108.

———. 2005/06. Correspondence: Striking the Balance. *International Security* 30 (3): 186–91.

———. 2008. *World Out of Balance: International Relations and the Challenge of American Primacy.* Princeton, NJ: Princeton University Press.

Brown, Michael E., Owen R. Cote, Jr., Sean M. Lynn-Jones, and Steven E. Miller, eds. 2000. *The Rise of China.* Cambridge, MA: MIT Press.

Broz, J. Lawrence. 2002. Political System Transparency and Monetary Commitment Regimes. *International Organization* 54 (4): 861–87.

Brzezinski, Zbigniew, and John J. Mearsheimer. 2005. Clash of the Titans. *Foreign Policy* 146 (January/February): 46–49.

Bueno de Mesquita, Bruce. 1990. Pride of Place: The Origins of German Hegemony. *World Politics* 41 (1): 28–52.

———. 2003. Neorealism's Logic and Evidence: When Is a Theory Falsified? In *Neorealism and the Balance of Power: A New Debate*, ed. John A. Vasquez and Colin Elman, 166–99. Upper Saddle River, NJ: Prentice Hall.

Bueno de Mesquita, Bruce, James D. Morrow, Randolph M. Siverson, and Alastair Smith. 1999. An Institutional Explanation of the Democratic Peace. *American Political Science Review* 93 (4): 791–807.

Bueno de Mesquita, Bruce, Alastair Smith, Randolph M. Siverson, and James D. Morrow. 2003. *The Logic of Political Survival*. Cambridge, MA: MIT Press.

Bull, Hedley. 1977. *The Anarchical Society: A Study of Order in World Politics*. New York: Columbia University Press.

Bush, George W. 2002. *National Security Strategy of the United States of America*. Washington, DC: Government Printing Office.

Bush, Richard C. 2005. *Untying the Knot: Making Peace in the Taiwan Strait*, Washington, DC: Brookings Institution Press.

Buzan, Barry, and Richard Little. 2000. *International Systems in World History: Remaking the Study of International Relations*. Oxford: Oxford University Press.

Callahan, William A. 2008. Chinese Visions of World Order: Post-hegemonic or a New Hegemony? *International Studies Review* 10 (4): 749–61.

Calleo, David. 1982. *The Imperious Economy*. Cambridge, MA: Harvard University Press.

Cappelen, Adne, Nils P. Gleditsch, and Olav Bjerkholt. 1992. Guns, Butter, and Growth: The Case of Norway. In *Defense, Welfare, and Growth: Perspectives and Evidence*, ed. Steve Chan and Alex Mintz, 61–80. London: Routledge.

Carpenter, Ted G. 2005. *America's Coming War with China: A Collision Course over Taiwan*. New York: Palgrave Macmillan.

Cha, Victor D. 1999. *Alignment Despite Antagonism: The United States–Korea–Japan Security Triangle*. Stanford, CA: Stanford University Press.

———. 2003. Multilateral Security in Asia and the U.S.-Japan Alliance. In *Reinventing the Alliance: U.S.-Japan Alliance Partnership in an Era of Change*, ed. G. John Ikenberry and Takashi Inoguchi, 141–62. New York: Palgrave Macmillan.

———. 2007. Currents of Power: U.S. Alliances with Japan and Taiwan During the Cold War. In *The Uses of Institutions: The U.S., Japan, and Governance in East Asia*, ed. G. John Ikenberry and Takashi Inoguchi, 77–129. New York: Palgrave Macmillan.

Cha, Victor D., and David C. Kang. 2003. *Nuclear North Korea: A Debate on Engagement Strategies*. New York: Columbia University Press.

Chan, Gerald. 1999. The Origin of the Interstate System: The Warring States in Ancient China. *Issues & Studies* 35 (1): 147–66.

Chan, Steve. 1988. Defense Burden and Economic Growth: Unraveling the Taiwanese Enigma. *American Political Science Review* 82 (3): 913–20.

———. 1993. *East Asian Dynamism: Growth, Order, and Security in the Pacific Region*. Boulder, CO: Westview.

———. 1995. Grasping the Peace Dividend: Some Propositions on the Conversion of Swords into Plowshares. *Mershon International Studies Review* 39: 53–95.

———. 1997. In Search of Democratic Peace: Problems and Promise. *Mershon International Studies Review* 41 (1): 59–91.

———. 2001a. Japan and the United States as Models of Development: Classifying Asia Pacific and Latin American Political Economies. *Comparative Political Studies* 34 (10): 1134–58.

———. 2001b. Liberalism, Realism, and Regional Trade: Differentiating APEC from E.U. and NAFTA. *Pacific Focus* 16 (1): 5–34.

———. 2004a. Can't Get No Satisfaction? The Recognition of Revisionist States. *International Relations of the Asia-Pacific* 4 (2): 207–38.

———. 2004b. Exploring Some Puzzles in Power-Transition Theory: Some Implications for Sino-American Relations. *Security Studies* 13 (3): 103–41.

———. 2005. Is There a Power Transition between the U.S. and China? The Different Faces of Power. *Asian Survey* 45 (5): 687–701.

———. 2008a. *China, the U.S., and the Power-Transition Theory: A Critique.* London: Routledge.

———. 2008b. Soft Deterrence, Passive Resistance: American Lenses, Chinese Lessons. In *Hegemony Constrained: Evasion, Modification, and Resistance to American Foreign Policy*, ed. Davis B. Bobrow, 62–80. Pittsburgh: University of Pittsburgh Press.

———. 2009. Commerce Between Rivals: Realism, Liberalism, and Credible Communication Across the Taiwan Strait. *International Relations of the Asia-Pacific* 9 (3): 435–67.

———. 2010a. An Odd Thing Happened on the Way to Balancing: East Asian States' Reactions to China's Rise. *International Studies Review* 12 (3): 386–411.

———. 2010b. Progress in the Democratic Peace Research Agenda. In *International Studies Encyclopedia,* Vol. 9, ed. Robert A. Denemark, 5924–42. New York: Wiley-Blackwell.

Chan, Steve, and Cal Clark. 1992. *Flexibility, Foresight, and Fortuna in Taiwan's Development: Navigating Between Scylla and Charybdis.* London: Routledge.

Checkel, Jeff. 1993. Ideas, Institutions and the Gorbachev Foreign Policy Revolution. *World Politics* 45 (2): 271–300.

Chin, Gregory, and Eric Helleiner. 2008. China as a Creditor: A Rising Financial Power. *Journal of International Affairs* 62 (1): 87–102.

Christensen, Thomas J. 1999. China, the U.S.-Japan Alliance, and the Security Dilemma in East Asia. *International Security* 23 (4): 49–80.

———. 2001. Posing Problems Without Catching Up: China's Rise and Challenges for U.S. Security Policy. *International Security* 25 (4): 5–40.

Christensen, Thomas J., and Jack Snyder. 1990. Chain Gangs and Passed Bucks: Predicting Alliance Patterns in Multipolarity. *International Organization* 44 (2): 137–68.

Chu, Yun-han. 2007. Taiwan's Politics of Identity: Navigating Between China and the United States. In *Power and Security in Northeast Asia*, ed. Byung-Kook Kim and Anthony Jones, 225–52. Boulder, CO: Lynne Rienner.

Ciorciari, John D. 2009. The Balance of Great-Power Influence in Contemporary Southeast Asia. *International Relations of the Asia-Pacific* 9 (1): 157–96.

Clark, Cal. 1989. *Taiwan's Development: Implications for Contending Political Economy Paradigms.* New York: Greenwood.

Claude, Inis L. 1962. *Power and International Relations.* New York: Random House.

Clayton, James L. 1976. The Fiscal Limits of the Warfare–Welfare State: Defense and Welfare Spending in the United States Since 1900. *Western Political Quarterly* 29 (3): 364–83.

Colaresi, Michael P., Karen Rasler, and William R. Thompson. 2007. *Strategic Rivalries in World Politics: Position, Space, and Conflict Escalation.* Cambridge: Cambridge University Press.

Cole, Wayne S. 1983. *Roosevelt and the Isolationists, 1932–1945.* Lincoln: University of Nebraska Press.

Collier, David, ed. 1979. *The New Authoritarianism in Latin America.* Princeton, NJ: Princeton University Press.

Cooper, John M. 1969. *The Vanity of Power: American Isolationism and the First World War.* Westport, CT: Greenwood.

Copeland, Dale C. 1996. Economic Interdependence and War: A Theory of Trade Expectations. *International Security* 20 (4): 5–41.

———. 2000. *The Origins of Major War.* Ithaca, NY: Cornell University Press.

Cossa, Ralph A. 2009. Evolving U.S. Views on Asia's Future Institutional Architecture. In *Asia's New Multilateralism: Cooperation, Competition, and the Search for Community,* ed. Michael J. Green and Bates Gill, 33–54. New York: Columbia University Press.

Craig, Campbell. 2004. American Realism Versus American Imperialism. *World Politics* 57 (1): 143–71.

Crawford, Timothy. 2003. *Pivotal Deterrence: Third-Party Statecraft and the Pursuit of Peace.* Ithaca, NY: Cornell University Press.

Crone, Donald. 1993. Does Hegemony Matter? The Reorganization of the Pacific Political Economy. *World Politics* 45 (4): 501–25.

Cumings, Bruce. 1981. 1990. *The Origins of the Korean War.* 2 vols. Princeton, NJ: Princeton University Press.

———. 1984. The Origin and Development of the Northeast Asian Political Economy: Industrial Sectors, Product Cycles, and Political Consequences. *International Organization* 38 (1): 1–40.

Daalder, Ivo H., and James M. Lindsay. 2005. *America Unbound: The Bush Revolution in Foreign Policy.* New York: Wiley.

Dabelko, David, and James M. McCormick. 1977. Opportunity Costs of Defense: Some Cross-National Evidence. *Journal of Peace Research* 14 (2): 145–54.

Danilovic, Vesna. 2001. Conceptual and Selection Biases in Deterrence. *Journal of Conflict Resolution* 45 (1): 97–125.

David, Steve R. 1991. *Choosing Sides: Alignment and Realignment in the Third World.* Baltimore: Johns Hopkins University Press.

Davis, David R., and Steve Chan. 1990. The Security–Welfare Relationship: Longitudinal Evidence from Taiwan. *Journal of Peace Research* 27 (1): 87–100.

Davis, James W., Jr. 2000. *Threats and Promises: The Pursuit of International Influence.* Baltimore: Johns Hopkins University Press.

Deger, Saadet. 1986. *Military Expenditure in Third World Countries: The Economic Effects.* London: Routledge.

Deger, Saadet, and Ron Smith. 1983. Military Expenditures and Growth in Less Developed Countries. *Journal of Conflict Resolution* 27 (2): 335–53.

DeGrasse, Robert W., Jr., with Elizabeth McGuiness and William Ragen. 1983. *Military Expansion and Economic Decline.* New York: Council of Economic Priorities.

Deng, Yong. 1997. *Promoting Asia-Pacific Economic Cooperation: Perspectives from East Asia.* New York: St. Martin's Press.

Deutsch, Karl W., Sidney A. Burrell, Robert A. Kann, Maurice Lee, Jr., Martin Lichtenman, Raymond E. Lindgren, Francis L. Loewenheim, and Richard W. Van Wagenen. 1957. *Political Community and the North Atlantic Area: International Organization in the Light of Historical Experience.* New York: Greenwood.

Deyo, Fred C. 1981. *Dependent Development and Industrial Order: An Asian Case Study.* New York: Praeger.

———, ed. 1987. *The Political Economy of the New Asian Industrialism.* Ithaca, NY: Cornell University Press.

Diehl, Paul F., ed. 1998. *The Dynamics of Enduring Rivalries*. Urbana: University of Illinois Press.

Diehl, Paul F., and Gary Goertz. 2000. *War and Peace in International Rivalry*. Ann Arbor: University of Michigan Press.

Doran, Charles F. 1989. System Disequilibrium, Foreign Policy Role, and the Power Cycle: Challenges for Research Design. *Journal of Conflict Resolution* 33 (3): 371–401.

———. 1991. *Systems in Crisis: New Imperatives of High Politics at Century's End*. Cambridge: Cambridge University Press.

———. 2003. Economics, Philosophy of History, and the "Single Dynamic" of the Power Cycle Theory: Expectations, Competition, and Statecraft. *International Political Science Review* 24 (1): 13–49.

Doran, Charles F., and Wes Parsons. 1980. War and the Cycle of Relative Power. *American Political Science Review* 74 (4): 947–65.

Downs, Anthony. 1957. *An Economic Theory of Voting*. New York: Harper.

Doyle, Michael W. 1983a. Kant, Liberal Legacies, and Foreign Affairs: Part 1. *Philosophy and Public Affairs* 12 (3): 205–35.

———. 1983b. Kant, Liberal Legacies, and Foreign Affairs: Part 2. *Philosophy and Public Affairs* 12 (4), 323–53.

———. 1986. Liberalism and World Politics. *American Political Science Review* 80 (4), 1151–69.

Dreyer, Edward L. 2007. *Zheng He: China and the Oceans in the Early Ming Dynasty, 1405–1433*. New York: Pearson.

Drezner, Daniel W. 1999. *The Sanctions Paradox: Economic Statecraft and International Relations*. Cambridge: Cambridge University Press.

———. 2009. Bad Debts: Assessing China's Financial Influence in Great Power Politics. *International Security* 34 (2): 7–45.

Edelstein, David M. 2002. Managing Uncertainty: Beliefs About Intentions and the Rise of Great Powers. *Security Studies* 12 (1): 1–40.

Elkins, Zachary, Andrew T. Guzman, and Beth A. Simmons. 2006. Competing for Capital: Diffusion of Bilateral Investment Treaties, 1960–2000. *International Organization* 60 (4): 811–46.

Elliot, John. 1984. *Imperial Spain*. New York: St. Martin's Press.

Elman, Colin. 2003. Introduction: Appraising Balance of Power Theory. *Realism and the Balancing of Power: A New Debate*, ed. John A. Vasquez and Colin Elman, 1–22. Upper Saddle River, NJ: Prentice-Hall.

———. 2004. Extending Offensive Realism: The Louisiana Purchase and America's Rise to Regional Hegemony. *American Political Science Review* 98 (4): 563–76.

———. 2009. Realist Revisionism. In *Rethinking Realism in International Relations: Between Tradition and Innovation*, ed. Annette Freyberg-Inan, Ewan Harrison, and Patrick James, 63–75. Baltimore: Johns Hopkins University Press.

Entous, Adam. 2009. Afghan Strategy Debate Exposes Split over Price. http://www.reuters.com/article (accessed on November 16, 2009).

Evangelista, Matthew. 1993. Internal and External Constraints on Grand Strategy: The Soviet Case. In *The Domestic Bases of Grand Strategy*, ed. Richard Rosecrance and Arthur A. Stein, 154–78. Ithaca, NY: Cornell University Press.

Evans, Peter. 1995. *Embedded Autonomy: States and Industrial Transformation*. Princeton, NJ: Princeton University Press.

Fairbank, John K., ed. 1968. *The Chinese World Order: Traditional China's Foreign Relations.* Cambridge, MA: Harvard University Press.

Fajnzylber, Fernando. 1990. The United States and Japan as Models of Industrialization. In *Manufacturing Miracles: Paths of Industrialization in Latin America and East Asia,* ed. Gary Gereffi and Donald L. Wyman, 323–52. Princeton, NJ: Princeton University Press.

Farnham, Barbara, ed. 1994. *Avoiding Losses/Taking Risks: Prospect Theory and International Conflict.* Ann Arbor: University of Michigan Press.

———. 1997. *Roosevelt and the Munich Crisis: A Study of Political Decision-Making.* Princeton, NJ: Princeton University Press.

Fearon, James D. 1994. Domestic Political Audiences and the Escalation of International Disputes. *American Political Science Review* 88 (3): 577–92.

———. 1995. Rationalist Explanations for War. *International Organization* 49 (3): 379–414.

———. 1997. Signaling Foreign Policy Interests: Tying Hands Versus Sinking Costs. *Journal of Conflict Resolution* 41 (1): 68–90.

———. 1998a. Bargaining, Enforcement, and International Cooperation. *International Organization* 52 (2): 269–305.

———. 1998b. Commitment Problems and the Spread of Ethnic Conflict. In *The International Spread of International Conflict: Fear, Diffusion, and Escalation,* ed. David A. Lake and Donald Rothchild, 107–26. Princeton, NJ: Princeton University Press.

———. 2000. Selection Effects and Deterrence. *International Interactions* 28: 5–29.

———. 2004. Why Do Some Civil Wars Last So Much Longer Than Others? *Journal of Peace Research* 41 (3): 275–301.

Feng, Huiyun. 2007. *Chinese Strategic Culture and Foreign Policy Decision-Making: Confucianism, Leadership and War.* London: Routledge.

Fischer, Fritz. 1967. *Germany's Aims in the First World War.* New York: Norton.

Fordham, Benjamin O. 2007. Revisionism Reconsidered: Exports and American Intervention in World War I. *International Organization* 61 (2): 277–310.

Fortna, Virginia P. 2004. *Peace Time: Cease-Fire Agreements and the Durability of Peace.* Princeton, NJ: Princeton University Press.

Frankel, Jeffrey A. 1993. Is Japan Creating a Yen Bloc in East Asia and the Pacific? In *Regionalism and Rivalry: Japan and the United States in Pacific Asia,* ed. Jeffrey A. Frankel and Miles Kahler, 53–85. Chicago: University of Chicago Press.

Fravel, M. Taylor. 2005. Regime Insecurity and International Cooperation: Explaining China's Compromises in Territorial Disputes. *International Security* 30 (1): 46–83.

Frederiksen, Peter C., and Robert E. Looney. 1983. Defense Expenditures and Economic Growth in Developing Countries. *Armed Forces and Society* 9 (4): 633–45.

Friedberg, Aaron L. 1988. *The Weary Titan: Britain and the Experience of Relative Decline, 1895–1905.* Princeton, NJ: Princeton University Press.

———. 1993/94. Ripe for Rivalry. *International Security* 18 (1): 5–33.

———. 2005. The Future of U.S.-China Relations: Is Conflict Inevitable? *International Security* 30 (1): 7–45.

Gartner, Scott S., and Randolph M. Siverson. 1996. War Expansion and War Outcomes. *Journal of Conflict Resolution* 40 (1): 4–15.

Gartzke, Erik A. 1999. War Is in the Error Term. *International Organization* 53 (3): 567–87.

———. 2003. The Classical Liberals Were Just Lucky: A Few Thoughts About Interdependence and Peace. In *Economic Interdependence and International Conflict,* ed. Edward D. Mansfield and Brian Pollins, 96–110. Ann Arbor: University of Michigan Press.

Gartzke, Erik A., and Kristian S. Gleditsch. 2004. Regime Type and Commitment: Why Democracies Are Actually Less Reliable Allies. *American Journal of Political Science* 48 (4): 775–95.

Gartzke, Erik A., and Quan Li. 2003a. How Globalization Can Reduce International Conflict. In *Globalization and Conflict*, ed. Gerald Schneider, Katherine Barbieri, and Nils Petter Gleditsch, 123–40. Boulder, CO: Rowman & Littlefield.

———. 2003b. War, Peace, and the Invisible Hand: Positive Political Externalities of Economic Globalization. *International Studies Quarterly* 47 (4): 561–86.

Gartzke, Erik A., Quan Li, and Charles Boehmer. 2001. Investing in the Peace: Economic Interdependence and International Conflict. *International Organization* 55 (2): 391–438.

Gaubatz, Kurt T. 1996. Democratic States and Commitment in International Relations. *International Organization* 50 (1): 109–39.

Gibbon, Edward. 1993. *The Decline and Fall of the Roman Empire,* 3 vols. New York: Knopf.

Gilpin, Robert. 1981. *War and Change in World Politics.* Cambridge: Cambridge University Press.

———. 2000. *The Challenge of Global Capitalism: The World Economy in the 21st Century.* Princeton, NJ: Princeton University Press.

Glaser, Charles L. 1994/95. Realists as Optimists: Cooperation As Self-Help. *International Security* 19 (3): 50–90.

Goddard, Stacie E. 2008/09. When Right Makes Might: How Prussia Overturned the European Balance of Power. *International Security* 33 (3): 110–42.

Goh, Evelyn. 2007/08. Great Powers and Hierarchical Order in Southeast Asia: Analyzing Regional Security Strategies. *International Security* 32 (3): 113–57.

Gold, David. 1990. *The Impact of Defense Spending on Investment, Productivity and Economic Growth.* Washington, DC: Defense Budget Project. Monograph.

Gold, Thomas B. 1986. *State and Society in the Taiwan Miracle.* Armonk, NY: Sharpe.

Goldstein, Avery. 2003a. An Emerging China's Emerging Grand Strategy: A Neo-Bismarckian Turn? In *International Relations Theory and the Asia-Pacific*, ed. G. John Ikenberry and Michael Mastanduno, 57–106. New York: Columbia University Press.

———. 2003b. Balance-of-Power Politics: Consequences for Asian Security Order. In *Asian Security Order: Instrumental and Normative Features*, ed. Muthiah Alagappa, 171–209. Stanford, CA: Stanford University Press.

———. 2005. *Rising to the Challenge: China's Grand Strategy and International Security.* Stanford, CA: Stanford University Press.

Gowa, Joanne. 1994. *Allies, Adversaries, and International Trade.* Princeton, NJ: Princeton University Press.

Green, Michael J. 2001. *Japan's Reluctant Realism: Foreign Policy Challenges in an Era of Uncertain Power.* New York: Palgrave.

———. 2002. Balance of Power. In *U.S.-Japan Relations in a Changing World*, ed. Steven K. Vogel, 9–34. Washington, DC: Brookings Institution Press.

Green, Michael J., and Bates Gill, eds. 2009. *Asia's New Multilateralism: Cooperation, Competition, and the Search for Community.* New York: Columbia University Press.

Grieco, Joseph M. 1988. Anarchy and the Limits of Cooperation: A Realist Critique of the Newest Liberal Institutionalism. *International Organization* 42 (3): 485–507.

———. 1997. Systemic Sources of Variation in Regional Institutionalization in Western Europe, East Asia, and the Americas. In *The Political Economy of Regionalism*, ed. Edward D. Mansfield and Helen V. Milner, 164–87. New York: Columbia University Press.

————. 1999. Realism and Regionalism: American Power and German and Japanese Institutional Strategies During and After the Cold War. In *Unipolar Politics: Realism and State Strategies After the Cold War*, ed. Ethan B. Kapstein and Michael Mastanduno, 319–53. New York: Columbia University Press.

Gulick, Edward V. 1955. *Europe's Classical Balance of Power*. New York: Norton.

Haas, Ernst B. 1953. The Balance of Power: Prescription, Concept, or Propaganda. *World Politics* 5 (4): 442–77.

————. 1958. *The Uniting of Europe*. Stanford, CA: Stanford University Press.

Haggard, Stephan. 1990. *Pathways from the Periphery: The Politics of Growth in the Newly Industrializing Countries*. Ithaca, NY: Cornell University Press.

Halliday, Fred. 2005. *The Middle East in International Relations: Power, Politics and Ideology*. Cambridge: Cambridge University Press.

Hamerow, Theodore S., ed. 1972. *Otto Von Bismarck: A Historical Assessment*. Lexington, MA: Heath.

Harding, Harry. 1987. *China's Second Revolution: Reform after Mao*. Washington, DC: Brookings Institution Press.

Harrison, Ewan. 2009. The Contradictions of Unipolarity. In *Rethinking Realism in International Relations: Between Tradition and Innovation*, ed. Annette Freyberg-Inan, Ewan Harrison, and Patrick James, 76–97. Baltimore: Johns Hopkins University Press.

Hartley, Keith, and Todd Sandler. 1990. *The Economics of Defence Spending: An International Survey*. London: Routledge.

Heginbotham, Eric, and Richard J. Samuels. 1999. Mercantile Realism and Japanese Foreign Policy. In *Unipolar Politics: Realism and State Strategies After the Cold War*, ed. Ethan B. Kapstein and Michael Mastanduno, 183–217. New York: Columbia University Press.

Hemmer, Christopher, and Peter J. Katzenstein. 2002. Why Is There No NATO in Asia? Collective Identity, Regionalism, and the Origins of Multilateralism. *International Organization* 56 (3): 575–607.

Herz, John H. 1950. Idealist Internationalism and the Security Dilemma. *World Politics* 2 (2): 157–80.

Hewison, Kevin. 1989. *Bankers and Bureaucrats: Capital and the Role of the State in Thailand*. New Haven, CT: Yale University Press.

Higgott, Richard, Richard Leaver, and John Ravenhill, eds. 1993. *Pacific Economic Relations in the 1990s: Cooperation or Conflict?* Boulder, CO: Lynne Rienner.

Hildebrandt, Gregory C. 1992. The Effect of Modernizing Soviet Machine Building on Defense and the Macroeconomy: 1995–2010. In *The Macroeconomic Dimensions of Arms Reduction*, ed. F. Gerard Adams, 217–33. Boulder, CO: Westview.

Hirschman, Albert O. 1945. *National Power and the Structure of Foreign Trade*. Berkeley: University of California Press.

Holsti, Ole R. 1962. The Belief System and National Images: A Case Study. *Journal of Conflict Resolution* 6 (3): 244–52.

Hopf, Ted. 1991. Polarity, the Offense–Defense Balance, and War. *American Political Science Review* 85 (2): 475–93.

Horowitz, Shale, and Min Ye. 2007. China's Grand Strategy, the Korean Nuclear Crisis, and the Six-Party Talks. In *Korean Security in a Changing East Asia*, ed. Terence Roehrig, Jungmin Seo, and Uk Heo, 33–52. Westport, CT: Praeger.

Houghton, David P. 2009. The Role of Self-Fulfilling and Self-Negating Prophecies in International Relations. *International Studies Review* 11 (3): 552–82.

Huang, Chi, and Alex Mintz. 1991. Ridge Regression Analysis of the Defense–Growth Trade-off in the United States. *Defence Economics* 2 (1): 29–37.

Hufbauer, Gary C., Jeffery Schott, and Kimberly A. Elliott. 1990. *Economic Sanctions Reconsidered*. Washington, DC: Institute for International Economics.

Hufbauer, Gary, and Yee Wong. 2004. China Bashing 2004. *International Economics Policy Briefs*, No. PB04-5; *http://www.iie.com/publications/pb/pb04-5.pdf*.

Hui, Victoria Tin-bor. 2004. Toward Dynamic Theory of International Politics: Insights from Comparing Ancient China and Early Modern Europe. *International Organization* 58 (1): 175–205.

———. 2005. *War and State Formation in Ancient China and Early Modern Europe*. Cambridge: Cambridge University Press.

———. 2008. How China Was Ruled. *The American Interest* (March/April): 53–65.

Huntington, Samuel P. 1968. *Political Order in Changing Societies*. New Haven, CT: Yale University Press.

Huntley, Wade. 1996. Kant's Third Image: Systemic Sources of the Liberal Peace. *International Studies Quarterly* 40 (1): 40–76.

Huth, Paul K. 1988. *Extended Deterrence and the Prevention of War*. New Haven, CT: Yale University Press.

Ike, Nobutaka. 1967. *Japan's Decision for War: Records of the 1941 Policy Conferences*. Stanford, CA: Stanford University Press.

Ikenberry, G. John. 2001. *After Victory: Institutions, Strategic Restraint and the Rebuilding of Order After Major Wars*. Princeton, NJ: Princeton University Press.

———. 2003. Is American Multilateralism in Decline? *Perspectives on Politics* 1 (3): 533–50.

———. 2006. *Liberal Order and Imperial Ambitions: Essays on American Power and World Politics*. Malden, MA: Polity Press.

———. 2008a. The Rise of China and the Future of the West: Can the Liberal System Survive? *Foreign Affairs* 87 (1): 23–37.

———. 2008b. The Rise of China: Power, Institutions, and the Western Order. In *China's Ascent: Power, Security, and the Future of International Politics*, ed. Robert Ross and Feng Zhu, 89–114. Ithaca, NY: Cornell University Press.

Ikenberry, G. John, and Michael Mastanduno. 2003. Conclusion: Images of Order in the Asia-Pacific and the Role of the United States. In *International Relations Theory and the Asia-Pacific*, ed. G. John Ikenberry and Michael Mastanduno, 421–39. New York: Columbia University Press.

Ikenberry, G. John, Michael Mastanduno, and William C. Wohlforth. 2009. Introduction: Unipolarity, State Behavior, and Systemic Consequences. *World Politics* 61 (1): 1–27.

Inglehart, Ronald. 1977. *The Silent Revolution*. Princeton, NJ: Princeton University Press.

———. 1990. *Culture Shift in Advanced Industrial Countries*. Princeton, NJ: Princeton University Press.

———. 1997. *Modernization and Postmodernization: Cultural, Economic, and Political Change in 43 Societies*. Princeton, NJ: Princeton University Press.

Inglehart, Ronald, Miguel Basanez, Jaime Diez-Medrano, Loek Halman, and Ruud Luijkx, eds. 2004. *Human Beliefs and Values*. Mexico: Siglo Veintiuno Editores.

Inoguchi, Takashi. 2007. Japan: Bilateralism at Any Cost? In *The Uses of Institutions: The U.S., Japan, and Governance in East Asia*, ed. G. John Ikenberry and Takashi Inoguchi, 51–73. New York: Palgrave Macmillan.

Inoguchi, Takashi, Akihiko Tanaka, Shigeto Sonoda, and Timur Dadabaev. 2006. *Human Beliefs and Values in Striding Asia*. Tokyo: Akashi Shoten.

Jacobson, Harold K., Robert D. Putnam, and Peter B. Evans, eds. 1993. *Double-Edged Diplomacy: International Bargaining and Domestic Politics*. Berkeley: University of California Press.

Jacoby, Neil H. 1966. *U.S. Aid to Taiwan: A Study of Foreign Aid, Self-Help, and Development*. New York: Praeger.

Jervis, Robert. 1968. Hypotheses on Misperception. *World Politics* 20 (3): 454–79.

———. 1976. *Perception and Misperception in International Politics*. Princeton, NJ: Princeton University Press.

———. 1978. Cooperation Under the Security Dilemma. *World Politics* 30 (2): 167–214.

———. 2003. Explaining the Bush Doctrine. *Political Science Quarterly* 118 (3): 365–88.

———. 2005. *American Foreign Policy in a New Era*. New York: Routledge.

———. 2009. Unipolarity: A Structural Perspective. *World Politics* 61 (1): 188–213.

Joffe, Joseph. 1995. "Bismarck" or "Britain"? Toward an American Grand Strategy after Bipolarity. *International Security* 19 (4): 94–117.

Johnson, Chalmers A. 1982. *MITI and the Japanese Miracle*. Stanford, CA: Stanford University Press.

———. 2000. *Blowback: The Costs and Consequences of American Empire*. New York: Metropolitan Books.

Johnston, Alastair I. 1995. *Cultural Realism: Strategic Culture and Grand Strategy in Chinese History*. Princeton, NJ: Princeton University Press.

———. 1999. Realism(s) and Chinese Security Policy in the Post–Cold War Period. In *Unipolar Politics: Realism and State Strategies After the Cold War*, ed. Ethan B. Kapstein and Michael Mastanduno, 261–319. New York: Columbia University Press.

———. 2003a. Is China a Status Quo Power? *International Security* 7 (4): 5–56.

———. 2003b. Socialization in International Institutions: The ASEAN Way and International Relations Theory. In *International Relations Theory and the Asia-Pacific*, ed. G. John Ikenberry and Michael Mastanduno, 107–62. New York: Columbia University Press.

Johnston, Alastair I., and Paul Evans. 1999. China's Engagement with Multilateral Security Institutions. In *Engaging China: The Management of an Emergent Power*, ed. Alastair I. Johnston and Robert Ross, 235–72. New York: Routledge.

Jones, Leroy, and Il Sakong. 1980. *Government, Business, and Entrepreneurship in Economic Development: The Korea Case*. Cambridge, MA: Harvard University Press.

Joo, Seung-Ho. 2007. Allies Under Strain: U.S.-Korean Relations Under G. W. Bush. In *Korean Security in a Changing East Asia*, ed. Terence Roehrig, Jungmin Seo, and Uk Heo, 171–91. Westport, CT: Praeger.

Kagan, Donald, ed. 1962. *Decline and Fall of the Roman Empire: Why Did It Collapse?* Boston: Heath.

Kahneman, Daniel, Paul Slovic, and Amos Tversky, eds. 1982. *Judgments Under Uncertainty: Heuristics and Biases*. Cambridge: Cambridge University Press.

Kahneman, Daniel, and Amos Tversky. 1979. Prospect Theory: An Analysis of Decision Under Risk. *Econometrica* 47 (2): 263–91.

———, eds. 2000. *Choices, Values and Frames*. Cambridge: Cambridge University Press.

Kamlet, Mark S., David C. Mowery, and Tsai-Tsu Su. 1988. Upsetting National Priorities: The Reagan Administration's Budgetary Strategy. *American Political Science Review* 82 (4): 1293–1307.

Kane, Tim. 2004. *Global U.S. Troop Deployment, 1950–2003*. Washington, DC: Heritage Foundation.

Kang, David C. 2003a. Acute Conflicts in Asia After the Cold War. In *Asian Security Order: Instrumental and Normative Features*, ed. Muthiah Alagappa, 349–79. Stanford, CA: Stanford University Press.

———. 2003b. Getting Asia Wrong: The Need for New Analytical Frameworks. *International Security* 27 (4): 57–85.

———. 2003c. Hierarchy and Stability in Asian International Relations. In *International Relations Theory and the Asia-Pacific*, ed. G. John Ikenberry and Michael Mastanduno, 163–89. New York: Columbia University Press.

———. 2003/04. Hierarchy, Balancing, and Empirical Puzzles in Asian International Relations. *International Security* 28 (3): 165–80.

———. 2007a. Causes and Consequences of North–South Cooperation. In *Korean Security in a Changing East Asia*, ed. Terence Roehrig, Jungmin Seo, and Uk Heo, 53–69. Westport, CT: Praeger.

———. 2007b. *China Rising: Peace, Power, and Order in East Asia*. New York: Columbia University Press.

———. 2009. Between Balancing and Bandwagoning: South Korea's Response to China. *Journal of East Asian Studies* 9 (1): 1–28.

Karabell, Zachary. 2009. *Superfusion: How China and America Became One Economy and Why the World's Prosperity Depends on It*. New York: Simon & Schuster.

Kastner, Scott L. 2009. *Political Conflict and Economic Interdependence Across the Taiwan Strait*. Stanford, CA: Stanford University Press.

Katzenstein, Peter J., and Robert O. Keohane, eds. 2007. *Anti-Americanisms in World Politics*. Ithaca, NY: Cornell University Press.

Kaufman, Chaim. 2004. Threat Inflation and the Failure of the Marketplace of Ideas: The Selling of the Iraq War. *International Security* 29 (1): 5–48.

———. 2005. Selling the Market Short: The Marketplace of Ideas and the Iraq War. *International Security* 29 (4): 196–207.

Kaufman, Robert G. 1992. To Balance or to Bandwagon? Alignment Decisions in 1930s Europe. *Security Studies* 1 (3): 417–47.

Kaufman, Stuart J., Richard Little, and William C. Wohlforth, eds. 2007. *The Balance of Power in World History*. New York: Palgrave Macmillan.

Kawasaki, Tsuyoshi. 2007. Layering Institutions: The Logic of Japan's Institutional Strategy for Regional Security. In *The Uses of Institutions: The U.S., Japan, and Governance in East Asia*, ed. G. John Ikenberry and Takashi Inoguchi, 77–102. New York: Palgrave Macmillan.

Kegley, Charles W., Jr., and Gregory Raymond. 1994. *A Multipolar Peace? Great-Power Politics in the Twenty-First Century*. New York: St. Martin's Press.

Kennedy, Paul M. 1981. *The Realities Behind Diplomacy: Background Influences on British External Policy, 1865–1980*. London: Allen & Unwin.

———. 1982. *The Rise of the Anglo-German Antagonism, 1860–1914*. London: Allen & Unwin.

———. 1987. *The Rise and Fall of the Great Powers: Economic Change and Military Conflict from 1500 to 2000*. New York: Random House.

Kent, Ann. 2007. *Beyond Compliance: China, International Organizations, and Global Security*. Stanford, CA: Stanford University Press.

Keohane, Robert O., and Joseph S. Nye. 1977. *Power and Interdependence: World Politics in Transition*, Boston: Little, Brown.

Khong, Yuen Foong. 2001. Negotiating "Order" During Power Transitions. In *Power in Transition: The Peaceful Change of International Order,* ed. Charles A. Kupchan, Emanuel Adler, Jean-Marc Coicaud, and Yuen Foong Khong, 34–67. Tokyo: United Nations University Press.

———. 2004. Coping with Strategic Uncertainty: The Role of Institutions and Soft Balancing in Southeast Asia's Post–Cold War Strategy. In *Rethinking Security in East Asia: Identity, Power, and Efficiency*, ed. J. J. Suh, Peter J. Katzenstein, and Allen Carlson, 172–208. Stanford, CA: Stanford University Press.

Khoo, Nicholas, and Michael L. R. Smith. 2005. Correspondence with David Shambaugh: China Engages Asia? Caveat Lector. *International Security* 30 (1): 196–213.

Kim, Woosang. 1989. Power, Alliance, and Major Wars, 1816–1975. *Journal of Conflict Resolution* 33 (2): 255–73.

———. 1991. Alliance Transitions and Great Power War. *American Journal of Political Science* 35 (4): 833–50.

———. 1992. Power Transitions and Great Power War from Westphalia to Waterloo. *World Politics* 45 (1): 153–72.

———. 2002. Power Parity, Alliance, Dissatisfaction, and Wars in East Asia, 1860–1993. *Journal of Conflict Resolution* 46 (5): 654–72.

Kim, Woosang, and James D. Morrow. 1992. When Do Power Shifts Lead to War? *American Journal of Political Science* 36 (4): 896–922.

Kindleberger, Charles P. 1973. *The World in Depression, 1929–1939.* Berkeley: University of California Press.

Kirby, Julius. 1920. *The Mesta.* Cambridge, MA: Harvard University Press.

Kirshner, Jonathan. 1995. *Currency and Coercion: The Political Economy of International Monetary Power.* Princeton, NJ: Princeton University Press.

———. 2003. States, Markets, and Great Power Relations in the Pacific: Some Realist Expectations. In *International Relations Theory and the Asia-Pacific,* ed. G. John Ikenberry and Michael Mastanduno, 273–98. New York: Columbia University Press.

———. 2010. The Tragedy of Offensive Realism: Classical Realism and the Rise of China. *European Journal of International Relations* (August): 1–23.

Kissinger, Henry A. 1973. *The World Restored: Metternich, Castlereagh, and the Problems of Peace, 1812–1822.* New York: Houghton Mifflin.

Kohut, Andrew, and Bruce Stokes. 2006. *America Against the World: How We Are Different and Why We Are Disliked.* New York: Times Books.

Kramer, Mark. 1999. Neorealism, Nuclear Proliferation, and East–Central European Strategies. In *Unipolar Politics: Realism and State Strategies After the Cold War,* ed. Ethan B. Kapstein and Michael Mastanduno, 385–463. New York: Columbia University Press.

Kugler, Jacek. 2006. The Asian Ascent: Opportunity for Peace or Precondition for War? *International Studies Perspectives* 7 (1): 36–42.

Kugler, Jacek, and Douglas Lemke, eds. 1996. *Parity and War: Evaluations and Extensions of The War Ledger.* Ann Arbor: University of Michigan Press.

———. 2000. The Power Transition Research Program. In *Handbook of War Studies II,* ed. Manus I. Midlarsky, 129–63. Ann Arbor: University of Michigan Press.

Kunz, Diane B. 1991. *The Economic Diplomacy of the Suez Crisis.* Chapel Hill: University of North Carolina Press.

Kydd, Andrew H. 1997a. Game Theory and the Spiral Model. *World Politics* 49 (3): 371–400.

———. 1997b. Sheep in Sheep's Clothing: Why Security Seekers Do Not Fight Each Other. *Security Studies* 7 (1): 114–55.

———. 2000. Trust, Reassurance, and Cooperation. *International Organization* 54 (2): 325–57.

———. 2005. *Trust and Mistrust in International Relations*. Princeton, NJ: Princeton University Press.

Labs, Eric J. 1992. Do Weak States Bandwagon? *Security Studies* 1 (3): 383–416.

Lake, David A. 2009. *Hierarchy in International Relations*. Ithaca, NY: Cornell University Press.

Larson, Deborah W. 1991. Bandwagon Images in American Foreign Policy: Myth or Reality? In *Dominoes and Bandwagons: Strategic Beliefs and Great Power Competition in the Eurasian Rimland*, ed. Robert Jervis and Jack Snyder, 85–111. Oxford: Oxford University Press.

Layne, Christopher. 1993. The Unipolar Illusion: Why New Great Powers Will Rise. *International Security* 17 (4): 5–51.

———. 2003. "The Poster Child for Offensive Realism:" America as Global Hegemon. *Security Studies* 12 (2): 120–64.

———. 2005. War on Terrorism. In *Balance of Power: Theory and Practice in the 21st Century*, ed. T. V. Paul, James J. Wirtz, and Michel Fortmann, 103–26. Stanford, CA: Stanford University Press.

———. 2006a. *The Peace of Illusion: American Grand Strategy from 1940 to the Present*. Ithaca, NY: Cornell University Press.

———. 2006b. The Unipolar Illusion Revisited: The Coming End of the United States' Unipolar Moment. *International Security* 31 (2): 7–41.

———. 2009a. The Influence of Theory on Grand Strategy: The United States and a Rising China. In *Rethinking Realism in International Relations: Between Tradition and Innovation*, ed. Annette Freyberg-Inan, Ewan Harrison, and Patrick James, 103–35. Baltimore: Johns Hopkins University Press.

———. 2009b. The Waning of U.S. Hegemony: Myth or Reality? A Review Essay. *International Security* 34 (4): 147–72.

Leblang, David, and Shanka Satyanath. 2006. Institutions, Expectations and Currency Crises. *International Organization* 60 (1): 254–62.

Lebovic, James H., and Ashfaq Ishaq. 1987. Military Burden, Security Needs, and Economic Growth in the Middle East. *Journal of Conflict Resolution* 31 (1): 106–38.

Lebow, Richard N. 1994. The Long Peace, the End of Cold War, and the Failure of Realism. *International Organization* 48 (2): 249–77.

Lebow, Richard N., and Benjamin Valentino. 2009. Lost in Transition: A Critical Analysis of Power Transition Theory. *International Relations* 23 (3): 389–410.

Legro, Jeffrey W. 2005. *Rethinking the World: Great Power Strategies and International Order*. Ithaca, NY: Cornell University Press.

———. 2007. What China Will Want: The Future Intentions of a Rising Power. *Perspectives on Politics* 5 (3): 515–34.

———. 2008. Purpose Transitions: China's Rise and the American Response. In *China's Ascent: Power, Security, and the Future of International Politics*, ed. Robert Ross and Feng Zhu, 163–87. Ithaca, NY: Cornell University Press.

Legro, Jeffrey W., and Andrew Moravcsik. 1999. Is Anybody Still a Realist? *International Security* 24 (2): 5–56.

Lemke, Douglas. 2002. *Regions of War and Peace*. Cambridge: Cambridge University Press.

———. 2003. Investigating the Preventive Motive for War. *International Interactions* 29 (4): 273–92.

———. 2004. Great Powers in the Post–Cold War World: A Power Transition Perspective. In *Balance of Power: Theory and Practice in the 21st Century*, ed. T. V. Paul, James J. Wirtz, and Michel Fortmann, 52–75. Stanford, CA: Stanford University Press.

Lemke, Douglas, and Ronald L. Tammen. 2003. Power Transition Theory and the Rise of China. *International Interactions* 29 (4): 269–71.

Lemke, Douglas, and Suzanne Werner. 1996. Power Parity, Commitment to Change, and War. *International Studies Quarterly* 40 (2): 235–60.

Levathes, Louise. 1994. *When China Ruled the Seas: The Treasure Fleet of the Dragon Throne 1405–1433*. New York: Simon & Schuster.

Levy, Jack S. 1984. The Offense–Defense Balance in Military Technology: A Theoretical and Historical Analysis. *International Studies Quarterly* 38 (2): 219–38.

———. 1987. Declining Power and the Preventive Motivation for War. *World Politics* 60 (1): 82–107.

———. 1996. Loss Aversion, Framing, and Bargaining: The Implications of Prospect Theory for International Conflict. *International Political Science Review* 17 (2): 179–95.

———. 1997. Prospect Theory, Rational Choice, and International Relations. *International Studies Quarterly* 41 (1): 87–112.

———. 2003. Balances and Balancing: Concepts, Propositions, and Research Design. In *Realism and the Balancing of Power: A New Debate*, ed. John A. Vasquez and Colin Elman, 129–53. Upper Saddle River, NJ: Prentice-Hall.

———. 2008a. Power Transition Theory and the Rise of China. In *China's Ascent: Power, Security, and the Future of International Politics*, ed. Robert S. Ross and Zhu Feng, 11–33. Ithaca, NY: Cornell University Press.

———. 2008b. Preventive War and Democratic Politics. *International Studies Quarterly* 52 (1): 1–24.

Levy, Jack S., and Joseph R. Gochal. 2001. Democracy and Preventive War: Israel and the 1956 Sinai Campaign. *Security Studies* 11 (2): 1–49.

Levy, Jack S., and William R. Thompson. 2005. Hegemonic Threats and Great-Power Balancing in Europe, 1495–1999. *Security Studies* 14 (1): 1–33.

———. 2010. Balancing on Land and at Sea: Do States Ally Against the Leading Global Power? *International Security* 35 (1): 7–43.

Lewis, Mark Edward. 1999. Warring States: Political History. In *The Cambridge History of Ancient China*, ed. Michael Loewe and Edward L. Shaughnessy, 587–650. Cambridge: Cambridge University Press.

Liberman, Peter. 1996. Trading with the Enemy: Security and Relative Economic Gains. *International Security* 21 (1): 147–75.

———. 1998. *Does Conquest Pay? The Exploitation of Occupied Industrial Societies*. Princeton, NJ: Princeton University Press.

Lieber, Keir A., and Gerard Alexander. 2005. Waiting for Balancing: Why the World Is Not Pushing Back. *International Security* 30 (1): 109–39.

———. 2005/06. Correspondence: Striking the Balance. *International Security* 30 (3): 191–96.

Lieber, Keir A., and Daryl G. Press. 2006. The End of MAD: The Nuclear Dimension of U.S. Primacy. *International Security* 30 (4): 7–44.

Lindblom, Charles E. 1965. *The Intelligence of Democracy: Decision-Making Through Adjustment*. New York: Free Press.

Lipset, Seymour M. 1963. *Political Man: The Social Bases of Politics*. Garden City, NY: Doubleday.

Little, Richard. 2007a. *The Balance of Power in International Relations: Metaphors, Myths and Models*. Cambridge: Cambridge University Press.

———. 2007b. British Neutrality Versus Offshore Balancing in the American Civil War: The English School Strikes Back. *Security Studies* 16 (1): 68–95.

———. 2009. Revisiting Realism and the Balance of Power. In *Rethinking Realism in International Relations: Between Tradition and Innovation*, ed. Annette Freyberg-Inan, Ewan Harrison, and Patrick James, 21–44. Baltimore: Johns Hopkins University Press.

Lobell, Steven E. 2007. The Second Face of Security: Britain's "Smart" Appeasement Policy Towards Japan and Germany. *International Relations of the Asia-Pacific* 7 (1): 73–98.

Long, William J. 1996. *Economic Incentives and Bilateral Cooperation*. Ann Arbor: University of Michigan Press.

Looney, Robert E., and Peter C. Frederiksen. 1988. Defense Expenditures, External Public Debt, and Growth in Developing Countries. *Journal of Peace Research* 23 (4): 329–37.

Luciani, Giacomo, ed. 1990. *The Arab State*. Berkeley: University of California Press.

Mack, Andrew, and John Ravenhill, eds. 1995. *Pacific Cooperation: Building Economic and Security Regimes in the Asia-Pacific Region*. Boulder, CO: Westview.

Mansfield, Edward D., and Jon C. Pevehouse. 2006. Democratization and International Organizations. *International Organization* 60 (1): 137–67.

Mansfield, Edward D., and Brian Pollins, eds. 2003. *Economic Interdependence and International Conflict: New Perspectives on an Enduring Debate*. Ann Arbor: University of Michigan Press.

Martin, Lisa L. 1992. *Coercive Cooperation: Explaining Multilateral Economic Sanctions*. Princeton, NJ: Princeton University Press.

———. 1993a. Credibility, Costs, and Institutions: Cooperation on Economic Sanctions. *World Politics* 45 (3): 406–43.

———. 1993b. The Rational State Choice of Multilateralism. In *Multilateralism Matters: The Theory and Praxis of an Institutional Form*, ed. John G. Ruggie, 91–121. New York: Columbia University Press.

———. 2003. Multilateral Organizations After the U.S.-Iraq War. In *The Iraq War and Its Consequences: Thoughts of Nobel Peace Laureates and Eminent Scholars*, ed. Irwin Abrams and Gungwu Wang, 359–73. Singapore: World Scientific Publishing.

Mastanduno, Michael. 1992. *Economic Containment: CoCom and the Politics of East–West Trade*. Ithaca, NY: Cornell University Press.

———. 1997. Preserving the Unipolar Moment: Realist Theories and U.S. Grand Strategy After the Cold War. *International Security* 21 (4): 49–88.

———. 2003. Incomplete Hegemony: The United States and Security Order in Asia. In *Asian Security Order: Instrumental and Normative Features*, ed. Muthiah Alagappa, 141–70. Stanford, CA: Stanford University Press.

———. 2007. Institutions of Convenience: U.S. Foreign Policy and the Pragmatic Use of International Institutions. In *The Uses of Institutions: The U.S., Japan, and Governance in East Asia*, ed. G. John Ikenberry and Takashi Inoguchi, 29–50. New York: Palgrave Macmillan.

———. 2009. System Maker and Privilege Taker: U.S. Power and the International Political Economy. *World Politics* 61 (1): 121–54.

Mastanduno, Michael, and Ethan B. Kapstein. 1999. Realism and State Strategies After the Cold War. In *Unipolar Politics: Realism and State Strategies After the Cold War*, ed. Ethan B. Kapstein and Michael Mastanduno, 1–27. New York: Columbia University Press.

McDermott, Rose. 1998. *Risk-Taking in International Politics: Prospect Theory in American Foreign Policy.* Ann Arbor: University of Michigan Press.

McDonald, Patrick J. 2007. The Purse Strings of Peace. *American Journal of Political Science* 51 (3): 569–82.

———. 2009. *The Invisible Hand of Peace: Capitalism, the War Machine, and International Relations Theory.* New York: Cambridge University Press.

McDonald, Patrick J., and Kevin Sweeney. 2007. The Achilles' Heel of Liberal IR Theory? Globalization and Conflict in the Pre–World War I Era. *World Politics* 59 (3): 370–403.

Mearsheimer, John J. 2001. *The Tragedy of Great Power Politics.* New York: Norton.

———. 2006. China's Unpeaceful Rise. *Current History* 105 (690): 160–62.

Mearsheimer, John J., and Stephen M. Walt. 2003. An Unnecessary War. *Foreign Policy* (January–February): 50–59.

Medlicott, William N. 1965. *Bismarck and Modern Germany.* New York: Harper & Row.

Melman, Seymour. 1974. *The Permanent War Economy: American Capitalism in Decline.* New York: Simon & Schuster.

Miller, Eric A., and Arkady Toritsyn. 2005. Bringing the Leader Back In: Internal Threats and Alignment Theory in the Commonwealth of Independent States. *Security Studies* 14 (2): 325–63.

Mintz, Alex, ed. 1992. *The Political Economy of Military Spending in the United States.* London: Routledge.

Mintz, Alex, and Chi Huang. 1990. Defense Expenditures, Economic Growth and the "Peace Dividend." *American Political Science Review* 84 (4): 1283–93.

———. 1991. "Guns" Vs. "Butter": The Indirect Link. *American Journal of Political Science* 35 (3): 738–57.

Mitrany, David. 1966. *A Working Peace System.* Chicago: Quadrangle Books.

———. 1976. *A Functional Theory of Politics.* New York: St. Martin's Press.

Modelski, George. 1987. *Long Cycles in World Politics.* Seattle: University of Washington Press.

Modelski, George, and William R. Thompson. 1996. *Leading Sectors and World Politics: The Coevolution of Global Politics and Economics.* Columbia: University of South Carolina Press.

Montgomery, Evan B. 2006. Breaking out of the Security Dilemma: Realism, Reassurance, and the Problem of Uncertainty. *International Security* 31 (2): 151–85.

Moon, Chung-in, and Chaesung Chun. 2003. Sovereignty: Dominance of the Westphalian Concept and Implications for Regional Security. In *Asian Security Order: Instrumental and Normative Features,* ed. Muthiah Alagappa, 106–37. Stanford, CA: Stanford University Press.

Moon, Chung-in, and On-taek Hyun. 1992. Muddling Through Security, Growth, and Welfare: The Political Economy of Defense Spending in South Korea. In *Defense, Welfare, and Growth: Perspectives and Evidence,* ed. Steve Chan and Alex Mintz, 137–62. London: Routledge.

Morgenthau, Hans J. 1948. *Politics Among Nations: The Struggle for Power and Peace.* New York: Knopf.

———. 1951. *In Defense of the National Interest.* New York: Knopf.

———. 1965. *Vietnam and the United States.* Washington DC: Public Affairs Press.

Morrow, James D. 1997. When Do "Relative Gains" Impede Trade? *Journal of Conflict Resolution* 41 (1): 12–37.

———. 2003. Assessing the Role of Trade as a Source of Costly Signals. In *Economic Interdependence and International Conflict*, ed. Edward D. Mansfield and Brian Pollins, 89–95. Ann Arbor: University of Michigan Press.

Mosher, Steven. 2001. *Hegemon: China's Plan to Dominate Asia and the World*. San Francisco: Encounter Books.

Most, Benjamin A., and Randolph M. Siverson. 1987. Substituting Arms and Alliances, 1870–1914: An Exploration in Comparative Foreign Policy. In *New Directions in the Study of Foreign Policy*, ed. Charles F. Hermann, Charles W. Kegley, Jr., and James N. Rosenau, 131–57. Boston: Allen & Unwin.

Most, Benjamin A., and Harvey Starr. 1989. *Inquiry, Logic and International Politics*. Columbia: University of South Carolina Press.

Mueller, Karl P., Jason J. Castillo, Forrest E. Morgan, Negeen Pegahi, and Brian Rosen. 2006. *Striking First: Preemptive and Preventive Attack in U.S. National Security Policy*. Santa Monica: Rand.

Murata, Koji. 2007. U.S.-Japan Alliance as a Flexible Institution. In *The Uses of Institutions: The U.S., Japan, and Governance in East Asia*, ed. G. John Ikenberry and Takashi Inoguchi, 131–50. New York: Palgrave Macmillan.

Nexon, Daniel H. 2009. The Balance of Power in the Balance. *World Politics* 61 (2): 330–59.

Niou, Emerson M. S., Peter C. Ordeshook, and Gregory F. Rose. 1989. *The Balance of Power: Stability in International Systems*. Cambridge: Cambridge University Press.

Nish, Ian. 1986. *The Origins of the Russo-Japanese War*. London: Longman.

Nitta, Keith A. 2002. Paradigms. In *U.S.-Japan Relations in a Changing World*, ed. Steven K. Vogel, 63–93. Washington, DC: Brookings Institution Press.

North, Douglas C. 1990. *Institutions, Institutional Change, and Economic Performance*. Cambridge: Cambridge University Press.

O'Donnell, Guillermo. 1979. *Modernization and Bureaucratic-Authoritarianism: Studies in South American Politics*. Berkeley: University of California Institute for International Studies.

Olson, Mancur, Jr. 1965. *The Logic of Collective Action: Public Goods and the Theory of Groups*. Cambridge, MA: Harvard University Press.

———. 1982. *The Rise and Decline of Nations: Economic Growth, Stagflation, and Social Rigidities*. New Haven, CT: Yale University Press.

Olson, Mancur, Jr., and Richard Zeckhauser. 1966. An Economic Theory of Alliances. *Review of Economics and Statistics* 48 (August): 266–79.

Oneal, John R., and Bruce Russett. 1997. The Classic Liberals Were Right: Democracy, Interdependence, and Conflict, 1950–1985. *International Studies Quarterly* 41 (2): 267–94.

Oren, Ido. 2003. *Our Enemies and US: America's Rivalries and the Making of Political Science*. Ithaca, NY: Cornell University Press.

Organski, A. F. K. 1958. *World Politics*. New York: Knopf.

Organski, A. F. K., and Jacek Kugler. 1978. Davids and Goliaths: Predicting the Outcomes of International Wars. *Comparative Political Studies* 11 (2): 141–80.

———. 1980. *The War Ledger*. Chicago: University of Chicago Press.

Osgood, Charles E. 1962. *An Alternative to War or Surrender*. Urbana: University of Illinois Press.

Owen, Roger, and Sevket Pamuk. 1999. *A History of Middle East Economies in the Twentieth Century*. Cambridge, MA: Harvard University Press.

Owens, John M., IV. 1997. *Liberal Peace, Liberal War: American Politics and International Security*. Ithaca, NY: Cornell University Press.

Papayoanou, Paul A. 1999. *Power Ties: Economic Interdependence, Balancing, and War*. Ann Arbor: University of Michigan Press.

Pape, Robert A. 2005. Soft Balancing Against the United States. *International Security* 30 (1): 7–45.

Paul, T. V. 1994. *Asymmetric Conflicts: War Initiation by Weaker Powers*. Cambridge: Cambridge University Press.

―――. 2005. Soft Balancing in the Age of U.S. Primacy. *International Security* 30 (1): 46–71.

Pempel, T. J. 2007. Japanese Strategy Under Koizumi. In *Japanese Strategic Thought Toward Asia*, ed. Gilbert Rozman, Kazuhiko Togo, and Joseph P. Ferguson, 109–33. New York: Palgrave Macmillan.

Peroff, Kathleen, and Margaret Podolak-Warren. 1979. Does Spending on Defense Cut Spending on Health? A Time Series Analysis of the U.S. Economy 1929–1974. *British Journal of Political Science* 9 (1): 21–40.

Petri, Peter A. 1993. The East Asian Trading Bloc: An Analytical History. In *Regionalism and Rivalry: Japan and the United States in Pacific Asia*, ed. Jeffrey A. Frankel and Miles Kahler, 21–48. Chicago: University of Chicago Press.

Pollack, Jonathan D. 2005. The Transformation of the Asian Security Order: Assessing China's Impact. In *Power Shift: China and Asia's New Dynamics,* ed. David Shambaugh, 329–46. Berkeley: University of California Press.

Pollins, Brian M. 1989. Does Trade Still Follow the Flag? *American Political Science Review* 83 (2): 465–80.

Porter, Michael E. 1990. *The Competitive Advantage of Nations*. New York: Free Press.

Posen, Barry R. 2003. Command of the Commons: The Military Foundation of U.S. Hegemony. *International Security* 28 (1): 5–46.

Powell, Robert. 1996. Uncertainty, Shifting Power, and Appeasement. *American Political Science Review* 90 (4): 749–64.

―――. 1999. *In the Shadow of Power: States and Strategies in International Politics*. Princeton, NJ: Princeton University Press.

―――. 2006. War as a Commitment Problem. *International Organization* 60 (1): 169–203.

Putnam, Robert D. 1988. Diplomacy and Domestic Politics: The Logic of Two-Level Games. *International Organization* 42 (3): 427–60.

Pye, Lucian W. 1968. *The Spirit of Chinese Politics: A Psychocultural Study of the Authority Crisis in Political Development*. Cambridge, MA: MIT Press.

Pyle, Kenneth B. 1996. *The Japanese Question: Power and Purpose in a New Era*. Washington, DC: AEI Press.

―――. 2010. Troubled Alliance. *Asian Policy* 10 (July): 3–9.

Qin, Yaqing. 2007. Why Is There No Chinese International Relations Theory? *International Relations of the Asia-Pacific* 7 (3): 313–40.

Qin, Yaqing, and Ling Wei. 2008. Structures, Processes, and the Socialization of Power: East Asian Community-Building and the Rise of China. In *China's Ascent: Power, Security, and the Future of International Politics*, ed. Robert Ross and Feng Zhu, 115–38. Ithaca, NY: Cornell University Press.

Rasler, Karen A., and William R. Thompson. 1983. Global Wars, Public Debts, and the Long Cycle. *World Politics* 35 (4): 489–516.

———. 1988. Defense Burdens, Capital Formation, and Economic Growth: The Systemic Leader Case. *Journal of Conflict Resolution* 32 (1): 61–86.

———. 2000. Global War and the Political Economy of Structural Change. In *Handbook of War Studies II*, ed. Manus I. Midlarksy, 301–31. Ann Arbor: University of Michigan Press.

Reed, William. 2003. Information and Economic Interdependence. *Journal of Conflict Resolution* 47 (1): 54–71.

Reich, Robert B. 2009. China and the American Job Machine. *Wall Street Journal* (November 17): A25.

Reid, Anthony, and Yangwen Zheng, eds. 2009. *Negotiating Asymmetry: China's Place in Asia.* Honolulu: University of Hawaii Press.

Reuveny, Rafael, and William R. Thompson. 2004. *Growth, Trade, and Systemic Leadership.* Ann Arbor: University of Michigan Press.

Reychler, Luc. 1979. The Effectiveness of a Pacifist Strategy in Conflict Resolution. *Journal of Conflict Resolution* 23 (2): 228–60.

Rice, Condoleezza. 2000. Promoting the National Interest. *Foreign Affairs* 79 (January/February): 45–62.

Richardson, Lewis F. 1960. *Arms and Insecurity.* Pittsburgh: University of Pittsburgh Press.

Ripsman, Norrin M., and Jack S. Levy. 2008. Wishful Thinking or Buying Time: The Logic of British Appeasement in the 1930s. *International Security* 33 (2): 148–81.

Risse-Kappen, Thomas. 1991. Did "Peace Through Strength" End the Cold War? Lessons from the INF. *International Security* 16 (1): 162–88.

———. 1994. Ideas Do Not Float Freely: Transnational Coalitions, Domestic Structures, and the End of the Cold War. *International Organization* 48 (2): 185–214.

Rock, Stephen R. 2000. *Appeasement in International Politics.* Lexington: University of Kentucky Press.

Rose, Gideon. 1998. Neoclassical Realism and Theories of Foreign Policy. *World Politics* 51 (1): 144–72.

Rosecrance, Richard. 1986. *The Rise of the Trading State.* New York: Basic Books.

———. 2001. Has Realism Become Cost–Benefit Analysis? A Review Essay. *International Security* 26 (2): 132–54.

———. 2003. Is There a Balance of Power? In *Neorealism and the Balance of Power: A New Debate*, ed. John A. Vasquez and Colin Elman, 154–65. Upper Saddle River, NJ: Prentice Hall.

Rosecrance, Richard, and Chih-Cheng Lo. 1996. Balancing, Stability, and War: The Mysterious Case of the Napoleonic International System. *International Studies Quarterly* 40 (4): 479–500.

Rosecrance, Richard, and Arthur A. Stein. 1993. Beyond Realism: The Study of Grand Strategy. In *The Domestic Bases of Grand Strategy*, ed. Richard Rosecrance and Arthur A. Stein, 3–21. Ithaca, NY: Cornell University Press.

Rosecrance, Richard, and Zara Steiner. 1993. British Grand Strategy and the Origins of World War II. In *The Domestic Bases of Grand Strategy*, ed. Richard Rosecrance and Arthur A. Stein, 124–53. Ithaca, NY: Cornell University Press.

Ross, Robert S. 1997. Beijing as a Conservative Power. *Foreign Affairs* 76 (March/April): 33–44.

———. 1999. The Geography of Peace: East Asia in the Twenty-First Century. *International Security* 23 (4): 81–118.

————. 2004. Bipolarity and Balancing in East Asia. In *Balance of Power: Theory and Practice in the 21st Century*, ed. T. V. Paul, James J. Wirtz, and Michel Fortmann, 267–304. Stanford, CA: Stanford University Press.

————. 2006. Balance of Power Politics and the Rise of China: Accommodation and Balancing in East Asia. *Security Studies* 15 (3): 355–95.

————. 2009a. China's Naval Nationalism: Sources, Prospects, and the U.S. Response. *International Security* 34 (2): 46–81.

————. 2009b. *Chinese Security Policy: Structure, Power and Politics*. London: Routledge.

Ross, Robert S., and Feng Zhu, eds. 2008. *China's Ascent: Power, Security, and the Future of International Politics*. Ithaca, NY: Cornell University Press.

Rossabi, Norris, ed. 1983. *China Among Equals: The Middle Kingdom and Its Neighbors, 10th–14th Centuries*. Berkeley: University of California Press.

Rothschild, Kurt W. 1973. Military Expenditure, Exports, and Growth. *Kyklos* 26 (4): 804–14.

Roy, Denny. 1994. Hegemon on the Horizon? China's Threat to East Asian Security. *International Security* 19 (1): 149–68.

Rozman, Gilbert. 2007. *Strategic Thinking About the Korean Nuclear Crisis: Four Parties Caught Between North Korea and the United States*. New York: Palgrave Macmillan.

Ruggie, John G. 1993. The Anatomy of an Institution. In *Multilateralism Matters: The Theory and Praxis of an Institutional Form*, ed. John G. Ruggie, 3–47. New York: Columbia University Press.

Russett, Bruce M. 1970. *What Price Vigilance? The Burdens of National Defense*. New Haven, CT: Yale University Press.

————. 1982. Defense Expenditures and National Well-Being. *American Political Science Review* 76 (4): 767–77.

Russett, Bruce M., and John R. Oneal. 2001. *Triangulating Peace: Democracy, Interdependence, and International Organizations*. New York: Norton.

Russett, Bruce M., John R. Oneal, and David R. Davis. 1998. The Third Leg of the Kantian Triad: International Organizations and Militarized Disputes, 1950–1985. *International Organization* 52 (3): 441–67.

Russett, Bruce M., Harvey Starr, and David Kinsella. 2009. *World Politics: The Menu for Choice*, 9th ed. Boston: Wadsworth.

Sabrosky, Alan N. 1980. Interstate Alliances: Their Reliability and the Expansion of War. In *Correlates of War II*, ed. J. David Singer, 161–98. New York: Free Press.

Samuels, Richard J. 1994. *"Rich Nation, Strong Army": National Security and the Technological Transformation of Japan*. Ithaca, NY: Cornell University Press.

————. 2007. *Securing Japan: Tokyo's Grand Strategy and the Future of East Asia*. Ithaca, NY: Cornell University Press.

Sartori, Giovanni. 1970. Concept Misformation in Comparative Politics. *American Political Science Review* 64 (4): 1033–53.

Sawyer, Ralph D. 1994. *Sun Tzu: The Art of War*. Boulder, CO: Westview.

Scalapino, Robert A. 1987. *Major Power Relations in Northeast Asia*. Lanham, MD: University Press of America.

Schroeder, Paul. 1976. Alliances, 1815–1945: Weapons of Power and Tools of Management. In *Historical Dimensions of National Security Problems*, ed. Klaus Knorr, 227–62. Lawrence: University Press of Kansas.

————. 1994a. Historical Reality Versus Neo-Realist Theory. *International Security* 19 (1): 108–48.

———. 1994b. *The Transformation of European Politics, 1763–1848*. Oxford: Clarendon Press.

———. 2003. Why Realism Does Not Work Well for International History (Whether or Not It Represents a Degenerate IR Research Strategy). In *Realism and the Balance of Power: A New Debate*, ed., John A. Vasquez and Colin Elman, 114–27. Upper Saddle River, NJ: Prentice Hall.

———. 2004. Embedded Counterfactuals and World War I as an Unavoidable War. In *Systems, Stability, and Statecraft: Essays on the International History of Modern Europe*, ed. Paul W. Schroeder, 157–91. New York: Palgrave Macmillan.

Schultz, Kenneth A. 2001. *Democracy and Coercive Diplomacy*. Cambridge: Cambridge University Press.

Schultz, Kenneth, and Barry Weingast. 2003. The Democratic Advantage: Institutional Foundations of Financial Power in International Competition. *International Organization* 57 (1): 3–42.

Schwarz, Benjamin. 2005. Comment: Managing China's Rise. *The Atlantic Monthly* (June): 27.

Schweller, Randall L. 1992. Domestic Structure and Preventive War: Are Democracies More Pacific? *World Politics* 44 (2): 235–69.

———. 1994. Bandwagoning for Profit: Bringing the Revisionist State Back In. *International Security* 19 (1): 72–107.

———. 1996. Neorealism's Status-Quo Bias: What Security Dilemma? *Security Studies* 5 (3): 90–121.

———. 1998. *Deadly Imbalances: Tripolarity and Hitler's Strategy of World Conquest*. New York: Columbia University Press.

———. 1999. Managing the Rise of Great Powers. In *Engaging China: The Management of an Emerging Power*, ed. Alastair I. Johnston and Robert S. Ross, 1–31. London: Routledge.

———. 2004. Unanswered Threats: A Neoclassical Realist Theory of Underbalancing. *International Security* 29 (2): 159–201.

———. 2006. *Unanswered Threats: Political Constraints on the Balance of Power*. Princeton, NJ: Princeton University Press.

Segal, Gerald. 1996. East Asia and the "Constrainment" of China. *International Security* 20 (4): 107–35.

Senese, Paul D., and John A. Vasquez. 2008. *The Steps to War: An Empirical Study*. Princeton, NJ: Princeton University Press.

Sexton, Jay. 2005. *Debt Diplomacy: Finance and American Foreign Relations in the Civil War Era, 1837–1873*. Oxford: Oxford University Press.

Shambaugh, David. 2004/05. China Engages Asia: Reshaping the Regional Order. *International Security* 29 (3): 64–99.

———, ed. 2005. *Power Shift: China and Asia's New Dynamics*. Berkeley: University of California Press.

Shih, Chih-Yu. 2005. Breeding a Reluctant Dragon: Can China Rise into Partnership and Away from Antagonism? *Review of International Studies* 31 (4): 755–74.

Shin, Gi-Wook. 2007. Regionalism and Nationalism in Northeast Asia. In *Cross Currents: Regionalism and Nationalism in Northeast Asia*, ed. Gi-Wook Shin and Daniel C. Sneider, 11–39. Stanford, CA: Walter H. Shorenstein Asia-Pacific Research Center, Stanford University.

Shure, Gerald H., Robert J. Meeker, and Earle A. Hansford. 1965. The Effectiveness of Pacifist Strategies in Bargaining Games. *Journal of Conflict Resolution* 9 (1): 106–17.

Silverstone, Scott A. 2007. *Preventive War and American Democracy*. London: Routledge.

Simmons, Beth A., and Daniel J. Hopkins. 2005. The Constraining Power of International Treaties: Theory and Method. *American Political Science Review* 99 (4): 623–31.

Simon, Sheldon W., ed. 1993. *East Asian Security in the Post–Cold War Era*. Armonk, NY: Sharpe.

Singer, J. David. 1987. Reconstructing the Correlates of War Dataset on Material Capabilities of States, 1816–1985. *International Interactions* 14 (2): 115–32.

Singer, J. David, Stuart Bremer, and John Stuckey. 1968. Capability Distribution, Uncertainty, and Major Power War, 1820–1965. In *Peace, War, and Numbers*, ed. Bruce M. Russett, 19–48. Beverly Hills, CA: Sage.

Smith, Alastair. 1996. To Intervene or Not to Intervene: A Biased Decision. *Journal of Conflict Resolution* 40 (1): 16–40.

Smith, Ron P. 1977. Military Expenditure and Capitalism. *Cambridge Journal of Economics* 1 (1): 61–76.

———. 1980. Military Expenditure and Investment in OECD Countries, 1954–1973. *Journal of Comparative Economics* 4 (1): 19–32.

Smith, Ron P., and George Georgiou. 1983. Assessing the Effect of Military Expenditure on OECD Economies: A Survey. *Arms Control* 4 (1): 3–25.

Snyder, Glenn. 1991. Alliance Theory: A Neorealist First Cut. *International Organization* 45 (1): 121–42.

———. 1997. *Alliance Politics*. Ithaca, NY: Cornell University Press.

Snyder, Jack L. 1991. *Myths of Empire: Domestic Politics and International Ambition*. Ithaca, NY: Cornell University Press.

Snyder, Scott. 2007. The China–Japan Rivalry: Korea's Pivotal Position? In *Cross Currents: Regionalism and Nationalism in Northeast Asia*, ed. Gi-Wook Shin and Daniel C. Sneider, 241–55. Stanford, CA: Walter H. Shorenstein Asia-Pacific Research Center, Stanford University.

Solingen, Etel. 2003. Internationalization, Coalitions, and Regional Conflict and Cooperation. In *Economic Interdependence and International Conflict: New Perspectives on an Enduring Debate,* ed. Edward D. Mansfield and Brian M. Pollins, 60–85. Ann Arbor: University of Michigan Press.

———. 2007. Pax Asiatica Versus Belli Levantina: The Foundations of War and Peace in East Asia and the Middle East. *American Political Science Review* 101 (4): 757–80.

———. 2008. The Genesis, Design and Effects of Regional Institutions: Lessons from East Asia and the Middle East. *International Studies Quarterly* 52 (2): 261–94.

Stein, Arthur A. 1993. Domestic Constraints, Extended Deterrence, and the Incoherence of Grand Strategy: The United States, 1938–1950. In *The Domestic Bases of Grand Strategy*, ed. Richard Rosecrance and Arthur A. Stein, 96–123. Ithaca, NY: Cornell University Press.

———. 2003. Trade and Conflict: Uncertainty, Strategic Signaling, and Interstate Disputes. In *Economic Interdependence and International Conflict*, ed. Edward D. Mansfield and Brian Pollins, 111–26. Ann Arbor: University of Michigan Press.

Stiglitz, Joseph E., and Linda Bilmes. 2008. *The Three Trillion Dollar War: The True Cost of the Iraq Conflict*. New York: Norton.

Stinnett, Douglas M., and Paul F. Diehl. 2001. The Path(s) to Rivalry: Behavioral and Structural Explanations of Rivalry Development. *Journal of Politics* 63 (3): 717–40.

Strange, Susan. 1987. The Persistent Myth of Lost Hegemony. *International Organization* 41 (4): 551–74.

Suh, J. J. 2004. Bound to Last? The U.S.-Korea Alliance and Analytical Eclecticism. In *Rethinking Security in East Asia: Identity, Power, and Efficiency,* ed. J. J. Suh, Peter J. Katzenstein, and Allen Carlson, 131–71. Stanford, CA: Stanford University Press.

Sweeney, Kevin, and Paul Fritz. 2004. Jumping on the Bandwagon: An Interest-Based Explanation for Great Power Alliances. *Journal of Politics* 66 (2): 428–49.

Taliaferro, Jeffrey W. 2004. *Balancing Risks: Great Power Intervention in the Periphery.* Ithaca, NY: Cornell University Press.

Tammen, Ronald L., Jacek Kugler, Douglas Lemke, Allan C. Stam III, Mark Abdollahian, Carole Alsharabati, Brian Efird, and A. F. K. Organski. 2000. *Power Transitions: Strategies for the 21st Century.* New York: Chatham House.

Tellis, Ashley J., Janise Bially, Christopher Layne, and Melissa McPherson. 2000. *Measuring National Power in the Postindustrial Age.* Santa Monica: Rand.

Tessman, Brock F., and Steve Chan. 2004. Power Cycles, Risk Propensity, and the Escalation of Great Power Disputes. *Journal of Conflict Resolution* 48 (2): 131–53.

Thayer, Bradley A. 2005. Confronting China: An Elaboration of Options for the United States. *Comparative Strategy* 24 (1): 71–98.

Thompson, Peter. 2007. The Case of the Missing Hegemon: British Nonintervention in the American Civil War. *Security Studies* 16 (1): 96–132.

Thompson, William R. 1999. Why Rivalries Matter and What Great Power Rivalries Can Tell Us About World Politics. In *Great Power Rivalries,* ed. William R. Thompson, 3–28. Columbia: University of South Carolina Press.

Thorson, Stuart J., and Donald A. Sylvan. 1982. Counterfactuals and the Cuban Missile Crisis. *International Studies Quarterly* 26 (4): 539–71.

Tomz, Michael. 2007. *Reputation and International Cooperation: Sovereign Debt Across Three Centuries.* Princeton, NJ: Princeton University Press.

Trachtenberg, Marc. 2007. Preventive War and U.S. Foreign Policy. *Security Studies* 16 (1): 1–31.

Treisman, Daniel. 2004. Rational Appeasement. *International Organization* 58 (2): 344–73.

Tucker, Nancy Bernkopf. 2005. Strategic Ambiguity or Strategic Clarity. In *Dangerous Strait: The U.S.-Taiwan-China Crisis,* ed. Nancy Bernkopf Tucker, 186–211. New York: Columbia University Press.

Van Evera, Stephen. 1998. Offense, Defense and the Causes of War. *International Security* 22 (4): 5–43.

———. 1999. *Causes of War: Power and the Roots of Conflict.* Ithaca, NY: Cornell University Press.

Vasquez, John A. 1993. *The War Puzzle.* Cambridge: Cambridge University Press.

———. 1996. When Are Power Transitions Dangerous? An Appraisal and Reformulation of Power Transition Theory. In *Parity and War: Evaluations and Extensions of The War Ledger,* ed. Jacek Kugler and Douglas Lemke, 35–56. Ann Arbor: University of Michigan Press.

———. 1997. The Realist Paradigm and Degenerative Versus Progressive Research Programs: An Appraisal of Neotraditional Research on Waltz's Balancing Proposition. *American Political Science Review* 91 (4): 899–912.

———. 2003. The New Debate on Balancing Power: A Reply to My Critics. In *Realism and the Balance of Power: A New Debate,* ed., John A. Vasquez and Colin Elman, 87–113. Upper Saddle River, NJ: Prentice Hall.

Vasquez, John A., and Colin Elman, eds. 2003. *Realism and the Balance of Power: A New Debate.* Upper Saddle River, NJ: Prentice Hall.

Vicens Vives, Jaime. 1969. *An Economic History of Spain*. Trans. Frances M. Lopez Morillas. Princeton, NJ: Princeton University Press.

Voeten, Erik. 2004. Resisting the Lonely Superpower: Responses of States in the United Nations to U.S. Dominance. *Journal of Politics* 66 (3): 729–54.

Von Stein, Jana. 2005. Do Treaties Screen or Constrain? Selection Bias and Treaty Compliance. *American Political Science Review* 99 (4): 611–22.

Wachman, Alan M. 2007. *Why Taiwan? Geostrategic Rationales for China's Territorial Integrity*. Stanford, CA: Stanford University Press.

Wade, Robert. 1990. *Governing the Market: Economic Theory and the Role of Government in East Asian Industrialization*. Princeton, NJ: Princeton University Press.

Wagner, R. Harrison. 1993. What Was Bipolarity? *International Organization* 47 (1): 77–106.

———. 2000. Bargaining and War. *American Journal of Political Science* 44 (3): 469–84.

———. 2007. *War and the State: The Theory of International Politics*. Ann Arbor: University of Michigan Press.

Waldron, Arthur. 1990. *The Great Wall of China: From History to Myth*. New York: Cambridge University Press.

Walt, Stephen M. 1987. *The Origins of Alliances*. Ithaca, NY: Cornell University Press.

———. 1988. Testing Theories of Alliance Formation: The Case of Southwest Asia. *International Organization* 42 (2): 275–316.

———. 1992. Alliance, Threats, and U.S. Grand Strategy: A Reply to Kaufman and Labs. *Security Studies* 1 (3): 448–82.

———. 2002. Keeping the World "Off Balance": Self Restraint and U.S. Foreign Policy. In *America Unrivaled: The Future of the Balance of Power*, ed. G. John Ikenberry, 121–54. Ithaca, NY: Cornell University Press.

———. 2005. *Taming American Power: The Global Response to U.S. Primacy*. New York: Norton.

———. 2009. Alliances in a Unipolar World. *World Politics* 61 (1): 86–120.

Walter, Barbara F. 2002. *Committing to Peace: The Successful Settlement of Civil Wars*. Princeton, NJ: Princeton University Press.

Waltz, Kenneth N. 1979. *Theory of International Politics*. Reading, MA: Addison-Wesley.

———. 1986. Reflections on *Theory of International Relations*: A Reply to My Critics. In *Neorealism and Its Critics*, ed. Robert O. Keohane, 322–46. New York: Columbia University Press.

———. 1988. The Origins of War in Neorealist Theory. *Journal of Interdisciplinary History* 18 (4): 615–28.

———. 1993. The Emerging Structure of International Politics. *International Security* 18 (2): 44–79.

———. 1997. Evaluating Theories. *American Political Science Review* 91 (4): 913–17.

———. 2000. Structural Realism After the Cold War. *International Security* 25 (1): 5–41.

Wan, Ming. 2003. Economic Interdependence and Economic Cooperation: Mitigating Conflict and Transforming Security Order in Asia. In *Asian Security Order: Instrumental and Normative Features*, ed. Muthiah Alagappa, 281–345. Stanford, CA: Stanford University Press.

———. 2007. Japanese Strategic Thinking Toward Taiwan. In *Japanese Strategic Thought Toward Asia*, ed. Gilbert Rozman, Kazuhiko Togo, and Joseph P. Ferguson, 159–81. New York: Palgrave Macmillan.

Wang, Yuan-kang. 2009. The Chinese World Order and War in Asian History. Paper presented at the annual meeting of the American Political Science Association, Toronto, September 3–6.

Ward, Michael D., David R. Davis, and Steve Chan. 1993. Military Spending and Economic Growth in Taiwan. *Armed Forces and Society* 19 (4): 533–50.

Waterbury, John. 1983. *The Egypt of Nasser and Sadat: The Political Economy of Two Regimes.* Princeton, NJ: Princeton University Press.

Weitsman, Patricia A. 2004. *Dangerous Alliances: Proponents of Peace, Weapons of War.* Stanford, CA: Stanford University Press.

Wendt, Alexander. 1992. Anarchy Is What States Make of It: The Social Construction of Power Politics. *International Organization* 46 (2): 391–425.

Werner, Suzanne. 1999. The Precarious Nature of Peace: Resolving the Issues, Enforcing the Settlement, and Renegotiating the Terms. *American Journal of Political Science* 43 (3): 912–34.

Werner, Suzanne, and Amy Yuen. 2005. Making and Keeping Peace. *International Organization* 59 (2): 261–92.

Whiting, Allen S. 1989. *China Eyes Japan.* Berkeley: University of California Press.

Williamson, D. G. 1986. *Bismarck and Germany: 1862–1890.* New York: Longman.

Wohlforth, William C., ed. 2003. *Cold War Endgame: Oral History, Analysis, Debates.* University Park: Pennsylvania State University Press.

Wohlforth, William C., Richard Little, Stuart J. Kaufman, David Kang, Charles A. Jones, Victoria Tin-bor Hui, Arthur M. Eckstein, Daniel Deudney, and William J. Brenner. 2007. Testing Balance-of-Power Theory in World History. *European Journal of International Relations* 13 (2): 155–85.

Woo, Jung-en. 1991. *Race to the Swift: State and Finance in Korean Industrialization.* New York: Columbia University Press.

Wu, Xinbo. 2009. Chinese Perspectives on Building an East Asian Community in the Twenty-first Century. In *Asia's New Multilateralism: Cooperation, Competition, and the Search for Community*, ed. Michael J. Green and Bates Gill, 55–77. New York: Columbia University Press.

Yarbrough, Beth V., and Robert M. Yarbrough. 1986. Reciprocity, Bilateralism, and Economic "Hostages": Self-Enforcing Agreements in International Trade. *International Studies Quarterly* 30 (1): 7–21.

———. 1992. *Cooperation and Governance in International Trade.* Princeton, NJ: Princeton University Press.

Yoon, Esook. 2007. Russian Foreign Policy and South Korean Security. In *Korean Security in a Changing East Asia*, ed. Terence Roehrig, Jungmin Seo, and Uk Heo, 137–54. Westport, CT: Praeger.

Zakaria, Fareed. 1998. *From Wealth to Power: The Unusual Origins of America's World Role.* Princeton, NJ: Princeton University Press.

Zhao, Tingyang. 2005. *The Tianxia System: A Philosophical Discussion on World Order* [in Chinese]. Nanjing: Jiangsu Education Press.

Zhu, Feng. 2008. China's Rise Will Be Peaceful: How Unipolarity Matters. In *China's Ascent: Power, Security, and the Future of International Politics*, ed. Robert S. Ross and Zhu Feng, 34–54. Ithaca, NY: Cornell University Press.

# Index

Italic page numbers indicate material in tables.

# Studies in Asian Security

Amitav Acharya, Chief Editor, American University
David Leheny, Chief Editor, Princeton University

The authorized representative in the EU for product safety and compliance is:
Mare Nostrum Group
B.V Doelen 72
4831 GR Breda
The Netherlands

www.ingramcontent.com/pod-product-compliance
Lightning Source LLC
Chambersburg PA
CBHW030644270326
41929CB00007B/191